The Scapegoat Generation

America's War on Adolescents

Mike A. Males

Common Courage Press

Monroe, Maine

Library of Congress Cataloging-in-Publication Data
Males, Mike A.
The scapegoat generation :
America's war on adolescents / Mike A. Males.
p.   cm.
Includes index.
ISBN 1-56751-081-7 (lib. bdg.) --ISBN 1-56751-080-9 (paper)
1. Teenagers--United States.   2. Adolescents--United States
I. Title.
HQ796.M2578 1996
305.23'5--dc20   95-53934
CIP

Common Courage Press
P.O. Box 702
Monroe ME 04951
207-525-0900
Fax: 207-525-3068

Third Printing

Contents

Tables and Figures

Acknowledgments

A number of people were most helpful in reviewing sections of this book. Dr. Andrea Zojourner read the initial draft and contributed many useful revisions, especially in her area of expertise (clinical psychology). Professors Kenneth Chew, Kitty Calavita and Ellen Greenberger of the School of Social Ecology, University of California, Irvine, read selected chapters and provided insightful critiques. Faye Docuyanan listened to more of my weird observations than anyone should have to and provided many good comments, especially on the concluding chapter. Dozens of adolescents, some quoted and some not, helped out immeasurably by invariably saying exactly what I did not expect.

In all cases, the handling of information and conclusions reached are the sole responsibility of the author.

Mike Males
Irvine, California
January 1996

1. Impounding the Future

Adolescent personality evokes in adults conflict, anxiety, and intense hostility (usually disguised as concern).

—Edgar Z. Friedenberg, *The Vanishing Adolescent*, 1959[1]

In this allegedly most child-centered of nations, we find it hard to care very much or very consistently about *other people's children*.

—John Demos, *The Changing American Family*, 1979[2]

America's legacy to its young people includes bad schools, poor health care, deadly addictions, and crushing debts—and utter indifference.

—*Time*, "Shameful Bequests to the Next Generation," 1990[3]

Maybe America, for all its prating about family values, hates its children. What else can explain the cruel abandonment of so many kids to such wretched circumstances?

—Sara Mosle, *The New Yorker*, September 11, 1995

The national crisis we face is unprecedented... our teenagers have lost their way.

—U.S. blue-ribbon medical, education, and health agency report, 1990[4]

Who are our children? One minute they are innocent. The next, they may try to blow your head off.

—Richard Rodríguez, editor, *The Los Angeles Times*, 1993[5]

California regards itself as the harbinger of America's future, the vision of its youthful vitality and promise. And so it is a bitter sign that in this thriving state, the future of the young is unrelentingly grim. Sketching the drastic deterioration in the conditions of California's children and adolescents over the last quarter century provides the prologue to examining America's spreading war against its youth, the official deceptions accompanying that war, and the social disintegration abandonment of the next generation portends as we enter the new millennium.

In 1970, when I was a Los Angeles adolescent, 825,000, or 12.5 percent, of California's children and youth lived in families with incomes below federal poverty guidelines.[6] The state then had six counties in which youth poverty exceeded 20 percent (but in no case approached 30 percent). All were interior valley counties dominated by squalid migrant-labor camps. Tragic, unacceptable, and immoral that human beings, especially children, should be living in such conditions, we Sixties activists thought. We fervently believed that our campus-cafeteria grape and lettuce boycotts backing strikes by César Chávez and the United Farm Workers and other successful anti-poverty campaigns would one fine day, a year or two at the outside, bring an end to these outrages.

A quarter-century later, Sixties kids, radical and otherwise, have achieved middle age and the kind of yuppie wealth enjoyed by no previous generation. But today, in 1995, 2 million, or one-fourth, of the Golden State's children and adolescents are growing up in poverty, twice as many as ripped at our young emotions in 1960s tales of Watts, Delano, Harlem, Montgomery, Appalachia.

California '95 now has 38 counties in which child and teen poverty rates top 20 percent, including 18 in which it exceeds 30 percent and four surging past 40 percent. Another 1 million California youth live barely above poverty conditions.[7] The explosion of child poverty in this wealthy state, and in other states of a nation dominated by affluent middle-agers and elders, accompanies the collapse of the public support for children, teenagers, and young families. The nightly news headlines youth violence, one expression of our abandonment of the next generation. We are not so eager to contemplate our own violence: that implicit in the abandonment itself.

In 1965, California's public schools ranked seventh in the nation in per-student funding. They were crowned by the finest free public college and university system in the world. In 1995, California schools ranked 41st nationally in funding and 40th in graduation rates.[8] The state is now second in classroom crowding and first in youth joblessness.[9]

From 1960 to 1980, California added 60 new college and university spaces per day. Since 1980, California has built 12 new prison beds every day. By the year 2000, the state will have 58 major prisons caging a quarter-million inmates. California's annual prison budget, $200 million in 1975, will top $10 billion by 2000.[10]

In the twelve months from January 1 through December 31, 1994, 26 percent of California's black, 15 percent of its Hispanic, and 6 percent of its white and Asian males ages 18-19 were arrested for felonies.[11] In 1993, 708,000 Californians were enrolled full-time in college; 930,000 were held on felonies or were in prison, on probation, or on parole.[12]

Two million children, one in four, are owed $4 billion in unpaid child support by absentee parents, mainly fathers. In 1994, 660,000 California children were reported abused, neglected, exploited, or abandoned.[13] Los Angeles was un-home to 10,000 homeless adolescents.

California is America's 11th richest state. Its economy is the tenth largest in the world. Its per capita wealth exceeds that of Sweden, the Netherlands, and Denmark. California householders age 40 and older report average incomes topping $50,000 per year, the most opulent generation in the history of this state or anywhere else.[14] Three-fourths of us own our own homes, valued at an average of over $200,000 each.[15]

As California adults have become richer, we have cut our taxes sharply. In 1973, state taxpayers shelled out $149 in state and local taxes per $1,000 of personal

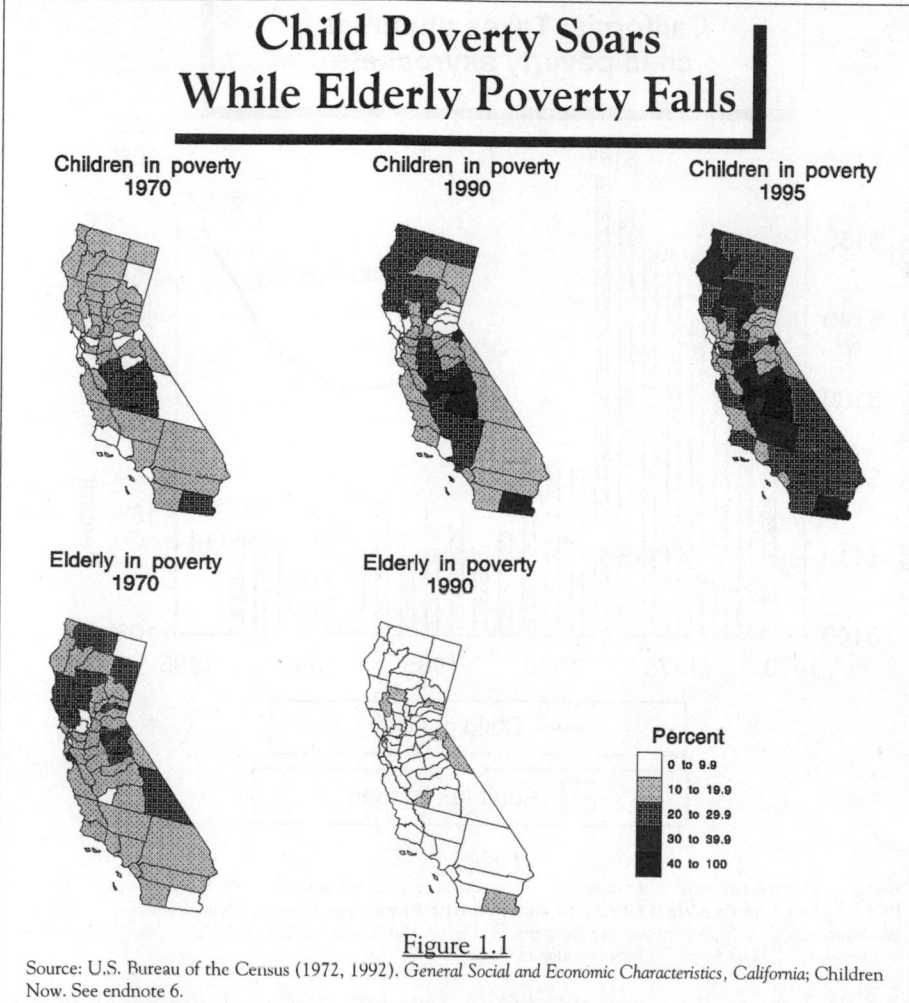

Child Poverty Soars
While Elderly Poverty Falls

Children in poverty
1970

Children in poverty
1990

Children in poverty
1995

Elderly in poverty
1970

Elderly in poverty
1990

Percent

☐ 0 to 9.9
10 to 19.9
20 to 29.9
30 to 39.9
40 to 100

Figure 1.1

Source: U.S. Bureau of the Census (1972, 1992). *General Social and Economic Characteristics, California;* Children Now. See endnote 6.

income. In 1992, that figure had fallen by a fourth, to $114.[16] In a continued downward spiral from the anti-tax Proposition 13 in 1979, California's state debt reached a record $41 billion in 1994, two counties with combined populations of 12 million were in or nearing multi-billion-dollar bankruptcies,[17] and all forms of social services (particularly those directed at young families) were drastically cut.

The relentless growth of child poverty in California is shown in Figure 1.1. The virtual eradication of poverty among the elderly over the same period is dramatic proof that government commitment through public assistance is a major force in ameliorating the demeaning social conditions of vulnerable groups. Figures 1.2 and 1.3 depict the orgy of tax-slashing, defunding of schools, and growth in prison populations in California in the last two decades—bitter trends also occurring elsewhere.

These figures chronicle a disaster much further advanced than Americans seem to comprehend, a war against children and adolescents whose growing peril

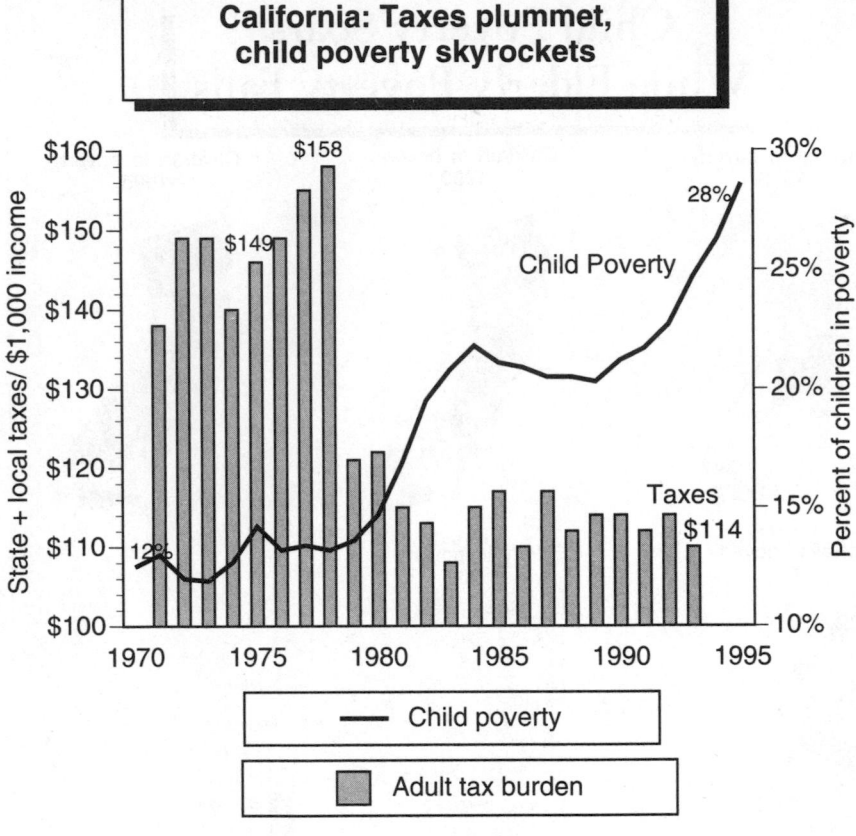

Figure 1.2

Sources: California Department of Finance (1995), *Statistical Abstract of California,* 1994, Sacramento, CA: Table P-2; U.S. Bureau of the Census (1992). Summary, Social Economic and Housing Characteristics—California, Washington, DC: U.S. Department of Commerce, Table 10; Kids Count (1995), *Kids Count Data Book,* 1995, Washington, DC: The Annie E. Casey Foundation, Appendix 3.

the follow pages will describe. If California is packing its prisons with the youth and young adults born in the 1970s and '80s amid poverty rates of 12 percent to 20 percent, how will it cope with the young of the 1990s as they mature into adolescence—a much larger generation raised with poverty rates of 25 percent to 30 percent?

By 1999, California will become a state with no majority race: Seven in ten of its 60 year-olds are white, six in ten of its 10 year-olds are nonwhite.[18] California prides itself as the apostle of the future. The future we are moving toward seems to be one in which aging America, without admitting it, declares that the racially-diverse younger generation is not really our kids, not deserving of our support. The attrition inflicted upon children and adolescents is an ominous development for which no precedent appears to exist in any society.

The popular official and media distortions of adolescent experience in 1990s America define a generation of parents and grandparents that seem not to know our own youth and, at worst, not to care what happens to them. The relentless defund-

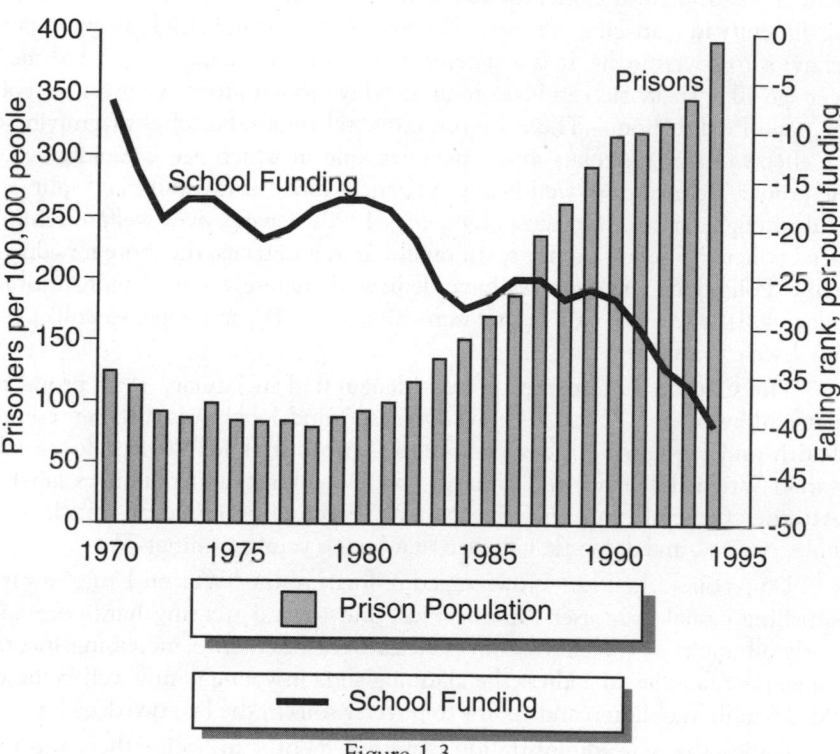

California: schools declining, prisons booming

Figure 1.3

Source: California Department of Finance (1995). *Statistical Abstract of California*, 1994, Sacramento, CA: Tables F-1, N-2

ing and dismantling of public and private support for the young by the richest generations of middle-aged and elders in American history is extreme and dangerous. It is peculiar for an older generation to display such punishing dislike for the youth we bred and raised and who, as will be shown, closely reflect our values and behaviors. Our divestiture of the coming generation is reflected in, and justified by, political and special interests who engage in blaming every social ill, from crime and violence and poverty and drug abuse to personal immorality, upon our most victimized adolescents.

Putting grownups first

In 1936, President Franklin Roosevelt urged 5,000 teenagers crowding the Baltimore armory to marshal their idealism to rescue the nation from an economic crisis brought on by cynical adults—a challenge backed by multi-billion-dollar youth education and jobs initiatives, which his New Deal wagered fully one-fourth of a strapped Depression-era budget to fund.[19] In 1994, President Clinton, soon to commit himself to a "welfare reform' bill projected to add 1 million children to poverty as the nation's older adults basked in record affluence, told an MTV audience that youths must change their ways to quit causing trouble for grownups.[20]

That the Clinton presidency dispenses the most virulent anti-adolescent sentiment is no accident. It coincides with a period in which adults are suffering increasing difficulty in managing our own lives, from marriage and child raising to personal behavior to government. It is a time of national detachment, in which Americans over age 40 or so are rich and becoming steadily more so, those younger are going in the opposite direction.[21] These are not universal trends, but ones magnifying existing effects of race and class into a new dynamic in which age is rapidly becoming the primary delineator of well-being. As generational seams strain and split, a powerful, though unspoken, philosophy guides 1990s debates over welfare reform and social policies: The less money spent on children and teens, the more for adults who count. Politicians and agencies have dedicated themselves to demonstrating that today's kids, whose poor are mostly nonwhite, are so beyond hope, so unlike us, that *they deserve punishment.*

The Clinton administration was inaugurated in January 1993 promising to "put children first." The Children's Defense Fund lobby was well represented in Health and Human Services appointee Donna Shalala, White House advisor Marian Wright Edelman, and Hillary. Top law enforcement nominees Janet Reno (Attorney General) and Louis Freeh (FBI Director) promised an attack on child abuse, poverty, and domestic violence that breeds young criminals.[22]

Drug policy chief Lee Brown urged re-focus of the "War on Drugs" away from punishing casual drug users, mostly kids, and toward treating hard-core addicts, nearly all adults.[23] Welfare reform policies were pitched to increasing income for young, poor families to address the alarming slide in young family well-being which added 6 million children and youths to poverty rolls in the last two decades.

It took the new administration but a few months to decide there was no percentage in '90s America for "putting children first"—except rhetorically. By early 1994, Clinton's welfare reform task force was urging a "Democratic family values" crusade against teen mothers with a punitive crassness chronicled in *The New York Times*.[24] Brown and Shalala, ignoring skyrocketing heroin and cocaine deaths among middle-aged adults, launched an ongoing media splash castigating kids for "casual use, single-time use" of marijuana.[25]

The president delivered a highly publicized sexual responsibility sermon to eighth graders, deplored "13 year-olds... with automatic weapons" to demand a crackdown on adolescent violence, and, carefully exempting adults from his proposals, demanded tougher penalties for teenage drunken driving and cigarette smoking.[26] Attorney General Reno won headlines for threats to federally regulate Beavis and Butt-head and other "violent media" she accused of corrupting youth.[27]

Like eating peanuts, preaching the Adolescent Apocalypse has proven hard to stop. Increasingly, Clinton's health and welfare policy has consisted of blaming teenagers for nearly all major social ills: Poverty, welfare dependence, crime, gun violence, suicide, sexual promiscuity, unwed motherhood, AIDS, school failure, broken families, child abuse, drug abuse, drunken driving, smoking, and the breakdown of "family values," the latest count as of this writing.

Republicans eagerly trumped Clinton's anti-youth measures. The 103rd and 104th Congresses became a veritable orgy of politicians representing adult genera-tions lambasting the teenagers they raised. A ludicrous spectacle—except that it is deadly serious. Where grayhairs and whippersnappers once swapped amiable snarlings about the other's morals and wry doubts about how the motherland could function with the other running it, today's adult attack on adolescents is angry and punishing.

In the past quarter century, American elders ("elders" signifying senior citizens and middle-agers generally over age 40) have made monumental progress in feather-ing our own aging nests. Note the present situation, even before the punishing attack on young family assistance promised by both parties as "welfare reform:"

- U.S. adults over age 40 are richer than adults in any nation on earth, other than enclaves such as Switzerland and Kuwait. We enjoy the highest real incomes and lowest poverty rates of any in U.S. history.

- U.S. adults enjoy the lightest tax burden of any developed nation, lower by far than any nation in the Organization for Economic Cooperation for Development. In 1990, U.S. tax revenue was 30 percent of our gross domestic product, compared to over 40 percent among similarly situated Western nations.[28]

- The U.S. has the highest rate of children and adolescents living in families with incomes below poverty guidelines ($11,522 per year for a family of three in 1993) in the industrial world, the result of spending fewer public resources on children than any other industrial nation.[29]

- In the last 20 years, U.S. child and youth poverty rose by 60 percent. In contrast, poverty among over-40 adults declined.

- Youths are by far our poorest age group; one in four is impoverished, twice the rate among grownups.[30]

America's level of adult selfishness is found in no other Western country (Figure 1.4). A 1995 National Science Foundation-funded study by the Luxembourg Institute reported that of 17 industrialized countries, the U.S. had the highest income per capita and the highest child poverty rates. (Table 1.5.)

Fashionable whining about the Japanese and Germans notwithstanding, the United States operates the most powerful economy in the world. The U.S. ranks first in per-person affluence, producing a higher gross domestic product with 250 million people than the other 17 nations, population 400 million, combined.

And the U.S., by an even larger margin, also ranks first in child poverty. With well below half the child population of the above nations, the U.S. accounts for 70 percent of the total number of poor children. America's child poverty rate is 50 per-cent higher than those of fellow frontier cultures, Australia and Canada, and two to eight times higher than those of Europe. We rank third from the bottom in percent of our wealth spent on education, topping only impoverished Ireland and non-secu-lar Israel.

In allocating the $1.5 trillion federal budget, the representatives of grownup

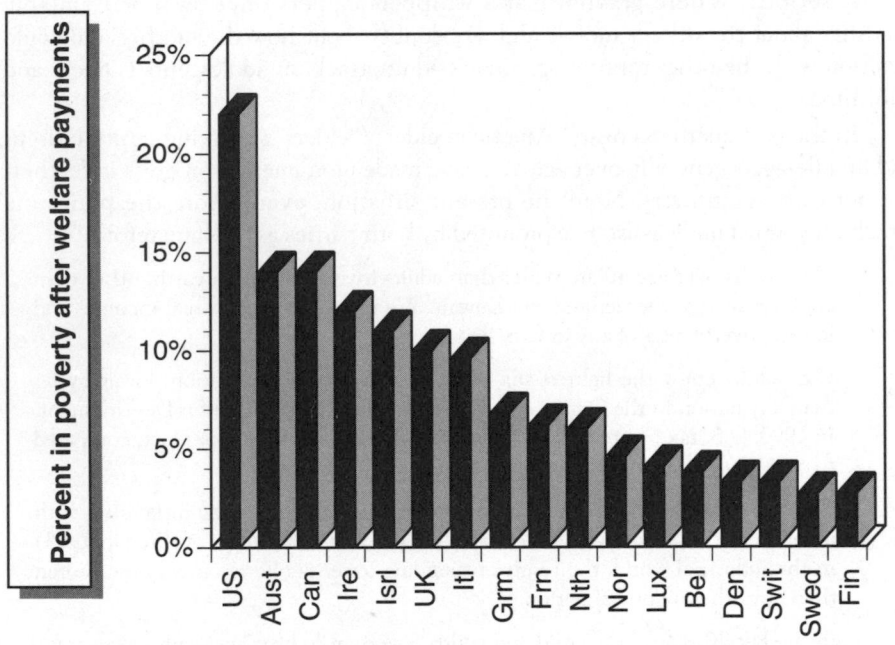

Figure 1.4

Source: Luxembourg Income Study (1995). See Table 1-5.

America insist that the 40 percent spent on public assistance for non-poor Americans ($612 billion in 1994), 25 percent spent on public assistance for the elderly ($400 billion), 20 percent spent funding the military ($280 billion), and 5% (by estimate of the conservative Cato Institute and the liberal Progressive Policy Institute, or $50 billion to $80 billion) donated in direct corporate subsidies are about right—but 7 percent spent for children and young families (about $100 billion) is bankrupting profligacy.[31] The insistence that welfare for indigent children, teenagers, and young families (unlike welfare for the elderly, middle-aged, or corporations) fuels moral breakdown and welfare dependence was first publicized by conservative social commentator Charles Murray and continues to represent Washington and media gospel even though Murray himself abandoned the claim.

Murray's admission in the Spring 1994 *Public Interest* that welfare doesn't cause much "illegitimate" childbearing after all was apt. If it did, we would expect that the 50 percent decrease in the real value of payments for Aid to Families with Dependent Children (AFDC) and Food Stamps over the past 20 years would yield much lower unwed childbearing rates today than in 1970 (in fact, they have risen by 80 percent). We would expect that Mississippi's stingiest-in-the-nation family welfare package (providing maximum benefits equal to only 40 percent of the state's

Table 1.5

The U.S. has a staggering child poverty rate compared to other Western nations—even after welfare payments are figured in:

Percent of children in poverty

	Pop. <18	Before welfare payments	After welfare payments	Number	Gross domestic product per capita
United States, 1991	68.8 mil	25.9%	21.5%	14.8 mil	$23,400
Australia, 1989	4.4	19.6	14.0	0.6	16,700
Canada, 1991	7.1	22.5	13.5	1.0	19,600
Ireland, 1987	1.1	30.2	12.0	0.1	12,000
Israel, 1986	1.9	23.9	11.1	0.2	12,100
Britain, 1986	13.2	29.6	9.9	1.3	15,900
Italy, 1991	11.2	11.5	9.6	1.1	17,500
Germany, 1989	15.6	9.0	6.8	1.1	17,400
France, 1984	13.9	25.4	6.5	0.9	18,900
Netherlands, 1991	3.3	13.7	6.2	0.2	17,200
Norway, 1991	1.0	12.9	4.6	0.05	17,700
Luxembourg, 1985	0.1	11.7	4.1	0.003	21,700
Belgium, 1992	2.2	16.2	3.8	0.08	17,800
Denmark, 1992	1.1	16.0	3.3	0.04	18,200
Switzerland, 1982	1.3	5.1	3.3	0.04	22,300
Sweden, 1992	1.9	19.1	2.7	0.05	16,900
Finland, 1991	1.2	11.5	2.7	0.03	15,900
Average (non U.S.)	80.5 mil	18.7%	8.4%	6.8 mil	$17,400

*Before and after measuring the effect of public welfare programs, as calculated using a standard measure.
Source: Luxembourg Income Study (1995). See Children: Progress elsewhere. *U.S. News & World Report* (1995, 28 August), p. 24.

median personal income) would produce the nation's lowest rate of unwed births (it has the nation's highest rate), and that Minnesota's most generous welfare benefits (providing up to 80 percent of its median personal income) would generate the most out-of-wedlock procreation (its rate is among the lowest). Across the 50 states and DC, higher AFDC and family welfare payments are consistently correlated with *lower*, not higher, rates of unwed childbearing among teenage mothers.[32]

The moral and practical arguments for cutting assistance to impoverished young families do not stand even the most casual scrutiny. They warrant even less favor in light of the fervor for maintaining much greater welfare largesse and expanding tax breaks for wealthier, mostly elder interests: 52 percent of the tax benefits of Republican proposals (by U.S. Treasury Department estimate at this writing) will go to the 10 percent of families earning over $100,000 per year.

The loudly-proclaimed desire to "reform welfare" for the benefit of its belea-guered recipients and society as a whole is thoroughly inconsistent with the destruc-tive child- and youth-punishing reforms close to approval. Rather, the unspoken principle that explains why the young should be the focus of such a seemingly illogi-cal and self-defeating attack, from the bipartisan slashing of student loans to the bipartisan cutting of teenage benefits, is that every dollar taken away from children and adolescents is one than can be given to a grownup.

Los Angeles Times contributing editor Robert Scheer delineated but a few mod-est examples of the young to old wealth transfer courtesy of the New World in Washington:

> Head Start is to be cut by $133 million, meaning that 50,000 kids will be eliminated from the program. Let me help you with the math here: $133 million pays for about 13 percent of one B-2 bomber. This Congress wants to build 20 more of those nuclear-war fighting planes, which have no strategic purpose now that the Soviet Union is history.
>
> Gone also is AmeriCorps, an excellent effort cut out of pure spite simply because President Clinton favored it. And forget the Summer Youth Employment and Training Program, which helped 600,000 kids get work experience. There will also be more homeless kids due to the $5 billion cut in HUD funding and the slashing of homeless assistance grants by one-third.[33]

The age-race connection

Where race, ethnicity, and gender were central to past social conflicts, today young age has become a major new factor. Three-fourths of all poor, unwed adoles-cent mothers, and three-fourths of all teenagers arrested for murder, are nonwhites (persons of Hispanic origin are referred to as "nonwhite" throughout). In California, 80 percent of all unwed adolescent mothers and 80 percent of all teens arrested for violence are minorities.[34]

President Clinton, California Governor Pete Wilson, House Speaker Newt Gingrich, and the media berate teenage mothers as welfare chiselers and cite "15 year-olds with guns" as the major threat to the social fabric. In practical '90s-speak, this means the behavior of nonwhites *causes* poverty, violence, and social costs. The racial statistics of what we call "teenage" motherhood and violence are as clear as the nearest volume of *Uniform Crime Reports* or *Vital Statistics of the United States*. It is evident to policy makers, as even the conservative American Enterprise Institute's Douglas Besharov pointed out, that punishing teenage mothers equals punishing blacks.[35]

That the issue is not "teenagers" or "adolescents" is shown by the low rates of pregnancy and violence among European and white American youths. So com-pelling is the race-age link that if California *adults of all races* experienced the same low rate of homicides and unwed births found among California *white teens* age 15-19, the state would have experienced 1,500 fewer murders and 50,000 fewer unwed births in 1993 than it did.[36]

The question Clinton and other liberal and moderates, academicians, and the media who hype "youth violence" and "teen pregnancy" evade is this: Is there something innately wrong with most minority groups, as Charles Murray claimed in *The Bell Curve,* or is there something wrong with the conditions in which minority groups live? In neither case is "teen age" a pivotal matter. In fact, it is a smokescreen, very much like the smokescreen of race or ethnicity raised in the past. This is a crucial point in understanding not just the evasions of today's social policy debate, but many points raised in this book. Because statistics usually are not available for income level in relation to unwed births, crimes, and other behaviors, race is substituted. That is because in the 1990s as in past decades, race remains a surrogate for poverty: The higher rates of unwed childbearing or violent crime among blacks and Hispanics relative to whites reflect the greater poverty of nonwhite populations. Where statistics on income are available, we find low-income whites also experience disproportionately high levels of these problems. The social policy debate's fixation on euphemisms such as "teenage childbearing" and "teenage violence," when what is really being deplored is "nonwhite or low-income childbearing and violence," has become a major impediment to analysis of issues in which neither race nor age, but social conditions, are paramount factors.

Whether one blames poverty on government or business or social or personal irresponsibility, no one (yet, anyway) blames 13-year-olds for their own impoverished conditions. Yet these conditions are crucial. A recent two-year Alan Guttmacher Institute study found six out of seven teenage mothers of all races were poor *before* they became pregnant.[37] The correlation between childhood poverty and later teenage childbearing is so strong that during the 1960-1993 period, the teen birth rate could be calculated with 90 percent accuracy from the previous decade's child poverty rate.[38]

Poverty also predicts the teen homicide and violent crime levels denounced in outraged bafflement by politicians before cameras and press. In an atmosphere of declining social support, youth raised in poverty—47 percent of black, 40 percent of Hispanic, and 17 percent of white youth in 1992[39]—without access to inherited wealth will be consigned to lifelong poverty. To a staggering extent, young age is like nonwhite race.

Regardless of race, grownups are only half as likely to be poor as their respective young. The rising poverty of the young is a doubly dangerous development because today, it is not always shared with adults. Thus modern adults find it ever-easier to blame adolescents for the consequences of the poverty adults profit from by imposing on them.

Wonderment as to why European teens experience so much less pregnancy and violence than U.S. teens is a major example of that modern American affliction: Social science tunnel vision.[40] U.S. teens who enjoy low youth poverty rates similar to those in Europe (whites and Asians in suburban Marin and San Mateo counties, California, for example) display low teenage pregnancy and low murder rates similar to those of Europe.[41]

The link between young age and nonwhite race provides a powerful insight into the singular hostility against youths expressed by elders, particularly in areas such as California, now experiencing the transition to a "majority minority" state. Often that link is direct: Shopping malls have dusted off vague laws once used for racial discrimination to institute teen bans to effect absence of (mainly) black youth.[42] The summer '95 hit film "Dangerous Minds" lionizes white ex-marine LouAnne Johnson for personally taming savage inner-city youth. Yet Johnson's book that served as the basis for the movie credited a "U.S. Government grant that pays for reduced class sizes" for her teaching success, a mundane tax-funded heroism not nearly as easy to sell to audiences as a white super-heroine.[43]

But race and white-savior myths are not the whole explanation. Anti-youth attitudes affect adolescents of all races and classes, even though different subgroups experience its consequences in different ways.

A visit to a major state youth prison such as California's "Chino," housing 2,500 violent youths, reveals a sea of black, Hispanic, and Asian adolescents. A trip to the ward of an upscale adolescent psychiatric hospital reveals a sea of white inmates running insurance-paid tabs of $1,000 per day or more. Just as the criminal justice system expands to cage more nonwhite teens for committing violent crimes, so the health and psychological establishments expand, concocting and publicizing new afflictions affecting more affluent youths (such as "conduct disorder," "oppositional defiant disorder," and "an epidemic of teen suicide") in a quest to make "adolescence itself a disease state" amenable to costly treatment.[44]

Getting an education

A 1995 University of California at Berkeley report found a sharp decline in voter support for school bond financing measures over the last three decades:

> Election results from the two periods, 1949-62 and 1986-94, provide a sharp contrast. The bond issues during the baby boom years passed in all 58 counties and most had statewide percentage voting "yes" of more than 70 percent. In the late 1980s, that percentage was closer to 60 percent and... in the 1990s, has dropped to 50 percent. In June 1994, a bond facility measure failed by 30,000 votes (and)... the number of counties supporting the proposals has fallen steadily to only 12 counties in June 1994.[45]

Across the continent, a prominent investigative team led by New York City businessmen inspected public school buildings and "expressed shock at the dilapidation... falling masonry, leaky roofs, crumbling beams, loose and broken windowpanes." Schools were in such disrepair that "it is probable that schoolchildren, teachers, and staff will be hurt or even killed in the near future." Liberal, 75 percent-Democratic New York City—whose average family income tops $60,000 and grew rapidly during the 1990s—chopped another $1 billion from its city school budget from 1994 to 1995 to save tax dollars. "Further huge cuts are as much a certainty as rising enrollments," wrote Sara Mosle in The New Yorker. Class sizes are projected to grow to 35 or more, and "the sense of futility verges on numbness."[46]

A bitter historical irony, not taught in schools, is that much of the wealth and middle-class stability among today's don't-tax-me homeowners is due to generous tax-funded welfare subsidies and government-enforced minimum wage boosts of the past. These government initiatives complemented the growing postwar economy to the benefit of low-income families. From 1950 to 1978, the real income growth among the nation's poorest one-fifth of families—overwhelmingly very young and elderly households—rocketed upward by 140 percent; among the richest fifth, by slightly under 100 percent. The real value (in constant 1995 dollars) of the minimum wage more than doubled, from $2.70 in 1950 to over $6.00 in the 1970s, benefitting millions of low-income young working families.[47] The GI Bill, the War on Poverty, and subsidized education, business loans, home mortgages, expanded Social Security and Medicare, and other social investments paid for by past American elders were crucial to boosting 10 million young families and 4 million aged out of poverty in the 1950s and '60s.[48]

But from 1978 to 1993, as elder generations consolidated their gains, the progress against poverty ground to a halt and reversed. Real family income growth increased 18 percent for the richest fifth, nearly all middle-aged and elders, but decreased by 16 percent for the poorest fifth (nearly all young families). The real value of the minimum wage declined by nearly a third, to $4.25 by 1995, benefitting millions of older business owners (particularly in the exploding service economy) at the expense of young workers. The government-sustained grownups of the 1990s are fortunate their postwar parents and grandparents harbored far less adult-centered attitudes than prevail today.

Robert McNamara's memoir *In Retrospect* recalls $52 in annual tuition at the University of California in 1937.[49] In 1965, a year of university education cost California Baby Boomers $219, one-twentieth of that era's per-capita income.[50] Large student loans were practically unheard of prior to the 1960s. "Strange as it may seem, the concept of borrowing for college is relatively new," wrote *New York Times* education editor Edward B. Fiske in 1986. "Up through the 1950s, most families paid for their children's education through savings and current income."

No more. In 1995, tuition for a year at the University of California reached $5,100, one-fourth of today's per-capita income, amid $342 million in budget cuts and the loss of 2,000 professors and 200,000 students from the system from 1991 to 1994. A gloomy analysis of California higher education concluded:

> As bad as things are now, they probably are going to get worse... The downsizing of the system is taking place just as California's college-age population is set to explode. The number of high school graduates is expected to climb by as much as 50 percent over the next 10 years. While 450,000 new students—40 percent of them members of racial and ethnic minorities—would pose a massive challenge to any higher education system, in California, where access to college is supposed to be a birthright, the increase is potentially political and social dynamite.
>
> Under the master plan, adopted in 1960, any California resident with a high school diploma is guaranteed a place in a public college or university... But as tuition increases outpace increases in financial aid and more students are priced out of the system, the 35-year-old master plan has begun to unravel... The already fierce battle over who will attend the state's best schools can only get worse. And the battle increasingly will be fought along racial and ethnic lines...[51]

In 1991, facing $300 million in budget cuts, California's community college and state university system laid off 1,000 full-time faculty and cancelled 9,000 classes. Low-income students were affected dramatically. Rising tuition and cancelled classes led to a 12 percent drop in black, Hispanic, and Native American freshmen in the university system in 1991, the first decline in a quarter-century.[52]

Note how drastically the California education picture has changed in less than three decades: From guaranteed free public education for every high school graduate in 1965 to a tuition-heavy, packed, deteriorating system in 1995 of which Patrick Callan of the California Higher Education Policy Center said: "The fact of the matter is that there is not enough room for everyone now, there won't be enough room later, and we have no plans for dealing with it."[53]

City University of New York, once the "Poor Man's Harvard," is slated to charge massive new tuitions.[54] Nationally, $32.5 billion in student debt was accumulated in 1994, up 57 percent since 1992. Congress's most recent budget includes slashing of $5 billion in student subsidies over the next seven years; Clinton's proposes cutting $6 billion, including freezes on Pell Grants for disadvantaged students.[55] Said the American Council on Education's David Merkowitz: "We've broken the historical promise we've had in higher education: That the current generation will help pay for the education of the next generation."[56]

"Obtaining the baccalaureate in the future will require 'education mortgages' analogous to home mortgages," the Council's *Investing in American Higher Education* reported in January 1995.[57] An "intergenerational shift in responsibility for funding higher education" has occurred, and low income students, especially minorities, are the most affected.

This shift became more pronounced as states cut university budgets and raised tuitions and federal student aid agencies increasingly shifted from grants to loans during the 1980s, the Council pointed out. This process has snowballed since 1990: University of California tuition doubled from $1,812 in 1990 to $4,103 in 1994. Unlike their parents, today's "students are now paying through borrowing" for higher education and "begin their careers in debt," the Council warned.

The reduction in adult support for education is both public (reduced tax support) and private. Today's parents, though wealthier than their parents, are paying less individually to help their children with college. This downward trend is partly due to the rise in divorce and family breakup and partly due to the growing reluctance of adults to continue the tradition of paying for the next generation's schooling. Concluded a special analysis on the soaring debt of today's students by *U.S. News & World Report*:

> Even very affluent families who earn $100,000 or more per year are thinking twice about depriving themselves of the fruits of their labors in order to underwrite higher education for their children. As Edwin Below, director of financial aid at Wesleyan University in Middletown, Conn., explains: "A lot of parents are in their 40s and ready to start enjoying the benefits of higher salaries and just don't want to pay a lot for college."[58]

A 1995 study of 3,000 households headed by University of Pennsylvania sociologist Frank Furstenberg found today's divorced parents, particularly fathers, are far less likely to help their grown children financially. These "intergenerational transfers" of wealth, as economists call them, have been essential to the stability past generations of Americans (including today's middle-aged and older adults) have enjoyed. But contrary to media reports of parents supporting Generation X as never before, fewer than one-fourth of today's young adult children received money from their parents. Only 28 percent of married parents provided financial help to their adult children; only one-eighth of divorced fathers and one-fifth of divorced mothers provided aid. "When men relinquish ties to their children during childhood, they rarely resume them later in life," researchers concluded.[59]

States have facilitated the growth of financial detachment by Baby Boom parents from their children. In the 1980s, while states were loudly raising legal drinking ages to 21 to "protect youth" from alcohol, they were quietly lowering from 21 to 18 the legal age at which parents would have to support their children. It is a standard pattern throughout the last quarter century: Teenagers are "adults" when convenient for adults and "children" when convenient for adults.[60]

Today's young are saddled not just with personal debts constricting their options, but also an ocean of red ink the richest cohorts of adults in American history are bequeathing them. Five trillion dollars in national debt; $400 billion in accumulated state deficits; $1.2 trillion in local IOUs and a roster of insolvencies, all rising. Massive debt is not a traditional American value. Five-sixths of the national debt was amassed since 1978; state and local deficits have snowballed since the 1980s. Wrote *Los Angeles Times* business columnist James Flanigan of Orange County's $2.5 billion-blowing bankruptcy:

> Orange County is not alone. Across the United States, municipalities have been piling on debt for years even as Americans have crowed about shrinking government. State and local government borrowings rose to $289 billion last year from $154 billion in 1991, according to the Federal Reserve System... Total municipal debt outstanding has risen to $1.22 trillion from $365 billion in 1980.
> ...What was the public purpose of those borrowings? It was to give county agencies, cities and school and water districts a little extra in their budgets. That way, government officials and county residents could get around the realities of life in a time of stern voter resistance to taxes and vocal protests about the size of government.[61]

Hidden budget shenanigans devised to fund government in this "no-new-taxes" era promise a bumper crop of Orange counties. Los Angeles County mortgaged its county courthouse, hospital, police stations, and public buildings, spent the money, and now faces $400 million in annual debt service and a bankrupting crisis.[62] Congress swiped the Social Security trust fund surplus that was supposed to cushion massive growth in future retirees, spent the money, and left an IOU for future congresses to figure out how to repay.[63]

"In the past two decades," University of Texas sociologist Norval Glenn understated, "American priorities have shifted away from promoting the well-being of children and toward promoting the well-being of adults."[64] We so-called adults have generously subsidized our own immediate well-being and pocketed the tax savings while dumping crushing debt, de-funded schools, and record poverty on the young.

Enter the new "generational politicians" such as California Governor Pete Wilson and President Clinton to tackle the one mission their tenure may be remembered for: Articulating the elder rationale for ripping off their young. The rationale is simple, repeated in an endless variety of ways: It's high time today's grownups, the salt of American decency, quit having to suffer personal heartache and fiscal drain taking care of such inexplicably rotten kids.

Political child abuse

Modern American hostility against adolescents has become so extreme compared to that of other societies that the most destructive deceptions easily achieve political and media currency. Few contemplate just what it means when a society's most affluent generations of elders choose to enhance our own well-being at the expense of attrition against our young.

In the United States in the 1990s, the attrition is hidden behind ringing bipartisan odes to "personal responsibility," "tough love," "fiscal conservatism," and "caring for children." Its practical policy consists of systematically eviscerating every social system, from aid to impoverished children to public schools and universities to employment opportunity to the most basic of constitutional rights upon which the future of the young depends.

Under the guise of "protecting children," the Clinton administration has managed a dismal evasion of the most fundamental realities of growing up American in the Nineties. The anti-youth bias of the Reagan and Bush years has now, in the Clinton presidency, erupted into an ephebiphobia[65] that indulges distortions with regularity.

Distorting "teenage pregnancy"

In his 1994 State of the Union address, Clinton incredulously ("Can you believe...?") painted the unwed teenage mother as a conniving welfare leech and demanded that her errant ways be punished by welfare cutoff and forced return to loving Mom and Dad.[66] Such mush-headed nostalgia might be expected from an offhand Reagan quip, but not from the policy encyclical of the Clinton camp.

Clinton and his Children's Defense Fund aides are well aware of the research showing large majorities of teen mothers suffered violent sexual and physical abuses at home,[67][68] that fewer than 5 percent of under-18 mothers live in homes where no adults are present,[69] that most "sexually active" girls under age 15 were initiated into sex by rape by older males[70] (often of the adult ages with whom Clinton joked about his own premarital El Camino truck-beddings), and that higher welfare payments are correlated with lower, not higher, rates of teen births (see Chapter 3).[71]

Shalala, who along with former Surgeon General Antonia Novello is the most simplistically anti-youth health official in memory, has been outspoken in blaming the existence of the nation's relatively small family welfare programs on "teenage pregnancy."[72] In fact, the average maternal recipient of Aid to Families with Dependent Children is 29 years old, had her first baby after age 20 in two-thirds of the cases,[73] was forced onto welfare rolls by job layoff or recent divorce, and is a victim of the father's failure to pay child support.[74] Ninety-three percent of all unwed births (including 60 percent among teens) involve at least one partner age 20 or older, as do 99.8 percent of all divorces.[75] Yet in cabinet debates, Shalala has taken a hard line on punishing teen mothers that she has never taken with adult fathers.[76]

In February 1994, Clinton (who has not publicly accepted "personal responsibility" for his own adultery) treated eighth graders at the inner-Washington Anacostia School to a lecture on sexual morality. Alone among commentators left to right, *The Nation's* Alexander Cockburn captured the hypocrisy of Clinton's cynical exercise:

> The kids, ready with questions about NAFTA and the Clean Water Act, were treated to homilies by this compulsive philanderer about "personal responsibility" and sex...An increasingly inegalitarian society pushes poor teenagers further and further to the margin and then blames them for lack of "responsibility."

If the president really wanted to prevent junior-high sex, he would lecture grownups. Among girls who give birth at age 15 or younger, vital records show that 40 percent of the fathers are senior high males and 50 percent are post-high-school adult men averaging five to six years older than the mothers.[77] Outrage at adult men impregnating and HIV-infecting junior high-age girls might have been a compelling subject for a presidential statement to the cameras. But that is not what Clinton means by "protecting children."

Added Cockburn:

> This is no secret to Clinton's advisers on these issues, such as Marian Wright Edelman of the Children's Defense Fund, Hillary Clinton, and Donna Shalala. They know that most pregnant teenagers come from abusive backgrounds and that the men who impregnate them, same as the men who give them AIDS, are mostly over 20. But they keep quiet as Clinton picks on the social group least able to defend itself.[78]

Not that the Children's Defense Fund, a seasoned Washington lobby, would make an issue of such impolitic child-defense topics as adult-youth sexual abuse and adult-teen sex. Its posters tacked to thousands of school infirmary walls nationwide deploy pure 1950s stereotypes to deride the teenage mother as a witless fool impregnated by the high school jock.[79]

The demeaning images of pregnant teenagers manufactured by supposedly child-centered Washington policy makers and lobbies betray a particularly vicious opportunism. Privileged official declaimers have proven too squeamish to face *even in concept* the childhood rapes and sexual abuses endured by most pregnant and parenting teens. "Rape in America is a tragedy of youth," the National Victim Center reported in 1992. Of their sample of 4,000 adult women, one in eight had been raped, 62 percent of these prior to age 18.[80] A *Los Angeles Times* survey of 2,600 adults nationwide found 27 percent of the women and 16 percent of the men had been sexually abused in childhood. The average age at the time of victimization was nine for victims, 30 for abusers. Half of the abusers were "someone in authority."[81]

Two-thirds of the pregnant and parenting teens in a mostly white Washington state sample had been sexually abused or raped. Victims averaged 10 years old at the time of abuse. Abusers averaged 27 years old, and most were adult male family members.[82] These results were similar to those found in a 1989 study of mostly nonwhite Chicago teen mothers.[83] Childhood sexual abuse was the single biggest predictor of teenage pregnancy over the past 40 years, a 1995 paper by University of Chicago sociologists found from their survey of 3,400 American adults.[84]

The prevalence of child rape has not stirred administration officials to confront adult-teen sexual issues. In June 1994, a Reuters reporter sought Shalala's opinion of an Alan Guttmacher Institute finding that a large majority of "sexually active" girls under age 15 were victims of rape by "substantially older" men. For most of these girls, a rape had been their only "sex."[85]

Here was a clear opportunity for the nation's top health official to promote public awareness of childhood's most devastating trauma. Shalala's dodge: "Teenagers need our help to avoid having sex while they are still just children themselves."[86] Equating rape with "having sex," blaming sexual violence on the victim's behavior, and ignoring the stark power issues manifest in intercourse between adults and 13-year-olds are classic "rape myths" past feminist activists would not have let a national figure get away with.

Not even the AIDS menace has spurred honest discussion among officials ever ready to single out adolescents, particularly high schoolers, for "high risk" behaviors leading to AIDS.[87] The recent San Francisco/Berkeley Young Men's Survey found 40 percent of their sample of 400 reported histories of forced sex, paid sex, and early sexual initiation—all indicators of adult-youth relations and bearing correspondingly high rates of HIV infection.[88]

Heterosexually-transmitted AIDS rates in girls are nine times higher for HIV infections acquired in childhood, and six times higher for infections contracted in adolescence, than corresponding rates among boys.[89] As Michigan Department of Public Health HIV epidemiologist Jim Kent reported in 1994, the evidence is clear that nearly all sexually-transmitted HIV among teens of both sexes is contracted from relations with adult men.[90] "We almost never see an AIDS case resulting from heterosexual sex where both partners are under age 18," he told me. While officials blame the spread of AIDS on young people's risky behaviors, their agencies' harsh statistics (detailed in Chapter 2) show it is overwhelmingly rooted in conditions of poverty, disadvantage, and social victimization. A black woman is 17 times more likely to contract AIDS than a white woman; Latino 50 year-olds are more likely to be infected than white teenagers.

Experts know this. When I contacted Patricia Fleming in 1994, then a chief Centers for Disease Control analyst and now the nation's AIDS czar, she was blunt: "Experts in the field have long known that adult men are responsible for a wide variety of [sexual] outcomes among teenagers," she said. "We talk about it in conferences all the time." But in the press? To Congress? To the public? "The media isn't interested in that fact," she told me. Perhaps the media would become interested if the Centers for Disease Control and AIDS preventers publicized it as forcefully as they do the myth that "teenage sex" means "sex between two teenagers."

Adult-teen sex is a crucial, complex phenomenon "as American as apple pie," to paraphrase H. Rap Brown. It is Humbert Humbert, Joey Buttafuoco, Something About Amelia, Charles Manson, and legacies of violated children and entrapped child brides from 12-year-old Pocahontas on; and it is Jimmy Carter, Teddy Roosevelt, and four other presidents, William O. Douglas, my Oklahoma grandfather, and happy 60-year marriages. But in the climate of 1990s social-science tunnel vision, obsessed with "teen age" as the sole issue, it is an inconvenient reality.

Adult-teen sex "is uncomfortable for adults to acknowledge," said Terri Wright of Michigan's Department of Public Health.[91] What many young girls face in real life politicians, experts, and health agencies refuse to discuss even in theory. The molding of "teen pregnancy" into an adult-sanitized myth yields much more political lucre than its decidedly unsexy realities.

After two years of relentlessly castigating juvenile mothers, Clinton, in a few sentences buried in an August 1995 anti-teen-smoking speech, mentioned that adult men are the issue. "It's child abuse," the president said. "It's not right."[92] As of this writing, no "adult father" policy has emerged; no "welfare reform" proposal to make men live under adult supervision; no public blamefest to match the many aimed at teen mothers.

The reluctance of the president and top officials to discuss the ugly truths of most "teenage pregnancy"— the backgrounds of poverty, of sexual abuse, of beatings, of initiation to sex by rape, of impregnation by older males, of abandonment by adult fathers with little child support—forms the chief fiction fueling the political malice termed "welfare reform." When a Democratic administration declares impoverished, nonwhite, abused, pregnant 15-year-olds the social policy equivalent of a free-fire zone, when a "liberal" health secretary dismisses the devastating trauma of child rape as "children ... having sex," the callousness of conservatives is no surprise. Senator Lauch Faircloth (R-North Carolina) recently derided the issues of rape, sexual abuse, and adult male pressures in teenage motherhood as "excuses" and demanded laws to stop young single mothers and their babies from "soaking up government largesse."[93]

Distorting "youth violence"

In the U.S. of the 1990s, 16 million children and teens live in poverty. Some 350,000 young are confirmed victims of violent and sexual abuses inflicted by caretakers (mostly parents) every year.[94] Given such conditions, teenage violence is not surprising; it is just like the adult violence from which it stems. In 1993, teenagers experienced three murders and 40 violent crime arrests per 1,000 teens living below federal poverty guidelines—the same rate as among similarly impoverished adults in their 20s and 30s.[95]

Violent youth crime is rising rapidly. Over the last decade, murder is up 50 percent, and violent crime arrests have doubled.[96] The orgy of adult outrage, shock, and self-righteous bafflement at juvenile violence is industrial phony. Youth violence is a straight-line result of the high and rising rates of poverty imposed on the young, a disastrous trend national and state policies have caused and exacerbated.

The poverty-violence link is not a new one. Dear-Abby myths of 1930s pastoral Americana aside, the same rising mayhem took place among our grandparents in the Great Depression. The U.S. murder eruption of 1930-34 was not eclipsed until the 1990s.[97]

Liberals and conservatives have joined in rampant escapism on "youth violence." The issue is not racial dysgenics and the debilitating effects of the welfare state, as conservatives claim, nor is it liberal scapegoats such as "media violence" and "gun availability." This kind of non-debate boils down to another social-sci-

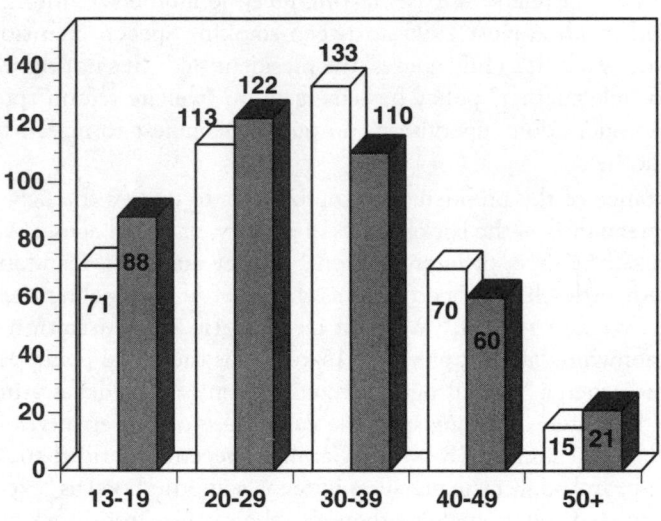

Poverty, not age or race, is the biggest factor in violent crime

Violence arrests per 1000 men in poverty, by age

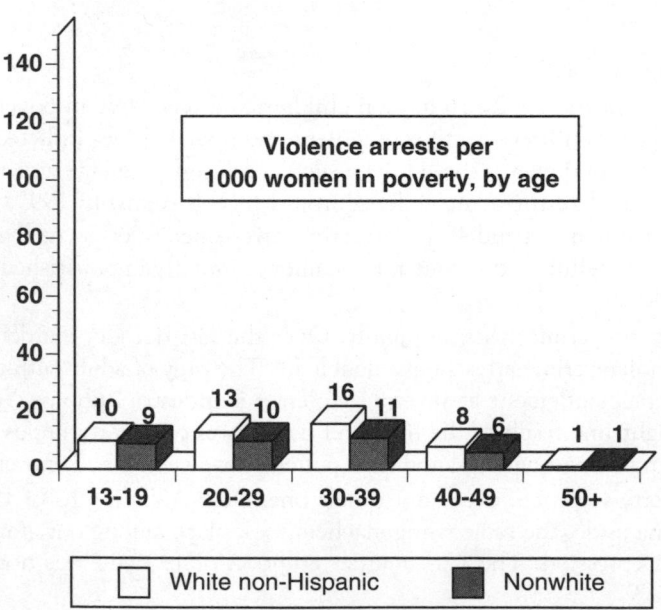

Violence arrests per 1000 women in poverty, by age

White non-Hispanic   Nonwhite

Figures 1.6, 1.7.

Sources: Law Enforcement Information Center (1994) *Crime and Delinquency in California 1993.* Sacramento: California Department of Justice, Table 33; U.S. Bureau of the Census (1995). *Poverty, Income and Valuation of Noncash Benefits 1993.* Washington, DC: US Department of Commerce, Table 11.

ence-blinded non-question over minorities' bad genes: Are nonwhite youth genetically more violent than white kids, or are they genetically more susceptible to violent TV, violent music, and itchy trigger fingers than white kids? Neither. Efforts to frame violence as a "teenage problem," as officials and a compliant media have done, fail before the stark reality that race, class, gender, era, family background, and locality are far greater predictors of violence than young age. In fact, when such factors are fully accounted for, young age doesn't predict much of anything about violence.

However, poverty does. Figures 1.6 and 1.7 show the rates of California violent crime (murder, rape, robbery, and aggravated assault) arrests in 1993 for males and females by age and race, expressed as a rate per 1,000 persons of each race, sex, and age group living on incomes below federal poverty guidelines. When poverty rates are equalized, suddenly a new pattern emerges.

Race disappears altogether as a factor. Whites (not including Hispanics) and nonwhites (blacks, Asians, Hispanics, and Native Americans) have very similar overall violence rates. Younger nonwhites age 13-29 are slightly more likely than young whites to be arrested, offset by the somewhat higher violence levels among older whites ages 30-49.

Equally dramatic is the effect on age and violence. When poverty rates are held constant, adults in their 20s and 30s have the highest rates of violent crime. Teens age 13-19 and adults over age 40 have unusually low rates of violence in relation to their poverty. The effects are very similar for males and females, as well as for whites and nonwhites: Violent crime tends to peak around age 30, a pattern very similar to that found in European countries whose poverty (and violence) levels are much lower than the United States'. Teenagers of all races, then, are not more violent than adults in their 20s and 30s; teenagers just suffer higher levels of poverty and its stresses than adults do.

The huge discrepancies unexplained by "expert" theories of youth violence are startling. First, an example of the statistics incessantly publicized in the media: In three major urban counties with a combined population of 2.5 million, Fresno, Sacramento, and San Bernardino, 84 teens were murdered in 1993.[98] Officials and experts reflexively blamed violent media, violent rap and rock songs, violent video games, gun availability, and innate adolescent savagery.

Second, the never-mentioned other side of the picture: Among California's 58 counties, 31, mostly rural and suburban, also with a combined population of 2.5 mil-lion, reported zero—*zero*—teens age 12-19 murdered. Same saturation in violent media (worse, given the greater subscription of wealthier families to blood-spewing cable channels). Same rock and rap depravity blaring into pubescent ears. Same video-screen slaughter (more among richer kids). Same guns scattered through every home and corner (more in rural counties). Same kids afflicted with presumed adolescent lunacy—200,000 of them blood hot and hormones raging. And in a whole year, not one teenager murdered anyone.

Eighty-four to zero. A high school football game with that score would draw more in-depth analysis. Over all, a simple statistic looms: The youth poverty rate is 70 percent higher in the three former urban counties with a teen murder every 100 hours than in the 31 mostly affluent rural and suburban counties with no teen killings in 12 months.[2] Poverty is not the whole story, of course. Even in California, 96% of all poor youths will not be arrested for a violent crime in any year.

Another part of the youth violence story is family violence. A recent study reported in *Science* found that 11 percent of U.S. children, some 7 million, are victims every year of a "severe violent act" (more serious than spanking or slapping, and including being "kicked, bit, punched, beat up, burned or scalded, and threatened with [or used] a gun or knife") inflicted by their parents. Abused children, the study found, were several times more likely to be violent themselves.[100] Family violence, like other forms of violence, is correlated with the stresses of poverty but is not completely explained by it.

The crucial factors of poverty and family violence share another trait—both are ignored by policy makers. While Clinton officials and Congress have repeatedly declaimed on "teenage violence," not one "urgent" press conference has been called to deplore the 2,000 fatalities and 350,000 substantiated sexual abuses and serious physical injuries inflicted on children and youths every year by parents and other caretakers averaging 31 years of age.[101]

No official "wake-up calls" greeted a 1994 Bureau of Justice report showing youths are six times more likely to be murdered by parents than the other way around.[102] The Centers for Disease Control, whose surveys have publicized the much-quoted "statistic" that "135,000 children bring guns to school every day," has issued no press releases on the pervasive in-home violence affecting youths. In 1995, a spokeswoman for the National Commission on Child Abuse complained that it was easier to get information from the CDC on soccer goalpost injuries than on the epidemic of adult violence against children.[103]

Distorting teenage drug use

The administration's increasing prevarication about teenagers escalated in late 1994 with a renewed "just say no" assault on an imaginary "epidemic" of teen drug abuse. "Urgent" press conferences in December 1994 and June 1995 featured Shalala, Education Secretary Richard Riley, and a host of Ph.D. consultants parading druggie t-shirts and reciting rock and rap lyrics to bewail what turned out to be a 3-percentage-point increase in occasional teenage patronage of mild hallucinogens.[104]

Especially condemned by Shalala was teens' "casual use, single-time use" of marijuana.[105] The image of cannabiphobic officials who owe their jobs to admitted former marijuana non-inhaler Clinton and former inhaler Vice President Gore would have been comic were it not for a tragic backdrop. Unmentioned federal health reports showed skyrocketing rates of cocaine, heroin, and pharmaceutical deaths among adults, reaching a record 13,000 fatalities in 1994.

Coroners' reports from 140 urban areas for 20,000 drugs cited in 8,500 drug overdoses, suicides, and drug-related accidents (ie, traffic crashes) in 1993 showed only 1.1 percent, involved children and teens. The figures directly from Shalala's own Drug Abuse Warning Network's *Annual Medical Examiner* data must be seen to be appreciated, (Table 1.8).

The adult drug death rate is nearly *ten times* higher than that of adolescents. A similar pattern shows up in DAWN's companion tabulation of drug-related hospital emergency room visits.[106] Out of 215,448 emergency treatments for abuse of heroin,

Table 1.8.

Teenagers account for just 1 percent of all U.S. illegal-drug deaths:

Drugs cited in deaths in 1993:

	Teen deaths*	Adult deaths*
Cocaine/"crack"	17	3,868
Heroin/morphine	12	3,777
Alcohol mixed with drugs	16	3,411
Narcotic analgesics	14	2,052
Antidepressants	20	1,397
Tranquilizers	3	1,120
Hallucinogens/marijuana	29	638
Amphetamines/"ice"	5	637
Barbiturates/sedatives	4	547
All other drugs	36	2,673
Total drugs cited	156	20,120
Deaths	98	8,445
Population, 1993 (millions)	20.8	188.9
Drug death rate/million pop.	4.7	44.7

*Note: Most drug-related deaths involve more than one drug; an average of 2.4 drugs per corpse.
Source: U.S. Drug Abuse Warning Network (1995). Annual medical examiner data, 1993. Series I, No. 13-B. Washington, DC: U.S. Department of Health and Human Services, Tables 2.01, 2.09.

cocaine, and marijuana in 1993, 6,158 (2.9 percent) involved children and adolescents.

Not that youths were immune to narcotic mishap. The drug found in the most teenage emergency room victims—four times more than the *total* involving cocaine, heroin, or marijuana—was aspirin and aspirin substitutes. These appear to result either from splashy "suicide attempts" to gain attention, or over-medication of the pain of the injury that really occasioned the ER trip. In the mean streets of the Nineties, the drug causing the most injuries to youth is dispensed not by a leering middle-school dropout or a Mr. T-sized alley pusher, but a Safeway checker? Officials neglected to mention a single Dr. Dre rap or t-shirt logo promoting Tylenol abuse.

The same reporters who no doubt indulged popular yuppie-era cocktail-party guffaws replaying the histrionics of the 1937 government anti-pot manifesto "Reefer Madness" solemnly publicized Brown's 1995 assertion that marijuana is an "extremely dangerous drug" that "can leave you fighting for your life in a hospital emergency room."[107] No one reported that DAWN's 1993 report on 8,500 drug deaths attributed only one to marijuana overdose. The few deaths in which marijuana was detected at all were in combination with stronger drugs such as heroin, cocaine, and alcohol, as were nearly all of the non-fatal emergency room treatments involving heavy use of marijuana (4,300 among teenagers and 25,000 among adults) in 1993.[108] The official and press imbalance contributes to that of the criminal justice system, further highlighting the drug war's race-age biases. A black teenager is only one-fifth as likely to die from drugs, but is 10 times more likely to be arrested for drugs, than a white adult.[109]

There are 20 million teens age 12-17 in the U.S. One hundred million Americans visit emergency rooms annually—300,000 every day. Four hundred thousand Americans die annually from tobacco; 100,000 from alcohol. Adult deaths from illicit hard drugs have risen 50 percent in the last five years to record levels. Long-term research has consistently shown that teenagers who occasionally smoke pot or use other mild drugs tend to be youths who are better adjusted than both their peers who abuse drugs and their peers who abstain from drugs[110] and are very unlikely to go on to harder drugs[111] (see Chapter 6).

Though constant whipping decoys for officials and the media, the evidence points to a startling conclusion: *Teenagers have not been a significant part of the nation's drug death or injury problem in nearly 20 years.* Yet the mid-1980s War on Drugs and "just say no" campaigns can't claim credit for the remarkable 80 percent teenage drug death decline since 1970, since all of it occurred prior to 1983.[112] Hysterical press splashes regarding the minuscule problems caused by adolescents with marijuana betray an administration more interested in manipulating a compliant press over an emotional non-issue than in facing the implications of a decade of failed policy.

Encouraged by the wildly enthusiastic media response to the fabricated "teen drug crisis," Clinton administrators in August 1995 proceeded to the next step: Full-scale misrepresentation. Clinton was in the forefront, hyping a "terrible" increase in teenage smoking.[113] In fact, National Institute on Drug Abuse surveys of tens of thousands of households over the past two decades show that in 1993, the percentage of 12-17-year-olds smoking within the past month was 62 percent lower than in 1974, 37 percent lower than in 1985, and 17 percent lower than in 1990. Teenage smoking plummeted nearly twice as fast as adult smoking both in recent years and in the long term.[114] By 1993, fewer than one in 10 youths age 12-17 had smoked within the past month, only one-third the level of smoking among their parents.

It is the Clinton administration's abysmal record on smoking by adults that raises questions about whether the administration's anti-teen-smoking campaign has anything to do with "protecting children from tobacco." Clinton health officials have retreated from even the weak Reagan- and Bush-era initiatives to protect children from the worst public health hazard created by tobacco: Smoking parents. In 1992, Bush's Environmental Protection Agency estimated from dozens of studies that smoking parents cause or aggravate 350,000 to 1.3 million respiratory diseases every year in the 25 million children exposed to household tobacco smoke.[115]

Clinton officials ignored the child health issue entirely in the executive summary of their 1994 Surgeon General's report on youth smoking and dismissed in one sentence the well-documented conclusion that smoking by parents promotes smoking among their children. The 275-page report dedicated only a few paragraphs to the issue and ignored the conclusions of two-thirds of the studies in its own research review: Parental, adult, and family smoking does encourage youths to smoke.[116] Recently, my own study of 400 Los Angeles middle school students found that compared to children of nonsmoking parents, children of smoking parents are three times more likely to be smoking weekly or daily by age 15 and much more resistant to anti-tobacco education.[117]

This issue was faced squarely by Bush's Office on Smoking and Health in 1989 ("75 percent of all teen smokers come from homes where parents smoke")[118] and Reagan's Surgeon General in 1986 (whose report found "the smoking habits of children... highly correlated with smoking habits of parents").[119] If, as Food and Drug Commissioner David Kessler declared to media headlines, smoking is a "pediatric disease," it is imperative that health officials move to stop parents from "infecting" children with nicotine in their own homes. Instead, fifty million adult voters who smoke speak louder to Clinton-era put-grownups-first health politics than confronting the health threats and behavioral influences that nicotine-addicted adults exert on children. So far, officials have acted to restrict smoking by grownups only in public buildings and workplaces where it offends nonsmoking adults.

Modern youth smoking policy benignly tolerates adults' forcing their children to inhale carcinogenic tobacco smoke for a dozen years, then berates teenagers for taking up the habit actively. The justification for singling out adolescents is that most adult smokers took up the habit before age 18. It is this kind of logic that has rationalized the last decade's growing official obsession with youth behaviors and corresponding exemption of adults from responsibility for the same or worse behaviors. Under this assumption, children and teenagers are indeed responsible for every social ill, and adults are blameless. Why punish adult criminals? All, from savings-and-loan crooks to convenience store bandits, committed their first anti-social act sometime in childhood. (If I hadn't been expelled from second grade, I'd probably never have written this book). There is no conceivable anti-social act committed by adults for which some kind of deterministic theory could not be constructed based on something done back in their youths.

Teen-focused tobacco and drug policy forms yet another social-science-blinded non-debate. As will be shown repeatedly in this study, the most important predictor of youth behavior is the behavior of adults around them. The most effective social and health policies recognize that youths cannot be reformed in isolation—at least, not by punitive measures. Adult and teen behaviors are inextricably integrated, have one and the same motives, and often (especially in the case of adult-teen sex) occur at one and the same time. They must be addressed together.

Present policy embraces the opposite strategy. Aides declared that "Clinton is considering no regulations affecting adult smoking."[120] Clinton even extolled adult smoking as "a reasonable decision" and assured tobacco-growing states that his campaign would be confined to teenagers. Health officials and the tobacco industry competed in public relations maneuvers to promote their virtues while branding adolescents stupid. In his September 10 news conference deploring the "awful dangers of tobacco" and the urgent need to "protect young people," the president announced his support for continuing the $25 million per year federal subsidy to tobacco farmers.[121]

When reporters asked the right questions, they found Clinton aides admitting the crusade was "calculated" to take advantage of "the mass appeal of a crackdown on teenage smoking," one in which "tobacco policy was driven by Clinton's political team."[122] Gone is Clinton's once-touted 75-cents-per-pack tax hike on cigarettes, the most effective approach to reducing teen and adult smoking. As the strongly anti-tobacco international medical journal *The Lancet* declared of Clinton's exercise: "Kicking the teenage habit... remains an ultimately cosmetic act... If governments really want to kick the public's smoking habit, they must begin to tackle adult tobacco consumption."[123] Predictably, the editors received a bagful of outraged letters from American health groups arguing, in effect, that adult and teen behaviors have nothing to do with one another.

The politics of distortion

A decade ago, University of Virginia law professor Richard Bonnie warned that health agencies were shifting "from information to persuasion," employing "propaganda" and "the regulation of information" to win political goals.[124] In matters adolescent today, the Centers for Disease Control and health agencies frame issues in ways most amenable for politicians to exploit. Issues selected for research and press publicity are tailored to suit the political pretense that teenage behaviors are wildly out of control, separate from those of adults, and demand uniquely vigorous management.

CDC behavior risk surveys, which form breathless newspaper headlines and lead broadcast stories, treat adolescent sex, violence, smoking, and drug use as bell-jar behaviors involving only "teenage peers" and adolescent-based influences, such as rock music, violent media, and tobacco advertising. The CDC and top health officials have proven manifestly uninterested in the most serious health threats to adolescents whose realities to do not conform to immediate political needs.

To the CDC, adult-teen sex—which accounted for 3.5 million babies, 20 million STD cases, and thousands of HIV infections in the last decade, which has shown up in national birth records for at least 90 years—does not exist. The entire issue in "teenage pregnancy" and "teenage AIDS" is promiscuity among "teenage boys and girls."[125] Teenage smoking is unrelated to adult smoking, and adult smoking presents no hazard to children worth mentioning. There is no such thing as child abuse or adult violence against children. Rape and sexual abuse are not factors in youth behavior worthy of any policy attention. Five thousand teenage suicide, drug abuse, and gun deaths merit incessant publicity; 50,000 adult suicide, gunshot, and drug abuse deaths every year receive no similar discussion.[126]

Modern American health and social policy sweeps aside a mountain of its own statistics and research and asserts: Nothing adults do has anything to do with what adolescents do. Inevitably, the CDC recommends more behavior education, prevention programming, mental health and drug abuse treatment, and law enforcement aimed solely at readjusting bad adolescent attitudes, claiming to the press that these are successful even when more stacks of studies and vital statistics show little or no effect. The result is a weird, manufactured image of teenagers living and acting in isolation from grownups and even their own parents, ideal for media and political assault, profitable to agency and private interest alike in terms of program advertising and funding.

The most far-reaching consequence of the administration's selective anti-teen campaigns is not health or safety or even electoral politics, but the economic and social effects of isolating the young. While fulsome in praise of the 1987 national minimum "drinking age" of 21 for "saving lives," administration officials (especially former Surgeon General Antonia Novello in 1989) revealed an ancillary goal: Restricting persons under age 21 from employment in millions of entry-level jobs in establishments serving alcohol.[127] Though of dubious life-saving merit, the barrage of "health" policies founded in discrimination against the young are serious contributors to today's rising youth unemployment, which itself carries life-threatening implications.

"One cannot ignore the apparent correlation of particular environmental, economic conditions and the emergence of the late 20th century adolescent myth," a recent study of policies toward youth noted. Crusades to decree teenagers "children" and push them out of the economy "for their own safety" during hard times (or, alternatively, to promote adolescents to "adults" when wars and economic booms demand expendable soldiers and cheap labor) are cyclical events in 20th century America,[128] predictably founded in advancing the fortunes of influential adults.

In 1990s politics, teenagers have become the ultimate grownup commodity. Note how easily the 1995 "family values" campaigns of Clinton, Gingrich, and Dan Quayle demean teenagers as "immature children" (not even grown up enough to drink a lite beer). You'd think these top political figures would have more gratitude toward adolescents. Just 25 years ago, the age group they now call "children" was drafted as "adults" and shipped to Vietnam en masse, 14,000 dying in combat before their 21st birthdays, to the inestimable benefit of these same three (and other) adult scholars, academicians, and National Guardsmen freed thereby to stay safely home to plot campaigns for high office.

Media and opinion-makers

Reviewing media distortions of adolescents would be redundant. The popular media seems to see its role as one of uncritically sensationalizing whatever assertions officials utter. Media spokespersons have uncorked their own fury at adolescents, revealing that anti-youth media distortions may not stem from poor journalism alone, but a large dose of personal hostility. A few examples:

So what if "many" unwed teenage mothers "have in fact been coerced into sex," Newsweek senior editor Jonathan Alter ranted: "Every threat to the fabric of this country—from poverty to crime to homelessness—is connected to out-of-wedlock teen pregnancy... The name of the game is shame."[129] ABC Prime Time Live anchor-exec Diane Sawyer, paid $7 million per year, went out on behalf of "taxpayers" who are "mad as hell" to personally "shame" teenage mothers (five out of six of whom grew up in poverty) as "Public Enemy No. 1."[130] 60 Minutes' producer Andy Rooney (who also has ethnic-baited) indulged in particularly ugly ridicule of teens mourning the suicide of Nirvana singer Kurt Cobain.[131] (Imagine the reaction if Rooney had demeaned the Clintons for mourning the suicide of Vince Foster.) The week of spring break, 1995, I counted a half-dozen afternoon talk shows featuring grown American adults, including famed hosts, berating, even shouting, at teenage mothers holding babies.

Democrats and liberals, no less than conservatives, seem to harbor a special anger at teenagers. It was not just right-wingers like Charles Murray who cast the impoverished teenage mother as agent of the apocalypse, but Clinton welfare reformers and liberal entities such as the Urban Institute.[132] It was not the Eagles Forum who concocted the statistically senseless notion that teen mothers were to blame for breeding 90 percent of all violent criminals, but Clinton's former Surgeon General Joycelyn Elders. Branding today's teens as "evil" emanates not from reactionary virtuist Bill Bennett (who portrays youths as dupes of corrupt adults), but liberal pundits like David Broder. Assailing welfare mothers as lazy leeches deserving cutoff was not simply a right wing crusade, but one of feminist columnist Ellen Goodman—as long as the mothers in question were teenagers.[133]

Goodman, at least, later lambasted the roles of adult men and sexual abuse in teen pregnancy, as did the Democrats' Progressive Policy Institute.[134] Interestingly, so did right-wing columnists such as Cal Thomas, Mona Charen, and spokespersons for the conservative American Enterprise Institute and Institute for American Values.[135] What is missing is the major media and political middle, which seems determined to cling to a profitable teen-bashing stereotype as long as it can.

No more slavish adherence to Clintonesque anti-adolescent myths has been forthcoming than on the moderate-liberal editorial pages of *The New York Times*, *Washington Post*, and *Los Angeles Times*; the rigidly right wing *Orange County Register* has expressed more skeptical attitudes than liberal editorialists. The outrageously inaccurate 1988 video *Rising to the Challenge*, blaming teen problems on their supposed pied-piper apings of rock and rap music barbarism, was popular among fundamentalist churchgoers, but its chief author was Democratic Vice President Gore's wife Tipper.

Though conservatives might applaud the scheme, it was former Robert Kennedy aide Adam Walinski who wrote in *Atlantic Magazine* that $30 billion more should be spent on law enforcement mainly to lock up black adolescents.[136] It was not the National Right to Life Association, but Planned Parenthood that created the image of an "epidemic of teenage pregnancy" in 1976 (when teen pregnancy was rapidly declining), one that has proven so useful to reactionary social policies.

When it comes to teenagers, adults right to left are reactionaries. "The disease is adolescence," *Rolling Stone* assured its 1993 yuppie readers, reprinted in *Utne Reader* for the New Aging.[137] *Utne Reader* printed the single most inflammatory and inaccurate teen-AIDS story, "AIDS explodes among U.S. teens," of any journal.[138] The viciously phony 1995 anti-teen film "Kids"—whose director congratulated himself for depicting "what's going on out there" as an endless array of blank-eyed, savage junior-high boys and brainless pushover junior high girls screwing, doping, raping, AIDS-spreading, beating, and savaging—was breathlessly lauded as "beautiful," "the teen movie America deserves," "important," "realistic," and "a wake-up call to America" by liberal reviewers in *LA Weekly*, *The Village Voice*, *Rolling Stone*, and *The New York Times*. While sensitive to crude racial and gender stereotypes, liberal commentators suddenly reverse themselves when teenagers are substituted—particularly when an image can be constructed of pregnant or violent or drug-using *white* teenagers.

The silence of 1990s feminists in the face of the punishing attack on teenage mothers is perhaps the most puzzling feature of liberal bigotry against the young. While Clinton aides and conservatives have resurrected primitive sexisms—that the female is solely responsible for pregnancy and parenthood, that mothers are at fault for breeding violent men, that rape is of little importance and can be blamed on young victims' behavior, that unwed mothers leech welfare and cause poverty, that female sexual behavior is irrational, that punishing mothers is the best way to effect social change—feminists (with a few notable exceptions) have been silent at best, and supportive of official prejudices at worst, so long as the campaign was restricted to *adolescent* motherhood.

Fabricating the "youth crisis"

Myriad government and private youth-management interests assert that they are simply responding to the unprecedented malaise of today's "generation at risk." Examination shows the real issue is whether these interests are abysmally ineffective or actually contribute to youth problems. Consider first what might be called the "pre-crisis" period, 1970 to around 1983. The trends in youth behaviors are the *opposite* of the impression given the public at the time of a building teenage catastrophe.

From the early 1970s (when today's 40 year-olds were adolescents) to the early 1980s, decreases ranging from 5 percent to 80 percent were recorded in adolescent murders, violent crime rates, self-destructive and self-inflicted deaths, violent deaths in general, birth rates, venereal disease, smoking, traffic deaths, and drug deaths.[139] Only unwed birth rates showed an increase, as they did among adults. Meanwhile, school graduation, college enrollment, and employment among teenagers all increased.[140] By a consensus of major indexes, youth of the early 1980s were the best educated and healthiest ever, experiencing long-term declines in nearly all problem behaviors and enjoying the best future prospects and longest life expectancies of any in history.

It was a singularly odd time for professionals, authorities, and the media to suddenly proclaim an "epidemic" of youth crises. Considerable evidence has been amassed that agency and industry self-interest, not the true conditions of teenagers, were the real motivators. As sociologist Robert Chauncey pointed out, the sudden "discovery" of the "teenage drinking problem" in the mid-1970s was concocted by the fledgling National Institute on Alcohol Abuse and Alcoholism as a ploy to win attention and funding. While NIAAA officials painted a grim picture of rampant youthful drunkenness and pre-teen alcoholism, no such epidemic appeared in arrest records or the NIAAA's own research review, which found no change in teenage drinking for at least 30 years.[141]

At the 1986 National Conference on Drug and Alcohol Abuse Prevention, the NIAAA and the National Institute on Drug Abuse painted mid-1980s teen drug abuse at "epidemic proportions," justifying expanded programming and agency funding. Claims of a "tripling" in teenage suicide over the past three decades are also common.[142] In fact, it appears much more likely that teen suicide is more accurately certified today than in the past.[143] As discussed in Chapter 8, the rates of teen and adult suicide and self-inflicted deaths (from firearms and poisons most likely to be suicides) show parallel patterns over the past 35 years, with both declining from the early 1970s to the early 1980s. Teenage drug deaths and drug suicides also diminished by 70 percent from the early 1970s to the early 1980s. Neither surveys nor statistics in the early 1980s revealed any serious teenage narcotics crisis.[144]

Never mind: Anti-youth hysteria was becoming profitable. In 1985 testimony to Congress, the National Association of Private Psychiatric Hospitals exaggerated the number of teenage suicides by 300 percent and portrayed self-destruction as a typical event among youth.[145] Hospital ads included scenes of teenagers putting guns to their heads and parents visiting graveyards.

In fact, fewer than one in 10,000 teens commits suicide in any given year, the lowest rate of any age group except children. Diagnoses of serious mental illnesses among adolescents showed no increase. "There is no great reason to believe that adolescents have more serious problems today than they once did," Brian Wilcox, who headed a 1987 American Psychological Association task force, concluded. But, the Task Force report noted, the medical industry was converting vastly overbuilt, economically disastrous private hospitals into profitable adolescent psychiatric units. "There were an awful lot of empty beds out there before they started pushing for teenagers," Wilcox said.[146]

The American Medical Association and National Association of State Boards of Education, in a 1990 tax-funded report in conjunction with the Centers for Disease Control, unabashedly doubled the number of teenage unwed births and claimed a wildly embellished "30-fold" increase in juvenile crime since 1950.[147] National highway safety officials have employed a variety of novel measures to imply that the teenage drunk driving death rate, which in fact is lower than among adults in their 20s and 30s, is several times higher than their own figures show it is.[148]

The unwillingness of American institutions to face the serious impacts of poverty, abuse, and adult behaviors on teenagers has crippled realistic policies. Child Trends' 1994 report on families, *Running in Place*, addressed these issues obliquely. But the main body of the report, using the absurd technique of contrasting parents' perfectionist *wishes* about how teenagers should act with the way imperfect human teenagers really *act*, blamed all unhealthy adolescent behaviors on "negative peer pressures."[149] Worse still, the October 1995 report on young adolescents released by the Carnegie Institute's distinguished Council on Adolescent Development, *Great Transitions*, represents abject evasion of critical issues in almost pure form.

Better termed "Great Escapisms," the Carnegie report declared half of all U.S. 10-14 year-olds "at high or moderate risk of impairing their life chances through engaging in problem behaviors." The report lists the usual teen horror-stats without mentioning the impacts of such crucial factors as sexual abuse of children, grinding poverty and racism, or the pervasive behavior examples and pressures of adults on teenagers. Ignoring five years of emerging research on the predominant adult role in "junior high sex," the report perpetuates the pretense that all pregnancy, childbearing, sexually-transmitted disease, AIDS, and rape (as well as drug and alcohol abuse and violence) among 10-14 year-olds are strictly a matter of unhealthy "peer group culture." Media corruption of youth wins a full chapter, "peer pressures" dozens of references, but just three sentences are spent on real-life adult violence against children.[150]

The Carnegie report's only positive notation is that teenagers are not really unstable, rebellious, or irrational, which is the youth-science equivalent of finding that blacks aren't really disposed to steal watermelons. Overall, the report's selective blindness (endorsed by such luminaries as William Julius Wilson, Michael Dukakis, Ted Koppel, and Senators Nancy Kassebaum, Daniel Inouye, and James Jeffords) perpetuates the investment of agencies' and programs' self-interested advertising masquerading as youth advocacy. Defense of traditional programmatic interests, ones which (in a misplaced medical model) strive to "treat" problems rather than prevent them, remains a major barrier to developing realistic measures to address youth problems at their roots in poverty and abuse.

The prescriptions for curing what is authoritatively diagnosed as "a generation at risk" have changed little in a decade, except to mushroom in size, funding, and scope: Behavior education, a variety of coordinated inter-agency interventions, mental health treatments, other professional remedies, and escalating suspension of legal and personal rights.[151] The hype has paid off. White kids were forced into treatment, dark kids to prison. Many more of both found themselves looking outward through bars.

Today, three times more teenagers are forced into professional readjustment regimens, four times more adolescents are mandated to drug and alcohol treatment, and six times more youths are confined to locked psychiatric wards than in 1980. A large majority of youths in psychiatric treatment were impounded under an exploding proliferation of new and vague diagnoses: "Conduct disorder," "transitional disorder," and other mental maladies unheard-of a decade before.[152] [153] A dozen times more states subject youths to a variety of scientifically-designed school behavior reform programs, from drug education to sexual abstinence and contraception programming to "values education," than in 1980.

In tandem, by the mid-1980s a majority of youth in jails, prisons, and detention facilities were nonwhite, incarcerated under criminal laws. Since 1980, arrests of juveniles have doubled. Twice as many teenagers are in jail, prison, other confinement; "a nation's children in lockup," a 1993 Los Angeles Times feature front-paged.[154] Predictable cycles of media publicity prompted by sponsors of each of these initiatives claim, in alternating regularity, "dramatic success" in fixing wayward youth, then that youth problems are skyrocketing, alarming, and "have never been worse."[155]

But has this decade of unprecedented, massive, costly, local-state-national-public-private-prevention-intervention-treatment youth reform and management strategy worked? Just the opposite.

Since the mid-1980s, youth homicide, violent crime, violent death, suicide and self-inflicted death, drug death, birth, and other problems that were previously declining all have risen, several rapidly. The upward trend in teen suicides and drug deaths from the early 1980s to the 1990s reversed previous declines (see chapters 6 and 8). Many trends, such as violent crime arrests and homicides, now stand at record levels. Unwed birth rates, previously rising, have risen faster. The "youth crisis," a fabricated cliche of self-interested groups in 1983, has become the genuine article under professional management in the 1990s.

Yet all the interests involved can do is propose more of the dismal same. "One side thinks we can reverse undesirable social trends through discipline and moral exhortation; the other side thinks that therapy and sensitivity will do the trick," wrote family historian Stephanie Koontz. "Both sides ignore the long-term structural changes that underlie many of the problems."[156]

Social science discovers the adolescent scapegoat

Pick up today's newspaper, tune in a talk channel, and chances are you'll encounter a view on teenagers similar to the one I found the day this was written. In the *Los Angeles Times*, University of Pennsylvania education professor Rebecca Maynard declaims on the subject of teenage sex:

> People forget that adolescents, regardless of income or social class, are risk-takers. They are impulsive. They feel invincible and they fail to plan ahead. So they don't think.[157]

As Harvard Professor of Geology and Zoology Stephen Jay Gould points out, American social science harbors a singularly lamentable history of looking for demographic scapegoats to buttress prevailing political needs. Compare Maynard's pronouncement on teenagers, typical of 1990s officials and social scientists quoted in the media, with the early-1900s socio-explanation for behavior by blacks:

> The Negro...(displays) instability of character incident to lack of self-control, especially in connection with the sexual relation; and there is lack of orientation... of self and environment.

The respected *American Medicine* of April 1907 editorialized against expanding rights for blacks who, being "without brains," could not comprehend the implications of their actions.[158]

Women lacked brains as well. Famed social psychologist Gustave Le Bon's 1895 "state of the knowledge review" indicates:

> All psychologists who have studied the intelligence of women... recognize today that they represent the most inferior forms of human evolution and that they are closer to children and savages than to an adult, civilized man. They excel in fickleness, inconstancy, absence of thought and logic, and incapacity to reason.[159]

Among the vast majority of social scientists, these myths of nonwhite, ethnic, and female brainlessness have been discarded. The same factless stereotypes applied to teenagers at the turn of the century have flowered, however. In psychologist G. Stanley Hall's *On Adolescence* (1904), which invented "*Sturm und Drang*" (storm and stress) as the driving feature of teenage behavior, adolescents and savages were the same thing: "Adolescent races."[160]

Today, both research findings and the electoral power of minority groups and women make it impolitic for most officials and experts openly to demean adult nonwhites and adult females. Even though research findings have just as solidly refuted the myth of teenage irrationality, social scientists bent on upholding prevailing political prejudices have not similarly banished teen-bashing to the landfill of bad-science anachronism.

The lazy, profligate, hypersexed "teenage mother" is a direct descendent of the black "welfare queen." "Youth violence" has its ancestry in the images of "Negro violence." "Teen suicide" and reckless teenage driving derives from the same impulsiveness once attributed to the hot-blooded minority male. Etc.

The popular social-science and media explanation, undressed of its academic nomenclature, for why teenagers act as they do is simple: Because they're stupid. They kill because Metallica puts the word on an album cover. They have sex because Madonna flaunts it. They smoke because a cartoon camel tells them to. They slash their wrists because a band calls itself "Suicidal Tendencies." They take drugs because of caps and t-shirts sporting marijuana leaves.

Do experts really believe the idiocy they declare in the press? If so, just consider how simple national health promotions would be if teenagers really were that dumb. Agencies would quit paying billions to PhDs and, instead, hire a crop of Madison Avenue marketers to churn out glitzy kid-fixing images. To stamp out crime, give McGruff a sax and shades. Drug and alcohol abstinence become the rage when DARE t-shirts display bitchen just-say-no logos. A rad anti-smoking dromedary, a studmuffin anti-gangsta, and goodbye teen smoking and gangs. Outfit a speed-metal band, "Pro-social Tendencies." A high-tech video game "Join the Rotary Club," a subliminal internet message, "turn in your cokehead mom," and goodbye epidemic social problems.

Assertions of adolescent irrationality display the selfsame affliction. Repeated studies find that modern medical and psychological experts will radically overestimate the prevalence of clinical disturbances among teenagers by a factor of *three*.[161] A 1987 *Sturm-und-Drang* throwback from the liberal medical journal, *The New Physician*, on teen suicide:

> Adolescence is a time of turbulence marked by rapid, physical, sexual, social and emotional development. It is a time of confusion and rebellion.[162]

Teen suicide rates are only one-fourth those of physicians.

Or note the explanation for teen smoking issued by the nation's leading anti-smoking official:

> The trend may be a reflection of what Michael Eriksen, director of the CDC's Office on Smoking and Health, calls "the perverse relationship between teens and adults."
> Smoking has always been an act of rebellion. As more adults frown on the use of tobacco, Eriksen says, it is possible that cigarettes have become even more "attractively illicit" to teenagers.[163]

Adolescent rebellion and perversity, of course, explain the 1989 finding of Eriksen's own Office on Smoking and Health that "seventy-five percent of all teenage smokers come from homes where parents smoke."[164]

Similar explanations by social scientists that AIDS cases contracted as HIV infections in teen years result from some kind of innate, "adolescent high-risk behavior"[165] fail on fundamental real-world counts. First, HIV infection rates are much higher among adults in their 20s and 30s (as measured by AIDS diagnoses, after the usual 10-year incubation period, among persons in their 30s and 40s). Second, most "teenage" HIV infections are acquired from sexual relations with adults.[166] Third, in contradiction to media myths, teenagers are not the fastest-rising group of HIV infectees, but among the slowest (see Chapter 2). The modern invention of "adolescent high risk behavior," an updating of Hall's "*Sturm und Drang*," is a circular non-explanation: High-risk outcomes result from high-risk behaviors which are *defined* as innate to adolescence.

What do researchers who have directly examined the question of adolescent "high risk" find? "Taken as a whole," one extensive review concluded of the standard stereotypes researchers have disproven for at least six decades, "adolescents are *not* in turmoil, *not* deeply disturbed, *not* at the mercy of their impulses, *not* resistant to parental values, *not* politically active, and *not* rebellious" (emphasis original).[167]

Another review found:

> Adolescents have been characterized as being particularly irrational in their behavior patterns. However, empirical tests have shown that adolescents are no less rational than adults. Applications of rational models to adolescent decision-making show that adolescents are consistent in their reasoning and behavior... (and) no more biased in their estimates of vulnerability to adverse health consequences than are their parents.[168]

Psychiatrist Daniel Offer and colleagues studied 30,000 teenagers and adults over 30 years, reaching conclusions that do not win talk-circuit billing or provide sensational media copy. They found 85 percent to 90 percent of teens held the same attitudes and risk perceptions as their parents, were not alienated, think about the future and work, were coping well with their lives, and did not display psychological disturbances:[169]

> Our youth are no healthier or sicker than we, their parents. They reflect us in their psychological defenses, beliefs, ideals, relationships, and behavior... We worry about the choices our teenagers make regarding drugs, sex, smoking, and drinking, yet decision making for adults is no different from decision making among teenagers.[170]

The mundane conclusion: Youths act like the adults who raise them.[171 172 173] For examples:

- In 1993, men accounted for 87 percent of all violent crime arrests among adults; boys accounted for 87 percent of all violent crime arrests among youths.[174]
- From 1940 to 1990, unwed birth rates rose 474 percent among teenage females and 510 percent among adult females ages 20-44; from 1975 to 1990, the increase was 78 percent among teens and 79 percent among adults.[175]
- Black adults are 45 percent less likely to commit suicide and 7.2 times more likely to commit homicide than are white adults, and black teenagers are 46 percent less likely to commit suicide and 7.7 times more likely to commit homicide than are white teenagers.[176]

Whether compared by state, era, or race, or combinations of the three, the mathematical correlations between rates of (and trends in) teenage and adult sexual, homicidal, suicidal, criminal, and other behaviors typically display near one-to-one correspondence.[177] In plain English, they act just like us. Maybe that's why we're so mad at them.

The courts: unchecked imbalance

Efforts to discern a judicial philosophy in the last 15 years of U.S. Supreme Court rulings on adolescent issues is fruitless. It is not one aimed at "protecting children." It is certainly not governed by "liberalizing rights." It is only quixotically founded in precedent. It is far from refreshingly eclectic.

The only central theme evident in recent Court decisions on youth is one of unrelenting hostility. Teenagers are decreed as "super-adults" subject to the harshest of punishments, or defined as "children" restricted by the most primitive of shackles, as will yield the most punitive result.

The Court has increasingly ruled from the late 1970s onward that juveniles have few, if any, constitutional rights and may be subjected to sterner punishments based on fewer procedural safeguards than adults are afforded. "You're dealing with children," Justice Antonin Scalia contemptuously dismissed an American Civil Liberties Union lawyer in a 1995 privacy rights case involving high school students. "You're not dealing with adults."[178]

Are teenagers children, then, meriting protection? Absolutely not. Alone among industrial nations, the U.S. executes "children." The U.S. has put to death 300 youths under age 18 in its history, including 125 under age 17—including three of the eight youths executed worldwide since 1979. (The only other nations still executing juveniles, according to Amnesty International: The enlightened democracies of Pakistan, Bangla Desh, Barbados, and Rwanda). In 1989, the U.S. Supreme Court specifically ruled that the execution of youths was constitutional.[179] Four of the nine justices, including Scalia, urged allowing states to extend the death penalty to "children" 15 and younger.[180]

Are teenagers adults, then, deserving of rights? Never. The Court ruled that self-interested psychiatrists and parents may decide whether juveniles can be committed indefinitely without even a hearing (as required for adult commitments) before an impartial state arbiter.[181] That ruling opened the door, literally, to an avalanche of costly juvenile psychiatric commitments—a majority of which were unnecessary, as shown by later assessments.[182]

Children, needing special safeguards? A 1977 opinion (in a case involving documented severe injuries to students, including hematoma and nerve damage, for trivial offenses) upheld school corporal punishment. The majority argued that the constitution's prohibition on "cruel and unusual punishment" is designed to "protect persons convicted of crimes... not children."[183]

Adults? Two 1980s rulings, effectively wiping out the standard of previous Courts that "students do not shed their constitutional rights... at the schoolhouse gate,"[184] granted school authorities unlimited power to censor student journalism[185] and expression.[186]

Children? The modern Supreme Court was not content simply to hold, in 1981, that juveniles may be tried and sentenced as adults.[187] Sweeping aside 1960s court rulings that juvenile justice forces the "worst of both worlds" upon youths by imposing arbitrarily stern sentence while denying basic rights,[188] the 1980s Court endorsed double standards aimed at punishing youths *more* than adults. In 1984, the Court allowed law enforcement sweeping authority to confine youths accused of crimes before trial, without hearings, on the mere suspicion that they might commit additional crimes.[189] In contrast, pre-trial detention is authorized for only the most dangerous adults, typically ones involved in organized crime, and only after an "adversary hearing."[190]

The effect of these double-standard rulings is that the popular myth that teens are treated leniently and "get away with murder" is the opposite of the truth. A 1993 California Department of Corrections study found juveniles were consistently confined for 60 percent *longer* than adults for the same crimes (nearly a year longer, on average: 26 months for youths, 16 months for adults), including wide sentencing disparities for murder (youth 60 months, adults 41 months) and other crimes.[191]

Children where convenient, adults where convenient, as will promote the most punitive outcome? This seems to be the new Court philosophy:

- In 1989, the Court specifically allowed states to deny juveniles individual rights because of their "immature age"—but to apply "individualized tests" in order to put them to death.[192]
- In 1981, the Court held that juveniles under age 18 may be punished for the "statutory rape" of another juvenile of the same age even if the sex was purely consensual.[193] In 1990 and 1992, the Court held that states may require juveniles to obtain the consent of both parents for an abortion even if one parent was absent or hostile.[194]
- In 1995, the Court (its "liberal" justices concurring) allowed schools unlimited authority to subject students to mandatory drug tests.[195] Justices repeated the inflammatory arguments of Clinton officials that "there is a nationwide drug problem in the schools."[196] Clinton, in turn, praised the Court's ruling—which permitted authorities to demand that student athletes urinate in front of them for drug testing—as "sending exactly the right message." The majority declared their belief that, in effect, simply *being* an adolescent constitutes probable cause to suspect wrongdoing. The majority's language indicated willingness to rule in any given case that teenagers have no constitutional rights whatsoever.[197]

Thus, in the courtroom as throughout America of the Nineties, young age has become an "aggravating factor" promoting higher standards of behavior, stricter judgment, and tougher penalties (accompanied by rhetoric of "caring" and "concern"), while adult age is a "mitigating factor" leading to lower expectations and more lenient sentences. The only coherent judicial philosophy tying these rulings together is an evident desire to sift out what ruling will inflict the maximum punishment on the adolescents at issue.

Generations

Government and private interests may exaggerate and exploit demographic scapegoats, as has happened many times in the history of the U.S. and other societies. They may manufacture misleading public information tailored to denigrate youths and flatter adults. But none of these institutions invented "adolescents" as the particular target for 1990s wrath. Today's adult public is especially attuned to the anti-youth agenda pursued by major interests and the media. Ultimately, the contradictions involved in an adult generation attacking the very young that it raised are so broad that the source of virulent youth-hating policies must be sought in public attitudes. The campaigns of politicians and special interests, which have bombarded the public with misinformation, explain a large share of today's anti-youth sentiment. But the unprecedented self-centeredness and detachment of many modern grownups who seem eager to receive such misinformation about their young also demands examination.

When older generations are criticized (occasionally and gently) for robbing the young, the focus of the attack has been on senior citizens simply because of the sheer amount of public resources now devoted to elder care and feeding. It is clear that allocating such an enormous share of the public welfare benefits for 35 million seniors, most of whom are well off, is far out of balance to their needs—especially when compared to that of 67 million children whose poverty rates are double those of the elderly and rising. But the problem is not the amount of money seniors receive from public coffers, even though senior welfare is so maldistributed that 12 percent of the nation's seniors (the highest rate in the industrial world) remain in poverty even after Social Security, Medicare, and the myriad of tax breaks are added in. The problem is the hostile attitudes today's seniors display toward extending the generous welfare they receive to younger families and children.

It is also clear that many seniors find the "greedy geezer" label occasionally directed their way baffling. Most survived the Depression in youth, fought two wars, and by their lights created the postwar wealth that defined a nation thought to have unlimited potential. The experiences of many of today's elderly belie the notion that their privileges and subsidies could diminish a shrinking pie for their grandchildren. They were brought up with the view that the American Pie had no limits. The idea that redressing disgracefully high rates of elder poverty in the 1950s with a comprehensive medical plan, Social Security checks of a few hundred dollars a month, and an array of mostly-small tax breaks and benefits could mushroom into a half-trillion dollar subsidy plan, a major factor bankrupting future generations, is incomprehensible.

Politicians curried just such complacency by assuring 1960s, 1970s, and 1980s workers that they were financing their own retirements through "accounts" accumulated from a kind of "insurance program" paid for by decades of FICA taxes withheld from their paychecks. In fact, nothing of the sort was the case. Today's seniors paid for only around one-fourth the costs of their retirements; just three of the dozen years they live, on average, past age 65. Social Security is not an insurance program and it involves no "accounts." It is simply publicly subsidized welfare, Aid to Dependent Seniors.[198] A large part of reducing today's manifest senior indifference to the well-being of younger generations, perhaps even deterring the growing willingness of over-65 voters to prefer cutting their own taxes to funding school bond issues and public assistance for the young, involves a clear message from political leaders that the welfare check seniors receive *today* is paid for by younger workers *today*.

This political "pyramid scheme" remained tenable as long as workers continued to enjoy rising wages and continue to outnumber seniors four or five to one. Neither is the case today. As will be shown, poorer young are subsidizing masses of richer old, an eventuality the opposite of that envisioned by Social Security's framers. That seniors and soon-to-be retirees seem unaware that their own welfare checks are directly tied to the welfare of the young families—the education youths receive, the jobs they land, the public aid systems that boost the young from dependence to wage-earner—is a direct result of the same climate of misinformation that leads the aged to fear and despise the young. Given the easily established mutual dependence of old and young, the manifest hostility of today's seniors toward youth interests is baffling and disturbing.

Detached seniors

America's senior citizens, who formed crucial constituencies for the New Deal and Great Society social reforms, have become steadily more conservative over the last 20 years—especially in states such as California, where large gaps have opened up between generally well-off seniors and poorer populations of young families and youths. Despite domination by women, who are usually compassionate on social issues, elderly voters in California have formed the biggest voting bloc backing a series of measures that have devastated the well-being of the young.

In 1979, two-thirds of Californian voters over age 65 voted to reduce their property taxes and cripple social services, hospitals, libraries, and schools. In 1992, voters over the age of 65 were the most enthusiastic supporters of an anti-welfare plan aimed at slashing benefits for the state's poorest young families, two-thirds of whose victims would have been children (it lost narrowly only due to opposition from voters under age 30). [199] In 1994, 68 percent of the seniors voted to boot the children of illegal immigrant parents (the same ones wealthier Californians typically employ) out of school and deny them basic health services, as did 65 percent of those age 40-65.[200] Again, only voters under age 30 opposed Proposition 187. In the 1994 elections, California seniors of both sexes were the most likely to vote for Republicans. A 1994 University of Michigan Institute for Social Research study found that while younger respondents solidly favored Social Secutity spending (despite the belief that it will be gone by the time they retire), only 47 percent of seniors supported increased federal funding for public schools even in theory. [201]

As a result of the publicly-underwritten 60 percent decline in elder poverty in three decades, the aged are no longer the impoverished "seniors on fixed incomes" of past liberal lore. They have amassed household net worths (assets minus debts) *averaging* $148,000 for couples, $64,000 for single men, and $60,000 for single women. Not only were the average net worths of seniors more than triple those of younger age groups, seniors were the only group to show an increase from the 1980s.[202] Yet most spent the wealth accumulated in their middle-age, when average household incomes topped $40,000 per year, so that today, half the elderly would be poor (poor, that is, if their massive personal assets, especially home ownership, are overlooked) were it not for government subsidies. These subsidies are paid for by younger workers attempting to repay school loans, start careers, buy homes, and raise children on much lower incomes and assets.

Today's seniors collect five to 20 times more Social Security, Medicare, and other senior subsidies paid by younger workers than they themselves paid into the system in taxes. While about $60 billion is spent every year on welfare benefitting 16 million poor children and their families (such as AFDC, Food Stamps, school lunch, Women Infants and Children, medical aid, and housing) and is shrinking, senior subsidy programs such as Social Security retirement and Medicare spend $400 billion annually and are skyrocketing. Even when public education costs are figured in, the average child in the U.S. receives about $5,000 in government aid annually; the average senior citizen, $15,000.[203] Unlike children's assistance programs, senior welfare programs cover most medical costs, are indexed to rise with inflation, do not diminish in individual payment as the number of recipients in a household rises, and are subject to no standards of "personal responsibility."

Since 1990, the average beneficiary of Social Security, age 70, has enjoyed a healthy monthly payment increase (from $603 in 1990 to $674 in 1994). But the average AFDC recipient, age 9, has suffered a loss in their already minuscule monthly benefit ($135 in 1990, $133 in 1994). It is time for liberal senior welfare advocates to pay attention. This imbalance is extreme.

In a particularly egregious double standard, welfare reformers insist that young single mothers raising children and running a household are not "working" and should be cut off welfare. Yet even divorced elderly housewives who (by the same logic) never "worked" a day in their lives are entitled to receive their former husband's Social Security checks because their domestic services are rightly considered "work." Welfare reform commentators, such as *The New Republic*'s Mickey Kaus, defend massive Social Security outlays but argue for slashing the 1.1 percent of the budget spent on AFDC because the former rewards "work" while the latter does not—that is, the average AFDC beneficiary, age nine, should damn well get a job.[204]

The chief representative of today's over-50 set is the 31-million-member American Association of Retired Persons, whose assets and commercial interests place it near the top of Fortune-500 tycoondom. The AARP demands full maintenance of Social Security (even the $75 billion in Social Security and Medicare paid to seniors with cash incomes exceeding $50,000 per year) and other senior welfare and tax breaks, even if the price is a million more children impoverished due solely to FICA deductions from their caretakers' paychecks.[205]

Today's children should not be surprised that today's grandparents tolerate 25 percent youth poverty rates. This is the generation that let its own grandfolks (the ones who paid the tab for Roosevelt's pro-youth welfare programs and the generous GI Bill) live out their twilight years in the 1950s and 1960s in abject penury, 40 percent scraping by on incomes below poverty levels.[206] The "sacred contract," which today's senior lobbies invoke to demand top-dollar subsidy from the young, is newly-discovered, one-sided, and expedient. Today's elderly recognize no similar "sacred contract" to pay for the best quality schools and assistance to support younger generations.

And children are not the only ones devastated by the avarice of those of age to be their grandparents. So are a sizeable chunk of their own-aged peers. Today's elder-welfare allocation system is so maldistributed that even after the U.S. spent one-third of its entire budget on the elderly, 12 percent of the seniors (blacks and Hispanics unable to accumulate property are heavily over-represented) live in poverty—two to three times higher than in more equitable and frugal industrial nations.[207] The maximum monthly family benefit for a worker retiring at 65 in January 1995 was $780 for workers making $11,000 in cash income per year, $1,564 for workers earning $25,000 per year, and $2,098 for workers earning $61,000 or more. As now structured, Social Security is a system for maintaining millions of elderly in poverty. Current elder-welfare defenders propose no schemes to relieve the poverty of these 4 million aged. Under Social Security's regressive benefit system, boosting the benefits of poor seniors to match those currently received by middle-income elderly would require boosting the benefits of wealthier seniors a like amount, costing $150 billion per year *more* for Social Security than is now being paid.

So, like children, adolescents, and young families, poorer seniors are victimized by an American welfare system that relentlessly rewards the rich. These impoverished U.S. aged are trotted out by condominium-senior lobbies to defend their own largesse. And no one has explained why poorer children and single mothers who receive public assistance should be stigmatized as welfare recpients and subject to cuts when wealthier seniors who receive more public aid are exempt from scrutiny.

If distributed equitably, spending one-third of the federal budget on the care of Americans over age 65 would be a fine idea. These grayed citizens have worked all of their lives and deserve some payback, one which would be easier to bear if the federal penchant for Aid to Perpetually Dependent Corporations (APDC) and Defense Industry Subsidy Stamps (DISS) weren't so potent acronyms for congressional protection. The problem is not caused by senior welfare per se, which (if made more progressive) would be a model for family assistance programs. The problem is that today's seniors are not responding to the unprecedented security they are provided at public expense with a like attitude of beneficience toward the young and the poor, but with hostility and contempt.

As a result, the exemplary social insurance for the American aged does not serve as a model for universal social insurance on the European scheme that many liberals have long championed, but as a major impediment to it. The removal (as of this writing) of Social Security, the nation's largest and fastest-growing welfare program, from budget review increases many-fold the pressure to cut remaining, smaller programs such as Supplemental Security Income, Medicaid, (both of which benefit many desperately poor and disabled seniors), Food Stamps, and AFDC. It has given the mass of senior voters whose needs are well taken care of by government a stake in opposing aid for the young, which they have done in rising numbers.

About one-third (demographic patterns ironically indicate that it is the poorest one-third) continue to vote to expand education and support assistance for young families. Others have dissented strongly from the AARP's hegemony and have backed groups whose goals benefit children even at the expense of reducing elder subsidies. They are the remnants of America's true grandparent generation—

unfortunately a minority. Their age peers need to be forcefully reminded that their welfare depends in a direct sense not on how stridently they can pressure politicians with their voting strength, but how well the younger generation, which funds their retirements, is succeeding in school and the job market.

Grabby Boomers

The put-seniors-first attitude of most seniors, deplorable as it is, is not the greatest menace to the young. Baby Boomers, my generation, the most massively subsidized age group in American history, is shaping up to be even worse. The menace goes beyond libertarian satirist P.J. O'Rourke's horror, horrible as it is, at tens of millions of "superannuated hippies." We have lost any semblance of our once-famed social conscience. Education forums report that Baby Boomers are more resistant to spending for education (now that our schooling is done). "We face the loss of more school bond issues and school support in the future as our population ages," the Institute for Social Research's Maris Vinovskis warned—and the attitudes of Baby Boomers are the reason "schools may go bust."[208]

It is not immediately clear why Baby Boomers, a generation famed for activism, anti-adult attitudes, and plenitude of high-risk behaviors in our own adolescence, should now represent such a virulently anti-youth claque of 30-50 year-olds. "A few years ago, a *Rolling Stone* survey of Baby Boomers said that boomers did everything, regret nothing and want their kids to do none of it," wrote columnist Ellen Goodman.[209]

But this is a bizarre turn of events. We were supposed to be the adults who could understand our kids' rock'n'roll, casual dope experimentation, sexual unconventionality, rebellion against prevailing values, and anti-adult attitudes. These were lifestyles from which we won grudging acceptance from our more conservative parents in the '60s and tolerance even from the likes of Barry Goldwater, David Rockefeller, and a blue-ribbon presidential panel formed to examine our dope-taking—one which recommended drug decriminalization and expanded youth rights![210]

Instead of tolerance, we display absolutist rigidity (for kids, not us). The Clinton administration's top health official singles out for special condemnation "one-time marijuana use... casual use" of the very type claimed by her bosses at 1600 Pennsylvania Avenue. A vice-president's wife circulates absurdly sensational videos blaming rock lyrics for teen suicide, violence, drugs, and sex. A president proposes absolute zero-tolerance for drinking alcohol by persons under age 21. It is tempting to say that the Clinton stance represents a retreat back to the wilds of 1970 when Vice President Spiro Agnew blamed the Beatles, Jefferson Airplane, and *Easy Rider* for "creeping permissiveness" among youth. But Agnew at least had the guts to include "pill-popping" parents and "growing adult alcoholism" for "setting examples for younger citizens to 'to do some experimenting on their own.'"[211] We display no such fairness.

Unlike the anachronism of elder views, today's Baby Boom self-fixation represents state-of-the-art hypocrisy. Here was a generation whose arrival on the scene in the late 1960s brought a doubling in violent crime, suicide, and murder, a tripling in venereal disease, a twelve-fold increase in drug arrests, and a drug death rate in 1970 five times that of today's young. Today, the drug death rate among Baby Boomer 40-year-olds is 15 times higher than that among '90s teenagers![212]

Baby Boomers' average marriage lasts only 80 months. Our males have set sky-rocketing records of child abandonment and deadbeat daddyism. Half of us admitted illegal drug use and nonmarital sex, and a similar number to driving drunk.[213] And Clinton and Gingrich threaten youths with dire punishments for violating *our* reverence toward "family values" and "personal responsibility," for experimenting with marijuana, for having sex before marriage? Could it be that this is self-exoneration of a Baby Boom generation afraid to face the damage of our own unrestrained self-indulgence?

Historians Neil Howe and William Strauss wrote in a much-deserved cold shower in the December 1992 *Atlantic*:

> Boomers might prefer to think of their generation as the leaders of social progress, but the facts show otherwise. Yes, the Boom is a generation of trends, *but all of those trends are negative*. [emphasis in original][214]

Boomers, who spent all our lives standing in lines, grew up with full knowledge of "limits" even before environmentalist Dennis Meadows and Jerry Brown made the term '70s mantra. But it went wrong. The relentless grab for yuppiedom combined with the disintegration of families in the '70s and '80s produced Baby Boomers' record-high levels of wealth and record-low commitments to coming generations. The mass of 1980s and 1990s absentee parents is a dozen times more likely to be up-to-date on their car payments than their child support payments.[215] The upwardly mobile adults able, for the first time, to shuck individual responsibilities to family and offspring also comprise an adult public willing to use government to hoard our own generational interests against those of the young.

A 1995 Rand Corporation survey showed fewer than half of Baby Boomers are putting aside savings from our high incomes (averaging over $50,000 per year per household for 40-65 year-olds) for our retirements.[216] We are paying for a lower proportion of our children's education, both publicly and privately, than our parents did for us.[217] While the credo of past parents and grandparents was to invest in the young and to sacrifice so that their children might live better, the '90s American grownup expresses outrage now that it is our turn to assume the normal duties of adulthood—including footing the bills.

On top of all that, we demand endless odes from politicians even when the result is fantasy (of the Stephen King rather than the Mother Goose type). California Governor Pete Wilson, the nation's most skilled Baby-Boomer/middle-ager apologist, spares little indignance at the "unfairness" of his graying constituents "who pay their own way" and "play by the rules," yet now have to "shoulder the tax burden" for young families and students.[218]

Middle age is too early for mass Alzheimer's. In ugly truth, Baby Boomers will be the first generation heavily subsidized by *both* its parents and its children. California elders and Baby Boomers paid little or nothing to attend a free college and university system guaranteed by a century of legislators prior to 1970. Raised on the generous education and welfare programs of the 1950s and 1960s, Boomers and their seniors have relentlessly refused to pay taxes for the government services they demand, ringing up federal, state, and local government deficits in the past dozen years totalling some $10,000 per family. Clearly, my over-40 American peers expect today's already impoverished, de-funded, and forcibly-indebted young to bankroll the huge Social Security and other elder maintenance payments demanded by our retiring 60 millions early in the next century.

Whatever is wrong with American youth is a predictable consequence of being raised by the over-40 cohort, which industrialist-emeritus Lee Iacocca called "the most selfish and irresponsible generation this country has ever produced."[219] The question is what is wrong with today's grownups—middle-agers and elders educated, aided, and prepared by a more beneficent postwar America to be the shining hope of the late 20th century. Why it is that we are leaving behind what Howe and Strauss accurately describe as "post Boom desertscapes" when we can well afford to support our successor generations?

Ironically, it is this detachment that may account for much of the anger and despair pollsters report among the older voters who lashed out angrily in the 1994 elections. Whatever can the richest, most pampered, most secure grayed and graying Americans in history possibly be so angry at? Today's elders, looking down from the hilltops and suburbs at the dark faces in city schoolyards, do not see ourselves reflected in today's young. Though we don't admit it openly, our anger must stem from the suspicion that "America" ends with us.

Erasing the bond

American adults have regarded adolescents with hope and foreboding throughout this century. What is transpiring today is new and ominous. A particular danger attends older generations indulging "they-deserve-it" myths to justify enriching ourselves at the expense of younger ones. The message Nineties American adults have spent two decades sending to youths is: *You are not our kids. We don't care about you.*

Adolescents and young adults do not organize constituencies effective in adult political arenas (the failures of Clean Gene anti-war brigades in 1968 are fresh; the suppression of 1936's radical youth lingers). If not provided for, they detach from adults as they perceive their elders have dissociated from them. The growth of gangs, runaway cultures, and shadow urban enterprises among the rising numbers of marginal youth—as well as anecdotes from teachers, social workers, and other "hands-on" adults that today's students seem extraordinarily "hard to reach"—testifies to detachment.

Its manifestation fuels the Golden State's biggest growth industry. California opened 2,916-bed Corcoran prison in 1988 at a cost of $280 million. In 1994, it held 5,387 inmates. Centinela prison opened in 1993 at a cost of $230 million for 2,208 guests; 18 months later, it housed 4,104. Ironwood, $214 million, opened in 1994 for 2,400; immediately the no-vacancy sign was out.

Seven more California prisons opened during 1989-93 at a cost of $1.3 billion to accommodate 16,000 more; today, they cage 28,000. During 1995-96, four new prisons for yet 8,600 more will open their doors, cost: $839 million. A new prison every eight months, full upon opening. Some incorporate second-generation names:

"Soledad II."

After 20 years of official declarations, professional pronouncements, psychological speculations, and media hyperbole regarding "teenage violence wild in the streets," California's sophisticated statistical harbingers boil down to a primitive and unoriginal point: Deny lots of kids a fair share of society's resources, expect lots of violence. Save money on schools, spend more on prisons. Erase the future of the young, they will return the favor by erasing our legacy. "The old get old, the young get stronger," Jim Morrison foretold in 1968.[220] A "generation war," pathetically easy for the old to declare, is impossible for the old to win.

2. Fertility Bites

My theory is, don't do it until you're 21, and then don't tell me about it.
—Hillary Clinton, 1995, on daughters having sex[1]

Elizabeth Monroe, Hannah Van Buren, Eliza Johnson, Alice Roosevelt, Rosalynn Carter.
—U.S. First Ladies who were pregnant teenagers

Sixteen year-old Elena related legal efforts to collect child support from the 24-year-old father of her baby. Carmen, 16, described how the 21-year-old father of her child refused to take responsibility. Seventeen year-old Jennifer, mother of two, tearfully recounted violence she feared both from her 23-year-old "boyfriend" and her own alcoholic father. Maggy, 16, and her 21-year-old husband handed their infant back and forth as they testified. An angry older mom described how her 14 year-old daughter was raped by an older teenager and her 16-year-old had a baby by a 24-year-old neighbor.

Soon, a shocked California Senate committee taking testimony at a Santa Ana alternative school in February 1995 was asking on cue, "How old is the father?" They didn't like the answers: Here and there a peer boy, but mostly men ages 20, 23, 24—in one case, 33 years old, with a 14-year-old lover. "Men are doing this," declared one conservative Republican senator, shaking his head. "These are *adults*."[2]

The Committee was seeing first-hand a major reality of "teenage" pregnancy, one officials and the media have ignored: Most of it is caused by adults. Men age 20 and older father 2.5 times more babies among senior high-age girls than do senior high boys, and four times more babies among junior high girls than do junior high boys.[3] This "adult" detail is only one of the crucial facts America's increasingly vitriolic furor over "teenage" sex has managed to overlook.

"Junior high sex" and other myths

America's penchant for hypocritical revulsion at adolescents reaches a crescendo on the topic of "junior high sex." The Centers for Disease Control, Alan Guttmacher Institute, and other media authorities incessantly lament that the amount of sexual activity among 12-14-year-olds has tripled over the past 20 years.[4] Suddenly in the 1990s, the president and every governor's wife and agencies left to right embraced the urgency of preaching chastity to eighth graders.

Honesty has little to do with discussions of "teenage sex," much less "junior high sex." As long as everyone assumed it meant a couple of seventh graders fumbling their way to intercourse—which battalions of top health officials and PhDs have deceived themselves and us into thinking—we're eager for details. Here is an issue to unite in one finger-pointing, moralizing mob condom and chastity devotee alike.[5] But the reality is far different, and it does not suit the needs of today's political sexologists.

Begin with the fundamental evidence offered for the existence of a "junior high sexual revolution." Surveys show that in 1970, only 20 percent of junior high boys and 4 percent of junior high girls claimed on self-reporting surveys to have had sex. In 1992, 27 percent of junior high boys and 10 percent of junior high girls.[6] Big news.

But, no one (except youth-at-risk expert Joy Dryfoos)[7] said, wait a minute. Three times more junior high boys than girls have had sex—at earlier ages, and with more partners? What does this mean? Are a few girls really getting around? Are boys having sex with aliens? Each other? Exaggerating—drastically, maybe? A 1995 long-term study of National Youth Survey data similarly found that 5.5 *times* more 13-year-old boys than girls claimed to be "sexually active"—but as the males aged into late adolescence, they consistently reported older ages of first sexual intercourse.[8]

And if rising legions of pubescents were "sexually active," how come the pregnancy rate among 10-14-year-olds hasn't similarly skyrocketed? In 1976, 3.2 babies, abortions, and miscarriages per 100 junior high girls; in 1988, 3.3.[9] Amid this supposed "junior high sexual revolution," 98 percent of the girls arrived at age 15 never having been pregnant. Junior highers must be America's most skilled condom deployers. Seventh graders should be enlisted to hold seminars for U.S. grownups, who sport the industrial world's highest rates of unplanned pregnancy.[10]

It looks like most of the "junior high sexual revolution" consists of junior high boys engaging in wild exaggeration in preparation for later gym class and barstool braggadocio. Except that politicians, academicians, and fundamentalists took them seriously. So much for the credulity of experts, who would be expected to harbor more skepticism about self-reported behaviors, especially on topics such as sex. And the contradictions get worse.

In the 1990s, California[11] and Maryland[12] became the first states to release comprehensive tabulations of fathers' ages in births among teenage mothers. The two states are very different demographically. California's pregnant-teen population is dominated by Hispanics and whites, Maryland's by blacks. Both states reported fathers' ages on 80 percent of the birth certificates for junior high mothers, leaving few unknowns. In the tabulation below, fathers' ages are arranged to correspond to ages of school attendance; 18-year-old males are thus classified as "school age" rather than as "adult" because most are in high school. (See Table 2.1).

In both states, junior high boys constituted fewer than 10 percent of the fathers in births among junior high girls. In California, adult, post-school men age 19 and older fathered a majority of births among junior high mothers; in Maryland, a little over one-third.

Maryland fathers tend to be younger than California fathers, reflecting the younger nature of black fathers. But in both states, men over age 21 father three times more births among junior high girls than do junior high boys. The GM workers Clinton swapped El Camino tailgate conquest tales with were more likely to knock up a junior high girl than the eighth grade boys the president sermonized on sexual responsibility a few days before.[13]

And another surprise: Of the 800 births fathered by California boys age 10-15 in 1994, only half involved mothers age 10-15. The other half involved mothers age

Table 2.1.

Fathers in births to junior high mothers are *not* peer boys:

Fathers' ages in births among mothers age 11-15	California, 1994		Maryland, 1994	
Age 13-15 (junior high)	372	8.0%	47	7.9 %
Age 16-18 (senior high)	2,017	43.2	341	57.4
Age 19-24 (adult)	1,982	42.5	185	31.1
Age 25-older (adult)	298	6.4	21	3.5
Total	4,669		594	

Sources: California Center for Health Statistics (1992-95). Resident live births by age of mother, age of father, marital status, race, county, 1989-94. Sacramento, CA: Department of Health Services. Horon IL (1995, 8 September). Paternal age for teen mothers less than 18 years of age. Baltimore: Maryland Department of Health and Mental Hygiene.

16 and older. Overall, 93 percent of California's four-year total of 25,000 births from 1990-93 involving at least one junior high-age parent involved a partner of senior high or adult age. A similar pattern is evident for Maryland. Kind of casts a pall on those wildly popular "mentor" programs in which adults and senior high students smugly team up to preach abstinence to younger teens. If senior highers and grownups are gung-ho to stamp out junior high sex, they should quit having sex with junior high kids.

The "minor" teenage mothers debated by welfare reformers also include those age 16 and 17. Figures from California and Maryland provide fathers' ages on 85 percent of all birth certificates for mothers age 16-17. Fathers' ages, again classifying 18-year-old males as "school-age" rather than as "adult" (Table 2.2), are:

Table 2.2.

Adult men, not boys, father a large majority of births among older schoolgirls:

Fathers' ages in births among mothers age 16-17	California, 1994		Maryland, 1994	
Age 13-15 (junior high)	258	1.4%	33	1.6%
Age 16-18 (senior high)	5,958	31.7	809	39.8
Age 19-24 (adult)	10,547	56.1	1,076	53.0
Age 25-older (adult)	2,044	10.9	103	5.1
Total	18,807		2,031	

Source: California Center for Health Statistics (1992-95) *op cit*; Maryland Department of Health and Mental Hygiene (1995), *op cit*.

Among mothers age 16-17, two-thirds of California fathers and nearly six in 10 Maryland fathers are post-school adult men age 19 and older. These figures are similar to those found by the Guttmacher Institute's study of 1988 birth records and self reports of fathers' ages in national surveys. That study found 80 percent of the births among girls ages 18 and younger are fathered by men 18 and older, and half by men age 20 and older.[14] Teenagers, in fact, are the only age group for which both sexes tend to marry older partners. National marriage records show that brides average 3 months older than the small number of teenage grooms; grooms average 3.5 years older than the much larger number of teenage brides.[15] Births among school-age mothers by age of partner are summarized in Figure 2.3.

For all the derogatory publicity on "children having children" and *People* magazine covers on "babies having babies," in only 8 percent of all teenage births and 1 percent of all births in the U.S. are *both* partners under age 18—that is, legally "children." The same health and media entities who have made the "child" age of the mother a cataclysmic headliner have shown no stomach for similarly featuring the "adult" age of 80 percent of the fathers. "Adults having babies with babies" is not the kind of crowd-pleaser America's pop-media is ready to spring on the supermarket checkout lines.

Is this adult-teen pattern a new and shocking degeneracy produced by the Sexual Revolution? Not even nearly. As turn-of-the-century feminist Anna Garlin

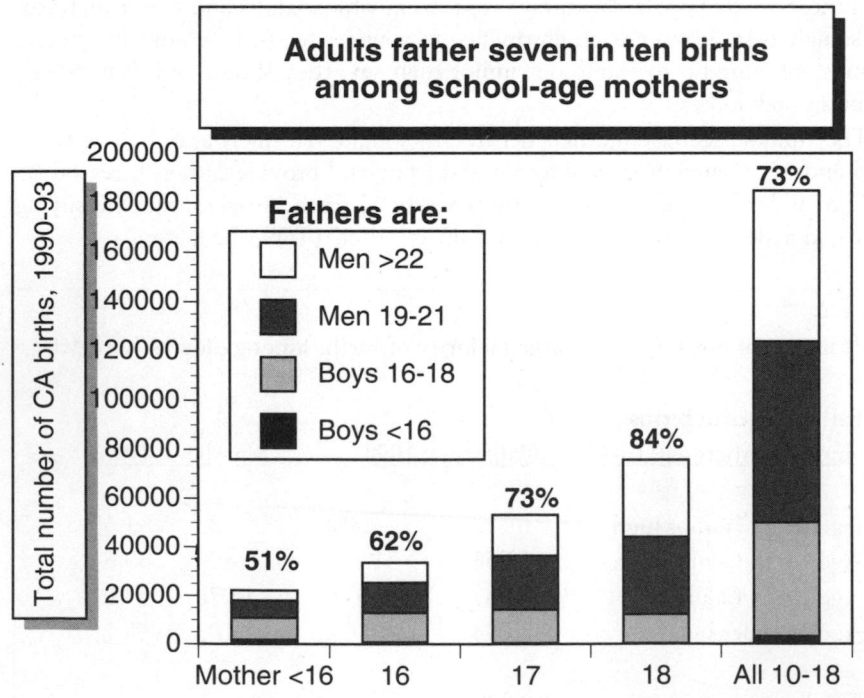

Figure 2.3

Source: California Center for Health Statistics (1995). See Tables 2-1, 2-2.

Spencer reported, statutory rape (or "age of consent") laws were initiated in the late 1800s to deal with a staggering volume of child prostitution. In 1858, a study found one prostitute for every 19 men living in New York City; three-eighths of the prostitutes were teenagers, and one-fourth were estimated to die from disease or violence every year. In most states, sexual relations between adults and girls age 10-13, and in some as young as seven, were legal at that time.[16]

Adult-teen liaison has shown up since U.S. birth records were first available. A tabulation by the Census Bureau from the first national birth registration area which covered more than half the nation's population, in 1921, showed that 70 percent of the moms age 10-14, and 90 percent age 15-19, reproduced with men 20 and older that year. Men over age 25 accounted for one-third of all "teenage" births (Table 2.4).

Table 2.4

Adult men have always fathered most of what we call "teen" births:

U.S. teen births, 1921	Mother age 10-14		Mother age 15-19	
Father age 10-14	11	1.5%	5	-%
Father age 15-19	210	28.2	13,570	9.3
Father age 20-24	311	41.7	82,625	56.5
Father age 25-older	214	28.7	50,114	34.3
Total	746		146,314	

Source: U.S. Bureau of the Census (1921). Birth, Stillbirth and Infant Mortality Statistics, 1921. Washington, DC: U.S. Department of Commerce.

In 1940—a year often cited by nostalgics as one of exemplary youth behavior—there were 304,000 births among girls ages 10-19. Just 12 percent of the fathers were also teenagers; 61 percent of the fathers were age 20-24, and 28 percent were age 25 and older.

Sexually-transmitted disease and AIDS

The popular myth, fostered in the media by health agencies and other experts, is that teenage girls and boys are spreading sexually transmitted disease (STD) and AIDS among one another like wildfire. Teens are declared to have the highest, or the most rapidly rising, sexual disease epidemics of any age group. Experts blame careless adolescent sex, a standard refrain.

In fact, teenagers are not the most at risk, and the ones who are being infected with STDs and AIDS typically have older, adult male partners. Records of gonorrhea and syphilis diagnoses going back to the mid-1950s have consistently shown that while rates of STD infection among adult men are 1.5 to two times higher than among adult women, STDs are three to four times more prevalent among 10-14 year-old girls than among 10-14 year-old boys. Contemplate the 1992 tabulation of

Table 2.5.

Many more younger teen girls than boys get STDs:

U.S. STD infectees, 1992		Male	Female	Percent female
Age	0-14	2,290	7,684	77.0%
	15-19	64,051	77,516	54.8%
	Total <20	66,341	85,200	56.2%
	20-older	232,037	139,164	37.5%

Source: CDC, printout on STD by age, race, sex, 1990-92. Cited in Males M (1993, December). School-age pregnancy: Why hasn't prevention worked? *Journal of School Health* 63, 429-432.

gonorrhea and syphilis cases by the Centers for Disease Control (Table 2.5).

Given that a substantial number of STD cases among younger males appear to result from relations with men, and since most STDs are more easily diagnosed in males than in females, the teenage female surplus is even more pronounced.

The silence of health officials on the damning patterns of adult-teen births and STDs is bad enough, but their complete failure to address the way adolescents get AIDS is nothing less than criminal. More than 1,000 diagnosed Acquired Immune Deficiency Syndrome (AIDS) cases among persons under age 20 in the U.S. (excluding those acquired in "Pattern II" nations such as Haiti) are attributed to heterosexual intercourse and are tabulated by the Centers for Disease Control. Since AIDS typically takes 7-10 years to develop from initial exposure to the human immunodeficiency virus (HIV), it's a safe bet that nearly all such cases were acquired from sex prior to age 15—childhood and junior high years. It's also a safe bet that many thousands of cases remain to be diagnosed.[17]

Of these heterosexually-transmitted child and pubescent AIDS cases, 91 percent are found in girls (Figure 2.6). In heterosexual sex, females are anatomically more vulnerable to HIV infection than males, so a surplus among females is not surprising. The AIDS rate among heterosexual adult women is 1.9 times the rate among heterosexual adult men. But that does not explain why the heterosexual AIDS rate among female and young-adolescent children is *more than 10 times higher* than among corresponding young boys (Table 2.7).

Among males, half the AIDS cases diagnosed between ages 12 and 25 (that is, excluding pediatric cases acquired from mothers at birth) are in nonwhites; among females, 75 percent. In fact, a 1995 study in *Science* magazine found enormous racial disparities in AIDS infections through January 1993: Black men were four times more likely to be infected than white men, and black women were 17 times more likely to be infected than white women, with Hispanics in between.[18] The U.S. House of Representatives' Select Committee on Children, Youth and Families pointed this fact out in a 1992 majority (Democrats') report: "Females and minorities represent [a] greater proportion of cases in youth than in adults." Oddly, the committee did not explore why this striking pattern, shown in Table 2.8, might be occurring.

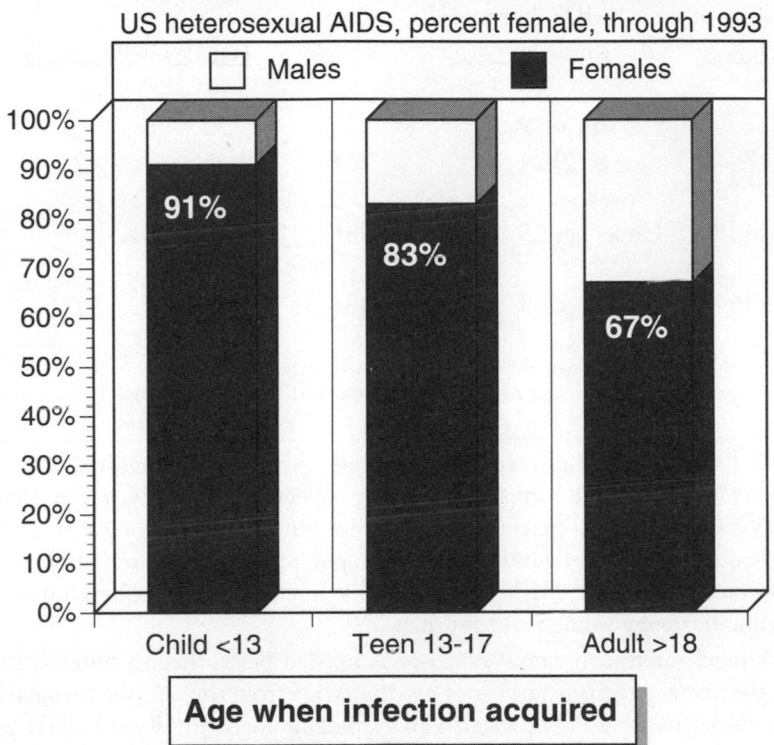

Six of seven heterosexual HIVs acquired by teens are in females

US heterosexual AIDS, percent female, through 1993

☐ Males   ■ Females

- Child <13: 91%
- Teen 13-17: 83%
- Adult >18: 67%

Age when infection acquired

Figure 2.6

Source: U.S. Centers for Disease Control and Prevention (1993, October). See Table 2.7

Black men and women in their 40s and 50s were substantially more likely to contract an HIV infection than were white teenagers. White females, even young ones, have very low risk of getting AIDS, but black females are nearly as much at risk as white males.

Nor have national health agencies publicly discussed AIDS as a disease of poverty, even though their own studies show this as well. In 1988-89, CDC researchers tested 150,000 15-24-year-old clients of sexually-transmitted disease, women's health, and drug treatment clinics. Even among these high-risk populations, HIV infection rates among the four-fifths of the 15-19 year-olds who were classified as heterosexuals with no risk factors were zero. Among 20-24 heterosexuals with no risk factors, HIV infection rates were 0.8 percent for men and 0.4 percent for women. Overall, HIV rates were more than three times higher among 20-24 year-olds than among 15-19-year-olds, with females showing higher rates than males among teenagers and males showing higher rates among 20-24-year-olds.[19]

Similarly, screenings of 270,000 low-income Job Corps applicants ages 16-21 found three in 1,000 infected. I must have heard this "alarming" statistic a hundred

Table 2.7.

Of heterosexual HIV infections contracted during teen years, six of seven are girls:

Probable age of HIV-infection:	AIDS diagnoses through 9/93:*	Cases diagnosed in: Males	Females	Pct female
Age 0-12	Age 0-19	21	225	91%
Age 10-17	Age 20-24	265	1,265	82%
Under age 18	Under age 25	286	1,490	84%
Over age 18	Over age 25	6,484	12,346	66%

*HIV infection assumed to occur an average of 7-10 years before AIDS diagnosed.
Source: U.S. Centers for Disease Control and Prevention (1993, October). *HIV/AIDS Surveillance Report 5*, Tables 4, 5, 7.

times from health authorities complaining about "promiscuous, high-risk kids," yet no one ever mentioned the most astonishing aspect of the study: From 1988 to 1992, HIV rates fell by 40 percent among males but doubled among females![20] A third study of disadvantaged youth, focusing on public clinics, runaway shelters, and detention facilities, found "HIV was generally low but... the highest rates were observed among young women and gay men..."[21]

How much more consistent evidence is needed before health officials recognize that the average teenage girl is not getting AIDS from the average teenage boy? Michigan Department of Public Health HIV epidemiologist Jim Kent looked at the pattern and drew the obvious conclusion. In 1994, Kent pointed out that "there's not enough (infected) teen-age males out there to account for" the surplus of HIV infections "teen-age girls are getting... from heterosexual sex." Teenage males and females "are both being infected by older males," he said.[22]

Despite repeated findings that low-income, minority heterosexual females are at particular risk of HIV infection, and occasional acknowledgment that this "may be related to sexual contact with older men,"[23] the CDC and other agencies do not list sex between adults and youths as a risk factor in the spread of AIDS. They don't talk about it, period. No effort appears to have been made to study the circumstances—including rape, prostitution, and "survival sex" (sex in exchange for food or shelter)—that produces the much higher risk of AIDS among poorer youth, particularly girls. Agencies continue to focus simply on "teenagers practicing high risk behaviors"[24] [25] and aim remedial programs at teenagers[26] as if adolescents cavorted in blissful isolation from adult society and its pressures and coercions.

"At any given time, Hollywood alone plays host to more than 5,000 runaways or throwaways whose life circumstances may include homelessness, physical and sexual abuse, substance abuse, survival sex, gang violence and a general sense of hopelessness," writes Stephen Knight of Hollywood's Free Clinic.[27] These teenagers, and poor and minority youth in general, are the ones getting AIDS—an issue buried

Table 2.8

AIDS is a disease of poverty:

AIDS cases per 100,000 population of each age and race, through September 1993:

Probable age HIV-infected:*	Age AIDS diagnosed:	Male AIDS rates			Female AIDS rates		
		White	Black	Hisp	White	Black	Hisp
5-younger	0-12	3	36	19	2	38	18
3-12	13-19	6	16	13	1	15	5
10-17	20-24	71	256	165	10	105	51
15-22	25-29	326	936	633	26	295	139
20-27	30-34	459	1427	1034	30	421	187
25-32	35-39	460	1619	1166	25	407	179
30-37	40-44	361	1312	991	15	270	133
35-42	45-49	259	966	729	9	154	84
40-47	50-54	181	668	520	7	110	63
45-57	55-64	97	368	307	6	58	36
55-older	65-older	21	86	84	4	17	12
Total, all ages		176	562	396	11	149	73

*HIV infection assumed to occur an average of 7-10 years before AIDS diagnosed.
Source: U.S. Centers for Disease Control (1993, September). *HIV/AIDS Surveillance Report*, Table 8.

in the false egalitarian zeal to portray all youth as afflicted with alleged teenage recklessness and therefore "at risk." A 1995 study by the Arizona Family Planning Council of 2,000 women ages 18-22 found that sexual abuse victims were twice as likely to have had an STD and to have engaged in sexual activity at an early age, which further enhanced the risk of contracting disease.[28] As occurs so often, the results of the hazardous conditions in which millions of youth are raised are officially portrayed as a teenage attitude and behavior problem.

The House Select Committee's AIDS report, falsely claiming that "HIV, the virus that causes AIDS, is spreading unchecked among the nation's adolescents, regardless of where they live or their economic status," attributed the epidemic solely to "sexually active... adolescent females and... adolescent males," and "high-risk behavior among youth," including alcohol use, drug use, and sex without condoms. But however beneficial sex education and condom distribution programs are, they will not cure the poverty, abuses, and abandonments that have created "alarmingly high" HIV infection rates ranging up to 17 percent "in certain groups of adolescents" concentrated in poorer runaway populations—while the mainstream teenage population displays levels of virtually zero.[29] The committee's report, "A Decade of Denial: Teens and AIDS in America," omitted the adult factor and itself became a contributor to the larger denial.

Instead, the committee, like other agencies and the media, depicted the main challenge as one of defeating teenage foolishness. It chose to emphasize the "alarming" increase in adolescent AIDS and warned that "teens... certainly will be the fastest growing group of persons with AIDS if we fail to act today." The press reverberated with this claim, though it is not true. From 1990 to the most recent figures available (September 1993), AIDS cases contracted during teen years rose at a slower rate than AIDS cases acquired during adult years (Table 2.9).

The ages most at risk of contracting HIV infection (diagnosed 7-10 years later as AIDS) are not teens, but adults in their 20s and 30s. The age group with the fastest-rising rates of HIV infection are Baby Boomers ages 30-45, who are displaying serious problems (see Chapter 6) with drug abuse as well. In addition to the never-mentioned issue of high-risk middle-agers, a number of features of the official AIDS tabulations shown in the tables demolish the official depiction of a teenage AIDS epidemic:

(a)   Adolescents are far from the most likely age group to acquire HIV infection. Teenage sex (even including some young-adult sex through age 22) is 60 percent less risky than sex among persons in their 20s, and 20 percent less risky than sex among persons in their 30s, to result in HIV infection and later AIDS diagnosis.

(b)   Teenagers are not the "fastest growing group of persons with AIDS," but among the slowest-growing. The growth in AIDS cases from 1990 to 1993 resulting from HIV infection at age 10-17 (up 106 percent) and at age 15-22 (up 118 percent) is faster than the growth in HIV infections acquired by persons in childhood (under age 12, up 104 percent), probably due to the reduction in HIV cases resulting from blood transfusions. But the growth in teenage-contracted HIV (up 115 percent for age 10-22) is slower than the growth in infection among persons in their 20s (up 129 percent), 30s (up 154 percent), 40s (up 131 percent), or 50s and older (up 119 percent).

(c)   The official position is that more programs "to reach youth" by "reducing high-risk behavior among youth" are the most effective strategies to quell "adolescent AIDS."[30] But adult-teen sex, not "teenage sex," is the biggest risk factor in HIV infection. The most critical factor in the spread of heterosexual AIDS among the young is not the "adolescent behavior... risk" blamed by health officials[31] and parroted by the media, but the vulnerability of very young, impoverished girls to rape, prostitution, and sexual relations with older infected males.

As is the case with many behaviors, the information-gathering and tabulation bureaus of health agencies have done terrific work. The statistics are sufficient to draw strong conclusions about the pattern of AIDS: Vastly higher and rising rates among young minority men and women, falling rates among young white men and older males.

And, as is the case with too many issues, the public information provided by health agencies with regard to AIDS has been highly politicized and seriously deficient. AIDS clearly is a disease of pervasive poverty, discrimination, and their consequences—prostitution, sexual abuse of young females, survival sex, poor health care, and hopelessness. The cures for the spread of AIDS, now diagnosed in 500,000 Americans, are intimately tied to the cure for these debilitating conditions. Yet how do officials and experts present the causes of AIDS, even as recently as November

Table 2.9

Teens are not the most "at risk," nor the fastest-growing age group, for AIDS:

Probable age HIV-infected:*	Age AIDS diagnosed:	AIDS cases diagnosed through: August 1990	AIDS cases diagnosed through: September 1993	Rate 1993**	Growth 1990-93
5-younger	0-12	2,525	4,903	10.0	+94.2%
3-12	13-19	568	1,415	5.9	+149.1
10-17	20-24	6,172	12,712	66.7	+106.0
15-22	25-29	23,437	51,006	252.6	+117.6
20-27	30-34	35,647	79,400	356.5	+122.7
25-32	35-39	31,932	75,534	358.0	+136.5
30-37	40-44	20,153	51,509	273.9	+155.6
35-42	45-49	11,356	28,477	185.4	+150.8
40-47	50-54	6,461	15,496	128.5	+139.8
45-57	55-64	6,359	14,119	67.5	+122.0
55-older	65-older	2,136	4,679	14.5	+119.1
Total, all ages		146,746	339,250	133.0	+131.2%

*HIV infection assumed to occur an average of 7-10 years before AIDS diagnosed.
**AIDS cases per 100,000 population for each age group.
Source: U.S. Centers for Disease Control (1990, 1993). *HIV/AIDS Surveillance Report*, August 1990, Table 7, and September 1993, Table 8.

1995 media statements by Philip Rosenberg of the National Cancer Institute, regarding his study published in *Science*? They are presented as "a rite of passage for young people" and a behavior problem of "young Americans" requiring more behavior-changing campaigns aimed at youths and young adults.[32] So committed are officials, as part of their age-based political agenda, to proclaim that the risk factor for AIDS is "young age" and its misbehaviors that even a deadly epidemic founded in poverty has proven insufficient to provoke reconsideration.

Rape

In 1989, I reviewed sentencing for sex offenses in the Montana college community of Bozeman and found a surprising result:

> Despite the long prison terms sometimes handed out to rapists or would-be sexual assailants of adult women... the reality of rape in Bozeman is that most sex crime victims are very young, and their assailants rarely wind up with stern sentences even if they are tried.
>
> A sample of 20 Bozeman-area rape and sexual assault cases that reached the courts since January 1986 shows... victims range in age from 3 to 52. The median age is 13 for both male and female victims.
>
> Sixty percent of the victims are female. Three out of four victims are under

the age of 16.

Assailants range in age from 13 to 62, with the average age 33. Nearly all are male.[33]

The much-larger National Women's Study of 4,000 women in 1992 found one in eight, a projected 12.1 million, had been raped. Of the victims, 62 percent were raped prior to age 18—and 29 percent prior to age 11. "The survey found that rape in America is a tragedy of youth, with the majority of rape cases occurring during childhood and adolescence."[34]

In a two-year study published in 1994, the Alan Guttmacher Institute (formerly the research affiliate of Planned Parenthood) thought to ask junior high girls what they meant by "having sex." Their answers are in Table 2.10.

Table 2.10

"Sexually active"? Many junior high girls say it was rape:

Type of "sex" experienced:

First intercourse at age:	Rape only	Rape and voluntary	Voluntary only
13 or younger	61%	13%	26%
14 or younger	43 %	17%	40%
15 or younger	26%	14%	60%
16 or younger	10%	14%	76%
17 or younger	5%	13%	82%
18 or younger	3%	12%	85%

Source: The Alan Guttmacher Institute (1994). *Sex and America's teenagers*. New York: AGI, p. 28.

For 40 percent of the "sexually active" girls under age 15, a rape had been their only "sex." The Guttmacher Institute reported that the male involved in these experiences was often "substantially older" than the female.[35] Labeling raped girls as "sexually active," as the CDC and experts routinely do, is akin to labeling robbery victims "criminally active."

The psychological effects of rape and sexual abuse of children and adolescents are as devastating as the physical effects. Studies of 445 mostly nonwhite teenage mothers by Chicago's An Ounce of Prevention[36] and of 535 mostly white pregnant and parenting teens by the Washington (state) Alliance Concerned with School-Age Parents[37] found large majorities had histories of sexual abuse, most of it rape, during childhood years. The Arizona Family Planning Council's 1995 study of 2,000 older teen women ages 18-22 of all races found that the one-fourth who had suffered rape or attempted rape were twice as likely to have been pregnant before age 18 than non-abused women.[38] In these studies, victimization occurred at an average age of 10—fourth grade. The victimizers were family members, male partners, and other men who, the studies found, averaged one to two decades older than the victims. Sexually abused girls were "sexually active" at much younger ages (1.5 to two years younger than non-abused girls) and tended to have partners five to six years older, factors which increased the chances of early pregnancy *four-fold*.

A 15-year-old I interviewed for a 1988 article, a victim of four years of sexual violence by her stepfather, had never been to therapy. But she had figured out the connection between her past and her current "promiscuity, drunkenness, falling grades, and a suicide attempt more to get attention than to die," behaviors so many experts seem unable to fathom:

> "When you start getting sexually abused, you hate it really bad, when you're 10, 11, 12, let's say.
>
> "But then you turn 13, and you start dating guys and stuff, and it enters your mind. You want sex more.
>
> "I started drinking when I was in fifth grade. I was going to parties in sixth grade, stealing alcohol, getting drunk, blocking it out of my mind.
>
> "The first time I fucked a boy—maybe a month after my 13th birthday—I got drunk so I could do it, so I could force myself to do something I didn't want to do. Something made me. I had to do it.
>
> "I don't know how to explain this, but I wanted guys to force me to have sex. I didn't want them to be nice and say, 'Will you kiss me? Is it okay if I hold your hand?'
>
> "I wanted boys to react exactly like I learned they should. Force me. Hit me around. Say, 'Bitch! Come over here!' I thought that was all I was good for."

Her first "boyfriend," at 13, was 20 years old. Raped or abused by an older male in childhood; "voluntary sex" with an older male shortly after puberty. The third step—a mother in high school—was avoided by this particular girl due, I think, to her extraordinary candor in facing her past.

The failure of health officials to directly confront the issue of rape of young adolescents by older teens and adult males betrays the hypocrisy surrounding this entire controversy. Health agencies trumpet surveys of the supposedly large increase in junior high sex when suitable to agency and program promotions They are quiet on surveys of young girls reporting they were raped. Perhaps self-reporting surveys (among both teens and adults, and especially on sensitive issues such as sexual behavior) harbor such serious flaws that they should be viewed with great caution, as this author believes. The most reasonable stance is that we don't know what young adolescents mean by "sexually active" or by "rape," and we have not been eager to find out. The only matter that is clear is that officials have selectively exploited junior-high sex surveys to advance their own interests while disregarding serious questions of violence and older male exploitation due to their political inconvenience.

Predictably, efforts have been made in media campaigns to blame children and youths for most or all sexual abuse of their peers. As Paul Okami of the UCLA Department of Psychology points out in a lengthy discussion, with rare exceptions, most of these alleged child-child abuses are peer explorations of a minor nature:

> Whereas concern over adult sexual abuse of children apparently reflects the actuality of genuinely widespread occurrences, research, writings, and activism related to "child perpetrators" appear instead to reflect symbolic concerns rooted in... adult overreaction to discovery of voluntary peer sexual interactions.[39]

A different kind of "voluntary"

Rafaela Herrera and Nancy Tafoya of the Las Cruces, New Mexico, La Clínica de Familia health centers, reenact the scenario of the seduction of a 15-year-old by her 23-year-old "boyfriend" at the November 1995 conference of the National Organization on Adolescent Pregnancy, Parenting and Prevention. This is the "typical" situation, they say. They contrast the skills and pressures, subtle and direct, exerted by experienced older males on younger girls (most of whom are from violent, sexually abusive families) with the inexperience of young adolescents in dealing with them. Citing the abuses and pressures from men, Herrera declares flatly that "teenage pregnancy is a social problem that is not caused by teenage girls."

The average duration of relationships from their beginning to first sex is three months, studies of the 565 teenage mothers who are clients of the centers show. Is this the voluntary "teenage sex" that officials berate? "Most of our girls are astonished to see what we call abuse," Herrera said. To many, hitting, slapping, even attempted rape, are not unexpected behaviors from boys and men in their families and their relationships. "If 35 percent admit to violence in their families, then conservatively, at least 50 percent experience it," Tafoya added.

"What is a 29-year-old guy doing with a 12-year-old?" Herrera shouts at one point, after recounting the facts of another young mother. "Why do we continue to allow it? What about male responsibility here?" She reads an interview with a 13-year-old mother who reluctantly describes the rape by which her father's stepbrother, age 19, impregnated her—and how her parents continued to let the man live at their trailer. "And who is getting punished?" Herrera asks after detailing the growing array of welfare and legal punishments aimed at adolescent mothers. "Does anybody see a boy or a man in this picture? Except, maybe, the little boy born to a teen mother?"

Herrera donates her services as a lawyer to help teen mothers through "the endless humiliations" of getting child support from the fathers. "It's amazing to see that guy who can buy the brand-new pickup and make those $450-per-month payments and $150 a month for insurance for that truck, but he can't come up with $250 in support payments for his child?"[40]

Adult-teen romances and sexual relationships are so common in American society that experts and officials have pulled no minor stunt in selling the myth that teenagers have sex only with each other. Only the miracle of modern social science enmeshed in political biases could get a simple behavior phenomenon so profoundly wrong. Disregard 18- or 19-year-olds paired with older men, which is along the lines of Jimmy and Rosalynn, William O. Douglas and wife, O.J. and Nicole, and millions of other such liaisons, exemplary to disastrous, from Congress to Compton—though the fertility from such diverse relationships today would be lumped together as part of "the epidemic of teenage pregnancy." The 1995 Guttmacher study found 74 percent of the births among 18-19-year-old women—some 220,000 per year—are fathered by men age 20 and older.

In this book, "adult-teen sex" refers to much-older men in relationships with young adolescents. Most adult-teen sex is not outright rape. What is meant by "voluntary" varies widely from relationship to relationship. In what appears to be a teen-sex first for the media, *Orange County Register* reporter Bonnie Weston empaneled a group of Newport Beach middle school girls and asked:

> So how old is too old when it comes to teen-age girls dating older guys?
> ... A group of girls 13, 14, and 15 threw out numbers that would likely make their parents wince: 20, 24, 28 and beyond.
> ... All of the girls said they have dated guys in their late teens or 20s at least for a little while. They all knew girls at [middle] school who have dated much older men, including several who ended up pregnant.
> Meeting older guys is easy. Among the likely sources the girls named were friends of older brothers, church, family gatherings, their neighborhoods, fast-food restaurants, and parties.
> "What do you mean, where?" [15-year-old Amber] Wester asked. "You just meet them walking down the street."
> The greatest age difference they cited was a 15-year-old schoolmate who dated a 28-year-old man. He broke it off because she said no to sex.
> The Bautistas [Rosa, 13, and Maria, 14] knew an 11-year-old who dated a 19 year-old. And several girls were acquainted with a 13 year-old newlywed. The girl and her 20-year-old husband are expecting a baby.
> ... [Fourteen-year-old Nadia] Flores had no illusion about why a 24-year-old man would date a girl her age: "For sex."
> ... Added Edna Morales, 14: "... older guys think they have all this power over you... You don't need status from some guy."
> ... Wester said, "I think older guys are more abusive. They think because they're older, they can push you around, walk all over you."[41]

Even where age gaps are considerable, the relationships I saw in a dozen years of working with adolescents were very diverse. In a wilderness summer work program, a 23 year-old supervisor was romantically involved with a 16 year-old crew member. A 37-year-old, a 21-year-old, and a 27-year-old had girlfriends who were 16-18 years old. A 20-year-old woman was aligned with a 17-year-old male employee. A 19-year-old leader had a relationship with a 15-year-old. Not all of these relationships involved sex, and no pregnancies resulted, though one later marriage did. In another low-income program, a 16-year-old moved in with her 21-year-old boyfriend, and another 16 year-old was dating a 25-year-old. These relationships seemed of an equal, if usually temporary, nature. Years later I have not heard complaints of exploitation from these couples' younger participants, now well into their 20s.

Others were not so equal. In one low-income-youth program I worked for, a 15-year-old girl was entangled with a 28-year-old paramour, separated from his wife and two children. A 16-year-old linked with a 32-year-old married man. Pregnancies resulted; one baby, one abortion. The men split. Suddenly, the independence (now expressed as mobility) of adult men became a disadvantage for teenage mothers—ingredients for a Children's Defense Fund poster you'll never see.

Involuntary older-younger sex was also prevalent among youths in these programs, as has been seen in research findings. Two sisters had been raped and sexually abused by their stepfather from age 7 to 12 (they reported it and were removed from home, but no prosecution took place). Another had been gang raped at age nine by a "friend of the family" and his friends (reported later, but no arrests). Another, a cheerleader, had been molested by cousins (not reported). Another had incest with her brother, six years older, from age 11 to 15 (not reported). Another was fondled in her bed by her drunken father at age ten (not reported; she didn't believe he knew who she was). Another was molested repeatedly by her grandfather from child years to her brother's wedding she attended at age 17 (her mother told her not to report it). Another had been molested in child and early teen years by a policeman and several of her five-times-married mother's "boyfriends" (not reported). Another had been raped at 14 by an unknown assailant who broke in to her bedroom (reported, no arrest).

Another was raped by her uncle on her living room floor when she was 13 (she reported it after he died). Another was raped at age 11 by her mother's live-in lover. The mother later told me she had been raped by him as well but continued to date him (neither rape was reported). Another 13 year-old was raped ("seduced," she put it) in elementary school by both her father and stepfather (she reported it, but no prosecution took place). A 9 year-old I interviewed for a newspaper report contracted herpes from rape by two of her mother's "boyfriends" (both were imprisoned after she testified against them in court at age 6 and 8). A 32-year-old program volunteer was convicted of molesting two boys, ages 11-13, he was assigned over a four-year period (he was sentenced to 30 days suspended, plus "counseling"). A mother and 14-year-old daughter shared the same 24-year-old "boyfriend" (reported but not investigated).

Adult-teen sexual harassment was also common. Some of it was really sexual assault. In one program, a 23-year-old leader was fired for grabbing the breasts and buttocks of five girls ages 15-17. In another, an adult employee was reprimanded for trying to button the bathing suit top of a 16-year-old. Other cases were simply brushed aside.

The finding of the American Association of University Women's 1992 "Hostile Hallways" survey—that 80 percent of all girls in grades 8-11 reported having been sexually harassed at school—was trumpeted in the media as proof of the hyper-sexuality of today's students. What was not publicized was the study's finding that 20 percent of the female students and 10 percent of the males said they had been sexually harassed by school faculty or staff.[42] This is a large number, given that adult males (96 percent of the adult harassers are male)[43] constitute fewer than 5 percent of all persons on school grounds.

An earlier survey of North Carolina high school graduates found that 82 percent of the females and 18 percent of the males had been sexually harassed at least once by school personnel, and 13.5 percent said they had sexual intercourse with a teacher while in junior or senior high.[44] Many argue that these reports are exaggerated or completely false, the inventions of young females. Yet a study of 225 school districts by Hofstra University Administration and Policy Studies professors, published in the national secondary school faculty journal Phi Delta Kappan, found that "false allegations constitute a small percentage of all allegations. It is more likely that students will fail to report actual incidents than that they will fabricate incidents." The most common incidents involved sexual fondling of students by male teachers or staff.[45]

The limitations of self-reporting surveys must be noted once again. Pinning exact numbers to sexual harassment incidence is difficult. Most of the students who reported being harassed by classmates said the incident involved sexual jokes, looks, gestures, or intimations of homosexuality.[46] The larger point is that once again, officials and the media were eager to believe the figures so long as students could be portrayed as harassing other students. It was the issue of adults sexually harassing youths that produced silence and denials.

Whether voluntary, forced, or something in between, "junior high sex" is not a separate or distinct issue. It is simply one part of "senior high sex" and "adult sex." Its only distinguishing feature is that it is much rarer. Similarly, at both the personal level (where most pregnancy and disease involve adult partners) and the societal level (where teenagers act like the adults around them), "teenage sex" is thoroughly intermixed with "adult sex." Even for the outcomes resulting from teenagers having sex with each other, pregnancy and disease trends are similar to those of adults around them.

The officially promulgated, popular notion that adult sex and teenage sex are very different, the former healthy and the latter disastrous, is demolished by figures from standard vital statistics reports. As Figures 2.11, 2.12 and 2.13 show, the trends in annual rates of births and of unwed births are identical for teenage (15-19) and adult (20-44) mothers over the 1940-1992 period, as are the trends in abortion rates for the 1972-91 period (the maximum time for which figures are available).[47] These teen and adult trends are uncannily alike, over decades of turbulent changes in sexual behaviors —the Depression, World War II, the postwar Baby Boom, the 1970s "Baby Bust," the legalization of abortion, the recent rise in family poverty. They demonstrate, through easily-available statistics in standard references such as *Vital Statistics of the United States*, that the official depiction of teenage motherhood and unwed motherhood are flawed at their core. Teenagers and adults occupy the same sexual worlds. The most ironic and sensational news about "teenage sex" is that it is exactly like "adult sex."

Poverty and teen birth rates

The Alan Guttmacher Institute's two-year study of teenage sexuality found pregnancy and birth were rare outcomes among American youth. When these did occur, poverty was the most profound influence. The study noted that in 1994, an appalling 38 percent of America's 15-19 year-olds were poor: They lived in families with incomes below or just above poverty guidelines. But of the one in ten teens who became pregnant or caused a pregnancy, 73 percent were poor. Of the one out of 25 teens who became parents, 83 percent were poor. And of the one in 40 teens who became parents while unwed, 85 percent were poor.[48]

California provides detailed figures on birth rates by age and race/ethnicity (in particular, separating white from Hispanic), which allows comparison of teen and adult trends by location as well. For the state's 24 most populous counties containing 22 million people and good representations of all races, the birth rates for adults are closely correlated with birth rates for teenagers, as they are for each separate race/ethnicity (Asian, Black, Hispanic, and White).[49] Geographic locations that have high rates of adult births also have high rates of teenage births.

The other major factor clearly influencing levels of teenage childbearing is

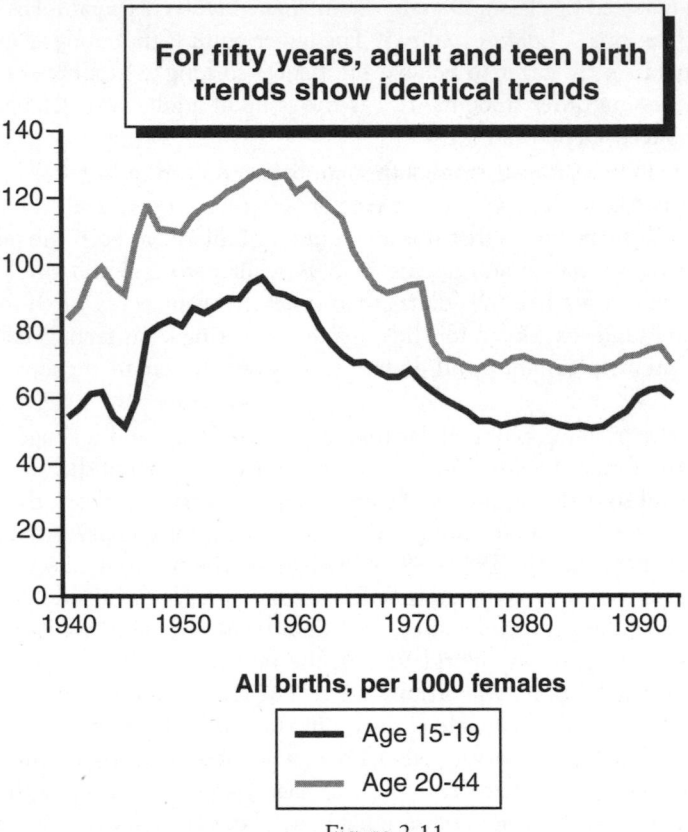

For fifty years, adult and teen birth trends show identical trends

All births, per 1000 females

—— Age 15-19

—— Age 20-44

Figure 2.11

Source: National Center for Health Statistics (annual). *Vital Statistics of the United States, 1940-1991*, Volume I, Natality. See Reference 52.

poverty, as the statewide California comparison for 1990 shows (Table 2.14).

Poorer black teens have higher birth rates than black adults, while Hispanic youth, almost as destitute, are close. Further, all of California's large increase in births among teenage mothers in the previous decade has been among Hispanics (up 45 percent) and blacks (up 31 percent), whose poverty levels have also increased rapidly, while white and Asian teen birth rates remain low and have not risen. Four in ten teenage mothers in California were born in second- and third-world nations and experience the crushing poverty of young, recent arrivals[50] that current anti-immigrant welfare reforms promise to exacerbate.

Opulent, suburban Marin County, California, which has the state's lowest rate of youth poverty, also has the state's lowest teen birth rate. Impoverished, migrant-worker dominated Tulare County, which has the state's highest youth poverty rate, has the state's highest teen birth rate. This pattern is evident on a national basis as well: States with higher youth poverty rates consistently have higher teenage birth rates.[51]

Only two factors, then, account for nearly all teenage childbearing levels and trends: adult childbearing levels and trends, and poverty (as reflected in race). These are intermixed as well: Poverty also correlates with higher birth rates among

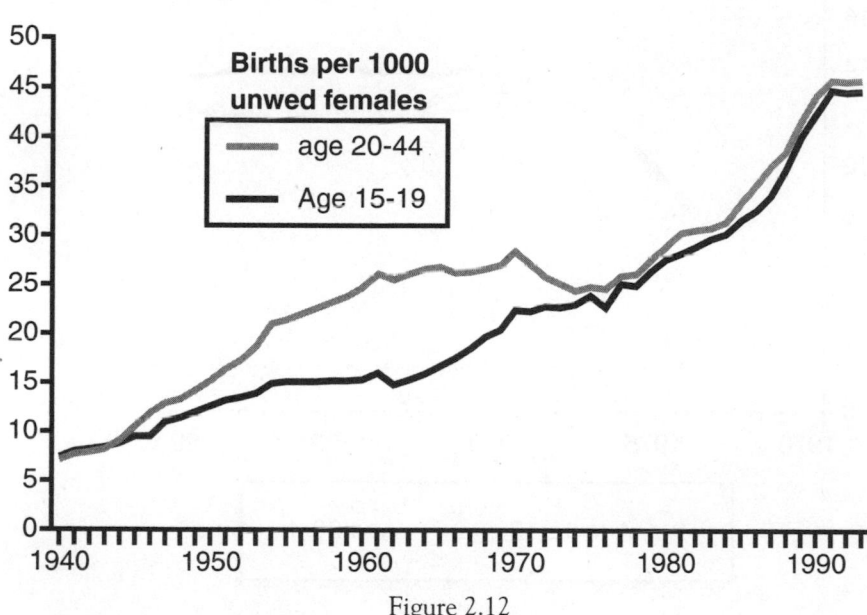

For five decades, adult and teen unwed birth rates are also identical

Figure 2.12

Source: See Table 2.11

adults. Again, there is no difference between teenagers and adults, no unique "teenage" factor (such as music or media or "peer pressure" or presumed adolescent irrationality) at work. The "peers only" vacuum in which "junior high sex" and "teenage sex" are presented by officials and experts does not exist.

See no evil

The prevailing image of "teenage sex and pregnancy" is a political invention. U.S. officials have had a long time to get used to the idea that the term "teenage pregnancy" is, overwhelmingly, a euphemism for "adult-teen pregnancy." Decades of birth, marriage, and sexual disease figures are consistent. One hundred thousand or more teenage females have given birth in the U.S. every year since at least 1915, and two-thirds to 90 percent of their partners have been men age 20 and older.[52] Adult-teen sex has presented a clear, long-term pattern that should have raised plenty of eyebrows in latter-day America's millions of scientific pages and bumper crop of hand-wringing dedicated to "teenage sex."

Yet in the two-volume 1987 *Risking the Future* study issued by the National Research Council's blue-ribbon panel on Adolescent Pregnancy and Childbearing, not a word is mentioned of adult-teen sex.[53] Nor is the topic broached in the blue-

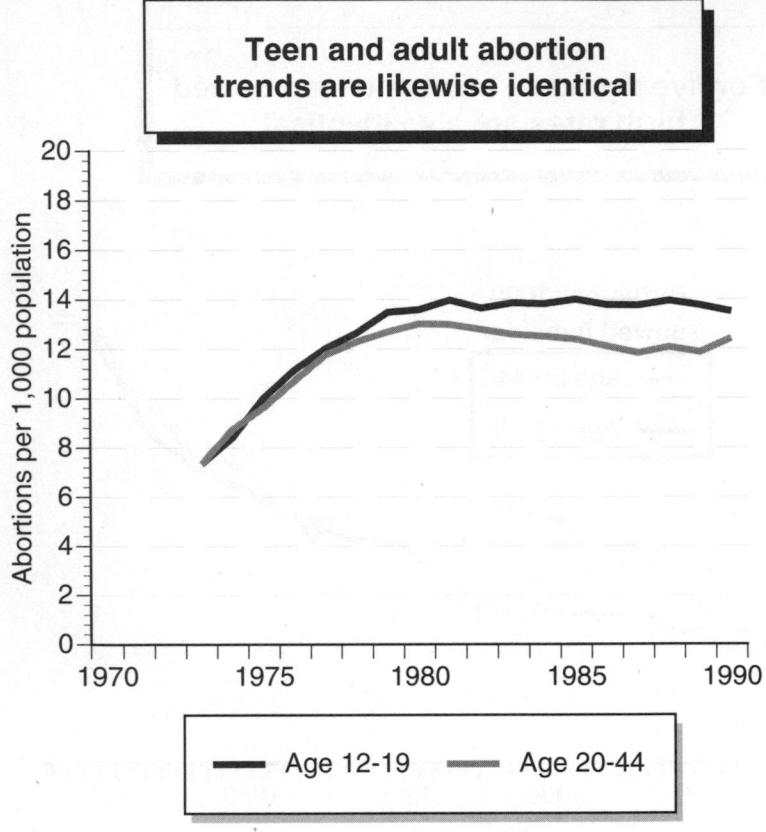

Figure 2.13

Source: The Allan Guttmacher Institute. In U>S. Bureau of the Census (1995). *Statistical Abstract of the United States 1995*, Washington, DC: U.S. Department of Commerce.

ribbon 1990 *Code Blue* study (headed by former Surgeon General Everett Koop and Illinois Governor James Thompson and issued by the American Medical Association, National Association of State Boards of Education, and Centers for Disease Control), which blamed "teenage pregnancy" on "sex... occurring at younger and younger ages."[54] Not a word by the Rand Corporation, one of whose top researchers argued for changing "teenagers' thinking" to prevent "children having children."[55] Not a word from the Carnegie Foundation, whose October 1995 report relentlessly evaded every serious adolescent sexual issue and blamed junior high sex on "peers" given too much unsupervised free time after school.[56]

Illustrative of the official and expert selective blindness to adult-teen sex is a comment from a leading population expert in a 1988 article in the nation's leading family planning journal: "I never heard of an adult who thought adolescents should bear children."[57] (Except for the adults who father 80 percent of all babies born to adolescents). And, needless to say, no mention of this uncomfortable issue has been publicly voiced by any of the officials charged with promoting public health: Not any Secretary of Health, Surgeon General, or other top health official in all the tor-

Table 2.14

Poverty is a major breeder of teenage and adult-teen motherhood:

California, 1990 Race/ethnicity	Birth rates* among Teens 15-19	Adults 20-44	Birth rate ratio Teen vs adult	Youth poverty rate
Black	103.8	81.9	1.27	30.3%
Hispanic	109.9	121.1	0.91	26.7
Asian	44.9	94.1	0.48	19.8
White	44.1	67.9	0.65	8.6
All	68.0	83.7	0.81	17.8%

*Per 1000 females in each age group, 1990.
Sources: California Center for Health Statistics (1992). Resident live births by age of mother, father, race, county, marital status, 1990. Sacramento, CA: Department of Health Services (printout); U.S. Bureau of the Census (1992). *Census of population 1990*. Social and economic characteristics. California. Washington, DC: U.S. Department of Commerce, Table 54.

rents officially uttered on "teenage sex." (Former Surgeon General Joycelyn Elders and unsuccessful nominee Henry Foster did write me letters privately acknowledging adult-teen sex as an important issue.)

Is adult sexual involvement with adolescents, even junior high girls, too trivial to merit notice, then? If so, then why isn't it routinely acknowledged before it is dismissed? Is it a natural, historical, normal liaison between older males and younger females? Why, then, is the result deplored as "teenage pregnancy" and condemned as an "epidemic social problem"? Why the universal effort to depict adolescent boys as the chief culprits in adolescent motherhood, a misconception that has misdirected two decades of policy planning and billions of dollars of effort?

"It's a real uncomfortable issue to deal with," replied Terri Wright, director of the Michigan Bureau of Child and Family Services. "It's uncomfortable for adults to acknowledge that other adults are having sexual relations with a child."[58] (As a 15-year-old I once interviewed said of her rape: "If it's hard for them to hear about, try having it happen").

The issue is more than grownup squeamishness. However common in real life, adult-teen sex demolishes what has been an AC-rated (Adult-Comfortable) "teen-sex" script to date. Discomfort with the fact of adult-teen sex also stems from the practical difficulty that the myriad of interest groups have no idea how to promote abstinence or contraceptive responsibility among the post-school adult men who cause most junior and senior high pregnancies and AIDS—though this presents a serious challenge that should have been faced years ago.

But the larger problem is more profound: Facing adult-teen sex means dismantling the Great Wall between "adolescent" and "adult" that advocates of all stripes had erected to keep the argument from intruding on taboo topics of grownup values, grownup maturity, grownup behavior, and grownup sex. To both conservatives and liberals, "teenage sex" has been an expendable issue, convenient to invoke in outraged tones to advance various social policy goals, easy to jettison when its realities prove inconvenient. Holding eighth graders 100 percent responsible has avoided the unsettling implications of the fact that adult sex and teenage sex are really one and the same phenomenon.

To conservatives, teenage promiscuity is just one symbol of America's larger moral decay from a mythical golden age of chastity. It offers a shot at easy political victories when moderates and liberals proved willing, as they typically do, to trade away adolescent rights in order to preserve adult rights—parental consent for minors' abortions, as opposed to a ban on all abortions, for example. Some conservative advocates of abstinence-only education invented results. The famed "80 percent reduction" in teenage pregnancy alleged to have occurred after the San Marcos, California, school system instituted its abstinence curriculum in the 1980s was cited favorably by conservative author William Kilpatrick in *Why Johnny Can't Tell Right from Wrong*[59] and by right-wing commentators for years. Yet investigation showed the results were fabricated; census figures showed the birth rate among San Marcos girls age 14-17 doubled over the period the program was in effect.[60]

Conservatives' cerebral insertion into the sand is cogently summarized by the right-wing-coalition, Focus on the Family's, "In Defense of a Little Virginity" ads in newspapers nationwide. Heavily concerned with "peer pressure," gays, and forcing teens to submit to "adult authority" on matters sexual, the lengthy ad text omits issues of adult partners, sexual abuse, rape, poverty, and adult example.[61] Despite conservative claims that "excellent programs have been developed" promoting sexual abstinence, independent evaluations of programs funded by Congress's chastity-promoting Adolescent Family Life Act of 1981 have consistently shown they are ineffective.[62] In the usual progression, each side produces its own propaganda from pencil-and-paper surveys showing its ideas are the key to success (fuel for future school-program debates) while vital statistics, ignored, show rising teen birth rates.

In many ways, liberals' record is even worse. To liberals, the teenage-sex myth has proven a safe target for "values" outrage and get-tough absolutisms on "right and wrong" too strident to aim at adult constituencies. Liberals, in fact, seem to bear a particular animus against adolescents that is not immediately explainable. Where conservatives are appalled at adolescent precocity—that teenagers seem to act as depraved as adults do—moderates and liberals have made vigorous efforts to portray adolescents as *more* reckless, *more* stupid, *more* in need of tough controls than grownups. Increasingly, moderate and liberal groups have portrayed lamentable adolescent behavior not simply as one part of American society's malaise, but as the *chief cause* of society's malaise. Liberals' willingness to trade away adolescent rights and well-being (ie, over abortion, the drug war, the subminimum training wage) in order to preserve various adult prerogatives is one in which right-wingers frustrated at the success of liberals and moderates in blocking efforts to legislate adult morality have proven only too happy to cooperate.

The role of moderate and liberal entities—Planned Parenthood, the Urban Institute, the Children's Defense Fund, and the Democratic administration—in creating an image of singular teenage misbehavior causing all manner of social costs to healthy adults has been pivotal. The Children's Defense Fund, in technical reports such as *Teenage Pregnancy: An Advocate's Guide to the Numbers* and *Child Support and Teen Parents*, at least mentioned (for those who looked hard) the roles of sexual abuse, adult fathers, and paternal abandonment in the lives of teenage mothers.[63]

But in its highly public poster and media campaigns, the CDF mentioned nothing of the sort, treating pregnant teens as witless fools knocked up by the high school jock, victims of MTV and their own adolescent delusions. The 1995 CDF myth of "teenage pregnancy" has advanced not one inch from the 1959 Philip Dunne film, *Blue Denim*: 16-year-old bad-girl Carol Lynley in a family way with the craven, horny basketball center. "Wait'll you see how fast he can run when you tell him you're pregnant," the CDF's 1990 poster reprise of their favorite athlete-impregnator theme warned over the picture of a sprinter looking like a fawn ready to bolt.

Another liberal entity, the Urban Institute, issued a 1986 report (discussed in the next chapter) alleging "tremendous social and financial costs... of teenage childbearing" and blaming teenage behaviors for costing a lot of public money.[64] It did not mention the two chief factors in the "costs" of teenage motherhood: That teenagers are many times more likely to be poor than adults *before* they become parents, and the failure of fathers (nearly all adults) to pay child support. We might imagine the enormous tab the UI (and similar "social cost" studies such as that by the General Accounting Office in 1993) might generate if it compared, straight across, the "public costs of minority-group childbearing" versus that of whites without mentioning such details as prior poverty and racial discrimination.

Similarly, Planned Parenthood and the Alan Guttmacher Institute have publicized the "epidemic of 1 million teenage pregnancies every year" since 1976. Yet it was not until the 1990s that their reports began to discuss the role of post-teen adult men in the sexual violence and reproductive collaboration that produced most of the "epidemic." Researchers simply adopted "the assumption that the partners of pregnant teenagers are also predominantly adolescents," AGI senior research associate David Landry wrote—an assumption contradicted by 70 years of national birth figures that, even though often incomplete, clearly pointed to adult partners.

When I raised the adult-teen sex issue with AGI in 1990, the response was one of curt dismissal. "That many if not most teenage women are impregnated by men who are not teenagers is a valid and accepted (point), although not much is made of it in the scientific literature," Jeannette Johnson, executive editor of the Institute's *Family Planning Perspectives*, wrote me in 1991. Adult fatherhood with 18 or 19 year-old mothers "would not really be of concern to most of society," she added.[65] If adult-teen reproduction was not of concern, then most of the "epidemic of teenage pregnancy" PP and AGI had raised for 20 years was not of concern, either.

However, a number of local Planned Parenthood personnel and sex educators have long recognized the seriousness of the adult-teen sex and sexual abuse issues and have been similarly frustrated by a political climate that refuses to deal with either. "Society needs an overhaul on some of its sexual views," said Angie Karwan of Michigan's Planned Parenthood, in a remarkable article by Jeff Green of the *Oakland Press* that for the first time confronted officials and programs as to why they won't discuss adult-teen liaisons. Said Karwan:

> "Teen-adult sex is not being dealt with. If the young girl isn't mature enough to say no, the adult should be."
>
> But Planned Parenthood programs are aimed at educating children and teens, not adults. Karwan said that's because federal grants mandate how program

money can be spent.

"We're locked in on a target population," she said. "That's how the money is awarded. We have to follow our grants."[66]

And there are a couple of decades of investment in traditional teen-targeted programs. AGI director Jeannie I. Rosoff acknowledged in 1990 that "most of the programs we have had have been preaching sex education" but "we now know that increasing knowledge does not necessarily affect behavior." The claim that sex education aimed at adolescents is the cure for "teenage pregnancy" persists because "sex education is something we know how to do," she said.[67]

In effect, those who postulate that abstinence or sex education is a panacea to "teen pregnancy" are contending that young girls, most with histories of poverty and sexual abuse, can be taught or persuaded to enforce abstinence or contraception upon significantly older male partners—some of whom don't take "no" for an answer. But, as Ruth Dixon-Mueller of the International Women's Health Coalition noted:

> Although reproductive health professionals have been concerned with women's ability to make contraceptive choices or to protect themselves from STDs, at the heart of these decisions lies a woman's ability to choose whether, when, and with whom to have sexual relations or engage in a particular sexual act. The question of choice is complex. What seems on the surface to be purely voluntary sexual activity, for example, may be driven by deep economic need.[68]

As Debra Boyer and David Fine, who research for the Washington (state) Alliance Concerned with School-Age Parents, concluded of the sexual abuse victims that form the majority of teen mothers:

> Voluntary and rational choices are unlikely to impinge on what has been a long course of involuntary action: For a large number of pregnant adolescents, a history of physical maltreatment and sexual victimization may have disrupted their developmental processes...
>
> The problems of the abused pregnant and parenting young women apparent in our findings are probably not related to any ineffectiveness on the part of prevention efforts in the adolescent pregnancy field. They are instead the consequences of long-term effects of sexual victimization for which the field of adolescent pregnancy prevention was not prepared.[69]

"There is no curriculum written to give a 14-year-old the skills to deal with a 20-year-old who wants to have sex with her," added Boyer.[70] A clear step forward, as AGI's Landry and Forrest declared, is for sex educators and service agencies to recognize that many younger girls face relationships with older partners, complicated by their own personal difficulties. Girls in such circumstances need specialized help "to protect themselves against unintended pregnancy and sexually-transmitted disease" as well as in assessing "the wisdom of the relationship."[71]

By 1992, the cumulating change was evident. The AGI's *Family Planning Perspectives* published a landmark study of sexual abuse and teen mothers, and in 1994, the Institute's *Sex and America's Teenagers* raised the issue of adult partners. In a careful 1995 study, the Institute became the first to document its predominance nationwide. Reported AGI researchers Landry and Jacqueline Darroch Forrest:

Age information for men makes it clear that some of the assumptions underlying many of the programs and policies aimed at reducing teenage pregnancy are not correct. Policies that equate teenage pregnancy with males under 20 miss many of the partners of adolescent women. Almost two-thirds of mothers aged 15-19 have partners who are 20 or older.

... Wide age gaps between young teenage mothers and older fathers merit some concern... (as to) very different levels of life experience and power and brings into question issues of pressure and abuse. Data from the National Survey of Children indicate that about 18 percent of women 17 and younger who have had intercourse were forced at least once to do so.[72]

Citation of the AGI's findings by President Clinton in an August 1995 speech[73] demonstrated the power of liberal lobbies to affect the debate. The AGI study and like advocacy by Senate Democrats' Progressive Policy Institute[74] may be a force behind the administration's gradual movement throughout 1995 away from punishing teen mothers and toward holding adult fathers more responsible. In both personal and practical terms, dealing with men is the crucial issue, one trivialized by a host of entertaining diversions captivating media presentations of teenage sexuality.

Cal and Trent made 'em do it

In 1991, I became president of the Montana Children's Trust Fund board and learned that the chief perk of that job, amid the futile task of persuading 1990s lawmakers that preventing several thousand Montana children from being beaten and raped every year amounted to a fundworthy state goal, was attending the National Conference on Child Abuse and Neglect. There, as in too many other forums, I saw the frivolous attitude toward teenage sexual issues that has preoccupied too many progressive and social-activist groups.

I wandered into a conference workshop by the March of Dimes, one of the hundreds of organizations that has taken up "teenage pregnancy prevention" as a top goal. The workshop began with a contrast between the Beatles' 1963 "I Want to Hold Your Hand," and a 1980s Color Me Badd hit, "I Wanna Sex You Up." A film on teen pregnancy carefully excised all references to poverty, sexual abuse, and older partners, with the result that teenage mothers wound up looking simply stupid. Sexy rock'n'roll plus dumb teen girls, organizers left us to conclude, equals more "teenage mothers" today than back in the halcyon days of '64. (Actually, we have fewer teen moms today). Another workshop I scouted claimed Calvin Klein Jeans ads are the culprit, as if Brooke Shields is every ghetto kid's role model. (If they really think media causes bad behavior, they should worry more about the effect on men of the nude scenes 12-year-old Shields performed as a child prostitute in the 1978 film "Pretty Baby").

MTV was dutifully raked: "Let's Go to Bed" by The Cure and Pat Benatar's "Stop Using Sex as a Weapon" (both real ardor-killers when listened to) made the blame list, along with the usual Parents Music Resource Center Most-Wanted: The Dead Kennedys, Guns'N'Roses, Madonna, and 2 Live Crew. A video caught Marian Wright Edelman, director of the Children's Defense Fund and Clinton advisor, on the porch of a hillside shack in a destitute West Virginia hamlet condemning rock music and TV sex for rural Appalachia's high teen pregnancy rates. Newsfilms warmed to the motley crew of former Reagan education secretary William Bennett giving blipped readings of Nine Inch Nails' "I wanna fuck you like an animal" alternative-radio lyrics (just not the same as the Trent Reznor version) alongside former NAACP civil rights activist C. Dolores Tucker crusading against corrupting Ice-T raps.

The solution these mostly liberal and moderate activists push is simple and cheap: "Teen pregnancy" can be curbed if we just cleanse the ditties, purify the big and little screens, and install comprehensive sexual behavior curriculums emphasizing abstinence, values, and contraception. Wholesale censorship is not demanded, but rather a kind of "abstinence-plus" regimen of legal-techno controls on kids: TV lockout gizmos, parents' advisories, minimum-age bans on "explicit" CDs and video sales (only grownups can rent naked, sixth-grade Brooke), late-night TV zoned for the violent and kinky to preserve the rights of "mature adults" while "protecting the children."

For the most part, these aren't Neanderthal right-wingers out to burn *Our Bodies Ourselves* or the former *Sassy* magazine for depraving innocent teenage girls with pictures of bare breasts. Most of the worst teen-sex escapism emanates from what remains of liberal activism in the '90s—the racially sensitive, feminist-informed groups that should be most in touch with reality.

Postulating a vast gulf between "immature adolescents" and "mature adults" is a crucial element in the formation of misguided youth policy. Sometimes the results of maximizing adult freedoms, "balanced" by maximizing youth restrictions, are ludicrous. For example, most states' statutory rape laws allow an adult to have sexual intercourse with a 16-year-old girl while obscenity distribution laws protect her from being corrupted by seeing a photograph of it.

But the cosmetic nature of "youth protection" laws is clear, not simply in the uniformly low ages at which youths can legally "consent" to sexual relations with grownups (which range from three to seven years younger than the age at which a youth can legally drink a lite beer), but in the fact that they're not meant to be enforced. The state of California, whose stern law prohibits adults from having nonmarital sexual contact with youth under age 18, prosecutes only around 600 statutory rape cases every year even though adults father more than 20,000 unwed births among under-18 mothers annually. With that many births, many times more potentially prosecutable cases involving abortion or non-pregnancy-producing sex exist.

The phoniness of "putting children first" and "protecting children" platitudes is evident in the fact that federal health and law enforcement officials have shown little interest in cooperating to design a consistent plan to protect even very young adolescents—those "too-young" pre-16-year-olds to whom White House aide William Galston wants to preach abstinence—from adult sexual pressures. Clinton authorities have proven more gung-ho to crack down on youths for smoking a cigarette after sex with adults.

Is, then, stricter enforcement of statutory rape laws the answer, as some conscientious moderates and liberals troubled by these contradictions suggest? The issue is not a simple one. The flaw in such "barrier policies" aimed at legally separating adults and teenagers is fundamental to the policy misdesign surrounding the issue.

Adolescents and adults are thoroughly intermixed in real life. They are intermixed because the maturity gap universally postulated between older adolescents and adults does not exist. If anything, American society considers teenage females *more* mature than adult men. If adults were considered the more responsible parties, a pregnancy involving an adult and a teenager would be called an "adult pregnancy" and the adult would be targeted for remedial action.

As the average age of puberty has decreased over the last two centuries—from around 17 in 1800 to 12 today for girls, and 13 today for boys[75]—teenagers have become increasingly adult-like. Recall the conclusion of Chicago researcher Daniel Offer and colleagues, whose three-decade study of 30,000 adolescents and adults found that both age groups operate at an average developmental and cognitive age of 16 years.[76] Insulting to grownups or not, the sexual reality faced by millions of 1990s American adolescents is that 1990s American adults cannot be counted upon to behave more maturely than teenagers.

It is within this day-to-day world that the Clinton administration's incessant campaign to flatter adults as "mature" and "responsible" and to denigrate adolescents as "children" wreaks its worst damage. The practical difference in maturity between a 16 year-old female and a 24 year-old male, if any, does not merit the enormous discrepancy in the rights and power that society grants. A generalized policy of prosecuting adult men for statutorily raping older adolescent girls (16-17) is doomed to fail due the sheer volume of such relationships and the fact that most are equal and consensual.

The danger is that vigorous pursuit of "barrier policies" contributes heavily to the artificial, government-created power imbalance that makes adult men more attractive to America's bumper crop of young girls seeking escape from poverty and abuse in the first place. The advantages adult men possess as a right of their adulthood, ones repeatedly cited by younger girls as paramount, are impressive: A car, an abode, the right to buy alcohol, the right to enter bars and nightclubs, freedom to travel without curfews—in short, independence. A man's adult rights, granted by society, become essential elements in his seduction of young girls, and thus society becomes a player in that seduction. If young girls are naive about adult men, it is a naivete today's adult-flattering laws and leadership encourage in "children." As will be shown on a variety of issues, the biggest downfall of 1990s teenagers is not that they rebel against adult values, but that they copy adult values only too well.

Forcing teenage motherhood

The price of conservative anti-abortion politics combined with liberal self-interest and frivolousness is borne by teenage girls in the three dozen states that require parental notification or consent before girls under age 18 can obtain abortions. Laws in liberal, Democrat-dominated Minnesota and Massachusetts in 1981 paved the way for a dozen years of documented trauma for young girls while accomplishing nothing of demonstrated benefit (voters in liberal Oregon, however, rejected such a law). In dozens of states, moderate and liberal lawmakers supportive of the right to abortion choice have voted for "parental consent" measures allowing parents or judges to force adolescent girls to secure illegal abortions or bear children against their will, results avoided only because of the skill of teens and their counselors in evading the law.

Predictably, the U.S. Supreme Court on three occasions during the 1980s and 1990s upheld such laws as "reasonable" to "protect" girls seeking abortions. The logic behind these decisions is that if girls under age 18 are too immature to obtain abortions, the remedy is to manufacture a legal runaround to force them to become mothers.

In its 1990 decision in *Hodgson v. Minnesota* (1990), U.S. Supreme Court justices ignored a painstaking record compiled by U.S. District Judge Donald Alsop of Minnesota. The District Court record included *unanimous* testimony from Minnesota judges who presided over 90 percent of the state's 3,000 "judicial bypass" proceedings (granting abortions to teenage petitioners in every single contested case) that the law was useless, cruel, and detrimental to family harmony. The record included exhaustive testimony from both pro- and anti-abortion judges. The judges who directly administered the law agreed that the law was a travesty. They reported that pregnant girls found bypass hearings "absolutely traumatic," involving "incredible amounts of stress," shaking, hand-wringing, "answering monosyllabically;" even consideration of suicide by the pregnant daughter of a prominent pro-life official, and testimony to a fear-induced spontaneous courtroom abortion.[77]

The record showed that following enactment of the parental consent law, approximately 1,100 teens from Massachusetts traveled to nearby states every year to obtain abortions.[78] In neither Minnesota nor Massachusetts did teenage pregnancy or abortion rates change due to the laws (in fact, teen abortion rates decreased faster when the laws were suspended due to court challenges than when they were in effect).[79] In neither state did the percentage of parents informed of their teens' abortion decisions exceed those of states without notification or consent laws.[80] [81] Literally no credible testimony supported upholding parental notification or consent laws.

No matter. The U.S. Supreme Court majority's opinion openly prided itself in ignoring the record. The Court opinion admitted with a shrug that "many minors in Minnesota 'live in fear of violence by family members' and 'are in fact victims of rape, incest, neglect, and violence;'" that no witnesses experienced with the law cited any positive effects; that parental consent laws increase the health risk to girls by promoting later-term abortions; and that local judges found "the young women... very mature and capable of giving the required consent."[82] Then six U.S. Supreme Court justices endorsed the Minnesota law as nothing more than a "minimal" burden on "the minor's limited right to obtain an abortion."[83] Justices even authorized states to protect the rights of long-gone fathers who had abandoned their children for years and provided not one iota of support to be notified, in evident hope that such fathers might step in and veto their daughters' abortions. The only factor evident in the Court's decision, wrote AGI director Rosoff, was "unreasoning hostility" against teenagers.[84]

A 1990 National Academy of Sciences study concluded that "parental notification and consent laws do not protect pregnant adolescents from harm. Rather, they often cause it."[85] Of course. *Harming minors is the purpose of such laws.* The legislative sponsor of Ohio's parental consent law told *Dateline NBC* that he regarded pregnant girls seeking abortions as akin to criminals who commit theft or vandalism, lucky that all they faced was embarrassment at having to discuss their sex lives with a judge.[86] The key to passage of such pointless and harmful measures has been "pro-choice legislators [who] joined anti-abortion supporters of the law."[87]

As has been pointed out, pregnant youths are not a random sample of adolescents. Only about 15 percent of all girls become pregnant before age 18. Half of these obtain abortions. Even without parental notification/consent laws, fewer than half of these—perhaps 3 percent of all teen girls—obtain an abortion without the knowledge of at least one parent.[88] A large majority of the latter are from fragmented, violent, sexually abusive family backgrounds. Girls' reasons for not telling their parents are poignant: Fear of violence, fear of abuse, fear of being disowned, fear of adding to family conflict and instability, fear of being judged a disappointment.[89]

Since it is unlikely that parents in such families can be counted upon to make better decisions than their adolescent children, the question is: Who should be empowered to make the decision? By their disregard of facts, compassion, and complexities, Supreme Court justices personify those who are *not* mature enough to be making such decisions for young girls. Example: Former Chief Justice Warren Burger asserted that having a baby "entails few—perhaps none—of the potentially grave emotional and psychological consequences of the decision to abort."[90]

Talk purity to me

In October 1994, American adults indulged an orgy of self-back-patting, courtesy of academicians and the media, when University of Chicago sociologists released the two-year *Sex in America* study of the sex lives of 3,400 men and women ages 18-59. "Faithfulness thrives," announced the *New York Times* front-page story; "surprising conservatism" (*L.A. Times*), "good news from the mainstream" (*USA Today*), and "fidelity reigns" (*U.S. News & World Report*), cascaded from the press.[91]

The surveyors, stung by right-wing criticism of past efforts to obtain funding for studies of Americans' sex lives, had made every effort to produce conservative results. They excluded those who lived in military barracks or college dormitories, used face-to-face interviews rather than anonymous questionnaires, sent out warning letters to prospective interviewees linking risky sex to AIDS, and even questioned one-fifth of their sample in the presence of spouses—techniques certain to minimize disclosure of promiscuity, infidelity, and unconventionality. In fact, the percentage of women reporting to the surveyors that they had ended their pregnancies by induced abortions during the 1975-88 period (13 percent, leading to an estimated total of 10.8 million abortions)[92] was half the number clinical records show really occurred during that time (25 percent, or 20.6 million abortions).[93]

Once again, self-reporting surveys are suspect—in this case, of respondents concealing behaviors others might not approve of. "Only" 25 percent of the husbands and 15 percent of the wives admitted extra-marital affairs, a finding trumpeted by survey authors as proof of Americans' "extraordinary fidelity in marriage" (the fact that the average marriage today lasts only seven years was not mentioned). But even this figure was diluted by newly-married young couples. Among men in their 50s, 37 percent admitted cheating on their wives. The average male age 18-59 reporting having had six sex partners in his life; the average woman, two. No one asked how this could be—especially since very few reported being gay.[94][95]

Imagine the way officials and the media would have handled this survey if it had used the same hype as for teenage sex: "25 MILLION AMERICANS CHEAT ON SPOUSES. Older Marrieds Worse for Affairs, Survey Finds. Experts Decry 'Alarming' Grownup Promiscuity, Infidelity!"

And so on. But the media and *Sex in America* surveyors perceived, correctly, that American adults are not open to entertaining bad news about our own behavior. The survey's tame results were headlined while its downers—such as 17 percent of the women and 12 percent of the men reporting childhood sexual abuse, or 21 percent of the women reporting forced sex (only 3 percent of the men admitted to rape)—were buried well below the sunny accolades to grownup purity. A few commentators compared surveyors' claims of U.S. sexual conservatism with those of Europe—again forgetting to mention that the U.S. suffers real-life levels of STDs, unwanted pregnancy, adult impregnation of teenagers, and divorce two to seven times higher than found in Western Europe.

American adults' self-proclaimed sexual responsibility was not backed up by solid measures of behavior outcomes. Yet, as in the case of loud public support for Prohibition amid widespread, quiet public drinking 75 years ago, the 1994 survey's public claims of fidelity quickly proved useful to politicians eager to claim that mainstream American adults observe "traditional" values. And once again, the penchant of American grownups to assert a strident personal morality while practicing the opposite is associated with extraordinary meanness toward those whose "sins" cannot be so easily concealed—such as pregnant, poor women, or persons with AIDS. Imagine how confusing it is to grow up in a such a society.

Unsexy realities

Because it is the myth, not the reality, of "teenage sex" that makes it hot political and media property, reasonable policy on the subject is likely to remove the issue from the spotlight. No prominent, and especially no official, interests have yet shown willingness to discuss openly the biggest factors in pregnancy, childbearing, abortion, STD, and AIDS among teenagers, which are themselves interrelated:

(a)   The sexual behaviors of American adults, which include the Western world's highest rates of non-marital pregnancy, divorce, single parenting, and STD,[96] both with other adults and with teenage partners,

(b)   The United States' staggering level of child poverty, which (as will be discussed in the next chapter) is the cause, not the result, of high rates of teenage childbearing, and

(c)   The sexual exploitation of very young females by older males, including sexual abuse, rape, coercion, prostitution, early sexual initiation, and default on paternal responsibilities, all of which are associated with child poverty.

The United States is not likely to reduce appreciably its level of teenage motherhood by sex education, condom distribution, abstinence lectures, welfare punishments, record ratings, or any of the avalanche of teen-fixing schemes which have been tried for a decade without success. Successes will be claimed, of course, mainly in terms of pencil-and-paper surveys or normal downward fluctuations in pregnancy rates eagerly touted by the same programs which have not claimed the upward ones.

In a typical example, Stephanie Ventura, spokeswoman for the National Center for Health Statistics, did not discuss poverty, abuse, or adult roles in teenage motherhood in a September 1995 press statement on the slight decline in teenage birth rates from 1992 to 1993 (which, as usual, paralleled the decline in adult birth rates). Instead, she attributed the drop to "messages about abstinence" and condom use "getting through" to teens. This statement was particularly dubious since the decrease in birth occurred only among 18-19-year-old mothers, not the younger teens most vigorously targeted for such "messages."[97] The standard effort by officials to take credit for any improvement overlooks the fact that teen birth rates declined by 45 percent over the 1959-86 period with few programs or "messages" aimed at them, and the 1980s and 1990s era of targeting teens has coincided with higher, not lower, birth rates.

For the long term, there is no painless programmatic cure-all to bestow on the U.S. the low rate of early childbearing found in other industrial nations. If the U.S. wants to emulate the lower teenage motherhood rates of Canada or Britain, or the very low rates of Norway or Sweden, the U.S. has to invest the greater resources that these nations do in social insurance programs to produce the same low child poverty rates these nations experience. The benefits paid by the U.S.'s small welfare system serve to reduce family poverty by only 17 percent, compared to 40 percent in Canada and the UK, 50 percent in Norway, and 60 percent in Sweden—and these latter nations, with their universal benefits, experience teen motherhood rates only a fraction of that of the U.S.[98] When child poverty is reduced, much of teen pregnancy and its motivations in escape and liaison with adult partners takes care of itself.

This conclusion is not an argument against sex education or open discussion of abstinence or contraception as means of protecting against unwanted consequences. In fact, school programs appear to contribute to the facts that three times more teen mothers graduate from high school today than in the 1950s, that babies born to poorer young mothers are healthier than in the past, and that most teens who are sexually active are practicing contraception responsibly and are at low risk of consequences.[99] Rather it is an argument for profoundly changing sex education to incorporate the crucial fact that many teenagers enter the adult sexual world at young ages due not to the pressures of peers, rock'n'roll, or their own hormones, but those of adults and older teens. Those programmers who claim that behavior education or "values" education (which usually means attempting to deceive students that American adults practice chaste behaviors the young can easily observe that we don't) or contraceptive devices can be deployed cheaply and easily to rescue policy makers from two decades of attrition against the young are doing profound and irresponsible disservice.

Along with poverty, the most important issue in "teen pregnancy" is sexual abuse. The chief "personal behavior" imperative—that of confronting exploitative male sexual behaviors—will become clear when interest groups finally begin listening to what junior high girls are saying about sex. Only 6 percent of 14-year-old girls report having had intercourse. Of this 6 percent, who our health officials brand as "sexually active," for half a rape was their only "sexual experience," and another one-sixth had experienced both rape and "voluntary" sex. That is, only 2 percent of all 14-year-old girls report having had purely voluntary sexual relations absent a history of rape.

What this seems to mean is that virtually all 14-year-old girls do not want to engage in sexual intercourse. They agree with abstinence promoters. They don't need to be lectured by camera-hungry politicians or subjected to don't-do-it "values" sermons. They need a social system committed to protecting them from rape and sexual pressure by substantially older males. They need access to sexual information and health care. And they need a political and health establishment whose officials have matured out of their current phase of blaming the nation's adult-caused sexual ills on eighth graders.

3. Breeding Doomsday?

Night puts a dark mask on this city's abandoned row houses, gutted factories and boarded shops... Camden is a city of children... boys who blind stray dogs after school... whores who get pregnant at 14 only to bury their infants.

— Kevin Fedarko, "Who Could Live Here?" *Time*, 20 January 1992

Welcome to prime time, bitch.

— Freddy Krueger, 1987

Images of the apocalypse are not invoked by teen mom Rosalynn Carter, nor by my Oklahoma grandmother, married at age 16 and pregnant at 17 at the outset of a 65-year union. No, the teenage cancer on society today's welfare reformers seek to excise are personified by black, 17-year-old LaSalla and 16-year-old Almonica, who described their teen motherhoods at the Florence Crittenton Center near downtown Los Angeles.

"I was watching five little brothers, sisters, cousins at home," LaSalla said. "Here, it's one, and I'm not getting hit around." She handed her tiny infant to me and displayed the scars on her calves where her drug-addicted mother beat her with an extension cord. After she graduates from the center's high school, she plans to marry her baby's 23-year-old father, who visits twice a week.

Almonica saw her mother set on fire and murdered by her stepfather during a drunken fight. The 21-year-old father of her child was a "friend of the family" who promised to get her out of a violent household where her life consisted of watching smaller siblings. She hasn't seen him in several months but did not appear distraught. "When I get out of here, I'll get a job," she said. "It won't be easy."

Seventeen-year-old mom Sabrina, at an Orange County alternative high school, is obnoxious. She is sarcastic and refuses to concentrate on lessons for the language and mathematics proficiency exams California students must pass to graduate. Finally she admits, "My baby was sick all last night. All I can think about is him. He won't eat unless I'm there." The teacher reassures her that all babies get sick, but Sabrina continues to fret. She is released from school at noon to go home.

Motherhood and high school don't mix, teen pregnancy preventers argue. They are half right. In the United States, particularly for lower-income women, motherhood and employment and careers don't mix, either. Since 1990, complaints to federal and state authorities by women who were fired or laid off by employers because they were pregnant or mothering have skyrocketed. Reported *U.S. News & World Report*: "Employers forced to squeeze more work out of fewer bodies may see pregnant staffers as unreliable—no longer able to log long hours, the first to rush home when baby gets sick—and thus less valuable."[1]

Conservatives are quick to point out the "social costs" of forcing employers, through the 1978 Pregnancy Discrimination Act and 1993 Family Leave Act, to rehire workers who take leave due to pregnancy. They might point out the personal costs as well: Such leave is typically unpaid. In America, alone among industrial nations in failing to establish a comprehensive family policy to provide for pregnant and parenting workers, there is no good time to have a baby—not high school, not college, not in jobs, certainly not in careers.

More aid = fewer teen babies

If policy makers want to reduce teenage motherhood and its alleged "social costs," the solution is clear: Give them more money. More public assistance, more child care allotments, more education and employment training subsidies, more child support (collected benignly or otherwise from mostly-adult fathers), more medical and housing aid, more assistance in dealing with childhood traumas such as rape and sexual abuse.

Realign welfare into a true social insurance program—as it is in Europe, as it was becoming in the U.S. around 1970 before two decades of slashings, as it is today, selectively, for the U.S. elderly. One that serves as an escape hatch for the young out of this nation's unconscionably widespread experience of childhood poverty. With more aid, it is likely that teenage parents (as noted in the last chapter, most teen mothers have adult partners age 20 and older) once again will become "early on, early off" recipients as they were two decades ago.[2]

The notion that generous public assistance promotes single motherhood is one of the most easily disproven myths of the welfare reform debate. In fact, exactly the opposite is the case. It is the sharp post-1970 cuts in family welfare that render it a bare-subsistence trap from which escape is increasingly difficult. American welfare is a poverty-maintenance system for a large fraction of its recipients. An exhaustive 1988 Urban Institute study of welfare systems in eight Western nations found that the U.S. seems "politically unable or unwilling to raise benefits high enough to be as effective in moving children out of poverty as universal and social insurance approaches."[3] The circumstances of the fraction of young families who remain on Aid to Families with Dependent Children for a long time (only 22 percent of recipients remain on AFDC for five years or more, often due to medical disabilities) merit specialized attention. But not the large majority whose dependence is short term (34 percent are on AFDC one year or less; 44 percent between one and five years) and is often due to sudden changes in circumstances, such as illness, layoff, or paternal abandonment.[4]

The idea of increasing aid to young families is not a soft-headed bleeding-heart lunacy; it is a hard-nosed proposal backed by solid data and track records. Western European nations pragmatically devote considerable resources to ensuring that, whatever the presumed misbehaviors of parents, children do not grow up in poverty. Europe has a startlingly low rate of births among teenagers (practically none among junior high-age girls), very low rates of welfare dependency among both single and married parents, and violence rates a tiny fraction of ours. Germany, whose gross domestic product per person is lower than the U.S.'s, has a teen birth rate one-fourth that of the U.S.—one that is falling while America's rises.

Conservative theorist Charles Murray's original conjecture that higher welfare payments promote more "illegitimacy" was praised by President Clinton as "essentially right."[5] Thus it is no surprise to find out it is absolutely wrong, especially for adolescents. From 1970 to 1994, the real value of Aid to Families with Dependent Children (the chief child welfare program) declined by 50 percent while the nation's rate of births per 1,000 single women rose by 80 percent.[6]

In a 1994 article, Murray agreed that "the AFDC benefit... in real terms has retreated to 1950s levels." In fact, AFDC fell from 1.4 percent of the federal budget in 1974 to 1.1 percent in 1994—and will be cut further. Murray's calculation of the welfare package (AFDC, food stamps, housing, and Medicaid subsidies) showed that the sharp decline in the real (inflation-adjusted) value of young family assistance programs after 1970 cut $400 in constant 1990 dollars out of the average monthly family welfare check. Yet the rate of unwed births more than doubled. Oh, well, "It seems likely that welfare will be found to cause some portion of illegitimacy, but not a lot," Murray admitted.[7]

In California, the average $178 per month of AFDC benefits in 1970 would have paid the rent on the $95-per-month apartment I occupied in Pasadena that year for seven weeks. A month of average AFDC benefits in 1993, $377,[8] would pay 1993's $550/month rent on that same apartment for just three weeks. In 1970, when welfare benefits were generous, California experienced 45,600 unwed births, 13 percent of the state's total births. By the logic governing today's welfare reform debate, the sharp cutback in benefits should have led to lower unwed birth rates. Yet in 1993, after two decades of plummeting aid, the state experienced 205,000 unwed births, 35 percent of the total births. The number of unwed births among California teenagers rose from 19,000 in 1970 to 49,000 in 1993, a time period during which the teen population rose by only 10 percent.[9]

I calculated the total "welfare package" more comprehensively (including AFDC, Food Stamps, subsidized school lunches, Women Infants and Children nutrition programs, other food subsidies, public housing subsidies, and Medicaid) available to qualifying families for each state in 1990. To determine how well a person could live on welfare in his/her particular state, I expressed the state's "total welfare benefit" as a percentage of each state's median personal income. This supposed "welfare incentive" was contrasted with each state's 1990 birth rate among unwed teenagers.

A consistent pattern emerged: *Higher* benefits were associated with *lower* rates of both teen births and unwed teen births. The association was statistically significant[10] and indicated that higher welfare payments act to reduce teen birth rates. The contrast in teen motherhood propensities between the five states in which families on welfare can enjoy the highest standard of living (78 percent as high as that of families living on the state's median income) versus the five states in which welfare families are the worst off (living on 45 percent of the state's median income) is striking (Table 3.1).

According to Murray and Clinton reformers, North Dakota teens (who can live nearly as well on welfare as if they worked full time and earned the state's median wage) should be breeding like flies, while Mississippi teens should be chaste in fear of that state's paltry dole—or migrating upriver to North Dakota to breed. But unwed Mississippi teens are four times more prolific than unwed North Dakota teens.

Table 3.1

Generous welfare systems promote *fewer* teen births:

1990	Welfare payments as percent of median income	Births per 100 females age 12-17	Child/youth Poverty rate
Most generous:			
North Dakota	89.4%	3.5	16.9%
New York	84.8	6.7	18.8
South Dakota	74.4	5.5	20.1
Utah	72.2	5.9	12.2
Montana	71.6	5.8	19.9
Avg, most generous	78.5%	5.5	17.6%
Least generous:			
Missouri	46.4%	9.4	17.4%
Mississippi	46.4	15.3	33.5
Alabama	46.4	12.3	24.0
Michigan	45.2	9.0	18.2
Texas	42.1	11.6	24.0
Avg, least generous	45.3%	11.5	23.4 %

Sources: U.S. Bureau of the Census (1993). *Statistical Abstract of the United States, 1992.* Washington, DC: U.S. Department of Commerce, Tables 147, 455, 591, 595; National Center for Health Statistics (1994). *Vital Statistics of the United States, 1990.* Washington, DC: U.S. Department of Health and Human Services, Table 1-59; U.S. Bureau of the Census (1992). *Census of Population 1990. Social and Economic Characteristics, United States Summary.* Washington, DC: U.S. Department of Commerce, Table 154.

There are, of course, differences between these states other than welfare beneficence that account for the twice-as-high teen birth rates in the least versus the most welfare-generous states. Statistical tests of association, which can be applied to estimate how much a factor like welfare is connected to another factor like teen birth rates, indicate that higher welfare payments account for 15 percent to 20 percent of the difference between the lower teen birth rates found in the most generous states versus the higher teen birth rates found in the stingiest states. The remainder is due to other differences between the states—the biggest of which is the higher youth poverty rates in the least generous states, which are partly a function of these states' lower levels of public assistance. (Note, however, that even the "most generous" states by American standards continue to have high youth poverty rates). The evidence remains that the politician/media creed that teen mothers have babies to collect welfare, the detour Charles Murray and Clinton welfare reformers have taken us on, is not just wrong, but ridiculous.

A similar pattern shows up over time, as Figure 3.2 shows. Over the time peri-

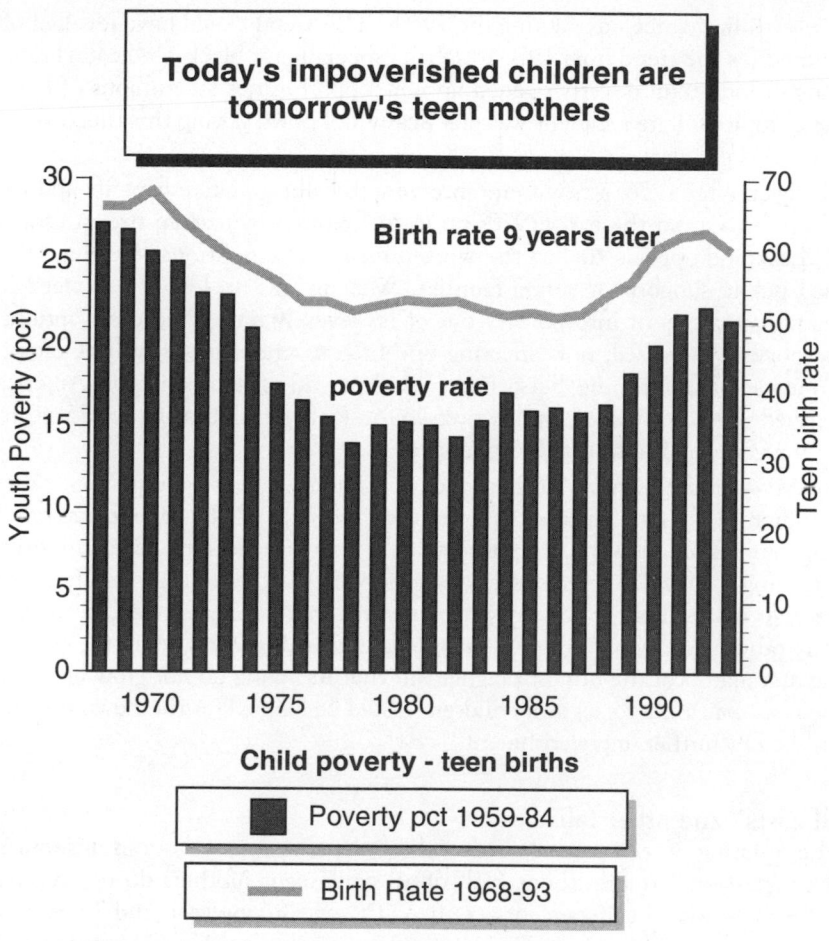

Today's impoverished children are tomorrow's teen mothers

Birth rate 9 years later

poverty rate

Child poverty - teen births

■ Poverty pct 1959-84

━━ Birth Rate 1968-93

Figure 3.2

Source: U.S. Bureau of the Census: *Poverty In the United States, 1992*; National Center for Health Statistics, *Vital Statistics of the United States* 1991 and advanced data. See Table 3.1

od for which poverty rates are available, 1959 through 1993, the rate of child poverty predicts the rate of births among teenagers nine years later with greater than 90 percent accuracy. That is, increases in child poverty are tied to increases in teen birth rates a decade later, so that the child poverty rate in 1965 closely predicts the teen birth rate in 1974. The pattern is a logical one. The average age of children living in poverty is nine; the average age of a teen mother at time of birth is 18.

The correlation between declining young-family welfare, rising youth poverty, and increases in teenage parenthood are strong and consistent, but not universal. For example, prior to 1970 there is no evident relationship—zero—between poverty rates and unwed childbearing rates among either teens or adults. It appears that the rise in unwed births over the last 50 years, shown in Figure 2.12 in Chapter 2, is the result of two very different trends. From 1940 to 1970, the increase in unwed birth rates was accompanied by rising welfare benefits and falling child poverty. It appears to have been part of the growing postwar family instability that culminated in the sudden growth in divorce rates during the 1960s. This trend would have levelled off and declined (as the trend from 1970 to 1976, especially for blacks, indicates) once the easing of long-term poverty opened up new opportunities for millions of families. The chronic welfare recipient was practically unknown during this time except among disabled populations.

However, after 1976, a new trend intervened. Falling welfare benefits and rising child poverty from the early 1970s on were followed by a steep rise in unwed births. This trend appears tied to the worsening social conditions resulting from decreased public support for young families. Welfare was no longer sufficient to boost young people born into poverty out of it, severely narrowing their options. Chronic poverty increased, now affecting one-fifth to one-third of welfare recipients. To argue that punishing "illegitimacy" will get rid of it is ludicrous. America has punished unwed, divorced, and poorer young-family childbearing for 25 years, creating the very conditions that breed more of it.

Poverty *precedes* teenage motherhood. A nation, state, or county that raises fewer children in poverty experiences fewer teen mothers. Higher public assistance for young families, and lower child poverty rates, work to reduce teenage childbearing by opening up a wider range of school and job alternatives to early family establishment. No matter how many ways this pattern can be demonstrated, no matter that every other wealthy nation in the world accepts its logic and dedicates itself to ensuring as a matter of the utmost pragmatism that its young do not grow up destitute, the U.S. continues to act as if children should be blamed for their own poverty and punished by further impoverishment.

"Social costs" and other fallacies

The equating of teen mothers with welfare dependency is a serious misnomer, several congressional studies show. Half of all adolescent mothers do not receive AFDC. Of those who do, 40 percent are off AFDC within one year, and 70 percent within four years, of giving birth. The average teen mother on AFDC, despite being poorer before becoming pregnant than the average adult mother, stays on the welfare rolls only one year longer than the average mother who gives birth in her 20s.[11] Those who are on AFDC received a whopping $376 per family, $133 per individual, per month in 1994. This is what the screaming over the "social costs of teen motherhood" is all about?

The extraordinary resentment of Americans at having to pay public money to support children and young families is revealed again in studies, from the Urban Institute to the General Accounting Office, alleging high "social costs" attributed to teenage motherhood. The 1986 review by UI economist Martha Burt is typical. It charges that families started by teenagers cost $16.7 billion in AFDC, Food Stamps, and Medicaid benefits in 1985. (The 1994 GAO figure is $34 billion). Examination of the UI review reveals that a similar number of families started by mothers age 20 and older would generate 60 percent as much welfare costs as those started by teens, but the "public costs of adult childbearing" are not highlighted.[12] So teen mothers (under unfairly harsh worst-case assumptions) actually cost $6 billion per year—the price of six B-1 bombers, or half the cost-of-living increase alone in Social Security and Medicare. Big deal! This is what liberal reform groups spend their time decrying?

Assume for the sake of argument that the figures are accurate and fair. Assume the maximum teenage contribution to welfare: 6 million children born to welfare mothers, whether teen or adult in 1994, who began their families as teenagers. Assume all teenage mothers stay on welfare for life (in fact three-fourths are off welfare within five years) collecting maximum benefits. Assume teenage mothers and their offspring contribute nothing in tax dollars for their entire lives (Urban Institute studies of the "social costs" of immigrants at least deduct taxes paid by immigrants). Under this beyond-worst-case scenario, $5,700 per year is paid in AFDC, all food, housing, and medical welfare, everything, to each impoverished child generated by a present or past teenage mother. That is $470 per child per month, including costs of the mother. If we wanted to boost every child born to every American women who ever had a baby as a teenager out of poverty, the total cost (called the "poverty gap") would be less than $10 billion per year.[13]

Big deal! The average 1991 Social Security check alone (not including Medicare or other senior subsidies) paid to each of 29 million elderly, most of whom hold more than $50,000 in personal assets and are not poor, was $629 per month.[14] In 1992, $75 billion in Social Security and Medicare was paid to 2.5 million elder households with cash incomes exceeding $50,000 per year—$2,500 in public payments going to each of the nation's wealthiest senior households every month. The cost of the 20 unneeded B-1 bombers added to the defense budget by Congress to provide welfare to hometown defense contractors is $20 billion.

And the loudest whining in Washington has been about the fraction of that sum paid for the care and feeding of impoverished four-year-olds? Because they had the bad taste to choose teenage moms?

The purpose of this comparison is not to begrudge the large majority of the elderly their modest subsidies—not if the large majority of the elderly whose own well-being is tied to welfare would forcefully inform politicians terrorized by elder voting power that the government better not begrudge poor children their more modest subsidies, either. Let's not try to argue that 70-year-olds deserve welfare but seven-year-olds born to dark-hued young moms deserve to go hungry in the streets.

The chief issue is the attitudes of the adults who run the American political system (managed by professional poll-preoccupied handlers) and their insensitivity to the fact that children and teenagers cannot vote, lobby, or bribe. There is no children's equivalent of the powerful American Association of Retired Persons, no American Association of Children of Past and Present Teenage Mothers, commanding Fortune-500 budgets and 30 million voters. If even a fraction of the aged were willing to put children's welfare on par with their own, we wouldn't see any more pseudo-scientific "social costs of teenage mothers" reports bewailing the fact that 2 percent of the $1.5 trillion federal budget is spent on a few million of the poorest children—the same children we 1990s adults expect to help pay off the $6 trillion tab for government deficits we put on plastic.

Note the logic welfare analyst Mickey Kaus of the erstwhile liberal *The New Republic* ascribes to reformers and the public:

When NBC and The Wall Street Journal polled voters right after the [November 1994] election, reforming welfare was the issue most often listed as the top priority...

How can welfare be so important? After all, the program that most people mean when they talk about "welfare"—Aid to Families with Dependent Children (AFDC)—only spends about $25 billion per year in federal and state money. Add in Food Stamps, and you're still talking about 3 percent of the federal budget. But it's a crucial 3 percent, both symbolically and substantively.

Poll-takers will tell you that welfare is a "values" issue. The values are work and family. Both AFDC and Food Stamps flout the work ethic, offering support to able-bodied Americans whether they work or not—the only major components of our "welfare state" that do this. Social Security's retirement benefits, in contrast, only go to workers. AFDC also seemingly undermines families, because it is available, by and large, only to single parents (mainly mothers).[15]

Social Security does not "only go to workers." It is paid (for example) to the former housewives of divorced or deceased husbands, women who—by the definition applied to single housewives on AFDC—never "worked" a day in their lives. It pays several times more in benefits than retired workers ever paid into it. The "values" underlying the popularity of Social Security is that aging adults receive or anticipate receiving it. The unpopularity of AFDC is due to the fact that aging adults cannot receive it. It is not unearned welfare that is repugnant. There is no "values" issue here. What rankles is the notion of young families collecting it.

Of course AFDC recipients don't "work." Two-thirds of its beneficiaries are children averaging nine years of age. One-third of the parents receiving AFDC are disabled. Thus at most, only one-fifth of AFDC beneficiaries are "able bodied" non-workers. The anachronism that women, single or otherwise, who maintain households and raise children do not "work" was buried until the AFDC debate resurrected it. The cure in most plans is to force AFDC mothers to go to "work" outside the home, at a minimum or sub-minimum wage job generating below-poverty income without day care, or lose benefits. The result is to punish 16 million children because of anger at what 8 million mothers are thought to have done.

It took right-wing columnist and Reagan advisor George Will (see below) to point out that most Americans are "socially costly." Most American's don't "work." Only 119 million of America's 260 million people were employed at paying jobs— "working"—all or part of 1993. It is perverse, and not without a measure of cruelty, to single out children for the test of "cost effectiveness" *while they are children*. Normally, an adult generation shoulders the costs—most obviously through tens of billions in income tax deductions for dependents taken by millions of middle class and wealthier income-tax-filing parents, or $250 billion in tax support of public schools—of the next generation, just as their parents paid their costs, and just as children grow up and assume costs for supporting their aging parents. Today's Baby Boom and elder generations hardly clawed our way up by our own bootstraps. We were and are generously subsidized by trillions of dollars in publicly-funded programs from the New Deal to the GI Bill to the Great Society to low-tuition education to homeowner mortgage deductions to Social Security—and by coming generations, through the enormous deficits today's elders are leaving behind.

The UI and GAO studies, in usual bell-jar fashion, which omits nearly every relevant context, simply compared welfare paid to families started by teen mothers to welfare paid to families started by adult mothers. Straight across. Ignored is the fact that due to the uniquely elevated level of poverty inflicted upon U.S. children by U.S. adults, five out of six teenage mothers were poor *before* they became pregnant.[16] At some point in this deadly serious debate, social analysts should confront the obvious: The poverty of teen mothers is an extension of their poverty prior to motherhood. Also ignored is the failure of unwed and divorced absentee fathers, nearly all adults, to pay child support. Also ignored is the role of sexual abuse in teen motherhood, which is related to emotional disturbance, drug abuse, and depression,[17] all factors affecting the mother's school success and employability.

Other than its political ease, why pick on teenagers? Social-cost students could more accurately and succinctly pursue the "social costs of low-income parenting," or "the social costs of parenting by sexual abuse victims," or the "social costs of adult male sexual behavior toward teenagers." Or why not just regress all the way to the standard demographic scapegoat: Since three-fourths of all single teen mothers on welfare are nonwhite, sum up the whole issue as "the social costs of minority-group childbearing." Such studies, inconsistently applied to malign the behavior of disfavored groups, are of orange-apple uselessness. And worse: By ignoring the large number of social and personal disadvantages that precede most teenage motherhood, researchers perpetuate the prejudicial notion that the only problem needing correction is bad attitude on the part of teenage females.

The "values" involved, then, are public and politician fury at providing money to what are perceived to be unwed teen mothers and their profligate broods. Never mind that the average AFDC mother is 29 years-old with two or fewer children, who is on welfare because she was recently laid off from work, divorced or separated, and who receives no support from the father.[18] The reason teenage mothers are targeted, as an aide to key welfare-reform Senator Daniel Moynihan (D-New York) reasoned, is that "teenage parents on AFDC" are "where, after all, the whole cycle of welfare dependency begins."[19] This is the Clinton, Congress, and media argument: Welfare dependency, like most every other national ill, is a teenage behavior problem.

If Generation Y, today's adolescents and children of school age and younger, harbored a volatile political wing, this is the kind of theory that would make them descend on Washington with machetes. *Welfare does not begin with teenage parents. Their welfare lives began before they were born.* Nearly all teenagers who have babies were on welfare *before* they had babies. They were subjected to a decade and a half of poverty by a wealthy society that saves its mostly older taxpayers money by raising 25 percent of its youth in penury and another 15 percent in near-poverty.

This is the society that, in Moynihan's own state, cut $1 billion out of New York City public schools, leaving them crowded and dilapidated and facing more cuts, and $200 million out of its chief public university in one year alone—to save older taxpayers money.[20] The society that already cut the real value of AFDC and Food Stamps in half over the last 25 years by refusing to index them to inflation—to save older taxpayers money. The society whose minimum wage (let alone the "subminimum training wage" for teenagers) paid for full-time full-year work would provide $2,000 less than a mother and two children need to escape poverty—to save

businesses money. In a society that weighed the interests of old and young generations on an equivalent balance, the question would be the social costs borne by
today's youths to subsidize today's adults.

At juncture after juncture over the past quarter century, Americans have
transferred publicly allocated resources away from children and young families and
toward the well-being of aging grownups. By the 1990s, welfare and minimum-wage
employment have become so stingy that neither provides a way out of poverty for
the increasing millions of youths raised in it. Suddenly, the consensus of the leaders
of both parties (representing older adults who profited the most from attrition
against young families) became that teenagers and children (the groups least responsible for creating their conditions) are the ones fully to blame for starting "the cycle
of welfare dependence." Even overlooking the sexual and physical violence most
teenage mothers experience due at least in part to the climate of poverty in which
so many spend their childhoods, the bleak opportunities of growing up young and
poor in a closing society leave few rewards other than starting and raising families.

Using age to mask inequality

Are children of teenage mothers more abused? More likely to be born with low
birth weights or other defects? Less likely to do well in school? More likely to be
hoodlums?

Again, we are not talking about teen-mom Rosalynn Carter's children. In
every instance where I have raised this question, those most adamant that teenage
mother = disaster have turned around and declared, "but Rosalynn's situation was
different." In other words, factors besides Rosalynn's "teen" age made her situation
different. What factors? The ones America is unwilling to address.

What 99 percent of the comparisons of the children of teenage moms versus
the children of adult mothers accomplish is further proof that yes, the progeny of
poorer nonwhites indeed do less well in American schools and society than do that
of wealthier whites. Yes, kids raised by parents with backgrounds of sexual and violent abuse tend to have more chaotic upbringings than kids whose parents were not
abused. In none of this does the age of the mother in and of itself show up as the
crucial factor.

Carolyn Makinson of Princeton's Office of Population Research reviewed several dozen studies from the U.S. and four other Western nations and found "remarkably similar" results:

> The most recent evidence indicates that the bulk of the adverse conse-
> quences of teenage childbearing may be of social and economic origin, rather
> than attributable to the effects of young age per se... Some evidence indicates
> that if maternal age has an effect, it is only among very young teenage mothers.[21]

An analysis of 7,100 U.S. children and their parents indeed found a small association between the child's intellectual development and maternal age—but concluded that the age of the mother was not the cause:

> The effects of parental age are apparently not biologic, but instead are due
> chiefly to the impact of sociodemographic factors and the tendency for young

mothers, especially blacks, to be overrepresented in lower socioeconomic groups and in female-headed households.[22]

In particular, teenage mothers are accused of producing babies with low birth weights, which in turn is the biggest predictor of poor infant health and development. Yet national vital statistics reports show the true cause of low birthweight babies is economic disadvantage, reflected in race (Table 3.3).

Table 3.3

Poverty, not maternal age, is the biggest factor in unhealthy babies:

| | Median birth weight* | | Percent low birth weight* | |
Age of mother	White	Black	White	Black
10-14	3,240	3,080	10.3%	15.7%
15-19	3,310	3,130	7.5	13.5
20-24	3,380	3,170	5.8	12.3
25-29	3,440	3,190	5.1	13.1
30-34	3,460	3,190	5.3	13.4
35-39	3,460	3,200	6.3	15.3
40-44	3,450	3,200	7.0	15.1
45-49	3,410	3,220	10.0	15.5
All ages	3,410	3,170	5.7%	13.3%

*In grams. Low birth weight is less than 2,500 grams (5.5 pounds).
Source: National Center for Health Statistics (1995). *Vital statistics of the United States 1990. Volume I, Natality.* Washington, DC: U.S. Department of Health and Human Services, Table 1-104.

The greater poverty of blacks and their lesser access to prenatal care has devastating effects on infant health. So much so that a white teenager—even a white junior high-age mother—is much less likely to have a low birth weight baby than a black adult at every age level. A black mother age 25-29, for example, is 40 percent more likely to bear a low birth weight baby than a white 15 year-old. Black infants weigh half a pound less at birth than white infants. Note also that there is little difference between black teens and black adults in the birth weights of their babies. The lesser effect of young maternal age on birth weights is explained by the fact that younger mothers, regardless of race, are more likely to be poor than older ones. Except for mothers younger than 15 and older than 40, the pattern reflects economic status, not the age or race of the mother.

Another study, which controlled for economic backgrounds still found a small relationship between mothers' ages and child development. The most important relationship was with mothers' scores on psychological tests of "malaise."[23] Since a history of sexual abuse and rape is closely linked both to teen motherhood and malaise, this may also be a key factor. The federally funded 1992 National Women's Study found that rape victims (60 percent of whom reported being raped before age 18) are three times more likely to report major depression, four times more likely to have contemplated suicide, six times more likely to have developed post-traumatic stress syndrome, and 13 times more likely to have attempted suicide.[24]

Common declarations that teenage motherhood is a "disaster" or a "calamity" or entails "tremendous social and financial costs" evade confronting the real issue: The devastating effects of persistent inequality imposed on nonwhite races and economic disadvantage imposed on the young. Makinson puts the issue more formally:

> Symptoms of social and economic inequality may be more visible than the inequalities themselves, and are probably more easily, if less fruitfully, eradicated. Many of the adverse consequences of teenage fertility are symptoms of this kind.

In other words, attacking "teen mothers" is a politically facile substitute for genuine efforts to eliminate racial and economic injustice—particularly that foisted on the young. There appears no health or child-rearing disadvantage related to the teen age of the mother except when the mother is very young (14 or younger). On the other hand, a history of poverty and abuse appear to be crucial factors. As Makinson points out:

> To the extent that young age is an intermediate variable between adverse consequences and root causes that are of social and economic origin, postponing childbearing until the risks are no higher than average might mean postponing childbearing permanently for many women who will remain socially and economically disadvantaged.[25]

That would be fine with conservatives such as Murray, vocal in his *Bell Curve* argument that childbearing by low-income mothers, mostly nonwhite, is (to use the 1920s term his book resurrected) "dysgenic."[26] Liberals who ascribe dire disadvantages to teenage motherhood, which is a surrogate for low-income motherhood, are making the same argument as Murray's without being as candid. If the parents are poor, there is no good age, no healthy age, no age at which "social costs" will not result from childbearing. Having a baby young disrupts schooling; having a baby old disrupts job and career.

As is so often the case when "teen age" is employed as a code word for "minority group" and "low income group," the conservative and liberal arguments boil down to the same unstated, circular set of premises and conclusions:

(a)   Older Americans are unwilling to spend the money to help poorer young Americans climb out of poverty, so

(b)   the poor (mostly nonwhites) should refrain from having children, but

(c)   if they do have children, the poor (mostly nonwhites) are to blame for their own poverty; therefore

(d)   older groups are justified in refusing to help poorer young people who cause their own problems.

Despite "values" assertions, welfare reform always returns to the same "bottom line:" transferring public resources away from children and toward middle aged and elder adults.

Punish the mothers

Normally, the case for a more generous welfare, or social insurance, system aimed at helping impoverished young families out of welfare would be made by Democrats and liberals. Such measures work handsomely in Europe. Such rapidly expanding welfare measures have worked handsomely to drastically cut elder poverty, down from 35 percent in 1959 to 12 percent by 1993. Such measures had worked handsomely in the 1960s, when the War on Poverty and expanding school and job sectors wrought dramatic results: Some 20 million young families boosted off welfare and a halving in the child poverty rate from 29 percent to 14 percent. As reduced numbers of children raised in penury matured into adolescents, the evidence for rapidly falling rates of nearly all social problems through the 1970s was evident.

Yet the most damaging rationale for slashing young family aid came not from Murray and Republican conservative welfare nemeses, but from President Clinton's welfare reform task force. The task force's priority was not welfare reform, but an unvarnished 1996 re-election strategy revealed by Jason DeParle of *The New York Times*:

> President Clinton's assistants have drafted a plan that urges him to lead "nothing less than a national mobilization" against teen-age pregnancy and promote some of the values that have historically been seized by Republicans, including sexual abstinence... It would use a Democratic bully pulpit to emphasize the importance of work, family and personal responsibility—the same themes that Republicans have often used in contending that the Democratic Party lacks mainstream values.
>
> The plan calls teen-age pregnancy "a bedrock issue of character and personal responsibility." It says the spiraling number of births among unwed mothers is the driving force behind many of the nation's problems, including poverty, crime, drugs and educational failure.[27]

Top Clinton officials were unrestrained in gloating over the potential for political gain from "dramatic Presidential events" blaming and lecturing youths:

> "I think what is important here is a Democratic President is saying it," said Donna E. Shalala, the Secretary of Health and Human Services, who contended that the Democrats have been unfairly accused in the past of neglecting such values.
>
> ..."This is, frankly, breathtaking," she said [of the plan].

The task force, reportedly envious of the attention garnered by former Vice President Dan Quayle's attack on the single motherhood of television character Murphy Brown, clearly stated the issue it wanted emphasized:

> The strategy envisions several... talks by the President, organized around the theme of "Putting Children First." It calls for him to make critical remarks about the role of the news media, especially television, "in sending young people damaging messages about sexual conduct, impulse control, and violence."

Speaking of damaging influences:

> The Clinton administration's welfare-reform task force intends to recommend that teen-agers who qualify for aid be prohibited from receiving it unless

they live with a parent or other responsible adult... The change is intended to eliminate what some analysts view as an incentive for unmarried young women to have children: the resources to establish their own households with the aid of welfare payments.[28]

Anthropologists will recognize this modern "welfare reform" as nothing more than resurrection of the ancient concept of "female supervision," in which social customs severely limited the freedoms of women (particularly young women) in order to keep them away from misbehaving men.

A particular cruelty of the Clinton plan, as with female-supervision customs throughout history, is the failure to recognize that some of the worst male misbehavior takes place within families. A 1992 Washington state study of 535 teen mothers illuminated the "parents or other responsible adults" which Clinton reformers would risk forcing teen mothers and their babies to live with: 66 percent of pregnant and parenting teens had been sexually abused, 44 percent had been raped, 59 percent had been hit with a belt or strap, 31 percent had been hit with sticks or other objects, 26 percent had been thrown against walls, 18 percent had been hit with closed fists, 5 percent had been burned with cigarettes or hot water. Overall, two-thirds had been sexually abused or raped, and 70 percent had been physically abused. Five percent of the births had resulted from rape. Most of the abusers were adult male family members. Nevertheless, 60 percent of the mothers under age 18 lived with parents (the real problem may be that too many, not too few, are living at home), nearly all others with husbands, relatives, or other adults. Those who did not live with parents consistently had suffered sexual abuses at home. The Washington study concluded that the physical and psychological effects of "sexual victimization may account for... consistently high rates teenage pregnancy."[29]

A 1994 study by Natalie Porter of the University of New Mexico School of Medicine found that 70 percent of pregnant teenagers receiving aid through social service programs had been sexually abused in their homes. "Yet the national drive for welfare reform aims to curb benefits for teen mothers, which will force many of them back into homes where they were victimized," Porter concluded.[30]

Clinton staffers are well aware of these studies. They are well aware of the 1990 Congressional Budget Office report showing fewer than 4 percent of mothers under age 18 live on their own, away from adults—and that most who can live with their parents already do so.[31] And of a 1994 report prepared for the General Accounting Office, Can They Go Home Again?, which found that "requiring minor parents to live at home is unlikely to reduce welfare dependency." The Center for Law and Social Policy concluded that the Clinton proposal might lead states to "inadvertently (or negligently) require a minor teen mother to return to an abusive environment."[32] The free-living teen welfare queen is as much a fabrication as the Cadillac-driving black welfare queen of past decades, only today's chief mythmakers are Democrats.

What is "breathtaking" about the Clinton "welfare reform" campaign is the depths of its dishonesty and cynical eagerness to whip up public anger at what may be America's poorest and most unfortunate young women. Perhaps the epitome of teen-sex deception Democrat-style was voiced by White House domestic policy aide William Galston, who won conservative applause with his "abstinence stance:"

"You might describe the emerging consensus as 'abstinence-plus.'"

Mr. Galston said that for teenagers 15 or younger, "the principal message has to be: don't, you're too young." For older teens, he said, "the principal message is still, 'don't, but if you do, act responsibly and make sure you don't do something that harms your future."[33]

Galston also endorsed plans to use "older students" as "mentors" to promote sexual abstinence among younger students.

It is impossible to believe that the president's top teen pregnancy expert, as well as a bevy of aides from the Children's Defense fund and other progressive child lobbies, could be unaware that 90 percent of the births among girls 15 and younger are fathered by "older teens" and adults—or of the predominance of rape and sexual abuse inflicted by "substantially older" males in the lives of "sexually active" girls under age 16. The Alan Guttmacher Institute study, *Sex and America's Teenagers*,[34] making just such points as these had been released to wide publicity the week prior to Galston's remarks.

The anti-youth policies pushed by Clinton were not initially embraced by Republicans. Then-Representative Rick Santorum (R-Pennsylvania), head of the House GOP task force on welfare reform, argued that any "signal" on welfare should be sent to all ages of recipients, not just aimed at the young. "It doesn't get at the long-term dependent population at all," Santorum pointed out, correctly.[35] Nevertheless, Santorum and other Republicans soon accepted the White House's invitation and trained their "welfare reform" guns not upon the special circumstances of the long-term adult dependents, which had formed the original impetus for reform, but on teenage mothers.

In short order, the designated scapegoat drew extremes of bipartisan invective. The teenage mother became a relentless destroyer of her own and future generations. She is worse than a homicidal gangbanger because teenage mothers are the *cause* of violent men. Not only that, 300,000 teen mothers are the source of *all* major social problems plaguing the United States, 1995's version of the Salem witches. The peak of absurdity came with former Surgeon General Joycelyn Elders' claim that 90 percent of all violent criminals were born to unwed teenage mothers. Even if every single son ever produced by every unwed teenage mother was arrested for a criminal offense every year, at most one-third of the young-male crime volume could be explained.[36]

The zeal to scapegoat teenage mothers masked the larger goal that couldn't be openly discussed: To punish welfare parents and impoverish children to save money for older taxpayers. "We've made great progress, and we're only touching the tip of the iceberg," bragged Wisconsin Governor Tommy Thompson (R) of his state's acclaimed welfare reform program that reduced AFDC caseloads by 21 percent while other states experienced increases. Progress as measured in 1990s light is grim progress indeed. The U.S. Bureau of the Census found that the proportion of Wisconsin children age 5-17 living in poverty mushroomed from 6.7 percent in 1987 to 16 percent in 1993, triple the national increase; 70,000 youngsters added to poverty roles under the nation's model "welfare reform."[37]

In a rare bit of sustained mass-media skepticism, *U.S. News & World Report* punctured "welfare reform miracle" bubbles coast to coast. *U.S. News'* analytical reports found that, yes, there are slothful bums on welfare, but most are hard-working. Most women on AFDC are victims of domestic violence, 40 percent are disabled, and others face misfortunes welfare reformers don't begin to perceive—and teenage mothers are only a small part of the larger, structural problems underlying chronic poverty.[38] Even more to the point, *U.S. News* declared in an apt pair of 1995 articles, "America's Other Welfare State" and "Getting Business Off the Dole," corporations are among the biggest soppers of public largesse, half of all American families are "on welfare," and "the payments get bigger as you move up the income scale."[39]

Teen motherhood: An opportunity

Ironically, and tragically in light of today's unreasoning welfare-reform invective, the teenage and young disadvantaged mother may be the most "cost effective" entity in society in which to invest substantial resources. The evidence is that early motherhood is an effort to escape from a past of violence and bleakness. As such, pregnant girls typically display dramatic improvements in behavior upon learning of their impending motherhood and represent good candidates for reinforcement, not punishment.

"Troubled, abused girls become more centered emotionally when they become mothers," Yale Gancherov, chief social worker at Los Angeles's Florence Crittenton Center for teen mothers and their infants, told me in 1992. "They often gain the attention of professionals and social services. Such girls are more likely to stay in school with a baby than without. Their behavioral health improves."[40]

Indeed it does, and dramatically. Perhaps the least-reported fact in an official and media zeitgeist of "teen mother tragedy" is the astonishing improvement in the previously troubled behavior shown by pregnant teens. When I raised this point to 150 school and community prevention experts who attended my workshop on poverty and adult fathers in teenage childbearing given to the November 1995 conference of the California Alliance Concerned With School-Age Parents, I expected a barrage of criticism. Instead, I saw heads nodding around the room. It isn't that a roomful of prevention providers were agreeing that early motherhood is an ideal solution to coping with poverty, abuse, and misery. It was acknowledgment that these girls don't come from ideal backgrounds with ideal arrays of options. There seems growing recognition that criticizing their choices stems from a position of luxury, and increasing humility that we may not fully understand its trade-offs.

In a 1990 study of 2,100 teenage females, Washington University and Harvard University researchers found "many of the problems of adolescent mothers are, in fact, those that are associated with the social and economic disadvantages of adolescents who have high rates of pregnancy, and thus, may not be due to child-bearing per se." Even though teen mothers come from "unstable family backgrounds," researchers found that "significantly fewer of those youths who are rearing children have recent (within the last year) symptoms of conduct disorder, alcohol or drug abuse or dependence, and depression, as well as suicidal thoughts, than their peers."

Their conclusion: "The adolescent mother, in contrast with the sexually active adolescent who is not a mother, feels better about herself and engages in fewer overt undesirable behaviors." The reason for this improved behavior among teen mothers is "independence" from past abuses, instability, and resulting self-destructive behaviors.[41] Exactly the independence from harmful past conditions that welfare reformers led by the White House seek most furiously to suppress.

A California pediatrics team administered interviews and clinical tests to 352 pregnant teenagers and found like results. Compared to pre-pregnancy rates, cigarette smoking declined by 80 percent, alcohol use by 85 percent, and illicit drug use by 75 percent among girls once they learned of their pregnancies—far more dramatic improvements than behavior education programs achieve. Though all categories of expectant mothers showed sharp declines in destructive behaviors, those who had been physically or sexually abused were somewhat more likely to continue smoking, drinking, or using drugs while pregnant—though only small minorities did so. The study found that high rates of drug and alcohol abuse and suicidal thoughts among violently and sexually abused young girls declined in "highly significant" fashion once they committed themselves to motherhood.[42] Clinical reports from 46 states for 1990 found that only 2 percent of teen mothers continued to drink during pregnancy, half the rate among mothers age 20 and older.[43] This despite the fact that teen mothers came from low-income backgrounds more likely to abuse alcohol.

Here, then, is an opportunity. The immediate improvements in behavior among troubled young girls in anticipation of motherhood provides a crucial window to reconnect them to education and services necessary to cement their positive changes.

The men
The United States has the Western world's highest rate of adult men impregnating teenage girls. (Not that all-adult, mostly-male policy makers would ever describe the "epidemic" that way). It also has the West's highest rate of fathers failing to meet paternal obligations to their children.

Teenage motherhood—and especially its poverty—can in large measure be termed an adult male behavior problem. Adult men (including older teens) are intimately involved at every negative stage: The psychological precursor of early sexual abuse, impregnation in adolescence, and default on fatherhood responsibilities after the birth. Men are not responsible for the prior poverty of girls they father children with, of course, but their failure to contribute financially to their families is a powerful factor in the continued poverty of young mothers. Thus, in tandem with the chief societal need to reduce children's poverty, the chief "personal behavior" issue in teenage motherhood is how to transform adult men into a positive force in the lives of younger females.

The reluctance to talk about fathers is paralyzing. Shalala repeatedly refers to teen mothers who "become pregnant." GOP House welfare reform quarterback, Representative Clay Shaw (R-Florida), argues for punishing teenage girls who "sleep with someone" and "get pregnant." Even when asked directly, Washingtonians want no part of complications that might cause their dead aim at teenage mothers to waver.

When I asked Jim Boriss, affable press secretary for Representative and Personal Responsibility Act crafter Jim Talent (R-Missouri), how "personally responsible" Congress planned to hold adult men who impregnate school-age girls, he replied: "That is a serious problem, we agree. But if the man isn't a fit father, the girl has to make a decision not to get pregnant." Even if she's 14 and he's 30? "These women do not have to have kids," Boriss declared.[44]

Republicans most certainly are not suggesting that girls get abortions. So here, again, is the contradiction: Teenagers (particularly girls), even very young ones, are super-adults, expected to enforce abstinence and safe sex upon adult men when "personal responsibility" is demanded. Yet these same girls are deemed too immature to obtain an abortion or receive welfare on the same terms as adults when "individual rights" are the issue.

The vaulting of biology-is-destiny into a special new dimension when the females in question are young adolescents has earned few protests from 1990s feminists. Yet consider the terminology of teen-mother theorizing: "Become pregnant." "By someone." "Girl make a decision." Until modern politicized-science took over, the male role in pregnancy was thought to be an active one. If the New Man of the '80s was sensitive, his counterpart of '90s is downright evanescent, the subtle and victimized impregnator.

California and national figures show that in over 90 percent of all unwed births, the father is 20 and older. But "illegitimacy" has been bashed enough. There is another cause of single motherhood that gets short shrift even though nearly half of all mothers receiving public assistance acquired their singlehood from it: Divorce and separation. Ninety-nine point nine percent of all divorced fathers—including all the famous ones, such as GOP luminaries Newt Gingrich and Phil Gramm—are 20 and older. Like unwed birth rates, divorce and marital breakup is rising, more than doubling since 1965.

The most recent tabulation shows 3.2 million mothers with incomes below poverty lines: 1.6 million below age 30, 1.6 million above age 30. Of these, 1.6 million were never married, and 1.6 million are divorced, separated, or still technically married.[45] The fathers with obligations to 97 percent of all poor children are adults past, and most more than a decade past, teenhood.

The amount fathers owe in child support is staggering: $40 billion in 1995. In Orange County, California, the nation's richest major county, where default is a personal value, 137,000 of the county's 600,000 children are listed by the District Attorney's Office as being owed child support by absentee fathers. The number is up from 97,000 in 1993 and 57,000 in 1991.[46] Nearly one in four fathers is in default and the subject of a child support enforcement order. In California, the scope of the problem taxes credulity: $5 billion is owed by absentee fathers to 3.4 million children, one-third of the state's total population under age 18. Eighty percent of the children on AFDC in California are owed child support; most would be able to survive without public assistance if it were paid.[47]

That the continuing poverty of teenage motherhood is largely an adult male issue is shown by the historical record as well. In the last 35 years, the rate of teenage females who become mothers has declined sharply, while the percentage who graduate from high school, attend college, and find employment has risen sharply.[48] Young female "personal behavior" has improved substantially. What has deteriorated is the behavior of their mostly adult male partners. While in 1955, 85 percent of the men who fathered babies with teenagers married them and took fatherly responsibilities (at least until the late 1960s, when divorce skyrocketed), in 1992, fewer than one third of the fathers appeared to be helping with the financial and parental duties toward the children of teen mothers.[49]

The modern absentee father has little to do with his children. A 1995 research review reported that "the overwhelming pattern is one of rapid disengagement by fathers following divorce." Fewer than half had seen their children more than a few times in the previous year, and fewer than a quarter saw their children on a regular basis.[50] Ironically, some evidence, from a study of 400 teens in 15 cities, argues that unwed adolescent fathers help more with childraising than adult fathers.[51] Wrote Guttmacher researchers:

> Teenage mothers whose male partners are in their 20s or older may not necessarily be better off economically than teenage mothers with partners of the same age. Some studies based on small numbers of couples suggest that older male partners of teenage mothers are more similar to teenage fathers than they are to their peers whose female partners are adults. Many of these fathers also have low educational attainment and inconsistent work histories. Programs that help young women who are pregnant or mothers complete schooling and obtain vocational training should also address similar needs of the fathers, to enable them to be personally and economically involved in their child's life.[52]

Is the "adult father" problem one of harsh social conditions like those affecting teen mothers—or is it bad personal behavior, or some combination? It would help if we knew something about him. Those who harbor illusions that academic America is independent of political-authority America would do well to study the research record on teenage pregnancy. Alongside a Manhattan-sized stack of studies of teenage mothers, only three studies of adult fathers with teen partners show up in literature indexes. Only one of these is within the past decade. Political grantors didn't want to know about adult men fathering babies with teenage mothers, and Ph.D.s spent two decades not troubling their funders with inconvenient details.

Fortunately, the one study of adult-versus-teen fathers available, that by Michael Lamb, M.D., and colleagues at the University of Utah School of Medicine, is highly informative.[53] The study reported the characteristics of teenage mothers and their partners for 125 couples of the same age (age gap of less than 15 months), 95 couples in which fathers were 15-36 months older than mothers, and 101 couples in which fathers were 42 or more months older than the mothers.

There were differences—not just between older versus younger fathers, but between mothers who choose older partners versus mothers who choose younger partners. Very mixed ones. Older males (average age at delivery, 22.5 years) who father babies with teenage mothers are somewhat more behaviorally troubled than younger fathers. Compared to teenage fathers, adult fathers with teen partners were significantly more likely to have a history of school failure, to smoke, to have been arrested, to react happily to the pregnancy, and to be employed at a higher wage.

Girls who chose older male partners were significantly more likely to report that the pregnancy was planned, their parents reacted happily to the news, they were casually involved with the father at time of conception, they used alcohol and drugs frequently, they had behavior problems at school, and they dropped out of school after conception.

The picture of a teenage mother (average age at delivery, 16.7 years) who allies with an older, adult father is consistent with that shown by Boyer and Fine's study of sexual abuse and teen mothers. She is often personally troubled, failing at school, "out of control," dependent, in need of emotional support, and quicker to become romantically involved. It is not surprising that Boyer and Fine found that sexually abused girls tend to have older partners.[54] There is more than a glimmer in these studies as to why some emotionally troubled younger girls and older males would coalesce in reproduction.

Teenage girls seek older partners as part of the pathology of past sexual abuse, as part of the remedy for it, and perhaps most importantly, for a mass of individual reasons. To lump the offspring of a wildly diverse array of peer-teen and of adult-teen liaisons under the derogatory "epidemic" label (labeling babies in terms of dangerous disease also appears to be uniquely American) is a key fallacy in the molding of teen motherhood into a ripe issue for politician's profit and media enjoyment. "Adolescent parents do not constitute a homogeneous population," Lamb and colleagues declared.[55]

Welfare deformed

The evidence shows that a more generous welfare policy toward young families works to decrease the birth rate by directly attacking the reason American teenage births are prevalent to begin with. Widespread child poverty and lack of education and career opportunity leave few other avenues of reward open to adolescents, particularly ones from abusive backgrounds, than early family formation. When other alternatives are available, childbearing is delayed.

These issues are typically ignored. To Shalala and others promoting programmatic or punitive "prevention" of teen pregnancy and motherhood, the sole issue is the mother's behavior and her involvement in unwed and "unintended" births that in turn are the cause of "welfare costs." "We will never deal with welfare reform until we reduce the amount of teenage pregnancy in this country," Shalala complained early in the debate.[56] But as Neal Deavitt, M.D. (1991), director of Santa Fe's La Familia Medical Center notes, the issue is a much more complex one of poverty, conditions, and opportunity:

> Many young women have told me that while they did not actively seek to become pregnant, they were not disappointed with the result ... Coming from a broken family in a substandard educational system, a teenage women loses little in the short-term by failing to plan to avoid pregnancy.[57]

For example, the uniquely sharp decrease in birth rates among nonwhite teens in the 1970s—a trend experts have never adequately explained—is closely correlated with the uniquely sharp rise in nonwhite youth enrolled in college. This trend, in turn, followed the reduced poverty and increased educational opportunity tied to

1960s War on Poverty programs that disproportionately helped young minorities. As public resources increasingly were transferred from younger to older generations beginning in the mid-1970s and accelerating in the 1980s and 1990s, youth opportunity evaporated and youth poverty rose. Teen birth rates reversed their decline and increased in the mid-1980s, particularly among nonwhites. A similar trend occurred among poorer adult mothers. With respect to teenagers in particular, a wealth of experience argues that a generous family welfare policy aimed at reducing child poverty and expanding youth education and job opportunity will sharply reduce birth rates. The effect of such a policy on unwed birth rates among persons of all ages is not clear, but there is no evidence that they would increase—and strong post-1970 evidence that the effect would be to reduce them.

A second aspect to reducing the poverty rate connected to unwed and divorced parenting revolves around a different kind of welfare reform—policies aimed at absentee fathers who fail to support their children. The "father problem" is a serious one, and not just with teen mothers. Men are increasingly detaching from their children and family obligations. In their zeal to punish the "sitting ducks"— the teen mothers whose acceptance of full responsibility for their behaviors makes them vulnerable to punishment—policy makers have bogged down in addressing the agents most in need of attention: The increasingly detached and violent men. Male violence and irresponsibility is evident not just through the stories of teenage mothers, but in a growing body of research and statistics as well. The rising criminality of young men resulting from rising youth poverty has been met by force and imprisonment, in which society pays a high price not just to cage them but to support their families as well.

The evidence is that welfare reform is best aimed not at the mothers—most of whom appear to be recovering from past victimizations, stabilized, caring for their babies, and benefitting primarily from increased social support—but at the mostly absentee fathers. In cases in which fathers want to support their families but are unable to, education and job training are indicated. In the fraction of cases in which fathers can pay but don't, law enforcement is the indicated response. The potential of an integrated solution involving enhanced opportunity for young men in tandem with mandates to participate in raising the children they father is promising but, in today's teen-mother-fixated and teen-punishing climate, is not now being adequately explored.

The role of new information emerging in summer 1995, spurred by the Guttmacher report, increased attention to sexual abuse studies, and stories in the *New York Times, Los Angeles Times, U.S. News & World Report,* and *USA Today* on the issues of sexual abuse and adult fatherhood, may have provoked at least a few doubts about demonizing teenage mothers. President Clinton, in an August 9 speech, acknowledged the roles of abuse and of adult men in fathering babies among girls age 17 and younger. In September, the president threatened to veto the House-passed welfare reform bill, which contained a ban on cash aid to unwed mothers under age 18.[58]

Some hopeful signs emerged in the U.S. Senate debate over welfare reform that followed. An amendment by Senators Kent Conrad (D-North Dakota) and Joe Lieberman (D-Connecticut) to the welfare reform bill finally addressed what the

latter senator called the "dreadful facts" that the "men" involved in "teenage pregnancy" are "are considerably older" and are "often abusive, exploitative, or overpow-
ering." The amendment directly encouraged states to "take statutory rape as a serious crime" in order "to deter adult men from committing a sexual act that will result
in a child born to poverty," as well as to collect "unpaid child support."[59] The discussion on the Senate floor revealed the continuing, extraordinary reluctance of top
Washington policy makers to discuss the role of adult men, and sexual abuse, in
"teenage" motherhood. Still, even if off the mark in its absolute reliance on statutory rape prosecution and especially in its misguided mandate that teenage mothers
live with parents or adults, the amendment represented a first step away from the
single-minded blaming of young mothers that has held center stage to date. (Or
maybe it was nothing more than a temporary respite from unreality. A few weeks
later, USA Today reported, while speakers at a Washington hearing attacked cuts in
federal aid for education and health clinics, Senator "Lieberman blamed [TV talk]
shows for the high teen pregnancy rate.")[60]

The excesses of the attack on young mothers and children became evident to
media commentators as well. In a searing column on September 14, conservative
George Will lambasted right-wing welfare cutoffs pushed by Senator Lauch
Faircloth (R-North Carolina) and presidential candidate and Senator Phil Gramm
(R-Texas):

> Phil Gramm says welfare recipients are people "in the wagon" who ought to
> get out and "help the rest of us pull." Well. Of the 14 million people receiving
> Aid to Families With Dependent Children, 9 million are children. Even if we get
> all these free riders into wee harnesses, the wagon will not move much faster.
>
> Furthermore, there is hardly an individual or industry in America that is
> not in some sense "in the wagon," receiving some federal subvention. If everyone
> gets out, the wagon may rocket along. But no one is proposing that. Instead, wel-
> fare reform may give a whole new meaning to the phrase, "women and children
> first."

Noting Moynihan's comparison of welfare reform with recent decades' disastrous deinstitutionalization of the mentally ill, which led to thousands of homeless
and their children sleeping on heating grates, Will continued:

> Actually, cities will have to build more grates. Here are the percentages of
> children on AFDC at some point during 1993 in five cities: Detroit, 67 percent;
> Philadelphia, 57 percent; Chicago, 46 percent; New York, 39 percent; Los
> Angeles, 38 percent. "There are not enough social workers," said Moynihan, "not
> enough nuns, not enough Salvation Army workers" to care for children who
> would be purged from the welfare rolls were Congress to decree (as candidate Bill
> Clinton proposed) a two-year limit for welfare eligibility.[61]

Similarly, U.S. News & World Report editors, in an October 2 editorial, went
against the welfare "blame and shame" grain of the other news magazines:

> Cut projected spending, shortchange job training and child-care needs, and
> abandon a national commitment to dependent children stretching back to the
> Depression. This is "tough love" without the love... A bill aimed at errant adults
> could thus wind up hitting America's children, already the poorest in the indus-

trialized world... Be prepared to spend more money—not less—and exercise more national leadership—not less—until we reverse this tide of poor children.[62]

The House bill had also eliminated the concept that children are entitled to be protected from abuse and neglect and abolished the requirement that federal funds help pay to support abused children in foster homes. It is difficult to imagine the thought process that led to such a provision. The Senate bill retained the "entitlement" of children to safe care and to protection from abuse and neglect.

The House bill's ban on cash aid to unwed teen mothers was also defeated, in a 76-24 vote, in the Senate, though conservatives such as Faircloth, Gramm, and Ralph Reed of the Christian Coalition vowed to revive it. Moynihan (whose top aide proposed targeting welfare reforms at teen mothers just 20 months earlier) criticized the House- and Senate-passed bills and the president's welfare plans as "abandonment of dependent children" and urged a veto of the entire bill. Moynihan's concerns: The Senate bill adopted a two-year assistance time limits and placed limits on benefits to legal immigrants. It also allowed states to decide whether to place "caps" on assistance paid to mothers who have babies on welfare and to teenage mothers, threatening a return to the Mississippi-standard of public assistance (right now, second or subsequent children born into welfare receive $10 per month in added benefits in Mississippi). As of this writing, the final bill is being negotiated in a conference committee of the two houses. Clinton at first said he would sign the Senate version.

In late October, *U.S. News* and the *Los Angeles Times* obtained a copy of a secret Department of Health and Human Services study projecting that the Senate bill's $38 billion cut in welfare over the next five years would force 1.1 million more children into poverty and markedly worsen the conditions of those already in poverty. As *U.S. News & World Report*'s analysis pointed out:

> Shortly before his endorsement of the bill, White House sources say, Clinton received a preliminary analysis of the legislation from HHS Secretary Donna Shalala that showed the bill would push some 1.1 million children into poverty. That was a conservative estimate: HHS analysts counted non-cash income like school lunches, food stamps and housing subsidies as cash in calculating whether a family was poor and assumed that no state, given the option to spend less on welfare, would actually do so... The administration tried to withhold the HHS report.
>
> ...Senate legislation... would have a devastating impact on the incomes of families with children. On average, they would lose $798 a family, or 6 percent of their cash income.[63]

The preliminary study, dated September 14 and concealed by the administration, revealed again Clinton's and Shalala's cynical indifference to the well-being of children, youth, and young families, a stance that appears moderate only in contrast to the draconian House measure that administration rhetoric invited in the first place. A late November 1995 roundup showed that Clinton's budget would severely cut programs for low-income families over the next seven years, including slashes in Medicaid ($54 billion in cuts by Clinton versus $163 billion in the GOP congressional budget), AFDC and Food Stamps ($34 billion under Clinton, versus $75 billion by Republicans), the earned income tax credit benefitting the working poor ($3 billion in Clinton cuts, versus $32 billion by Republicans), and student loans ($6 billion by Clinton, more than the $5 billion cut proposed by Republicans).[64] Clinton is no friend of the poor and young; positioning for the 1996 elections is his sole consideration. "There's a lot of pressure to produce some kind of welfare reform bill and not to be seen as opposing welfare reform in general," explained former Clinton welfare advisor Ira Sawhill of the administration's motives in trading more children in poverty for political gain.[65]

The final report, released November 9, estimated the Senate bill would put 1.2 million more children in poverty; the House bill, 2.1 million. The amount of money necessary to boost *all* U.S. children out of poverty? About $16 billion today ($20 billion if the Senate bill becomes law)[66]—less than the cost of the B-1 bomber program Congress added to the defense budget over the protests even of the Defense Department.

As of this writing, the signs are that Clinton may reverse again. An open letter to the *Washington Post* on November 5 by Children's Defense Fund president Marian Wright Edelman was particularly influential in inducing the president to take a "second look" at the bill's damaging effects on children, a senior White House official said.[67] The welfare bill hammered out by House-Senate conference committees turned out to be harsher than the Senate version. At this point, shifting administration welfare plans are impossible to predict. As on so many issues, they seem driven by the narrow prospects of immediate political gain rather than on any discernible principles.

Social service agencies expect the worst. "It's important to say that both the Senate and the House version are going to drastically curtail economic assistance to children," said Peter Digre, Los Angeles County director of Children's Services. "It's going to be a different world in terms of the economic well-being of millions of children."

Digre's office serves 650,000 children on AFDC in Los Angeles County, including 60,000 now in foster care. Half of these children, some 300,000 to 350,000, are projected to lose their economic assistance due to the reform law's time limits. Digre's forecast:

> When a family's economic assistance is curtailed, people start to get their utilities cut off. They can't pay the rent, so they are forced from their housing and end up homeless.... We see a lot of children being reported for neglect. They don't have food. They don't have a place to live. They don't have medical care. They don't have adequate clothing...
>
> As people go into that downward spiral from poverty to destitution, we start to see an increase in physical abuse. When AFDC was cut about 6 percent in 1992, in the year after we saw a bump of about 10 percent more kids in the child welfare system, and about 20 percent more child abuse reported... As families come under increased stress, they become more desperate—and they become more violent.[68]

4. Wild in Deceit

...Adult life appears, dignified and capable, but in reality enmeshed in the same evil as the symbolic life of the children on the island. The officer, having interrupted a man-hunt, prepares to take the children off the island in a cruiser which will presently be hunting its enemy in the same implacable way. And who will rescue the adult and his cruiser?

—William Golding,
commentary on *Lord of the Flies*, 1954[1]

Younger and younger children... thirteen and fourteen... are becoming involved in... the most wanton and senseless of murders... and mass rape.
Four youths ranging in age from fifteen to eighteen... poured gasoline on one (derelict) and flipped a lighted match at him, turning him into a human torch... burned and beat another and... shoved him to his death in the East River.

— Chairman, U.S. Senate Subcommittee on
Juvenile Delinquency, 1956[2]

Children as young as 13 are shooting other young people for a bicycle or a leather jacket, setting fire to homeless men and women, participating in gang rapes.

— Governor's Commission on Youth Violence,
New York, June 1994[3]

If children are not protected from their abusers, then the public will one day have to be protected from the children.

— Nancy Gibbs, *Time*, 8 October 1990

When a 3-year-old Los Angeles girl was murdered in an apparent gang killing in September 1995, the press headlined the story and President Clinton rightly called a "day of mourning" for child victims of street violence. When a 3-year-old Beverly Hills boy was murdered by his 37 year-old father three weeks later, the story drew little attention or politician outrage. When a national child abuse commission reported in April 1995 that 2,000 American children per year are murdered by their parents and caretakers, Clinton and other leaders didn't bother to comment.[4] But the September 1995 decision by Time-Warner Records to cut loose its rap music label was widely hailed by politicians as a victory over youth mayhem. The official view must be that the words of rap songs are a bigger incitement to teen violence than the fists, sticks, sexual assaults, and other substantiated physical brutalities inflicted on 350,000 children and adolescents every year by the adults they should be able to trust the most.[5]

Inflicted not simply by parents, but by official caretakers as well. "For years, certain officers had been beating up the kids of the community, and no amount of protests or complaints filed seem to stop the abuse," *Los Angeles Times Magazine* reported of Pico/Aliso, the largest public housing project west of the Mississippi. Today: "According to statistics compiled by the Los Angeles Police Department, Pico/Aliso is one of the city's most violent neighborhoods."[6] Police violence and domestic violence are subjects of occasional condemnation, primarily when sensational cases intrude or politicians curry favor with women's groups. But the daily reality of children and youth becomes an issue only when they begin to practice what American adults have long taught them.

And violence against the young is inflicted not simply by the front-line caretakers such as families and police, but up the scale as well. Youth violence is a hot topic, exploited by pols and pundits and the same public officials who studiously sidestep the predictability of its eruption from well-known roots—the same ones that breed adult violence. Adult violence against children is a muted issue, subject of zero "urgent" press conferences and few magazine covers unless its import can be trivialized by media preoccupation with accused celebrities such as Woody Allen or Michael Jackson, spectacular cases such as Susan Smith's, or a "recovered memory" furor.

So frenzied has the media hype of juvenile violence become that the September 1994 Gallup Poll of 1,000 adults found wildly exaggerated views of its prevalence, and majority demands for executing juveniles who commit murder:

> Perhaps because of recent news coverage of violent crimes committed by juveniles, the public has a greatly inflated view of the amount of violent crime committed by persons under the age of 18. Official crime statistics show that juveniles commit only about 13 percent of all violent crimes. But the average estimate of that statistic by Americans in the recent poll is more than three times that high, at about 43 percent. And almost two-thirds of Americans believe that juvenile violence accounts for more than 30 percent of all violent crimes.

In fact, one-fourth of the poll respondents believe youths accounted for more than half the nation's violent crime. The most exaggerated notions of juvenile crime were found among the youngest adults (age 18-29) in the sample.[7]

From the Washington and media depiction, no one would guess another fact shown in FBI figures[8] year after year: Two-thirds of all murdered youths are slain by adults, not by other youths. In a 1993 tabulation of 11,000 murders by age of victim and killer, the FBI reported that 70 percent of the murderers of children/youths and 92 percent of the slayers of adults were adults. But grownup voters and media patrons don't want to hear about that, so it is not officially talked about.

At one time, before these two officials came to mirror the nation's collective, selective outrage over a mythical construct known as "youth violence," Attorney General Janet Reno and FBI Director Louis Freeh did want to know. At the dawn of their careers as President Clinton's top law enforcement professionals, they vowed to make war on the "home violence"[9] and "terrible poverty and hopelessness in our urban areas" that breed young so dehumanized that by age 15 "nothing can be done but to incarcerate them for the rest of their lives."[10] Tap tap: The '90s did not sign up for lectures from Sociology of the Swarthy Urban Child. Reno and Freeh found themselves relegated to a few paragraphs in the inside pages, and brief lines before the half-hour newsbreak, stirring no policy debate.

Then Reno, a quick study in media trial by fire after the Branch Davidian tragedy at Waco, bayed the usual federal censorship threats at Hollywood mayhem (especially Disney and Beavis and Butt-head) for inciting cherubs to unprecedented barbarism. Instant stardom: Front-page banner lines, lead-story status, features and furor, editorial and political plaudits.[11] Spurred by pure American escapism and the pseudo-science of that century-old foe of adolescents, pop psychology, today's debate over a deadly issue proceeds with exactly this much acumen: Witnessing a fictional murder on TV, a rape on celluloid, a gundown on the video screen, has more effect on a child's psyche than actually *being* beaten or raped or growing up in bitter poverty.

I recently asked a guard at Chino, a prison 40 miles east of Los Angeles stuffed with 2,500 of California's most dangerous 16-24 year-old rapists, murderers, and batterers, how many had been violently abused at home. "One thousand percent," he said. I asked the same question 1,200 miles away and a few years earlier of the superintendent of Montana's Pine Hills youth detention center, Al Davis:

> "All of our kids at Pine Hills have been neglected or abused in one way or another," Davis said. "...In most cases, we should leave the kid home and send the parents to Pine Hills."[12]

A remarkable study in Sacramento, California, found that while only 1.4 percent of the county's children ages nine to twelve had come to the attention of child protective authorities due to victimization by abuse or neglect, the same 1,000 children accounted for half of the city's arrests for crimes committed by youths in that age group.[13]

Bureau of Justice Statistics reports show that while youths predominate in street violence, adults are the aggressors in home violence. Parents are six times more likely to murder their teenage children than the other way around.[14] And like nearly all youth and adult behaviors, the two are linked. A 1992 National Institute of Justice Study found that child abuse is a factor in at least 40 percent of the nation's violent crime.[15]

President Clinton vows to punish his stock villain, "13-year-olds... with automatic weapons,"[16] but neglects to discuss the fact that 49-year-olds (Clinton's age) murder twice as many people.[17] In the equation of rising American brutality, young age is the most politically expedient characteristic to blame—and among the least-important real-world characteristic. There is no such thing as "youth violence," except in the same sense that there is "Sagittarian violence" (One in 12 killers! Tripled since 1960!) or "Smith violence" (The leading name of U.S. murderers!) or "Brown-eyed violence" (don't even calculate).

Most people, especially experts, would find such a statement—"there is no such thing as youth violence"—incredible. They would point to the doubling in homicide and 70 percent rise in violent crime arrests among 13-19-year-olds in the last decade, the gangland drive-bys, the 135,000 school gun toters, the pipe-stabbings and wildings and cold-eyed sixth grade shootists. Yet all of these are predictable results of the doubling in youth poverty over the past 20 years. A nation that adds 6 million young to its poverty rolls—especially under circumstances in which older age groups are becoming richer—can expect an increase in street violence among youths compared to adults. It is a tragic and unnecessary development. But it is not one that should be generating the pious shock and bewilderment among those familiar with the causes of violence.

Youth violence is primarily a sociological issue, flowing from the larger conditions in which minority youths are raised. The stresses and violence of growing up impoverished push marginal youth toward violence, as the 16-fold higher murder arrest rate for black Los Angeles teenagers compared to white L.A. teens (discussed below) demonstrates. Adults subjected to similar levels of poverty are similarly violent. Yet national and state youth violence policies continue to mistreat it as a "psychological" problem located within the heads of adolescents, a strategy that guarantees no option other than to lock up ever-growing numbers of nonwhite youths under conditions in which most can never be released to society. *The most effective anti-violence policy that can be adopted is to raise fewer children in poverty.*

What violence trends really show

Most people, regardless of age or income, are not habitually violent. Fewer than 1 percent of the teen population age 13-19 is arrested for a violent crime in any one year. Only one in 3,000 teens is arrested for homicide. Even though teenagers as a group are not violent, teenagers are arrested for more violent crimes than any other age group except persons in their 20s. In 1993, violent crime arrests, including homicide, rape, robbery, and aggravated assault, peaked at age 18—as they did in 1955.[18]

Trends in youth violent crime arrests show a relatively level and low pattern from the 1940s to the early 1960s. Prior to 1960, the FBI's annual *Uniform Crime Reports* tabulated only a fraction of the nation's arrests, and juvenile arrests were especially understated. The reports were based on incomplete fingerprint records, the FBI warned, exacerbated by the fact that many jurisdictions did not fingerprint juvenile offenders then.[19] While the FBI reported only 34,599 juveniles arrested in 1950, investigation by the U.S. Senate's juvenile delinquency subcommittee found 300,000 to 400,000 juveniles arrested that year —ten times more than reported by the FBI.[20] Yet unconscionably, a 1990 blue-ribbon panel assembled by the American Medical Association, the National Association of State Boards of Education, the Centers for Disease Control, numerous national luminaries, and 300 expert reviewers issued a straight-line comparison of haphazard 1950s figures with comprehensive 1980s figures compiled under uniform national reporting systems, and hysterically announced: "The number of teenagers 14-17 arrested per year has increased nearly thirty-fold since 1950."[21]

The level of violence arrests has quadrupled (not risen thirty-fold!) among youths and doubled among adults age 20-44 since the 1950s (Figure 4.1). In addition to better tabulation from more police agencies around the country, much of the apparent increase in violent crime arrests can be attributed to better police work and record-keeping. Interestingly, the number of crimes reported by victims to FBI surveys has not increased, but arrests have. In 1973, arrests equalled 12.8 percent of victim survey reports; in 1992, 23.5 percent.[22] This indicates that much of the sup-

**Rising modern teen poverty promotes
rising teen violent crime**

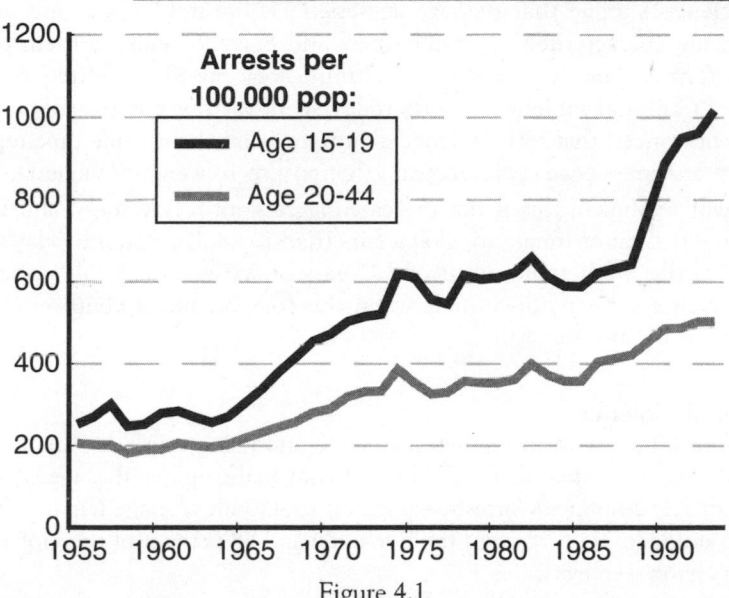

Figure 4.1

Sources: FBI, *Uniform Crime Reports for the United State*s (155-1993). See Reference 8.

posed increase in crime in recent years results from more victims reporting crime and police making more arrests.

Even with the qualifications of better reporting and more efficient law enforcement, youth violence arrests have increased during two recent periods: 1963-74 and 1985-93. Figure 4.1 shows raw violent crime arrest rates for teens age 15-19 and adults age 20-44 for the 1955-1993 period, adjusted for the proportion of the nation's population covered by each year's annual FBI crime report. Violence arrests rose from 250 per 100,000 15-19-year-olds in 1963 to 620 in 1974, a jump of 140 percent. This 1960s rise was accompanied by a 100 percent increase in adult violence arrests.

From 1974 to 1985, youthful violent crime rates were stable and fluctuating, falling to 590 per 100,000 in 1985. This respite was accompanied by a similar stabilization in adult violence arrests. Since then, hell has broken loose in the nation's urban centers.

After 1985, youth violence arrests skyrocketed, rising to over 1,000 per 100,000 youths by 1993. This 73 percent increase in youth violence was accompanied by a 41 percent rise in adult violent crime arrest rates. Note that while violent crimes are billowing among both teens and adults, the rise in adolescent violence arrests over the last three decades greatly exceeds the rise in adult violence arrests. While in 1963, teens age 15-19 were 25 percent more likely than adults age 20-44 to be arrested for a violent offense, by 1993 teens were twice as violence arrest prone.

It is this recent increase that has provoked the most attention. Political and media pronouncements harbor an angry, baffled, and frantic tone devoid of analysis of the environmental components that amply explain the trend. Some American "social scientists argue that teenage aggression is natural," reads one review.[23] Teenagers are characterized by "recklessness and bravado" making them prone to violence, former American Society of Criminology president Alfred Blumstein declared.[24] Criminal violence experts today seem to waver between two highly inconsistent stances: that teen violence is "innate," and at the same time represents America's "lost innocence" (which means that past teens were not violent).

As will be shown, this is not the case; aggression, recklessness, and violence are no more natural or innate to adolescents than to adults. Rather, today's "youth violence" is the predictable result of 20 years of self-serving adult policies and behaviors that are clearly discernible when the components of youth violence are examined one by one.

Gender and violence

Violent crime, both in its high incidence and rising trend, is a male issue. In 1993, FBI *Uniform Crime Reports*[25] showed that males under the age of 20 were involved in 7,180 homicide arrests, compared to 430 for teenage females. Teenage males accounted for 94 percent of the homicide and 88 percent of the violent crime arrests involving teenagers.

Females age 15-19, in contrast, had lower murder arrest rates than men in their 50s. Further, while murder arrests among teenage males have skyrocketed since the mid-1980s, those among females have been stable. In 1993, females age 10-19 accounted for 8 percent of the nation's over-10 population, but less than 2 percent of its murder arrests and just 3 percent of its violent crime arrests. Teenage female violence, while occasionally media sensationalized, is not a threat to public safety.

Violence is not simply a male, but an adult male issue. Like teenage males, adult males accounted for nine in ten violent crime arrests involving adults in 1993. Adult men over age 20 accounted for two-thirds of all violent crime arrests in 1993. Of particular concern, men ages 20-44—the age most likely to be parents—accounted for just 24 percent of the over-10 population, but comprised 55 percent of the nation's homicide and 57 percent of its violent crime arrestees. No presidential commissions, Congressional hearings, or *Newsweek* cover stories on middle-aged male slaughter.

Predictably, officials have sought to blame the least culpable group—teenage females—for male violence. In 1994, Surgeon General Joycelyn Elders claimed that children of unwed teenage mothers account for nearly all crime. This claim was based on the "evidence" of a few hours' of uncontrolled surveys in a New York central-city ward where virtually all parents are severely impoverished blacks or Hispanics. And as usual, the media tagged along. *Time* magazine, citing no reason and zero documentation, blamed "14 year-old mothers" for "all these 16-year-old predators."[26] Perfect: The whole violence enchilada, from alpha to omega, birth to murder, is the fault of teenagers.

Except that the statement is factually ridiculous. The proportion of young men arrested (a staggering 25 percent per year for 18-24 year-olds)[27] far exceeds the proportion ever born to unwed teenage mothers (8 percent per year).[28] Even if every unwed teen mom's son grew up to be a thug and was arrested every year, only one third of violent crime could be explained thereby. Teenage mothers are no more likely to raise poorly-developed children than adult mothers from similar backgrounds.[29] Yet it is likely that offspring of teenage mothers are disproportionately likely to be arrested, just as it is known that children of poorer, nonwhite mothers comprise a large majority of violent crime arrests. Further, in a nation in which 95 percent of all births involve at least one partner over age 20, it is absurd to blame any significant share of social problems on "teenage mothers." The officials so eager to blame male violence on teenage mothers have never publicly discussed the adult male violence victimizing teenage mothers[30] [31]— nor have 1990s feminists called their hand.

Elders' accusation and the media's approving circulation of it forms the most recent instance of a long history of selectively invoking legal and social support systems to punish teenage females' "immorality." As University of Hawaii sociologist Meda Chesney-Lind (an exception to the feminist silence) points out, girls are routinely incarcerated at rates many times higher than boys for sexual misconduct and related "immoral" behaviors. Forced gynecological examinations on young female offenders to determine virginity were routinely pursued by law enforcement. The bitter irony in the punitive efforts to enforce female virtue is that most girls and women in prison for serious crimes were themselves victimized by prior sexual violence, which was rarely addressed.[32]

Three out of four homicide victims are male. Teenage boys tend to kill adult men, and vice versa. Prior to 1980, research indicated a majority—63 percent in one study[33]—of all murders by boys age 11 to 19 dispatched adult men who were abusing their mothers or other family members. Today's rise in gang violence reduces that figure considerably while raising a new issue: Do teenagers invent violence (as those who promote the popular "innate" or "intrinsic" theories hold), or do they learn it from adults in family and social contexts?

Poverty and violence

The official/media-generated crisis of "children killing children" (and innocent adults) collapses in one simple calculation: Divide the arrest rate for murder or violent crime (which includes murder, rape, robbery, and aggravated assault) for each age group by the number of persons in that age group living in poverty. The result: The fact that teenagers are more likely to live in poverty than adults in their 20s and 30s fully explains the higher rates of murder and violent crime among teenagers. Let us take 1992 as the most recent year for which both crime and poverty figures are available (Table 4.2).

For every 1,000 persons living in poverty, 1.2 murder and 35 violent crime arrests can be expected for teens, a rate lower than that of persons age 20-24 and similar to that of persons age 25-34. In older age groups, violent crime declines geo-

Table 4.2

Poverty has similar effects on teenage and adult violence:

Age	Arrests for: Homicides	Violent Crimes	Population below poverty level	Arrests per 1,000 persons living in poverty: Homicides	Violence
9-12	40	11,011	3,440,000	0.1	3.2
13-19	6,693	196,135	5,550,000	1.2	35.3
20-24	6,109	157,179	3,120,000	2.0	50.4
25-34	5,920	240,335	5,540,000	1.1	43.4
35-44	2,766	113,930	3,940,000	0.7	28.9
45-59	1,393	40,091	3,320,000	0.4	12.1
60-older	408	8,895	5,100,000	0.1	1.7

Sources: U.S. Federal Bureau of Investigation (1994). *Uniform Crime Reports for the United States, 1992*. Washington, DC: U.S. Department of Justice, Table 38; U.S. Bureau of the Census (1994). *Poverty in the United States, 1992*. Current Population Series P60-185. Washington, DC: U.S. Department of Commerce, Table 5.

metrically, as do poverty rates. Poverty does not seem to provoke the same kind of public violence (the kind usually resulting in arrest) among persons over age 40 as among persons in their teens, 20s, and 30s, perhaps because most habitually violent people have been killed or incarcerated by that age. Or it may be that poverty is not a straight-line predictor of violence. Above a certain threshold—with respect to blacks and Latinos ages 15-34 in particular—widespread poverty appears to foster a "critical mass" of groups who operate outside the law (i.e., gangs) and who therefore enforce their interests by means of violence,[34] increasing the violent crime rate more than poverty alone would predict.

There is no discernible difference in violence between adolescents and the adults of the age groups who are raising them. Teenagers do not respond to poverty more or less violently than do grownups; teenagers just experience more poverty. Once the poverty factor is removed, "teen violence" disappears, and with it all the agonized why-why-why saturating the media and political landscape (usually fanned by experts who should know better) whenever the cameras roll to another teen murder scene.

The uniquely rising rate of poverty among youths parallels the unique rise in violent crime among youths. This trend shows up most clearly in the disparity in poverty between young and old. In 1959, children were 1.4 times more likely than adults to live in poverty. By 1969, after the successes of the war on poverty, the child/adult poverty ratio bottomed out at 1.2. For a brief five years or so, the U.S. flirted with the standard of other industrial societies in having only a slightly higher child than adult poverty level. It was a standard the rising self-centeredness of post-1970 grownups could not sustain. As young-family poverty programs were selectively dismantled in the 1970s and '80s while adult anti-poverty measures retained generous funding, the number of children living in poverty rose by 6 million.

In 1992, children were 2.1 times more likely as adults to live in poverty, a gap wider than any in the decades in which statistics have been kept. By the late 1980s, these rising numbers of tots born into poverty from the mid-1970s on were maturing into teenhood. Predicting a rise in youth violence beginning in the late 1980s from that pattern is not exactly sociological rocket science.

In California of 1993, one in four black, and one in five Hispanic, males ages18-24 is arrested for a felony every year. This is many times the white and Asian arrest rate.[35] The large disparity in poverty among racial/ethnic groups is the single most consistent social factor explaining the large difference in violence among these groups. Poverty should not be misunderstood as some kind of imperative, however. Most poor people are not violent. As Table 4.2 indicates, 96 percent of all poor people will not be arrested for a violent offense and 99.9 percent will not commit murder in a given year. But the ongoing criminological debate over whether poverty *causes* an *individual* to be violent is not as important to the study of youth violence as is its effect on entire populations. No serious observer disputes the larger fact that if 6 million poor are added to any population (as we have done for youth since 1970), that population will display more violence.

This is not a concept we have trouble grasping when adults are impoverished. What Los Angeles County Children's Services director Peter Digre reports from practical experience is what research has amply showed: "We've learned from past experience that whatever undermines the economic well-being of families immediately translates into increased child abuse."[36] Nor is it new. The link between poverty and violence was clear in the Great Depression, when murder rates among today's white great-grandparents in their younger days erupted to record heights. In 1935, scholars George Leighton and Richard Hellman deplored the harsh new American-scape of teens with guns:

> A migratory worker who has traveled back and forth across the country for twenty years has described the comparatively recent appearance of firearms among the young bums. "In my day," said he, "gats were almost unheard of... It's different now... you find high school kids armed."[37]

The Great Depression's murderous violence, which peaked in 1933 at 9.7 homicides per 100,000 population,[38] was unexcelled until the Great Youth Depression of the 1990s (in 1993, the U.S. murder rate reached 10 per 100,000 population). If the U.S. wants less juvenile violence, serious consideration needs to be given to the societally-inflicted violence of raising three to 10 times more youth in poverty than other western nations.[39]

Race and violence

California is the arch-violent state. It is home to one in six American teen murder arrestees. Its largest county, Los Angeles (population 9 million, mostly urban, the equivalent of the entire state of Michigan), accounts for half of California's homicides. L.A. County has experienced a 370 percent explosion in teen murders since 1970 and is the former home of *one-sixth* of all murdered junior high kids in the United States. Its records of murder arrests are detailed by age, sex, and race and, unlike national records, provide separate statistics for Hispanics. If we can't find a singular phenomenon of "teen violence" in Los Angeles, it can't be found.

Let us focus on the violence among teens under age 18 that arouses so much fear in the political byways and media (Table 4.3).

Table 4.3
Teen murder arrests show large race/ethnic differences attributable to poverty:

Los Angeles County, 1994	Murder arrests: Male	Female	Total	Age 13-17 Population	Murder arrests per 100,000 pop.
White	10	2	12	190,000	6.3
Asian	25	4	29	85,000	34.1
Hispanic	102	4	106	370,000	28.6
Black	81	4	85	85,000	100.0
Total	218	14	232	730,000	31.8

Source: Law Enforcement Information Center (1995, 14 July). Sex and race/ethnic group of felony arrestees, 1994, by category, offense, and age. Los Angeles County. Sacramento, CA: California Department of Justice (printout); U.S. Bureau of the Census (1992). *Census of Population 1990. Characteristics of the Population - California.* Washington: U.S. Department of Commerce, Table 54.

Add up the school-age murder toll in hyper-violent L.A.: 95 percent of the 264 males, and 86 percent of the 25 females, were nonwhite, exactly those groups whose youth poverty rates exceed those of whites five-fold. Figure 4.4 shows the race and age breakdowns for homicide. A black 60-year-old is twice as likely to be involved in a homicide than is a white teenager. No more powerful example of the influence of poverty on violence could be imagined.

In yet another racial differential, virtually all of California's increase in youth homicide and violent crime from the mid-1980s to the early 1990s was among blacks (violence arrests up 50 percent), Hispanics (up 100 percent), and Asians (up 60 percent) and followed similar rises in youth poverty rates. Among white, non-Hispanic California teens, the violence increase was very small (up 10 percent) over the period. Nearly all the youth violence increase that has occurred nationwide over the past decade has been among nonwhites, a fact obscured by national crime totals that do not separate whites and Hispanics.

Guns and violence

From the magazine covers, news broadcasts, and politician broadsides, the tragedy of "kids and guns" is a staple—so much of one that Americans could easily think kids are the only ones who commit firearms mayhem. Like so much else that everyone knows about teenagers at the behest of myriad authorities, that would be wrong.

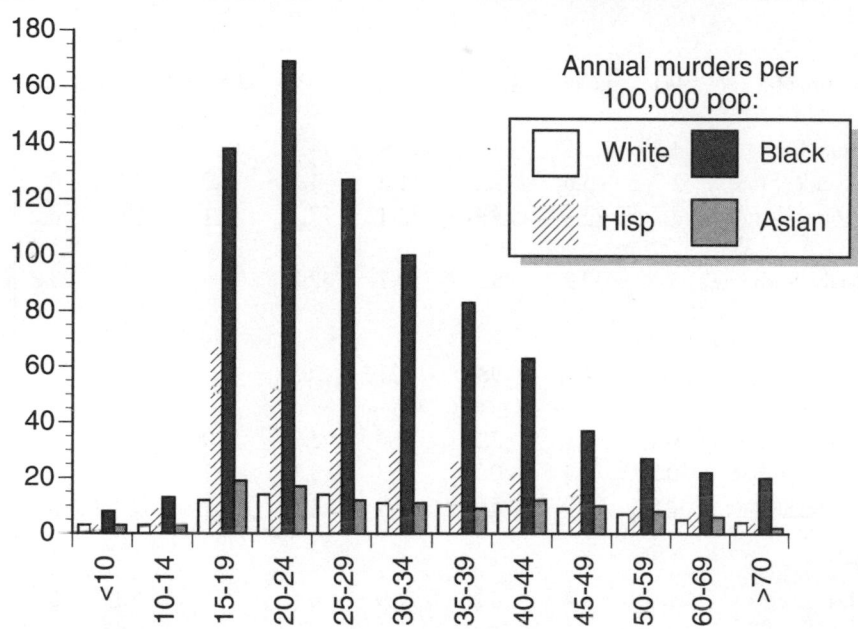

Poverty and disadvantage, not teen age, promote high murder rates

Fig 4.4

Source: Center for Health Statistics, California Department of Health Services (1995). See endnote 105.

It is indeed an American tragedy that in the most recent reporting year (1990 as of this writing), 4,690 youths age 10-19 were killed by firearms.[40] But it is also a tragedy, one unaccompanied by headlines and breathless documentaries, that firearms took the lives of 10,275 Americans ages 20-29, 7,651 ages 30-39, and 4,630 in their 40s. The most commonly repeated phrase during the Congressional non-debate (the measure passed with only one dissenting vote) on outlawing gun posses-sion by youths under age 18—"kids and guns don't make sense"—could be more jus-tifiably phrased "Americans, particularly American men, and guns don't make sense."

Once again, the hard figures on the American gunshot toll do not support the notion that teenagers, even older teens, are the highest-risk group for gun violence. Gunshot violence is shared by adult age groups as well (Table 4.5).

The most striking aspect of Americans' firearms toll is not the teenage risk—which for 15-19-year-olds is less than among adults age 20-24 for males and less than all adult groups under age 40 for females—but the male risk. Females at every age level suffer less than one-fifth as many gunshot deaths than males at *any* age.

Table 4.5

U.S. firearms deaths are highest among adults in their 20s, not teens:

Firearms deaths*	10-14	15-19	20-24	25-29	30-34	35-39	40-44	45-49
Number of Male deaths**	441	3,656	4,707	4,253	3,557	2,811	2,203	1,606
Suicide rate	1.2	12.5	16.5	14.9	14.3	13.5	13.8	14.9
Accident rate	1.7	3.6	2.4	1.6	1.2	1.0	1.0	0.7
Homicide rate	2.2	23.7	29.4	23.3	17.2	14.1	10.6	8.0
Male death rate	5.0	39.9	48.3	39.7	32.7	28.6	25.4	23.8
Number of Female deaths	119	474	586	729	703	580	459	362
Suicide rate	0.4	2.1	2.2	2.6	2.7	2.9	2.7	2.9
Accident rate	0.2	0.3	0.3	0.3	0.2	0.2	0.1	0.0
Homicide rate	0.8	3.0	3.7	3.9	3.5	2.7	2.4	2.2
Female death rate	1.4	5.4	6.2	6.9	6.4	5.8	5.1	5.2
Number of Male and Female deaths combined	560	4130	5293	4982	4260	3391	2662	1968
Suicide rate	0.8	7.4	9.5	8.7	8.5	8.1	8.2	8.8
Accident rate	1.0	2.0	1.4	1.0	0.7	0.6	0.6	0.3
Homicide rate	1.5	13.7	16.8	13.7	10.3	8.4	6.4	5.2
Both sexes, death rate	3.3	23.1	27.7	23.4	19.5	17.1	15.1	14.3

*In 1990.
**Death rate is per 100,000 population.
Source: National Center for Health Statistics (1995). *Vital Statistics of the United States 1990.* Volume II, Part A, Mortality. Washington, DC: U.S. Department of Health and Human Services, Table 1-27.

The teenage (age 15-19) risk of homicide by firearms is less than that of adults in their 20s. The teenage firearms accident rate is the highest for any age group, but the teen gun suicide rate is the lowest.

A solid case can be made that guns are much too available in American society and wind up in violent and careless hands. But the real issue is not age. From a safety standpoint, the same mortality statistics persuasively argue that if it is too risky for adolescents to have guns, it is too risky for adults to have guns. From a practical standpoint, there is no way to allow adults the freedom to own and possess firearms—especially not 200 million of them—and at the same time to keep them away from youths. Justice Department studies indicate that only a small number of youths obtain guns by buying them from dealers. The violent groups of most concern, urban gangs, are typically run by adults in their 20s, 30s, and older, who easily obtain firearms for their members no matter what laws apply to youths.[41]

Adult violence against youth

The only political candidate I have encountered who made adult violence against children a major campaign theme was Mike McGrath, the Lewis and Clark county attorney who ran for the office of Montana attorney general in 1988. "In my years in law enforcement, I have never seen a serious criminal who wasn't abused as a child," McGrath told me. "Most were physically abused, some were sexually abused, and all of them were emotionally abused. People are raised to be criminals."

Here is how grown adults reacted to veteran prosecutor McGrath's dose of reality:

> McGrath and observers at his speeches agree that the topic of child abuse, particularly sexual abuse, makes audiences uncomfortable. "As soon as he mentions it, they look down, very ill at ease," one Democratic candidate said.
> "They don't want to hear about it," McGrath agreed. "But I'm going to keep child abuse as the focus of my campaign."[42]

McGrath lost, though not by a wide margin. Analysts agreed with McGrath that the child abuse theme was not a vote-enhancer. Not like, say, blaming Beavis and Butt-head.

However uncomfortable it makes adults to hear about it, along with poverty, household violence against children and teens is the foundation of youth crime. Yet officials seem unable to comprehend that violence, like cigarette smoking and other behaviors, does not *begin* with adolescents. It is the manifestation of years of negative childhood experiences and conditions. Within the official and media preoccupation with youth crime as the major category of violence, adult violence against children and teenagers is distinctly downplayed, except when celebrities or spectacle are involved. It is under-investigated, under-reported, and under-prosecuted.

The U.S. Advisory Board on Child Abuse and Neglect reported in April 1995 that violence, mostly by adult parents and caretakers, kills 2,000 children and seriously injures 140,000 more per year. Worse still, the Board found, was the indifference:

> When it comes to deaths of infants and children... at the hands of parents or caretakers, society has responded in a strangely muffled, seemingly disinterested way... Little money has been spent to understand this tragic phenomenon. The true numbers and exact nature of the problem remain unknown, and the troubling fact of abuse or neglect often remains a terrible secret that is buried with the child.[43]

No presidential addresses or multi-cabinet press conferences ensued. Shalala and the Centers for Disease Control continued their tradition of silence on the issue of child abuse, symptomatic of an official dereliction that did not go unremarked in the Board's "scathing assessment" of child protective services and federal responses.

"You can call the Centers for Disease Control and Prevention and find the number of children who had a brown recluse spider bite last year, but you certainly can't get correct information on child abuse and neglect," University of Oklahoma child abuse expert Barbara Bonner testified.[44] The board found that professionals— doctors, teachers, social workers—failed to report seven in 10 cases of suspected child abuse to authorities. Those that were reported, even homicides, were "routinely" reduced to lesser charges or not prosecuted at all.

Of the 1 million cases of physical or sexual abuses of children and youths reported to overworked child protection authorities in the most recent available year (1993), 232,061 cases of physical abuse and 139,326 cases of sexual abuse of children were substantiated.[45] False reports are believed to be very few; lack of investigative resources accounted for most of the reports not substantiated. Under-reporting is much more likely. A 1985 survey of 2,600 adults nationwide found 22 percent had been sexually abused as children at an average age of 10 by abusers who averaged around 30 years old.[46] A dozen years of tabulations of child abuse and neglect cases by the American Humane Association likewise consistently found offenders averaged over 30 years old. Substantiated cases of violent abuse and sexual offense against children by their parents and caretakers quadrupled from 1976 through 1993.[47]

The 370,000 confirmed cases of violent and sexual offenses in 1993 against children and youths, overwhelmingly by adult offenders, can be compared to the 350,000 arrests of children and youth for violent and sexual offenses (including all violent crimes plus misdemeanor assaults and sex offenses) reported by the FBI for 1993.[48] Although adult violence against children/youth and crimes of violence by children/youth are both distinctly under-reported, crimes against juveniles are more often unreported than crimes against adults.[49] The enormous hype surrounding "youth violence" (primarily in public locations) can be contrasted with the muted official and media concern regarding what appears to be an equivalent or greater volume of adult violence against juveniles (primarily in homes).

The cliché that the American home is a violent place for children is suggested from a number of sources:

> Interviews with national probability family samples reveal that a full 18 percent of children have been the object of a "severe violent act" (more serious than spanking or slapping... [including being] kicked, bit, punched, beat up, burned or scalded, and threatened with or used a gun or knife) by their parents at some time in their lives, with 11 percent experiencing an event in the past year.[50]

This works out to 7 million children subjected to at least one "severe violent act" by their parents every year, not including spanking and whipping (which the U.S. Supreme Court has ruled would constitute "cruel and unusual" punishment if inflicted on adults). Assuming (absurdly conservatively) that none of these 7 million parentally-assaulted children suffered more than one violent assault per year, that would be approximately 19,000 kickings, beatings, bitings, burnings, punchings, and threats or attacks with weapons aimed *against* American children by their parents *every day*.

A 1985 study of 1,000 families by family violence researcher Murray Straus found that parents inflicted nearly twice as many severe, and nearly four times as many total, violent acts on their teenage children than the other way around.[51] Other studies indicate Straus's findings may be conservative. A 1988 survey of 1,146 parents found that 80 percent of the children under age 10, two-thirds of the 10-14-year-olds, and one-third of the 15-17 year-olds were hit or struck by their parents within the previous year. Parents are nearly four times more likely to commit simple assault, and twice as likely to commit severe or aggravated assault, against their teenage children than the other way around. Two thousand to 5,000 children are killed by their parents every year, with most called "accidents."[52]

Widespread official attention and legal initiatives are brought to bear against family violence when adults are victimized. Health Secretary Shalala's call for "zero tolerance" for domestic violence aimed at women has been matched by her "zero commentary" on the issue of child abuse. Clinton's radio address condemning domestic violence, in the wake of the O.J. Simpson verdict and the eve of Louis Farrakhan's Million Man March on Washington, focused almost exclusively on spousal violence and mentioned child victims only in passing.[53] Los Angeles Police Chief Willie Williams had harsher words for "young people" who commit violence "against their parents or their grandparents" than for the 170,000 cases of child abuse and neglect inflicted on children by the city's parents and caretakers the previous year.[54] Battered children are a constituency with even less power than battered women.

But though women get more attention because they organize and vote and children don't, their issues are the same. The evidence is that "parents are more violent to their children than to each other," in fact, "roughly double" so.[55] The high incidence of rape and sexual abuse inflicted on the young,[56] primarily by adults, was cited in Chapter 2.

While youths are more likely to murder than be murdered outside the family, the reverse pattern applies within families. The 1994 Bureau of Justice Statistics survey of 1,300 family murders in 33 major cities showed youths under age 20 were 55 percent more likely to be victims than killers. When parents over age 20 and children under age 20 are examined, parents were six times more likely to murder their children than the other way around.[57]

Adults are the chief murderers of children/youth in all circumstances, in fact. California has the nation's highest ratio of youth to adult murder arrests and harbors one in six youth killers nationally. Yet even in the nation's leading youth-murder state, 64 percent of the murdered youths under age 18 were slain by offenders over age 18 (national tabulations indicate that figure is well over 70 percent). The accompanying Table 4.6 is compiled from matching a cross-tabulation of 1,600 murders by age of victim and offender provided by the California Department of Justice for 1993 with murder arrest and homicide death statistics by age.

Adults over age 20 accounted for two-thirds of the murders of children under age 12, one-third of the murders of teenagers 12-19, and 80 percent of the murders

Table 4.6

Adults, not youths, are the chief murderers of youths
Age of murderer by age of victim, California 1993

| Murderer | Age of Murderer | | | | |
	≤12	12-17	18-19	20+	Total
Total murderers	2	578	514	2,698	3,792
Age of victim:					
<12	0	24	30	101	155
12-17	2	155	69	126	351
18-19	0	118	85	127	331
20-24	0	97	139	491	728
25-34	0	97	101	848	1,047
35-64	0	81	74	880	1,035
65+	0	5	15	125	145

Sources: Law Enforcement Information Center (1994). Willful homicide crimes, 1993, age of victim by age of offender (printout). Sacramento, CA: California Department of Justice. Center for Health Statistics (1993). Microcomputer Injury Surveillance System (MISS), 1990. Sacramento: California Department of Health Services (diskette). Calculations cross-matching arrestees, victims, and homicide tolls by age are by the author to estimate victims/offenders of unstated age.

of adults 20 and older. Teenagers are not unusual in that every age group, with the exception of young children and the elderly, is most likely to be victimized by its age peers.[58] That teenagers accounted for 29 percent of California's murder arrestees in 1993 (white teens for 3 percent, nonwhite teens for 26 percent) is tied to the fact that teens comprise 30 percent of California's poverty population among persons over age 10.

Legal adult violence

The above discussion of adult violence against youth does not include corporal punishment, legal in the United States but in no other industrial nation. American parents freely hit their kids. The 1990 National Longitudinal study of youth found that 61 percent of the 3-5-year-olds were spanked in the week preceding the interview, and these an average of three times. Two of three adolescents reported having been legally hit by their parents or other adults at least once while in their teens.[59] Thus the kind of violence that would bring misdemeanor or felony assault charges if inflicted upon an adult occurs hundreds of millions of times every year in the lives of American children—and is not reflected in child abuse statistics cited.

The benefits of corporal punishment promised by its advocates do not materialize in fact, a point well reviewed elsewhere. To the contrary: Legally spanked and beaten children are "associated with an increased probability of several psychosocial problems" including educational failure,[60] problem drinking,[61] adult depression and spouse abuse,[62] reduced occupational and economic achievement,[63] increased aggression and violence,[64] [65] and even a greatly-enhanced probability of winding up on death row.[66] In a logic not yet grasped by lawmakers, the Supreme Court, the police in the Pico/Aliso district, or six in ten American parents, beating children (legally or illegally) produces children who beat.

No matter. Academics can study and report, logicians can reason, civil libertarian hearts can bleed. Hitting children is not a subject to which rational debate applies. It is another manifestation of Americans' unique exploitation of children as models for absolutist behavior standards and austere punishments that grown adults would not impose on themselves. Advocates of corporal punishment (such as the Orange County, California, legislator who proposes to paddle juvenile graffitists) portray themselves as "tough." Yet Singapore, whose policy of caning criminals American advocates of spanking juveniles recommend as a model, administers 95 percent of its legal beatings to adults—especially to corrupt politicians. In contrast, the U.S. appears to be the only nation that authorizes the hitting of juveniles while shielding even adult criminals from physical punishment. This breathtaking anti-child hostility was reflected in a 1977 Supreme Court decision:

> An examination of the Amendment and the decisions of this Court construing the proscription against cruel and unusual punishment confirms that it was designed to protect those convicted of crimes. We adhere to this long-standing limitation and hold that the Eighth Amendment does not apply to the paddling of children as a means of maintaining discipline...[67]

The Court's decision came in a Florida case in which junior high students, for offenses as trivial as "being slow to respond," were beaten. One suffered a hematoma requiring medical attention and absence from school for several days, the other lost the use of one arm for a week. Not only did the Court uphold corporal punishment of youths, it allowed schools to inflict it without hearing, notice, or review. It is difficult to read the majority opinion without concluding that justices were delighted with their "toughness" in dismissing every significant fact of the case.

To rejoin, as did the Court's four dissenters (all now retired), that "where corporal punishment becomes so severe as to be unacceptable in a civilized society, (we) can see no reason that it should become any more acceptable just because it is inflicted upon children," is polite understatement. As in the case of social policy, we American adults through our institutions and courts are imposing Third World conditions of poverty and legal violence upon our children while demanding First World protections for ourselves.

The question is less whether corporal punishment is barbaric, futile, or even counter-productive than its extraordinary hypocrisy. If beatings are effective in deterring misbehavior, and if deterrence is the goal, then American grownups (especially the Bible-quoters who freely cite "spare the rod" admonitions but overlook whole verses of Deuteronomy mandating harsh physical punishments of adult criminals) should demand an even heavier schedule of paddlings, spankings, and other physical punishments for adult drunk drivers, child molesters, white collar criminals, racketeering legislators, and other adult miscreants than it would impose upon children who are "slow to respond." And televise the lashings for maximum deterrence and viewing pleasure: The Caning Channel.

Rambo for real

The "legal violence" inflicted in war is perhaps the most devastating adult brutality against children. As Ramapo College psychologist Roger Johnson pointed out, the deliberate killing of civilians, including high proportions of children, has increasingly become a tool of war policy makers. Prior to World War II, the overwhelming majority of wartime casualties were soldiers; during and after World War II, civilians.

The Japanese rape and slaughter of 100,000 citizens of Nanking in 1938 was designed to subdue the population quickly to preserve its own troops for further conquests. Mass murders of civilians were also committed by the Russians, Germans, and British. The American atomic bombings of Hiroshima and Nagasaki were likewise designed to end the war and enhance diplomatic positioning vis-à-vis the Soviets at the expense of 200,000 civilians, without risking further American lives. Forty percent of those killed by American incendiary and anti-personnel bombs in Vietnam were children. Nearly 100 million people have died in 20th century wars, Johnson writes: "Today, the targeting of civilians is routine."[68]

In early 1993, a Harvard University Medical team found that as a direct result of the Persian Gulf War and the bombing of power and water treatment plants by American and United Nations forces, 46,000 Iraqi children under the age of five died from water-borne diseases (typhus and cholera) and malnutrition in the first six months after the war. U.S. health authorities estimated 170,000 would die. The toll of children, a predictable result of destroying infrastructure facilities in a developing nation, far exceeded the 100,000 Iraqi soldiers killed in the armed conflict.[69] In a 59-day war, more pre-school Iraqi children died than the child body count from 10,000 years of U.S. gang violence at 1993 levels.

Likewise the 25,000 Americans killed in Vietnam who were sent to the war as teenagers is equal to a 10-year toll of all teenage homicides at today's elevated rates. The aged warmakers—Saddam Hussein, George Bush, United Nations commanders, Lyndon Johnson, Richard Nixon—were never personally at risk. As Clinton declared, civilized nations do not use "assassination" as a foreign policy tool. Those who have fought in and died by the hundreds of thousands in war, both as combatants and as civilians, were children, teenagers, and young adults—the same youngsters that grownups and government officials wax misty over caring about when war is not at hand. Vietnam was the nation's first major war fought mainly by teenagers. Half the 55,000 killed were under age 21. Nearly all had been sent to the war right out of (or in) high school.

The rationales for such wartime policies are unstated and simple. As Phil Ochs sang a quarter century ago, sending the young to war saves the old. Killing civilians advances the war effort while minimizing the risk to military combatants. In this respect, governments and urban gangs—in their territoriality, their amoral pursuit of constituent interests, their hyper-sensitivity to affront—are remarkably alike. The gang brutality that occasionally kills Los Angeles 3-year-olds and the American tactical bombing that killed thousands of Vietnamese and Iraqi 3-year-olds stem from the common sentiment that the interests of the older are legitimately served by forcing lethal risks on the younger. That Americans' murder, drug abuse, and suicide increase sharply during and after wars is discussed in Chapter 6.

Noted *Nation* columnist Alexander Cockburn:

> The prime model for violence is not TV or heavy metal but the U.S. military, and the attendant militarist culture. Diminish state-sanctioned violence and, in the end, you diminish the generalized social violence that derives from it.[70]

"Violence begets violence"

"Teenage" violence is so interrelated with adult violence that analyzing it separately obscures more than it illuminates. As Straus notes, "family training" is the genesis of violence.[71] Children who are violently and sexually abused are three times more likely than non-abused youths to behave violently themselves, even when such variables as parental income and marital status are held constant.[72] Teenage mothers,[73] incarcerated youths,[74] and other youth populations at risk were victimized by severe violence and sexual abuse while growing up at much higher levels, typically 60 percent to over 90 percent.

Pre-teen years appear to be the time in which a storehouse of rage builds up in abused children.[75] From age 10-12 to age 13-14, the rate of homicide arrests multiplies nine-fold. It jumps another five-fold by age 16, and redoubles yet again by age 18. Thus an 18-year-old is 100 times more homicidal than an 11-year-old. Even so, 1,999 out of every 2,000 18-year-olds will not kill anyone.

Violence rises in late teenage years as youths acquire the strength, skills, and independence to retaliate against previous victimizations. This latter potential illustrates the tragedy of misdirected reprisal. The hostility of abused children is not usually brought to the door of the abuser.

The link between adult and youth violence has been well established. A 1992 National Institute of Justice comparison of the criminal records of 908 abused/neglected youths with 667 non-abused youths found that "violence begets violence... being abused or neglected as a child increased the likelihood of arrest as a juvenile by 53 percent, as an adult by 38 percent, and for a violent crime by 38 percent." The study reported that in addition to being more crime prone:

> The abused and neglected cases were also more likely to average nearly 1 year younger at first arrest (16.5 years versus 17.3 years), to commit nearly twice as many offenses (2.4 percent versus 1.4 percent), and to be arrested more frequently (17 percent of abused and neglected cases versus 9 percent of comparison cases had more than five arrests).[76]

Thus teens and adults who were abused or neglected as children not only commit 40 percent more crimes than non-abused persons, they commit twice as many crimes per criminal than their non-abused counterparts. This indicates that the overall crime volume among individuals abused or neglected as children is approximately 2.4 times higher than those whose childhoods were free of violence and neglect. The NIJ findings should be considered conservative, since the absence of "official records" of abuse or neglect in the non-abused sample does not guarantee at least some of the control group had been abused as well. Child abuse and neglect, as noted, are notoriously under-reported.

A 1990 study of 300 students reported in *Science* magazine likewise found that abused children were nearly three times more aggressive than non-abused children even when other factors such as family income, divorced and single parenting, and family discord were taken into account. Abused children committed 30 percent more aggressive acts in real life and were rated as consistently more violent both by their teachers and peers. Due to probable "under-reporting of abuse" in the so-called non-abused sample, "our estimates of the magnitude of the effects of abuse may actually be underestimates," the authors said.[77]

Repeated studies in Philadelphia, Los Angeles, and other cities found that while most youth and young-adult gangs are not violent, so-labeled "scavenger" or "territorial" gangs are. Of those that perpetrate most gang violence:

> The research indicates without question that most gang members are impoverished school drop-outs with a history of violent victimization at home and in their communities, who commit crimes to get by, and whose affiliation with their gang may be the only reason they have for liking themselves and feeling proud.[78]

Instead of focusing on the adult violence that precedes youth violence, the official response has been to "suppress gangs"—with concomitant growth in their size and violence.

A similar official delusion that "crime begins with teens" operates to the detriment of girls. Sociologist Chesney-Lind deplores the role of law enforcement in "criminalizing girls' survival strategies" such as running away, prostitution, and vagrancy with incarceration while the same officials "neglect the reality that most of these behaviors were often in direct response to earlier victimization, frequently by parents, that officials had, for years, routinely ignored:"

> In a society that idealizes inequality in male/female relationships and venerates youth in women, girls are easily defined as sexually attractive by older men. In addition, girls' vulnerability to both physical and sexual abuse is heightened by norms that require that they stay home where their victimizers have access to them... As they run away from abusive homes, parents have been able to employ agencies to enforce their return. If they persisted in their refusal to stay in the home, however intolerable, they were incarcerated.[79]

It is not surprising that the few cases of teenage female violence result from such situations (females who had been abused were 77 percent more likely to commit crimes than non-harmed girls, the NIJ study found). Still, the same news media that hypes imprisoned girls and women, such as *Newsweek*'s 1993 cover story, tends to bury at the end of sidebars the fact that "nearly every single one of them in there has probably been abused."[80]

Adult violence against youth often remains a hidden, family crime; violence by youth is both public and subject to emotional anecdote. For example, while the media and officials claim school violence has risen drastically and that "135,000 kids bring guns to school every day,"[81] the annual *Monitoring the Future* report of over 2,000 public high school seniors finds no rising trend. In 1976, 5.0 percent of the white seniors and 6.7 percent of the black seniors reported being injured by someone with a weapon at school. In 1993, these figures were 4.3 percent and 6.4 percent, respectively.[82] "Victimization rates of high school seniors changed little between 1976 and 1993," the National Center for Education Statistics reported.[83] Reports of other types of school violence and crime were similarly stable.

The "adult factor" explains why theories that blame violence on youth procliv-ities, while popular, inevitably fail fundamental real-world tests of validity. While all adolescents are exposed to equivalent levels of youth-based influences, such as media violence or "peer pressure" real-world violence is highly concentrated in cer-tain demographic groups. Why, in fact, do boys commit nine times more violent crimes than girls? Why are murder rates among black male youths ten times higher (and rising several times faster) than murder among white, non-Hispanic male youths? Why are California teenagers a dozen times more likely to commit murder than Montana teenagers? It is here that efforts to explain "youth violence" as a phe-nomenon separate from "adult violence" fail most profoundly across a wide variety of pragmatic tests.

The difference is that black, male, urban, California youth are exposed to far different kinds of adult influence and conditions than are rural, white, Montana teens. Correlations of youth violence rates with corresponding violence rates of adults of their gender, race, era, and region reveal powerful associations.[84][85] Both over time, for the last four decades, and by geographic region of the U.S., youth vio-lent crime arrests and adult violent crime arrests are almost perfectly correlated: Where one is high, the other is high also.[86] These near one-to-one correlations indicate that 90 percent of the youth violence rate over time and by geographic location is explained by the same factors that cause adult violence. In short: *Youth violence and adult violence are not separate behaviors; they are one and the same phenom-enon.*

But the parallel nature of youth and adult behavior described throughout this book is not automatic. If conditions between the young and old become sufficiently divergent, separate youth trends may emerge. Beginning in the mid-1980s, during a period of intensive legal and programmatic efforts to combat "teen violence," youth violent crime arrests began to climb rapidly. Crime among California teenagers rose earlier, and more rapidly, than among youths nationwide, even though (perhaps partly because) the state pioneered "get tough" policies in the 1970s.[87] The poverty rate among California youth also rose at a record pace during this period, from 15 percent in 1980 to 29 percent by 1995. The demographic variables underlying both youth and adult violence rates are so decisive—and converge around the variable of "poverty"—that they dwarf the "age" factor unfortunately chosen to name the issue.

Escapisms: Hollywood, hormones, hot blood

American health and social scientists have too often been prominent in trivili-azing the social conditions underlying youth violence. The American Medical Association has garnered far more publicity demanding tighter movie regulations than it ever has denouncing the rape, beating, and neglect of children.[88] The American Psychological Association claimed in a 1993 report that "antisocial behaviors tend to peak during adolescence" as a result of—not poverty, not abuse, not adult example—but teenage "developmental crises" (turn the clock back a cen-tury to G. Stanley Hall). The APA listed four individual experiences as "preeminent... in the development of violent behavior:"

- Access to firearms;
- Involvement with alcohol or other drugs;
- Involvement in antisocial groups; and
- Exposure to violence in the mass media.[89]

Let us examine the nature of the person described here. An individual who would commit an act of violence merely because he or she (a) witnessed a fictional act of violence in the media, a comic book, a music lyric, or on a video screen, (b) has an intoxicating substance or instrument of violence available, and/or (c) because other anti-social people authorized it, is both stupid and a lunatic. The argument that immediate factors such as "media violence" or gun availability *cause* youth violence is simply a restatement of the century-old adult prejudice that adolescents are dangerously dumb.

Prejudicial stereotyping is not known for its originality of thought. The stereotypes of violence and mental vulnerability used to describe teenagers today closely resemble those aimed at blacks and other minorities in previous decades. A century after Hall, American pop-media psychology still seems unable to resist the dead-end non-theory (called the "fundamental attribution error" by social psychologists) that if an unpopular group such as teenagers displays some bad behavior, it must be *innate* to that group. (The corollary of the fundamental attribution error, routinely applied to adults, is that if a favored group displays that same or worse behavior, it is due to bad luck affecting otherwise well-behaved individuals in unfortunate circumstances).

What those who blame "youth violence" on the intrinsic flaws of adolescents and the deleterious stimulations adolescents purportedly crave are really disparaging is black, Hispanic, and poorer Asian teens. These groups account for 88 percent of the teen murders and 80 percent of the teen violent crimes in California, for example, a state in which whites are the plurality race among adolescents by a considerable margin.[90] Nationally, blacks, who comprise only one in six teenagers, accounted for *twice* as many homicides and more violent crimes than all white, Hispanic, and Asian teens put together in 1993. And black adults in their 20s are even more likely to commit murder than are black adolescents.[91]

This is the official claim, an old one, for which the new "youth violence" crisis serves as a smokescreen dressed up for modern times: Racial/ethnic minorities are particularly violent. Not one commentators to the left of Charles Murray would express so baldly in the 1990s (and even Murray derides his own genetic-deficiency non-science as not mattering much). Thus, the all-purpose '90s-friendly codeword, "teenage," is substituted for "black" or "Latino." Note, for example, how some liberal reviewers who criticized conservative author Dinesh D'Souza for his argument, in *The End of Racism*, that white fears of black violence constitute "rational discrimination," not racism, nonetheless agreed that whites' "distrust of black *teenagers* can be viewed as rational" (emphasis added).[92] This race-to-age transfer of discriminatory attitudes was anticipated 30 years ago by Edgar Friedenberg in his 1964 work, *The Dignity of Youth and Other Atavisms:*

In our society there are two kinds of minority status. One of these I will call the "hot-blooded" minorities, whose archetypical image is that of the Negro or Latin. In the United States, "Teen-agers" are treated as a "hot-blooded" minority. ...The minority stereotype... develops to fit the purposes and expresses the anxieties of the dominant social group.[93]

If teenagers, particularly dark ones, are homicidal maniacs for no reason, the simplest bad influences (a rhyme in a song, a celluloid hero shooting up a streetful of villains, a video Mortal Kombat game) can set them off. Blaming the media for inciting youth violence has become the latest mass evasion, typically embraced in tandem with "family values" crusades. Hillary Clinton weighed in to urge Americans to "stay away from the theaters and turn off our sets because we are so offended by the gratuitous violence, sexual degradation, and bad taste we are subjected to on the screen." Candidates, on the advice of their professional handlers and poll-scanners, have donned the mantle of Dan Quayle, from President Clinton vs. Sister Solja and Calvin Klein to Senate Majority Leader Bob Dole gunning at the movie/rap corruptors.[94]

High on the list of escapists is William Roper, former director of the same Centers for Disease Control and Prevention that has never compiled research or issued a major statement on the hundreds of thousands of real injuries to children inflicted by adults every year. Yet Roper waxes on scary youth violence statistics and the media's role.[95] Roper is yet another among top health officials, presidential candidates, and candidates' wives who had nothing to say about the rapes, violent abuses, and murders of millions of children documented in the *Rape in America* and U.S. Advisory Board on Child Abuse and Neglect reports.

Most of the media-blamers seem to be liberals and moderates seeking to recapture some of the coveted "values" field from conservatives such as Quayle, Dole, and former Education Secretary and top-virtuist William Bennett: Columnists Ellen Goodman and Colman McCarthy, Senator Paul Simon (D-Illinois) and Edward Markey (D-Massachusetts), *Mother Jones* magazine, and liberal editorialists from the *Los Angeles Times* to the *New York Times*. Each devoted far more attention to the oft-repeated assertion that "the average American child sees 8,000 murders and 10,000 acts of violence on television before he or she is out of grammar school" than to the rarely-examined fact that millions of American children experience *real* rapes and beatings before they are old enough to get out of grammar school.

The frivolous attitude of many liberals toward the genuine causes of youth violence paralleled liberal escapisms toward teenage sex. Columnist Carl Rowan was a lonely dissenter:

> I'm appalled that liberal Democrats... are spreading the nonsensical notion that Americans will, to some meaningful degree, stop beating, raping, and murdering each other if we just censor what is on the tube or big screen... The politicians won't, or can't, deal with the real-life social problems that promote violence in America... so they try to make TV programs and movies the scapegoats! How pathetic![96]

Media-blaming, like the media itself, is prime escapism. *Newsweek* carried no fewer than five cover stories on the dangers of rap and rock music in four years.

Major newspapers such as *The Los Angeles Times* devote many times more space to "media violence" issues than to real adult violence against children. The claim that "3,000 studies" document that violence in TV programs and movies promote societal violence has become a fallback for those reluctant to discuss harsher social realities. For example: If media is any kind of significant cause of youth violence, we should find violence levels among different subgroups of youth, all of whom are exposed to similar amounts of media influence, quite similar. After all, any teen can tune in *NYPD Blue*, watch *A Nightmare on Elm Street*, or buy Guns'N'Roses and Geto Boys.

Yet youth violence levels are extremely dissimilar. Black youths, as noted, are a dozen times more likely to commit murder than are white youths; males are nine times more violent than females; Washington, DC, teens are 22 times more likely to be arrested for homicide than Washington state teens. "Media violence" theories, like many psychological findings that become hopelessly confused when attempts are made to extend them outside the laboratory, are noteworthy for their inability to explain real world behaviors.

When examined, media violence research is murkier than its proponents admit. Studies done in laboratories usually show an effect of media violence on aggression; studies done in real-life settings tend to be inconclusive. The large-scale studies that have attempted to correlate the media preferences of thousands of students with their aggressive behaviors have found only low-level effects, typically averaging 0.1 to 0.2, on a scale of 0 to 1.0. This weak association would indicate that at most, media violence explains 1 percent to 5 percent of the violence in society not explained by other factors. (Of course, it may be the other way around: Youths who are already violent may be somewhat more attracted to violent media).[97] In no case do the findings on media violence effects come close to the tight correlations between adult violence and youth violence (typically over 0.9) or the two- to three-fold higher rates of violence among abused children. It should be noted that research reviews that have found media violence effects on youths have also found similar effects on adults.[98] This suggests that restrictions on marketing or programming should be aimed not just at youths, but at adults.

Sometimes embarrassments occur. In 1994, Morality in Media, a New York City media watchdog group, rushed to the press to blame a Beavis and Butt-head episode for causing a troubled youth to drop a bowling ball off a freeway bridge, shattering a car windshield and killing an eight-month-old baby. Investigation showed the tragedy was an accident and that the youth did not have cable TV and had never seen the Beavis show in question.[99]

In its 1988 video, "Rising to the Challenge," Tipper Gore's Parents' Music Resource Center blamed rock-and-roll for rising youth suicide, pregnancy, and crime. The video is both fraudulent and, for its slick production, astonishingly ignorant of rock music. Its authors distorted the words to Ozzy Ozbourne's 1981 song "Suicide Solution" to make it appear pro-suicide (the song is not about suicide; "suicide solution" refers to the deadly dangers of alcoholism) and butchered statistics wholesale. To prove it wasn't stodgily anti-rock, the PMRC singled out two artists as "healthy and inspiring" for youths. One was Bruce Springsteen, whose earlier music is replete with realistic and evocative drug, sex, and violence themes (his

1982 work "Nebraska" describes a murder spree by teenagers as "fun"). The other PMRC-approved group was the Irish band U2. U2's song "Pistol Weighing Heavy" would be cited in 1991 by psychologist Park Deitz as prompting a deranged fan to murder actress Rebecca Schaeffer (the song is not about murdering actresses).

Even a researcher who buys into the notion of innate teenage recklessness, Jeffrey Arnett of the University of Chicago, was unable to connect violent rock music to teenage violence. His 1991 study of 50 young "metalheads" who patronized heavy metal groups such as Anthrax, Megadeath, Slayer, Ozzy Ozbourne, Dokken, Metallica, Queensrÿche, Iron Maiden, and Stryper (the last a self-proclaimed "Christian heavy metal" band!) found most youths were attracted not just to the fast-paced music, but to the "social consciousness" of the lyrics.

They had a point. My own examination of the heavy metal albums that a group of low-income junior high boys I worked with in the 1980s told me they most admired turned up a surprising array of well-worded songs that strongly criticized racial oppression, economic inequality, war, drug addiction, child abuse, environmental destruction, and suppression of free speech. The biggest single theme of the metal groups I listened to was anti-victimization. Metallica's 1986 *Master of Puppets* and 1988 *And Justice for All* albums contained powerfully-worded songs condemning heroin and cocaine addiction, the deaths and maimings of young soldiers in war, the oppressions of psychiatric treatment, and corporate destruction of the environment. Queensrÿche was astonishing for the bitterness of its anti-fascist lyrics in sophisticated thematic albums such as *Rage for Order* (1986) and *Operation Mindcrime* (1988). Popular bands such as Metal Church and Megadeath unsubtly counseled the young in enraged individualism. A major feature of heavy metal music turned out to be the least expected—a large contingent of politically aware invocations which actively resurrected the mantle of radicalism raised by '60s anti-establishment rockers such as Jefferson Airplane, Steppenwolf, and The Doors, and '70s punkers like the Clash, the Ramones, the Cure, and the Sex Pistols. The intergenerational synthesis of Right On and Rad.

Concluded social scientist Arnett from his study:

> Perhaps the most striking finding of the study was that for many of these adolescents, heavy metal music served a purgative function, dissipating their accumulated anger and frustration. They listened to it especially when they were angry, and it consistently had the effect of making them less angry, of calming them down. This result certainly does not lend itself to an argument that heavy metal music is dangerous and should be banned; ironically, it would seem more appropriate to advocate subscribing to heavy metal music for adolescents who show evidence of a propensity for aggression.[100]

"Not even one subject," Arnett found, "reported that the music tended to make him feel sad or hopeless." We 40-somethings should listen to it more.

Conversely, there is no accounting for what snaps the twigs of true maniacs. For example, the Clintons, like most aging Baby Boomers, extol the Beatles—yet the Beatles' 1969 *White Album* was cited by Charles Manson as his inspiration for the "Helter Skelter" killing spree (the song "Helter Skelter" is not about slaughter, but refers to a British amusement park ride). Noted media violence researchers have even blamed "Sesame Street" for inciting aggression in youths.[101] But oddly, they have ignored the most common media inspirations spurring a multitude of fanatics to initiate various holy wars, murderous devout cleansings, and repeated instances of not suffering witches to live: The Bible, Koran, Torah, and other religious works (which typically contain clear admonitions against killing).

Two things are clear from the muddled picture and our current deficient knowledge. First, the media-blamers have sold their escapism well: A 1989 Time/CNN survey showed 67 percent of Americans declared that TV and movie violence was "mainly to blame" for real-life violence among teens.[102] Second and more realistically, what societal violence, if any, that the media does inspire is thoroughly unpredictable. Charles Joseph Whitman, who gunned down 16 people with a high-powered rifle from the top of the University of Texas tower, was (as singer Kinky Friedman eulogized) an Eagle Scout nurtured on the *Boy Scout Handbook*. Albert DiSalvo, the Boston Strangler, had an appetite for bloodshed whetted by Anglican religious services. Maybe we should look at the issue the other way around: Hundreds of millions of American youth have patronized John Wayne, James Cagney, and Schwartzenegger, tuned in Megadeath, the Beatles, and Ice-T, pored over the Bible, and even become Eagle Scouts—and haven't murdered anyone.

This profitable, never-ending campaign against print and airwave trash will certainly be extended into cyberspace, as magazine covers announce the techno-defilers from which youth must now be rescued by ethereal adults from ethereal adults: Internet smut, e-mail filth, virtual-reality porn, modem mayhem. The late-night lure of the Compuserve-pederast becomes the latest excuse for not facing the fact that the real danger lies two doors down the hall.

In 1991, Montana 4-H director Kirk Astroth and I decided to achieve some youth-at-risk-conference notoriety by screening Tipper Gore & Co.'s "Rising to the Challenge" to the teen and grown conferees, then scrutinizing the X-rated PMRC video's profuse statistical and lyrical fibbings point by point. Naturally, our workshops drew huge crowds and were full of explicit debates on whether metal, rap, and punk tunes (which we dissected line-by-line on overheads) propelled kids to maraud, rape, and kill. A good vacation from reality was had by all.

A thrash-metal band singled out for particular opprobrium by the PMRC was rebellious junior-high headbanger favorite Metallica and its vivid album cover, "Kill 'Em All!" In the spirit of scientific hypothesis testing, I attended a Metallica concert in Oklahoma City to witness first-hand, ears cottoned from row 443, how music warps kids' minds. There was the usual set lit like Morlock holes from hell and the characteristic over-amped rat-a-tat jet-landing slamming and shrieking and obscene exhortations to the strobed-churning mob in front of the stage. The final encore— perfect for my experiment—turned out to be "Kill 'Em All!" After that ten-minute episode of aural mayhem ended the show, 25,000 young people ages 11 to 21 and heavily male emerged from the Myriad Arena looking properly menacing in ripped jeans, stringy hair, and t-shirts announcing untoward thoughts. They poured into an empty 1 a.m. downtown which tempted them with dozens of glass and steel towers and upscale businesses and no visible police (or parental) presence whatsoever. I waited for central-city Okie Armageddon. The thousands thronged through the dark streets to their cars, departed. Not even a parking meter was kicked. I drove a tattooed eyebrow-ringed 16-year-old hitchhiker to his home in a decaying part of town and asked whether, after four hours of deafening musical savagery, he was planning to do some damage. "Nah, man," he said. "I feel really mellow."

Where teens aren't violent

The theory of many American social scientists' that violence is a naturally occurring, innate feature of teenagers[103] is another in a long list of this country's psychological theories deployed to blame disfavored demographic groups for the behaviors stemming from social iniquities. As such, it is ill-suited to explain basic facts. Within America's closest sister nations—United Kingdom, Canada, Australia, Germany, France, and Italy—some 20 million teens (age 15-19) dwell. In 1990, 300 of them were murdered.[104] Of the U.S.'s 17 million teenagers, 3,000 were murdered that year. The U.S. teen murder rate was twelve times that of other major urbanized, industrialized societies; six times higher even than that of our fellow frontier cultures Canada and Australia. The U.S. adult murder rate is likewise seven times higher than that in the other six nations. We kill more and younger. While in the U.S., teens accounted for one in eight of our 24,000 murders in 1990, that proportion was one in fifteen of the 4,500 murders in the other six Western countries.

Teenagers are innately violent? Japan has 10 million teens. In 1990, 30 Japanese teenagers were involved in murders, a rate *one-fiftieth* that of the U.S. The very low murder rate among Japanese and European teens is evidence enough that adolescents, even modern Western ones, are not intrinsically barbaric. Further, the U.S. murder gap is far too high to blame more than a small share even on the officially-designated chief culprit: America's widespread gun availability.

We don't have to examine other Western societies to find non-violent teens. We have even better proof right here in our teen- and gun-infested homeland, right in the middle of the Gundown State. Thirty-one suburban and rural California counties with a population of 2.5 million, in which a quarter-million teenagers reside, experienced zero teenage murders in 1993.[105] Zero. No small trick in a year in which 4,000 people died at the hands of their fellow Californians.

Same rock'n'roll furies, same rap conceits, same TV barbarisms (worse, since suburban and rural families are more likely to subscribe to graphic cable channels), same guns on every block (more in rural towns), no shortage of drug and alcohol involvement, no lack of opportunity to form anti-social groups for youths who so desire, the same teenagers bearing whatever innate "high risk" teenage qualities and "crises" of growing up experts offer as all-purpose explanations. But no killings.

Yet central Los Angeles census tracts with the same youth population as these 31 counties experienced more than 200 youth murders. How on earth would the American Psychological Association, William Roper, and Tipper Gore explain that? Would they mention that the youth poverty level of these 31 counties is only a fraction that of central Los Angeles?

Do violent teens make the headlines in suburban papers? Certainly. The recent shooting death of suburban Lakewood, California's, Spur Posse chief won the usual media frenzy; his pathetic wanabee-gang of middle-class white rapists was briefly the nation's most famous. Indeed, the media seem embarked on a frantic campaign to convince adults that no one is safe from their rampaging young. And in fact, of California's 1 million white teenagers, 70 were arrested for murder in 1993, generating better than a headline a week. Many more per slaying, in fact, than the 600 nonwhite youths arrested for murder.

That the news media hyperventilates over every white suburban high school murder to prove it is "not racist" (that is, it is even-handedly anti-youth) does not erase the enormous surplus of violence among nonwhite young and the racism inherent in failing to scrutinize why that is. *The Los Angeles Times* follows a predictable protocol typical of the mainstream media. Murder committed by a suburban youth, usually white, is exhaustively autopsied. Reporters and editorialists point out the "good family," "loving parents," and "advantages"—the benign backdrop for inexplicable barbarism by an adolescent maniac. Proof that teenagers are unpredictably hyper-violent, society's Rottweilers needing shorter leashes. Also, perhaps, reflective of the greater value society places on the lives of suburbanites versus ghetto dwellers.

In years of working with families, I learned to be skeptical of superficial "good family" reportage, but leave that for a later chapter. The point is that the moderately liberal *Times* is loathe similarly to dissect, especially editorially, why 19 City of Angels nonwhite teens commit murder for every one white teen. The price of the media's refusal to examine the racial—that is, the poverty—aspects of "teenage violence" is that ever-harsher penalties are inflicted on nonwhite youths. The "liberal" media—from *The Los Angeles Times* to *Rolling Stone*—may hype "white youth" violence out of sense of racial even-handedness, but the practical result is to create a climate for more punitive approaches aimed overwhelmingly at minority adolescents whose violence rooted in social disadvantages remain unexamined and unrelieved.

An example of the public's fascination with teenage brutality is the 1989 Central Park "wilding," in which four black teens maimed a white jogger and left her brain-damaged and in a coma for weeks. There are some 25,000 murders and 750,000 felony assaults in the United States each year, many of equal or greater viciousness, but the "wilding" became an instant media cover hit. Why that particular brutality? Why not another, bizarrely similar attack around that same time by two black men, age 23 and 32, on a white female jogger in Syracuse, New York, in which the victim was raped, stabbed 11 times, left tied to a stake in the ground, and told by one of the attackers, "Die, bitch, die"—which received virtually no press?[106]

Because violent incidents are singled out to prove a point. Tipper Gore and the PMRC's point, for example, was to use the "wilding" to blame their favorite scapegoat: Rock and rap music. Proof, said Gore, was that one of the Central Park assailants was humming a rap tune "Wild Thing" (a song that has nothing to do with raping and beating young women).[107] While Gore and the PMRC deplore the "new" threat of uniquely evil heavy metal, punk, rap, and depraved media influences over the last decade, they are 40 years behind the times. A U.S. Senate report on the August 1954 "reign of terror" in a New York City park by four teens age 15-18 that left two dead dedicated a chapter to "exposing horror comics:"

...Subsequent investigations disclosed that the pattern of sadism followed by this Brooklyn youth gang had been blueprinted almost word for word and act for act in a cheap pulp publication entitled *Nights of Horror*. A complete file of *Nights of Horror* was found in [leader] Jack Koslow's possession. It had been well-thumbed... Even Koslow's words, which had so shocked our nation—"This night has been a supreme adventure for me"—were parroted from the lips of a character in *Nights of Horror*.[108]

Others blamed killer teens of the day on diabolic blues lyrics, in which all sorts of coded (and not so coded) meanings were found, and of course there would soon be Elvis. The difference is that today we have major remedial industries to serve. Tipper and colleagues apparently had no points to make about violent 32-year-olds. Other interests highlighted the "wilding" to push their particular youth-fixing solutions—popular political remedies, profitable treatment programs, rock'n'roll record labelings and bans, all manner of tougher laws.

Given the assumptions behind them, it is not surprising that the record of youth-targeted cure-alls is bleak. The unpopular reason is evident: "Youth violence" does not exist as a singular "youth issue" separate from "adult violence." This fact explains why decades of legal and programmatic interventions aimed at youths—which mushroomed over the last five to ten years—have not only failed, but may be contributing to today's record youth violence, and worse, today's adult exoneration.

Going easy on the grownups

In my few years as a crime reporter and youth worker, I saw a number of instances illustrating the bizarre American penchant for excusing adults. It isn't just that sentences for adults tend to be more lenient, as shown in the California figures that youths consistently receive jail and prison terms 60 percent longer for the same crimes than adults (Table 4.7).[109] Or even that the U.S. Supreme Court has, in several decisions also reviewed in Chapter 1, authorized harsher treatment of juvenile offenders than adult offenders. Courts and institutions are notoriously gentle on grownup violent offenders *when the victim is young*.

In 1987, the Bozeman, Montana, school district stripped the track letter from a student alleged to have held a party at which other students drank alcohol; the same district took no action when a 31-year-old coach pleaded guilty to drunkenly assaulting a 19-year-old woman outside a tavern. A 16-year-old served a year in jail for exposing himself to women and writing a bad check; the 32-year-old youth program worker who had sexually molested the boy for four years was sentenced to 30 days suspended, community service, and counseling. The admitted molesting of a 12-year-old girl and scrawled notes from a half-dozen young girls who had been victims of attempted rape failed to persuade a judge to sentence the assailant to prison; when the man later brutally raped two adult women, he received 70 years as a "repeat" offender.

Mary Ann Abraham, a Bozeman rape victims' advocate and law student, told me her review of sentencings found that elk poaching and bad check writing consistently brought lengthier terms than sexual assaults against children. "A kid goes through the horror and embarrassment of testifying in a rape or molesting case, and the guy gets 30 days?" she said. "I'm livid about that! What good is all this education

Table 4.7

Youths serve sentences 60 percent longer than adults for the same crimes:

	Average months served in California		
	Adults	Juveniles	Youth excess
Homicide	41	60	+46%
Kidnaping	42	49	+17
Robbery	25	30	+20
Assault	21	29	+38
Burglary	18	21	+17
Theft (non-auto)	11	18	+64
Auto theft	13	17	+31
Forcible rape	43	58	+35
Other sex crimes	34	40	+18
Narcotics	14	22	+57
Other offenses	11	20	+82
Average	16	26	+63%

Source: California Department of Corrections and California Youth Authority, cited in Harris, Ron (1993, 22 August). A nation's children in lockup. Los Angeles Times, p. A20.

in the school system about 'good touch, bad touch' when our legal system doesn't validate kids when they are molested or raped?"[110]

In 1987, a nationwide American Bar Association study found that sentences were consistently tougher when the victims of sexual offenders were adults than when they were children or youths. The majority of sentences given to adults who had sexually violated children were less than one year, and 30 percent were less than six months. When the victims were adults, 77 percent of the sentences were more than one year, and 40 percent were more than 10 years. Courts were twice as likely to grant probation when the victims were children than when they were adults. Parents who sexually abused their children consistently received shorter sentences than strangers who did so.[111]

No Newsweek cover stories on "Adults: Wild in the Homes," or New York magazine splashes on "How the Justice System Lets Grownups Get Away with Rape and Murder" to match their features on teenagers. No Governor's Commission on Adult Violence Against Youths to go with the youth-violence commissions sprouting nationwide. No White House declarations of mourning for child victims of their own parents and caretakers amid nonstop denunciations of school and gang violence, no Shalala or Surgeon General press conferences on child rape. No Diane Sawyer televised shamings of adult rapists of child victims or judges who let them off the hook. No Centers for Disease Control surveys or press on the "risk factors" for hundreds of thousands of confirmed child and youth victims of sexual and violent abuses by parents and caretakers every year.

No, indeed. Priorities are priorities. In May 1994, nine bills aimed at television violence, all sponsored by Democrats as "pop culture takes the rap," were pending in Congress.[112] The adolescent scapegoat had been identified in punitive measures as well. It was time to teach these inexplicable, infuriating, fearsome kids a lesson.

Getting tough on teens

At the beginning of Governor Ronald Reagan's second term in 1971, California initiated popular, harsher incarceration standards against juveniles. This "get tough" policy quickly led to greater proportions of imprisoned juveniles than found in any other state. By 1992, 450 of every 100,000 California youths were incarcerated, tops in the nation. A California Department of Corrections/California Youth Authority report showed that convicts under age 18 consistently were incarcerated for terms averaging 60 percent *longer* than adults convicted of similar crimes (Table 4.7).

More than 13,000 teenagers were arrested in 1992 under California's strict weapons control laws,[113] the strongest effort to restrict gun availability of any state. More than 1,100 new state laws were passed in a dozen years requiring more mandatory and longer prison sentences. In 1992, National Council on Crime and Delinquency president Barry Krisberg reported that California's overall incarceration rate, with a record 130,000 behind grillwork, was the highest in the world.[114]

According to "get tough" proponents, California should have waltzed into the mid-1990s a crime-free New Eden. But New Eden bore a striking resemblance to 1928 Chicago. The teen population rose only marginally, but youth homicides rocketed from 350 in 1970 (below the national average) to 1,055 in 1994 (double the national average). Other juvenile violent crime mushroomed in California earlier, and more dramatically, than in any other state. Today California youth violence stands at record levels, as does the state's proposed new prison budget to contain it. California built 32,000 new prison spaces from 1989 to 1994, all filled to capacity within a few weeks of opening.

The lessons of California seem to have been lost on other states, which have increasingly adopted similar strategies in recent years with similar results. From the *Houston Chronicle*, some doubts about "the huge prison expansion" that leaves Texas "doomed to a vicious cycle of crime and punishment:"

> Those concerned about crime and getting tough on criminals should be paying particular attention to a sobering new study that indicates Texas, despite a five-year, $2 billion prison expansion program, cannot keep pace with its inmate population, which likely will begin overflowing the prisons again as early as next year.
> ...The state will have 146,000 correctional beds when work on the present program is completed next year, and another 12,000 spaces will be added by mid-1997. That is triple the number of prison spaces the state had as recently as 1990.
> ...When all the construction dust temporarily settles next year, there will be more than 100 separate lockups... The annual cost of operating Texas' prisons and state jails is now more than $1 billion —and growing.
> Factors include the tougher parole policies, recent penal code reforms that

doubled the minimum time that violent offenders will have to serve behind bars, and a juvenile crime problem that has become a crisis... thousands of teen-age criminals... graduating to—and filling up—adult prisons.[115]

It isn't working. From 1980 to 1994, teenage violent crime rates rose by 60 percent, while violent crime rates among the adults of age to be their parents (30-49) rose by an even more alarming 76 percent.[116] With record tens of thousands of its adolescents behind bars under ever-tougher sentencings, the United States still experienced a record 7,500 murder and 230,000 violent crime arrests of teenagers in 1994.

And it isn't going to work. Officials, with the help of a compliant media, will continue to exploit temporary and trivial statistics to generate press for claims of success. For example, California Attorney General Daniel Lundgren credited the state's "three strikes" law for a decline in violent crime in 1994 that was actually attributable to gang truces and the effects of the Northridge earthquake, which briefly interrupted northwest Los Angeles's normal violence patterns. No matter what the dismal experience, the criminal justice experts getting the most attention—such as UCLA's James Q. Wilson, the Brookings Institute's John DiIulio, and Northeastern University's James Alan Fox—continue to push for ever more police, tougher laws, more prisons, more gun law enforcement targeting youths, and more behavior-modifying "prevention programs" to meet the coming "crime wave storm" in youth violence[117] [118] instead of facing fundamental conditions of poverty and society-imposed violence and disadvantage.

The criminology establishment promotes more of the dismal American social science doctrine of programs to protect privilege. The fact is—by the stark, consistent, and easily-countable measure of homicide—the United States is in a record phase of violence. It now exceeds the murderousness of the Great Depression. It is teenagers and their young adult cohorts, record numbers of whom are trapped in rising poverty, hopelessness, and childhood violence not inflicted by adults in any other opulent western society, who are in the forefront. It is not going to abate until America's most-affluent adults of today learn to share society's resources with the young as past generations shared with us.

5. Nicoteen Fits

Adults are capable of making a decision to smoke or not.

— President Clinton, News Conference, 10 August 1995

Only adults should ever face the decision to smoke or not.

— R.J. Reynolds Tobacco Company ad, 10 October 1995

Children have never been very good at listening to their elders, but they have never failed to imitate them.

—James Baldwin

In March 1994, 300 students at Moss Landing Middle School north, of Monterey, petitioned a surprised U.S. Congressman Sam Farr (D-California) to take legislative action against parents whose smoking damages the health of children. "We're secondary smokers, and we have more of a risk of dying... because we're young and developing," eighth grade student president Maureen Bomactao told Farr. "Children of heavy smokers are exposed to smoke daily and suffer the health consequences."[1]

Bomactao, age 14, initiated the petition because both of her parents smoked. She was worried about the effects on her brothers and sisters and other children of smokers. Of 480 students, nearly all signed, she said. "It was a project for me. Those who weren't serious, who didn't care, I didn't let them sign."

"I write letters, but nothing happens," she complained. Lawmakers and health officials don't take action, so youths take their own. Bomactao pamphleteered and organized her siblings. "I talked to my parents, put pamphlets on their bed. They don't smoke in the house any more. When they light a cigarette in the car, my brother starts choking and pulls his shirt over his face. They put it out." Her sister is allergic to smoke. "It definitely affected me in track," she said. "If it hurts my lungs, I can't run."

"Most of us are not even doing it, but we're at risk for diseases, like chronic bronchitis," she said. "They talk about kids' smoking, but we can't talk about adults'."

In a single gesture, Bomactao and her young petitioners cut through the smokescreen of the tobacco industry and national health agencies to the true issue: The greatest tobacco danger to children and youths is the smoking of adults. But the adult smokers she and middle-school signers were petitioning to control are important. They constitute 50 million customers, 50 million voters. In contrast, the young are second-class citizens, tacitly viewed as undeserving of health protection in their own homes but ever-handy to blame in the political arena by the very health proponents charged with protecting them.

So hypocritical is the campaign to "protect children from tobacco" that tobacco giants like R.J. Reynolds and Philip Morris, which profit in the tens of billions from contributing to the deaths of 400,000 active smokers and the diseases of hundreds of thousands of children forced to passively breathe adults' smoke every year, can piously declare in a nationwide ad campaign that youths take up smoking due to "peer pressure" and that "minors should not have access to cigarettes. They should not smoke. Period."[2] R.J.R. and Philip Morris know, but do not admit, what research amply shows: Smoking kids are the products of smoking parents, smoking adults, and a smoking culture, not "underage sales" or "peer pressure" or some compulsion to nicotine unique to adolescents.

President Clinton's stance on tobacco likewise is a study in the deployment of emotional anti-youth rhetoric to hide his administration's continued tobacco promotion policies. In his campaign "against" teenage smoking, Clinton repeatedly invoked dire images of the "awful dangers of tobacco" to youth and the urgent need "to protect young people." In the next breath, he extolled tobacco producers and their addicted millions as vital to the economy and explicitly endorsed the industry views: Smoking by "children" is "terrible," but smoking by adults is "a reasonable decision," declared the president. Clinton admitted that he is an occasional cigar smoker who has disregarded his own health and daughter's pleas to quit.[3] His aides affirmed that "Clinton is considering no regulations affecting adult smoking."[4]

Reporters who burrowed in to the genesis of the new crusade found the usual politics at the core. Wrote the Associated Press's Richard Fournier of the White House's expectation of a "calculated... political windfall":

> Political advisors were buoyed by independent and internal polling that showed mass appeal for a crackdown on teenage smoking, even if it's despised in the South... [and] calculated it into a tobacco policy that was driven as much by Clinton's political team as his domestic policy shop.[5]

Behind the president's rhetoric of urgency and danger, genuine but politically-risky measures against smoking were being jettisoned. Dropped from health policy was the 75-cent-per-pack cigarette tax, proposed by Clinton during the 1992 campaign and bitterly opposed by the tobacco industry—for the very reason that higher taxes are by far the most effective policy to reduce both teenage and adult smoking.[6] When asked if he would end federal tobacco crop subsidies, Clinton backpedaled again: "I've always supported the tobacco program," which funnels $25 million per year to tobacco growers, he said, repeating the usual industry-generated guise of preserving "family farms."[7] It is the support from the 90,000 federally-subsidized "family tobacco farms" concentrated in 11 states that provides the grass-roots underpinning of the tenacious political clout the tobacco industry wields in Washington.

Academics and health officials, aided by a compliant media, have sought to weave an ever more fantastic scenario of gullible youth lured into smoking by cartoonish Old Joe camels, grizzled Marlboro cowpokes, and evil young peers. Smoking, top officials tell the media with increasingly narrow insistence, begins when a stupid teenager sees a colorful tobacco ad; no other factor need be considered. Meanwhile, the same health officials ever diligent in guarding adult non-smokers from the hazards of second-hand wisps in public buildings and workplaces have maintained silence on the hazards inflicted by the daily clouds of smoke (an EPA-declared carcinogen) suffered by 25 million children and adolescents of smoking parents in their homes.

Mature "adult smoking"

Why do teenagers smoke? The best evidence is: Because their parents and nearby adults do. The indignant and increasingly anger-tinged bafflement among experts that "3,000 kids take up smoking every day" is yet more politically-manufactured hypocrisy.

The vast majority of health damage done to children and youths from tobacco abuse is not from their own smoking, but from that of their parents and other adults. The retreat from confronting the impact of parental and adult smoking on the young by Clinton health authorities is further evidence of the degree to which health protection has become an element of popular politics.

However tentatively, health officials in the Bush and Reagan regimes at least openly discussed adult-smoking issues. Studies are conclusive that the largest proven effect of "passive smoking" is on the health of young children and adolescents exposed to high levels of adult smoking. The Surgeon General's landmark 1986 report, *The Health Consequences of Involuntary Smoking*, notes:

> In general, the evidence on active smoking in combination with the dosimetry of involuntary smoking leads to the conclusion that the effects of ETS [environmental tobacco smoke] on a population will be substantially less than the effects of active smoking. The effects of ETS on infants and young children are an important exception.[8]

Dozens of studies have now established serious health damage to children caused by parents' smoking. As summarized in the above report, these include low birth weight, "increased frequency of hospitalization for bronchitis and pneumonia," "increased frequency of acute respiratory illnesses and infections, including chest illnesses...bronchitis, tracheitis, and laryngitis," "chronic respiratory symptoms," "chronic cough and phlegm," "chronic middle ear effusions," chronic and acute asthma, reduced lung capacity, and higher risk of cancer (including leukemia and lung cancer) compared to children of nonsmoking parents.[9] That parents' smoking may be deadly to their children was reinforced by a 1990 Yale University School of Medicine study of 191 non-smokers diagnosed with lung cancer. Researchers found that exposure to second-hand cigarette smoke at home during childhood and adolescence *doubled* the risk of contracting lung cancer in adulthood even if the child never took up active smoking.[10]

The 1986 Surgeon General's report noted that exhaled smoke is actually more dangerous than what goes into a smoker's lungs: "Sidestream smoke is characterized by significantly higher concentrations of many of the toxic and carcinogenic compounds found in mainstream smoke, including ammonia, volatile amines, volatile nitrosamines, certain nicotine decomposition products, and aromatic amines."[11] Children have higher rates of respiration and metabolism than adults, as well as lower body weight, multiplying the effects of constant, concentrated, "passive" cigarette smoke damage.

In 1991, the National Center for Health Statistics reported that children in households of smoking parents were 70 percent more likely to be in "fair to poor health" than children of nonsmokers. This finding elicited a weak demurrer from Health Secretary Louis Sullivan that adults should "consider" not smoking around children.[12] In 1992, Bush's Environmental Protection Agency spent dozens of pages summing up the most recent findings on the health effects of parents' smoking on their children. Its conclusions demolished the notion that adult smoking is a "reasonable decision." Using conservative procedures, the EPA found:

> In children:
> ETS [environmental tobacco smoke] is causally associated with an increased risk of lower respiratory tract infections (LRIs) such as bronchitis and pneumonia. This report estimates that 150,000 to 300,000 cases annually in infants and young children up to 18 months of age are attributable to ETS.
> ETS exposure is causally associated with increased prevalence of fluid in the middle ear, symptoms of upper respiratory tract infection, and a small but significant reduction in lung function.
> ETS exposure is causally associated with additional episodes and increased severity of symptoms in children with asthma. This report estimates that 200,000 to 1,000,000 asthmatic children have their conditions worsened by exposure to ETS.
> ETS exposure is a risk factor for new cases of asthma in children who have not previously displayed symptoms.[13]

Prevention magazine's Children's Health Index 1995 found the exposure of children to household smoke widespread and damaging. Forty-three percent of children lived in households with one or more adult smokers, and children in households where tobacco smoke was present were nearly twice as likely to be rated as unhealthy according to the magazine's indexes.[14]

In my years of working with families, I repeatedly encountered scenes of apartments and houses and trailers, the atmospheres of which were blue with smoke as parents and grown relatives and friends puffed away despite the visible effect on babies, children, and teenagers. "You see I start gasping for air when I have to run down the full court," complained one 15-year-old basketball player whose games I attended. Her pleas to her parents to quit smoking or go outside were ignored. She started sleeping outdoors while in training to avoid the smoke. Out of scores of families with smoking parents, I met only one—a father whose daughter was in track—who would smoke outdoors to avoid damaging his children's health.

These are the mature grownups the tobacco industry guards like a grizzly sow protecting its cubs, the president panders to as "reasonable," and health agencies and lobbyists make excuses for not addressing—except when their smoking offends adults in public. Whether or not a ban on smoking around children (as the National Research Council suggested) could be enforced is not the question yet, though legal approaches would be fully justified. Officials have not even mounted a serious publicity and education campaign to persuade adults of the hazards of blowing smoke down their kids' throats.

Adult smoking is not only a serious health hazard to youths, but a psychological impetus to smoke as well. Rather than being a "pediatric disease" as defined by Food and Drug Commissioner David Kessler, smoking is more accurately viewed as an "adult contagion" transmitted from parents and other influential grownups to children. Some of this transmission may be physical. Parental smoking may induce a "pre-addictive" effect, inferred from the blood levels of cotinine, a derivative of addictive nicotine, which can actually be measured in children exposed to household tobacco smoke.[15] Certainly the nervousness, irritability, and behavior problems children of smoking parents often display at school are consistent with nicotine withdrawal.

While Clinton aides call breathless press conferences over increases in youth smoking, a 1994 Centers for Disease Control report that found a 5 percent to 12 percent increases in smoking among adult women of age to be parents (18-44) since 1990, which was particularly marked among the better-educated women age 25-44, received no notice or concern as to its potentially harmful effects on children.[16] In fact, when studies were issued several years ago on the damaging effects of adult smoking on children, anti-smoking activists such as director Joseph Banzhaf of Action on Smoking and Health vowed to use the data to push for banning smoking from "the work environment and public places" to protect nonsmoking *grownups*.[17] Likewise, the American Public Health Association's policy statement on indoor smoking ignores children and argues only for measures to restrict smoking in the workplace and public places. The disgraceful record: In a decade, public health groups initiated no effective action—not even a minimal publicity and education campaign—to carry out the National Research Council's 1986 recommendation for "eliminating tobacco smoke from the environments of young children."[18] Should they ever decide to do so, I will be happy to donate a prize-winning slogan for health promoters to aim at parents and other adults who marinate children in nicotine haze: "If you won't quit, take your butt outdoors."

Kids! You're too stupid to smoke!

Following my employment by the American Cancer Society in 1990 to coordinate a petition drive to place an initiative to raise Montana's state cigarette tax by 25 cents,[19] I worked with health groups to plan anti-smoking strategy for the 1991 session of the state legislature. The tactical switch I had seen before, in anti-drunk driving politics of the early 1980s, was taking place: When adults get rough, re-focus the attack on kids.

Health lobbies united behind a modest bill to impose a ban on tobacco sales to youths under age 18 and a $50 fine on retailers who sold cigarettes to them. Why? Montana adolescents, who lived in a state which gave them the same rights to buy and use tobacco as adults, were substantially *less* likely to smoke daily by their senior year of high school (11 percent vs 18 percent nationally), less likely to try tobacco (61 percent) than youths nationally (66 percent), less likely to continue smoking if they did (18 percent vs. 27 percent nationally), and less likely to emulate adult examples to smoke. In particular, Montana teens were less likely to use tobacco in any form (including both smoking and chewing) than teens in Minnesota, a state cited by health lobbies as having a model anti-youth-smoking law![20] I notified health lobbies that I would testify against the bill as unfair, unnecessary, and ineffective (a threat that did not seem to terrify them). I wanted renewed efforts to raise cigarette taxes and control illegal sales of tax-free cigarettes from Native American reservations in order to raise the price of smoking for all age groups.

The national Tobacco Institute and several major companies introduced their own bill to ban sales of tobacco to youths. Surprisingly, it was much more punitive than the health lobbies' bill. It provided fines of up to $1,000 against stores who sold cigarettes to kids—and against youths who bought or possessed cigarettes. Throughout the process, the tobacco industry seemed intent on punishing teenagers who smoked as viciously as possible. Its lobbyists were adamant in their insistence that teens were "too immature to make an *adult* decision to smoke."[21]

Although there were ample reasons to doubt the industry's motives on other provisions of the legislation, this aspect of their campaign was singularly puzzling. It is an article of faith among health lobbies that if 70 percent (reported in a 1991 nationwide Gallup Poll) to 90 percent (health agency estimates) of the adults who smoke first took up the habit during adolescent years, smoking can be brought to a crashing halt if teenagers can be kept away from stogies. If that was true, the industry should have been frantic about efforts to cut off its teen market.

Self-destructive industries being rare in my lobbying experience, I wondered what the tobacco industry's exhaustive research into why youths take up smoking[22] was telling them. After all, health lobbies' spirited public-interest crusade against smoking was only one of their many interests, but tobacco sellers' *livelihoods* depend on knowing why people smoke. Why would an industry bring the hammer down with harsh fines and demeaning rhetoric against its future customers—especially in light of the repeated claims by anti-smoking groups that if persons don't take up smoking by age 18, they never will?

As I viewed industry ads and publications, some reasons surfaced. The Tobacco Institute provides free to parents a booklet, "How to Discourage Your Child from Smoking." Since we can be sure that tobacco marketers don't really want to discourage smoking, the subtler message is of interest. Cigarette sellers advise parents to "impress" upon teenagers that they are too "immature" to attempt such a sophisticated "adult" habit and need to be "protected" by laws and concerned parents. In 1990, the Tobacco Institute mailed out sleek red packets to all stores on "preventing" tobacco sales to persons under 18, complete with signs stating that the store would not sell tobacco to minors because, "It's the Law!"[23] Not surprisingly, this campaign by tobacco sellers had no effect in reducing tobacco sales to youths, a study by Massachusetts Medical School researchers found.[24]

Recent industry ads have continued this combination of flattery of adulthood and adult maturity—thematically linked to smoking, intelligent decision-making, and personal freedoms—with denigration of "minors'" immaturity, similarly linked to non-smoking, stupidity, and restrictions on freedoms. If there is a way (deliberately or inadvertently) to promote smoking as a desirable habit among teenagers, the motley tobacco industry, health lobby, and presidential campaign to portray cigarettes as For Mature Grownups Only—a symbol of urbane adulthood and well-deserved personal rights—couldn't be slicker.

From passive to active smoking

In most cases, active smoking in adolescence is simply a continuation of passive smoking in childhood. That parents' smoking is the biggest single factor in youth smoking was a point well established by research and publicized by health officials during the Reagan and Bush administrations.

In 1986, the Surgeon General's report noted that "smoking habits of children are highly correlated with smoking habits of parents."[25] The U.S. Office on Smoking and Health's excellent 1989 *Smoking, Tobacco & Health Fact Book* points out that "seventy five percent of all teenage smokers come from homes where parents smoke." Further, "there are smokers living in 40 percent of all homes where babies are present."[26] Taken together, those factors predicted a future adult smoking rate of about 30 percent, which was very close to the true number among persons in their 20s and 30s in 1994.

In contrast, Clinton health officials have backed away from publicizing the health and behavioral hazards to children presented by adults' smoking. No major reports have been issued on the subject during the Clinton years, and only one mild statement by Surgeon General Joycelyn Elders even mentioned parents' smoking. The 1994 Surgeon General's report, *Preventing Tobacco Use Among Young People*, gave short shrift to parental smoking as a health danger to youths or a factor in youth smoking. The summary report devoted only one sentence to dismissing the issue.[27]

Instead, Clinton health officials blame youth smoking on tobacco advertising and "peer pressure," the latter an echo of the tobacco industry's favorite scapegoat. The "peer pressure" claim, in particular, has become a health-lobby/tobacco-industry cliché. When asked, youths in general don't report much of it—but the small share of youths who smoke do! Only 14.8 percent of the teenagers in a 1995 study of a "high risk adolescent population" (that is, low income, who are more prone to smoking than more affluent teens) reported that they felt any peer pressure "to try cigarettes."[28] Since that is about the percentage of low-income 12-17-year-olds who smoke, that figure makes sense.

Yet the 1991 Gallup Poll reported that 44 percent—three times as many—of the smokers ages 18-29 cited peer pressure as the reason they began smoking (16 percent cited family influences, a negligible 1 percent cited tobacco advertising, less than 1 percent cited tobacco sample promotions, and 34 percent cited other influences).[29] Clearly, the fraction of kids who smoke tend to hang around with the fraction of kids who smoke, as any glance at junior or senior high (or adult, for that matter) social groupings shows in actuality. Is that just the merest of coincidences, as both the tobacco industry and 1994 Surgeon General's report blaming "peer pressure" for youth smoking would have us believe? Or is there some reason these youths choose each other for "peers" in the first place?

Studies emphasizing peer pressure[30] as a motivator in youth smoking have been mixed or inconclusive, especially as to generality of effect,[31] and typically do not examine the competing hypothesis and context of parental smoking. Nor do they consider the fact that parental smoking *predates* peer smoking influences by a decade or more. Nor do they consider research (and common sense) showing that choice of compatible peers typically *follows*, not precedes, choice of the lifestyle peers are supposed to accept.[32] While most of a person's friends have habits similar to those important to adolescents, and adults, it appears that choosing to associate with smoking peers is the result of a person's choice to smoke, not the cause of smoking—or, more accurately, the result of a number of prior conditions and choices about lifestyle of which smoking is only one element.

The effects of tobacco advertising on youth smoking are similarly murky. As noted, only 1 percent of the respondents age 18 and older in the 1991 Gallup Poll cited tobacco ads as an influence on their decision to smoke, but assume for the moment that people are not always aware of the larger influences on their decisions. Research has clarified the issue, but not in the way either tobacco sellers or health lobbyists seem to want to admit. A series of studies in the *Journal of the American Medical Association* in 1991 indicated that tobacco advertising influences cigarette brand choice among beginning smokers (heavily-advertised Marlboro is favored among all age groups, though Joe-Camel-advertised Camels are making much larger gains among teen smokers than among adult smokers, whose brand choice has been established).[33] [34] Interesting in terms of internal industry competition, but so what?

None of the studies answered the crucial question: Whether tobacco advertising induces youths to take up smoking *who would not otherwise*. Health lobbies have made a terrific effort to show that and so far have failed. In fact, the *JAMA* study directly addressed to the subject, a self-reporting survey of teenagers' reactions to Camel promotion, found that while Camel sharply increased its market share among youths who smoke, overall smoking among young people actually *declined* during the 1986-1990 study period.[35] Further, both of the surveys officials regularly cite, the National Household Survey and Monitoring the Future, showed declines in youth smoking during the Camel promotion.

In 1995, the CDC issued a report which concluded that the 6 percent smoking initiation rate among teenagers in 1988, compared to 4.6 percent to 5.5 percent during other years of the 1980s, was due to the introduction of Old Joe. No other factors were examined, nor was the contradiction with other surveys explained. For example, smoking within the previous month by 12-17-year-olds fell by 24 percent (including a decline of 67 percent among 12-13-year-olds) from 1985 to 1990 in the two Household Surveys bracketing the 1988 introduction of the Joe Camel campaign,[36] and by 3 percent among high school seniors from 1987 to 1989 in the Monitoring the Future survey.[37] Even taking the CDC report purely at face value, attributing to it 100 percent accuracy and correctness in its author's conclusion that 1988 represented a "Camel hump" in youths beginning to smoke,[38] perhaps 1 percent of all teens who would not smoke (6 percent versus 5 percent) otherwise were induced to do so by Old Joe. That is roughly one-tenth the percentage induced to smoke by smoking parents (16.3 percent versus 5.6 percent in the Los Angeles survey, shown below) under the same dubious assumption of singularity of cause.

My view of tobacco ads is that they constitute deceptive consumer information and should be restricted to prominently emphasizing that the primary effects of the drug they market are addiction, disease, and death.[39] But when I challenged study authors, in a 1992 letter exchange in *Journal of the American Medical Association*, to show where their research demonstrated that tobacco ads cause youths to smoke, they replied: "It will be another 5 years before we are able to document, with any degree of certainty, the change in the incidence of initiation in teens as a result of this [Camel advertising] campaign."[40] In other words, it hadn't been demonstrated. This is not the way the issue has been portrayed in the press, where tobacco ads are flatly depicted as the reason that adolescents smoke.[41]

But if tobacco ads influence brand choice among beginning smokers, that would explain why cigarette companies design ads to appeal to youths and frantically defend them. It does Camel no good if a teen smoker puffs Marlboros. So yes, tobacco ads are aimed at adolescents to induce those who smoke to pick a particular brand, and the tobacco industry is loathe to admit that its ads are indeed aimed at youths. (The industry would be stupid to target them at anyone else. Very few established smokers switch brands). Further, ads contribute to the general climate, reinforced by the social acceptability of adult smoking, that tobacco addiction is a legitimate and approved habit in the U.S. But there is little or no evidence that ads induce any appreciable number of youths to smoke who would not otherwise. Neither the industry nor health lobbies want to discuss tobacco advertising in light of the evidence that the true issues are the acceptability of adult smoking, the exalted nature of adult status, and the connection of smoking to these two desirable conditions by all interests involved.

Blaming tobacco ads for teen smoking is not a tactic of censorious right-wingers on the same model as, say, blaming MTV for teen sex. Rather, the notion that youths are marionettes of corporate advertising tends to be an argument by those on the left. Note the single-cause concept of teen smoking argued by the corporate-accountability organization In Fact in replying to one of my recent articles:

> In decrying President Clinton's "failure to address adult smoking," Males ignores the addictive nature of nicotine. Virtually all new smokers start before their 18th birthday; their average age is about 14. One million teens will be hooked as new tobacco industry customers this year, and half of them will eventually die from tobacco-related illnesses.
>
> The real breakthrough of Clinton's proposal—and the part most likely to be gutted by a Congress bent on deregulation—is its willingness to go after the *appeal* of tobacco to youth. The parental influence Males blames for youth smoking is, like peer pressure, a red herring brought to us by Philip Morris and RJR Nabisco—intended to obscure and deny the profound social and cultural effects of $6 billion per year in tobacco advertising and promotion. With foes so rich and powerful, why make enemies of 50 million adult smokers?[42]

This is like saying that censoring rock or rap music, which is far more ubiquitous in adolescent lives than tobacco ads, would prevent teenage drug use, violence, and pregnancy—but we should avoid making enemies of adults who are addicted to drugs, who violently abuse youths, and who exert sexual pressures on adolescents. Health groups and agencies demand that heroin, crack, and gambling addicts cease and desist when their habits imperil others, they demand that addicted teenage smokers stop immediately or face fines and penalties, and they demand that addicted adult smokers refrain from smoking where it offends nonsmoking adults. Yet they excuse the damage to children and youths caused by adult smokers because adults are addicted.

Excusing adult smoking behaviors in order to retain public support is more evidence that adolescents are invoked because they are politically powerless, available to buttress whatever larger political point a group, right or left, is trying to make. The price of scoring a point against a destructive industry is that the complexity of adolescent decision-making is swept aside, youths are portrayed as robotized, and the simplistic solution of censoring or restricting what youths can see or do becomes the only solution for which health groups show any enthusiasm.

All teenagers are exposed to the $6 billion per year tobacco advertising barrage, though only a fraction smoke. All teenagers are exposed to "peer pressure," though only a fraction seem to take it seriously. All teenagers are exposed to their own teenagerness. What, then, makes the fraction which smokes different from the majority that seems well able to resist these universal "pressures"?

There is no one answer; even studies that investigate a variety of factors still find that the biggest motivators are individual. But the largest, most logical, most research-pinpointed (and most never-mentioned-by-health-officials) reason for youth smoking appears to be smoking by adults, itself a complex phenomenon. Teen smoking is highly concentrated among certain demographic subgroups—low income, mostly white and Hispanic youths from backgrounds in which adults smoke. Among 26-34-year-olds, 53 percent of those with less than a high school education, and 37 percent of those with a high school diploma but no college (that is, the low-income group) are smokers.[43] This is the prime age group raising kids on housefuls of airborne Carolina carcinogen, and this is indeed the demographic group where most adolescent smokers are found as well—another coincidence!

The interconnection between teen and adult behaviors shows up not just in studies of children of smoking parents, but in larger surveys by sex, race, community, and region as well (Table 5.1). The correspondence between teen and adult smoking across a variety of populations is remarkable. Note that with the fascinating exception of blacks, the ratio of youth to adult smoking is very similar—that is, the youth smoking rate consistently centers around one third of the adult smoking rate—across a variety of region, city size, racial, and gender variables. To guess from the failure of officials and experts to discuss the matter, 25 million children choking on parents' nicotine fog from utero to puberty doesn't make a whit of difference in their health or their decisions to take up the cancer stick.

Yet research has shown that smoking by parents is a significant, general factor promoting youth smoking,[44] [45] strongly affecting elementary[46] and school-age youth, exerting greater influences than peer smoking[47] and socio-economic status,[48] and even displaying continuing, though lesser, effects on smoking by teens as old as college age.[49] Even a 1989 paper rating parents' attitudes more important than parents' behaviors found that children of *smoking* parents who *disapproved* of smoking were more likely to smoke than children of *nonsmoking* parents who *did not disapprove* of smoking.[50]

In 1993, I undertook a direct investigation of the effects of parental smoking on youth smoking. In a survey of 407 Los Angeles and suburban Van Nuys students ages 10-15, I found a discouraging 36 percent came from homes where parents smoke. Those students from homes where parents smoke were three times more likely to be smoking on a daily or weekly basis by age 15 than students from non-smoking households (Table 5.2).

Nineteen out of 20 children of non-smoking parents managed to resist the allures of Old Joe, the Marlboro Man, pressuring peers, and their own adolescent

Table 5.1

Teens smoke like the adults of their sex, race, locale:

Monthly smoking*	Age 12-17	Age 18-34	Ratio youth:adult
Males	9.3%	31.2%	.30
Females	10.0	28.1	.36
Whites	11.0	31.8	.35
Blacks	4.0	23.9	.17
Hispanics	8.4	25.1	.33
Other	10.1	23.6	.43
Large metro	8.1	26.1	.31
Small metro	12.0	30.4	.39
Nonmetro	9.1	36.8	.25
Northeast	10.5	31.6	.33
North Central	11.1	29.1	.38
South	8.4	30.8	.27
West	9.0	26.4	.34
All	9.6%	29.6%	.32

*Data from 1993.
Source: U.S. Substance Abuse and Mental Health Services Administration (1994, October). *National Household Survey on Drug Abuse. Population Estimates 1993.* Washington, DC: U.S. Department of Health and Human Services, Tables 1A-1C, 14A-14H.

stupidity and refrained from the killer weed. Note that this study did not examine the influences of influential adults other than parents, such as stepparents, foster parents, parents' live-in lovers, relatives, brothers and sisters, teachers, coaches, and other "mentors." Other studies have suggested the behavior of these adults may have significant impacts on specific types of youth tobacco patronage, more than peers or tobacco ads.[51]

One would expect that parental smoking would receive much more attention among officials and in the media than tobacco advertising in motivations of teens to smoke. Not at all. Even though Surgeon General Joycelyn Elders and the Office on Smoking and Health authors of the 1994 *Preventing Tobacco Use Among Young People* report admit that research to date does not demonstrate that tobacco advertising is a "causal" factor in youth smoking, its "effects foster the uptake of smoking."[52] In other words, it is officially-decreed as the chief causal factor whether it can be shown as one or not. Research to follow.

Table 5.2

Smoking parents are three times more likely to have smoking kids:

Los Angeles survey of student smoking, 1993	Either or both parents smoke	Neither parent smokes	Odds ratio
Has tried cigarettes	46.1%	28.2%	2.2
Smokes weekly/daily by age 15	16.3	5.6	3.4
Smokes weekly/daily by age 13	13.8	3.8	4.1
Smokes now/will smoke in future	5.0	1.5	3.4
Non-smoker/will never smoke	50.3	71.8	0.4
Education resistance*	25.3	11.8	2.5
Number surveyed (407 total)	141	266	

*Student reported that they would or might smoke in the future after hearing anti-smoking presentation. Results based on 407 students surveyed in four North Los Angeles middle schools, 1993. All results statistically significant by chi-square analysis at $p < .01$.

Source: Males M (1995, August). The influence of parental smoking on youth smoking: Is the recent downplaying justified? *Journal of School Health* 65, 228-231.

Just as the authors of the report were willing to highlight faulty causal factors research does not conclusively support, so were they willing to ignore more genuine causal factors that research does delineate. The report dismissed the issue of parental smoking in its executive summary and devoted only one page to discussing the issue in the body of its report. But the report's own review of 34 studies found that 23, or two-thirds, showed family smoking and adult smoking influences were important inducements for youths to smoke. Instead of focusing on that issue as past federal health reports have done, the 1994 report downplayed it and gravitated toward blaming tobacco ads and youthful "peers" for causing teens to smoke.[53]

Smoking by parents is not 100 percent of the reason teens smoke, either (as the example beginning this chapter and the survey above indicates). It is simply a major risk factor. Surveys indicate that 90 percent to 95 percent of the children of non-smoking parents manage to resist some $100 billion in tobacco advertising during their childhoods and adolescences, they seem to avoid having peers who smoke, and they seem to resist "peer pressure" even if their peers do smoke. In contrast to the dubious and derivative effects of peer pressure and tobacco advertising, parental smoking has shown up as a powerful primary influence on youth smoking in a variety of studies. While only one-sixth of adult smokers cite family members' smoking as an influence on their decision, the practical fact is that studies continue to show that large majorities of teen smokers come from homes where parents smoke, numbers much too high to be dismissed as a coincidence either statistically or as a matter of research.

Teen smoking is not an adolescent irrationality. Rather, it closely follows the particular patterns of smoking adults of their place and time.

Except when teens do better...

Not that the official/media teen-bashing establishment would admit it, but teenagers display by far the largest *decrease* in smoking, and in 1994 display the *lowest* smoking rates, of any age group (Figure 5.3). The percentage of 12-17-year-olds who reported smoking one or more cigarettes within the past month stood at 25.0 percent in 1974, 15.3 percent in 1985, 12.0 percent in 1990, and 9.8 percent in 1994.

Official assertion: Teenagers are risk-takers bamboozled by tobacco ads. Now explain the 61 percent decline in adolescent smoking in two decades, during a period in which the tobacco industry spent well over $100 billion in advertising (Table 5.4).[54]

Manipulating surveys

The above tables, as well as claims about how many people smoke or whether it is going up or down, must be swallowed with a large grain of salt. It is time to discuss one of the most misleading official/media manipulations involving adolescent behavior: The self-reporting survey. Smoking is merely one of the worst examples of the misuse of surveys by officials eager to manipulate public and legislative opinion.

The pattern of survey dissemination through the media is telling. When advocates want to promote more programs or agency appropriations, surveys are selected to show a rise in unhealthy teenage behavior even if other evidence is contradictory. When advocates want to demonstrate their particular policy was a "success," surveys are produced to show the youth behavior is declining even if the results are highly flawed.

Self-reporting behavior surveys are unreliable tools, likely to produce misleading results. A great deal of the misleading picture of modern adolescents is due to the increasing deployment of self-reporting surveys by self-interested groups. Adding to the false picture they can present is the tendency of agencies, which conduct a variety of surveys of adolescent behavior, to micro-analyze insignificant changes and to mix-and-match to produce convenient results. Rarely are the weaknesses of surveys mentioned in the news media, which regularly prints them as cold, hard truth.

Forty years of research on self-reporting surveys have shown that subjects lie about every conceivable matter, generally in the direction of confirming whatever notions the surveyors hold or whatever the subject perceives as the most agreeable answer.[55] Hundreds of examples are found in the research. The 1994 *Sex in America* survey, discussed in Chapter 2, shows that even in a careful, state-of-the-art, anonymous survey of Americans' sexual habits, respondents under-reported their abortions, and probably sexually-transmitted diseases, by a huge amount—50 percent or more. A 1995 *Prevention* magazine survey found that 97 percent of the parents responding declared that their children were fully up to date in their immunizations, while clinical surveys have shown the true figure is around 75 percent.[56] Not surprisingly, children and teenagers are most likely to give answers gauged to please adults, who have the power to reward and punish.[57][58]

The tobacco industry can find from its survey that children connect its advertising logos with anti-smoking sentiment, while health lobbies find that children

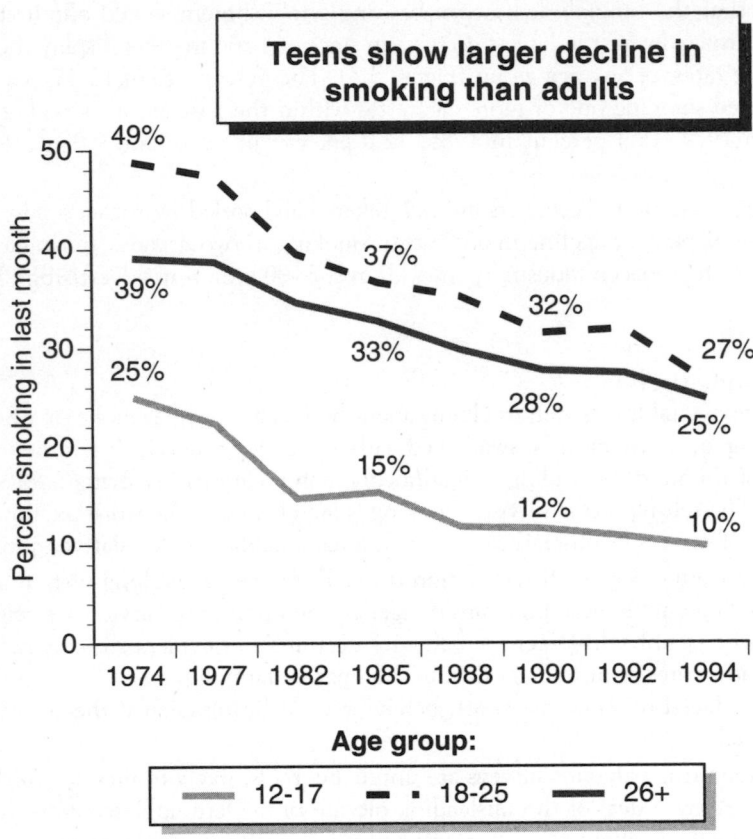

Figure 5.3

Source: *National Household Survey on Drug Abuse*, (1995). Substance Abuse and Mental Health Services Administration, U.S. Department of Health and Human Service See Table 5.4.

view tobacco ad characters as pro-smoking.[59] In neither case do surveyors employ outright deception. They don't have to. The subtle pressures on survey respondents to answer in a manner pleasing to the surveyor are called "demand characteristics" by professionals, and they work to bias results in the desired direction. In the large majority of behavior surveys, questions and interviewing techniques are not deliberately biased, but many subjects are able to detect the idea behind the survey and respond accordingly. A legendary expert on psychological research design, Donald Campbell, has published tongue-in-cheek, yet solid scientific "advice to trapped administrators" on how to use demand characteristics to ensure that any survey proves their programs effective.[60]

Even though surveys are cited in this book, warnings are issued at periodic points in the volume to readers: Self-reporting surveys range from the reasonably truthful to the worst of fiction. The key question for readers of surveys to ask is: What motivations do subjects have to conceal the truth? Embarrassment, disclosure of sensitive behaviors, desire to please the surveyor, avoidance of punishment, perceived social stigma, and many others that might not come immediately to mind

Table 5.4

Teenage smoking has declined faster, and is rarer, than adult smoking:

Decline in smoking:	from 1974 to 1994	from 1985 to 1994	from 1990 to 1994	1994 smoking rate
Age 12-17	–61%	–36%	–18%	9.8%
Age 18-25	–46%	–28%	–17%	26.5%
Age 26-34	–44%	–29%	–15%	28.5%
Age 35+	–33%	–21%	–14%	23.5%

Source: Substance Abuse and Mental Health Services Administration, *Preliminary Estimates from the 1993 National Household Survey on Drug Abuse*, Advance Report No. 7, Dept. of Health & Human Services, July 1994, Table 14B.

affect responses in serious ways.

We would not, for example, expect girls and women who report on surveys that they were raped to claim such a terrifying, humiliating experience if it did not occur. Conversely, we might expect men and young boys to claim sexual achievements when they have not occurred, since promiscuity is often seen as a male value. Smoking, drug use, alcohol use, sexual behavior, and other topics on which adults question teenagers, often in detail and in environments such as schools where students are keenly aware of punishments for not giving "right answers," may produce responses that are anything but the truth and in all different variations from it. Particular skepticism is justified when survey results do not accord with real, measurable "outcomes"—such as births or deaths—a point that is cited repeatedly in this book. When efforts are made to determine the accuracy of self-reports, such as implying to students that their responses would be subject to independent verification, answers can change dramatically.

The popularity of self-reporting surveys persists for a good reason (they are often the only way to obtain information on certain behaviors, such as smoking) and two bad reasons: They provide a numerical, scientific-appearing veneer to program promotion and evaluation, and they often can be counted upon to produce results favorable to the surveyors.[61] In a series of famous studies, Robert Rosenthal and his colleagues at Harvard demonstrated that experimenters subtly (and inadvertently) influence subjects to give the answers and behaviors they expect to find, a powerful biasing influence that he labeled "expectancy effects." These affect not simply psychological experiments. A newspaper reporter who expects to finds high schools full of drugs and violence can be counted upon to find students who will affirm that predisposition.

A particularly egregious, and relevant, example of dubious survey work is a 1991 study by De Paul University researchers published despite its obvious flaws in the *Journal of the American Medical Association*. The study found that "active enforcement" of laws against tobacco sales to youths produced a miraculous decline of 70 percent in youth smoking in the Chicago suburb of Woodridge in just two years.[62] So ecstatic were anti-smoking groups at the prospect of a cheap and easy law enforcement solution to teen smoking that no one examined what the survey really showed. The initial March 1989 survey found self-reported "regular smoking" among affluent Woodridge eighth graders (16 percent) *five times* the national average (3 percent). Uniformed police officers were then repeatedly brought in to schools to lecture students on how they would be searched and arrested and fined for smoking, as 50 youths actually were. In March 1991, a second survey revealed regular smoking among Woodridge eighth graders had dropped to "only" 2.5 times the national average (5 percent versus 2 percent). No "control group" was used to see whether youths in similar communities might have experienced similar reductions in youth smoking without such "active enforcement" techniques, as national surveys indicated were indeed occurring in similar fashion among eighth graders not subject to police lectures and searches.[63] The more realistic conclusion is that Woodridge kids were playing with the surveys, not reporting real behaviors.

Playing with surveys is common. In my survey of Los Angeles middle school youth, I built in questions to determine if subjects were lying. Six classes with 286 students took the survey on their smoking behaviors. Students then heard an anti-smoking lecture by a speaker forced to use a voice enhancer because of a smoking-caused laryngectomy, provoking a horrified reaction (even some shrieks) among students to the prominent hole in his throat. After the lecture, students then took the same smoking survey immediately.

As expected, there was a 41 percent decrease in the proportion of students who said they would or might smoke in the future. Good. That's what an anti-smoking lecture is supposed to do. But there was also a 21 percent decrease in the proportion of students who said they smoked within the previous week. Since it is impossible to change a *past* behavior, especially on surveys administered 45 minutes apart, one-fifth of the students who reported smoking were exaggerating on the initial survey or minimizing on the second one.[64] Either that, or the presentation achieved a milestone in super-effectiveness: Retroactive smoking cessation.

Similar serious discrepancies have emerged in official surveys. The Household Surveys noted above report a large, continuous decline in youth and adult smoking over the past 20 years. The University of Michigan's *Monitoring the Future* surveys of high school seniors and young adults in school settings report a decline in smoking through the mid-1980s, then a levelling off and slight rise in the 1990s, for both age groups.[65] Thus the two major surveys show very different results. Rather than analyzing these differences or even pointing them out to the press, agencies and officials have chosen to cite whatever results best fit their needs.

A case in point is this morning's (5 October 1995) *Los Angeles Times*, which contains yet another bewailing of the supposed "increase of nearly 20 percent" in smoking among California youths in the last three years.[66] In absolute terms, this meant a rise of less than 2 percent in the low level of California youth smoking. Surveys are not accurate enough to document behavior changes with that kind of precision, as the following shows.

The National Institute on Drug Abuse's National Household Survey is potentially the most accurate—or least inaccurate—to use to compare youth and adult smoking. It employs a sampling technique designed to reach a cross-section of households, interviews youths not in school, and interviews youths and adults under roughly the same conditions over the longest period. Yet in its 1994 report, this survey uncovered a factor that should cast doubt on whether surveys accurately reflect true behaviors.

How subjects answered questions on smoking depended on how they were asked (Table 5.5). Whoops. One in five subjects lied in one interview or the other, including substantially larger numbers of adolescent and young adult subjects than older subjects. Complete privacy of response revealed a lot more smokers, who could have been more truthful, or more prone to exaggeration, because of complete anonymity. As noted in discussing sex surveys, subjects may use anonymity to embellish as well as conceal.

Table 5.5

Are smoking surveys really accurate?

Smoked in past month		Asked face to face	Asked in private questionnaire
Age	12-17	9.8%	18.9%
	18-25	26.5	34.6
	26-34	28.5	32.4
	35-older	23.5	27.9
	Total	23.4%	28.6%

Source: Substance Abuse and Mental Health Services Administration (1994, October). *National Household Survey on Drug Abuse* (1994-B Sample). Rockville, MD: U.S. Department of Health and Human Services, Tables 14A, A14A.

If officials are going to present such self-reports as fact, they should at least point out that both the Household and Monitoring surveys show teenage smoking declining faster than adult smoking over the past two decades. Currently, however, the Office on Smoking and Health compares surveys of students taken in school with those of adults taken over the telephone. When surveys employing different settings and techniques are mixed and matched, real distortions can occur. There are now a number of different surveys of smoking and different combinations available, allowing various interests to arrive at whatever conclusion they want.

Every social problem is a "teenage problem"

The singular misdirection of American anti-smoking policy has been its preoccupation with the relatively unimportant fact that most adult smokers took their first drag during adolescence. Since it would be difficult to cite any behavior by adults that does not have some root in child or teenage years, every problem in society thus becomes a "teenage problem." Because adults are presumed to be "addicted" or entrenched in their behaviors, they become exempt from scrutiny or responsibility, except when their smoking annoys non-smoking adults (then self-control is demanded).

The simplistic youth-blaming fixation is reflected in former Surgeon General Joycelyn Elders's letter summing up the *Preventing Tobacco Use Among Young People* report:

> The public health movement against tobacco use will be successful when young people no longer want to smoke... When young people no longer want to smoke, the epidemic itself will die.[67]

Elders could have said that the smoking epidemic will abate when giant industries are no longer allowed by her government to secure billions of dollars in annual profits from freely marketing in millions of retail outlets an addictive and dangerous product that is publicly subsidized, undertaxed, and misleadingly advertised. She could have blamed state and federal authorities knuckling under to the enormous economic power and the legal bribes of tax revenues and private contributions from the tobacco industry. She could have criticized public health officials for lacking the most skeletal backbone to confront smoking adults over the serious diseases and irresponsible modeling that careless practice of their nicotine addiction inflicts on children. She could have ordered her own disease control agencies to stop slanting reports to excuse smoking adults, enable their continued addiction, and hold out futile promises that restrictions on youths will prevent their smoking without inconveniencing grownups.

Elders could have announced a major campaign to demand that adults finally display adult maturity by quitting smoking or accepting restrictions on their practice of it that clearly communicate the seriousness of smoking to children. She could have argued for measures to reduce youth poverty, since the report and surveys show that poorer youths and adults are two to three times more likely to smoke than are wealthier ones.[68] As the nation's top health officer overseeing the nation's leading anti-smoking agency, Elders could have accepted full adult responsibility for the perpetuation of tobacco addiction and targeted adults for the solution, instead of petulantly blaming primarily low-income "young people" for creating the "epidemic." But that would have required genuine leadership and health policy, not the scapegoating electoral politics the Clinton administration has substituted for serious analysis and planning.

The more important issue is that smoking remains an acceptable behavior for adults to practice cheaply and with few restrictions, which gives it the stamp of official approval—particularly to those youths whose closest grownup role models also recommend it by their behaviors. To argue, as top health advocates do, that "adolescents are the tobacco issue," or that "by addressing teens, you could effectively solve the smoking problem,"[69] ignores the interconnection of teenage and adult behaviors. It also claims to know the unknowable. We do not know whether the *individuals* who smoke, even if we had forcibly prevented them from smoking during adolescence, would have taken up the habit in adulthood. A great deal of the impetus to smoke, even for those predisposed by social and family influences, resides in a welter of individual characteristics we know little about.

The worst aspect of the official claim—that because teenagers are responsible for the smoking epidemic, teenagers should be singled out to end it—is that it removes a powerful motive for grownup behavior improvement: To safeguard their own health, as parents, and that of their children exposed to their behaviors. It is discouraging that a recent study found decreased parental involvement in children's decisions to smoke,[70] which coincides with a growing school and health campaign whose message is: "Science, education, and laws can prevent teenage smoking; parents need not be involved."

It's discouraging because the healthiest influence teenagers have on adults is that youths do not accept grownup rhetoric, but grownup behavior, as their model. Through 1988, 50 percent of the adult smokers reported having quit,[71] some 40 million. Adolescents respond not to assertions and sermons, but to that kind of day-to-day reality of their observations of how grownups act. Their greater connection to reality is why teenagers are so often accused of defying hypocritical official morality crusades.

A society that attempts to enforce a doctrine that tolerates, even justifies, unhealthy behaviors among adults but angrily denounces teenagers for emulating them is promoting harmful lifestyles among both age groups. The most vigorous measures to reduce adult smoking, including higher taxes and increasingly stringent campaigns to prevent adult smoking around youths, should be paramount. The best ways to reduce adolescent smoking are to signal true social disapproval by raising the cost and inconvenience of smoking, and to reduce the number of adolescents growing up in households where adults smoke. The evidence is that many teenagers would be allies in a campaign to reduce parents' smoking if official timidity at offending grownups could be overcome.

The most pathetic rationale I hear from teenage smokers is their belief, repeated many times in recent press reports, to wit: "If cigarettes were that dangerous, they wouldn't let stores sell them." Typically, officials are quoted expressing incredulity that teens could still take up smoking after all the official warnings and ridiculing as naive the adolescent notion that tobacco must not really be that addictive and harmful.[72] Indeed it is naive. If any education system was reckless enough to employ me as a health consultant, I would make such adolescent naivete my prime target.

If there is one point school and community health programs should stress above all, it is that today's youths cannot rely on adults to look out for the interests of the young. It is amusingly idealistic for any young person to believe that today's grownups, including health agency chiefs and top tobacco executives, are concerned about anything except our immediate grownup selves. It is disastrously naive for teenagers to believe that today's health officials would take the expected vigorous action—such as sharply higher taxes, restrictions on misleading advertising, tough enforcement of laws against illegal tobacco smuggling and tax-free sales, and strict rules about smoking around nonsmokers even when the latter are children without political power—against a product that addicts and injures millions and kills 400,000 every year. American adults have amply demonstrated that we can't handle the freedom to use a product as addictive and contagious as cigarettes without harming ourselves and the kids who depend on us. Frankly admitting that would be the first step in a realistic campaign against tobacco.

Welcome to Marble-Row Country

That smoking in past aeons has been an enviable habit for youths to take up can be seen from literature of the day. Note peer admiration for Huckleberry Finn's habit. Temperance reformers also rallied against cigarettes, and fourteen states passed general cigarette prohibition laws from 1895 to 1914. Prior to World War II, smoking remained a more genteel and casual habit, widespread but not intense.[73]

The emergence of nicotine as a prevalent drug of addiction turned up in the 1940s and 1950s. Soldiers returning from World War II and Korea sported full-blown habits nourished by free cigarette distribution at military posts. As cigar-chomping comedian Alan King reminisced of his former habit, Bogey, Bacall, the Duke, Murrow, everyone in the public eye sported a stick. Smoking peaked in 1960s, with surges in adolescent and adult usage in 1963 and, to a lesser extent, in 1973.

Smoking was known to be unhealthy. Cigarettes, labeled "coffin nails" in *Scientific American* as early as 1926, were so described when I was in elementary school in 1956. We smoked frequently (without inhaling), mostly stealing our parents' smokes one or two at a time. I quit by age eight and became a vicious activist against the habit, joining with small friends in planting chemically-treated wood splinters in our addicted parents' cigarettes so that they would explode upon igniting (unwise, since severe corporal punishment was a family value in 1958 Oklahoma). *Mad* magazine's 1966 "Famous Marble-Row Funereal Black" satire—"you get a plot you like" with "our famous 'flip-top' box," backed by a western graveyard where "we've planted young cowboys who died from those cigarette slugs in the chest"[74]—caused much parental annoyance and was tacked to many a juvenile wall.

Still, before the 1960s, the devastating respiratory and heart damage in mostly older adults caused by cigarette smoking had not yet emerged to serve as deterrent to teenage initiation or adult continuation. At that time, perhaps 40 percent of all teenagers and 50 percent of all adults smoked. What followed this deadly excess is instructive to those who believe government must force and propagandize youth to produce change.

Throughout health, and particularly smoking, campaigns, authorities have repeatedly tried to tie behaviors to major public events. The idea that individuals can make decisions on their own observation or for reasons unconnected to either pro- or anti-smoking media images (such as my own decision in elementary school not to smoke because of irritation at the habits of my smoking parents) is too often dismissed, and with it important insights into why people take up, don't take up, or give up bad habits. The 1964 Surgeon General's report on *Smoking and Health* is credited with initiating the decline in postwar smoking rates. It may have, but in the short term smoking surged upward in the late 1960s.

The large subsequent decrease in adolescent smoking during the 1970s has never been convincingly explained. The biggest declines in smoking began in the mid-1970s amid stark evidence that heavy postwar smoking rates were beginning to take their toll. Adult respiratory disease deaths tripled from 1950 to 1975. Glamorous images of smoking media stars of 1955 were replaced by cancerous checkouts among aging notables of 1975. Few families were spared the tumbrels of the black nicotine plague.

In the 1970s, two million smokers died of cancer and chronic obstructive pulmonary disease—my father, uncle, and grandfather among them. Millions of America's vast "smoking generation" hooked in postwar years set themselves to kick the killer weed before it booted them. Millions of nonsmokers vowed to help them via nicety or mayhem.

As a result, an unusually large number of young 1970s adolescents thinking of taking up malignancy sticks were privileged to witness, in their own living rooms, the agony of millions of adults (to wit, their parents) going through the nervous, fumbling, fuming, morosely cursing stopping-and-backsliding ordeal of quitting. Any household who has harbored a quitting smoker knows the enlightening drama these children watched their beloved role models undergo.

But quit many did. As psychologist Lawrence Bauman points out, concern for children is a major incentive for parents to quit smoking to set "an indelible positive example."[75] By 1988, the Centers for Disease Control reported that 37 percent of the 18-34-year-old and 47 percent of the 35-49-year-old former smokers had quit—some 25 million people, mostly parents.[76] Some of this may have been Mark Twain-style quitting—so easy it can be done every week. Those who didn't, more often than not, joined the skyrocketing toll of the "smoking boom" generation, setting a less positive but also effective example.

With such powerful in-home education going on, it is no surprise that surveys of the mid and late 1970s documented rapidly rising numbers of teens realizing the dangers of smoking—and acting on that knowledge. *Senior Scholastic* reported in 1981 that "puffing is passé," citing a rise to 75 percent of all 1980 teens who believed their peers disapproved of smoking: "The kind of social approval (for non-smoking) that influences people of all ages."[77] The 1970s were also a period in which the 1960s decline in child poverty was beginning to pay dividends. Sharply increased college enrollment and job opportunity among teens escaping from poverty was paralleled by sharply declining misbehaviors, of which smoking was one.

Clearly, this kind of rapid, major attitude change and health success story among the young should have drawn excited attention from health authorities. It did not.

The fascinating drop in youth smoking did not fit into the prevailing 1980s theory that teenagers are so irrational that force, government initiative, and program persuasion are required to improve youth behavior. It did not coincide with any formal educational measures, which in the 1970s had not changed much from those of previous decades, or law enforcement efforts—in fact, laws against teen smoking were universally unenforced during this period. The tobacco industry tried to lure new smokers, spending $40 billion on advertising from 1975 to 1985. Yet during that period, the Monitoring survey showed puffing among high school seniors fell 20 percent, while the Household survey showed overall adolescent smoking rates dropped by 40 percent.[78]

The facts were there: Four million fewer teens were smoking in 1981 than in 1970. Adolescents were still trying tobacco, but they were rejecting it on a massive scale: Three out of four who tried smoking did not continue it.[79] They were rejecting it on their own without being forced, arrested, lectured, or compulsively treated.

The growing irrationality and degeneration of "prevention" programs shows up most clearly in the anti-teen-smoking campaign, which began in the late 1980s and copied the anti-teen-drinking campaign's increasingly shrill and punitive stance. States and localities instituted and added bite to anti-smoking measures aimed at teens. Whole new arrest categories were created. In one city, juveniles were forcibly searched for tobacco after being stopped for even minor traffic tickets. In another, locals offered to provide guards for cigarette vending machines to make "citizens' arrests" of juveniles caught buying. Fines for youth smoking were implemented, then raised, with local communities in states like Minnesota free to add on tougher penalties still.[80]

Demands for more laws, stronger sanctions, and tougher enforcement (including "stings" and vigilante arrests) against youthful smoking accompanied intensifying education regimens. Schools began kicking students out of extra-curricular activities and requiring substance abuse courses of those who used tobacco at all. These types of tactics won the approval of U.S. Secretary of Health and Human Services Louis Sullivan, who declared that practically any measure was justified to stop youths from the "slow suicide" of tobacco addiction—any measure that didn't inconvenience adult smokers or the tobacco industry, that is. Did it work? Officials' own Household and Monitoring surveys reported that the rapid decline in teen smoking during the 1970s and early 1980s slowed in the late 1980s and leveled off in the early 1990s.[81]

The Montana Student Tobacco Referendum

If health lobbies jettisoned their blind hostility against teenagers, they would realize youths are their greatest allies in the anti-smoking struggle. When asked to decide policy, even restrictions on their own behavior, rather than being ridiculed and subjected to adult manaclings, adolescents *as a group* (not just the sycophantic teens grownups elevate as the "voice of youth") can be counted upon to endorse startlingly radical and reasonable measures. An example:

In October 1991, 51,000 junior and senior high students in sparsely-settled "Marlboro Country" trooped to vote by secret ballot at school polls in a unique "student tobacco referendum" held by the Montana Legislature and Office of Public Instruction. The relentless advocacy of several legislators and high school lobbyists led by the bill's sponsor, Democratic State Representative Dorothy Bradley, pushed the issue through. Many thought it was a terrible idea. "If they vote wrong, this could be a major promoter of smoking and chewing among kids," one prevention official declared at a meeting in the state capitol, echoed by other professionals in attendance.

The student referendum followed on the heels of a spectacularly successful December 1990 secret-ballot vote by 2,000 junior and senior high students in Bradley's city of Bozeman. Eighty percent resoundingly prohibited all tobacco smoking and chewing by students, teachers, staff, and visitors, regardless of age or status, on school grounds anywhere anytime, across-the-board policies recommended as particularly effective.[82] The delighted Bozeman School Board ratified the sweeping tobacco ban in which student, staff, and teacher votes melded in a vehement anti-nicotine landslide. "Our kids and staff acted very, very responsibly," Superintendent Paula Butterfield announced.

Butterfield and Bozeman student leaders, along with the state 4-H clubs and initially skeptical anti-tobacco health lobbies, backed the statewide student referendum proposed by Bradley's bill in the 1991 Legislature. "Students will comply more with a law that comes from them," Bozeman senior president Jennifer Pohl told lawmakers and the press. "It's up to us to pass the law and them to follow it," fumed a conservative legislator, a smoker. "We can't let children make policy." The student tobacco referendum was killed, reinstated, killed, resurrected, finally passed the Senate by five votes and was signed by Republican Governor Stan Stephens.

Three hundred and fifty-eight Montana schools conducted the referendum in the first two weeks of October 1991. Some, like Missoula's April Hill School, celebrated the vote with fanfare, formal debates, and official polling booths. Others tersely handed out the ballots and counted them in open resentment over a state mandate.

When the secret ballots were counted in a state which had become the tobacco industry's chief symbol of "Marlboro Country" rugged smokerism, teenagers declared a flat "no" to their generation using tobacco. Of 51,233 students in grades 7-12 who voted (80 percent of those enrolled), 30,244 endorsed a voluntary plan by which store owners would refuse to sell cigarettes or tobacco to those under age 18. In Bozeman, student support for the youth tobacco ban, while supportive by a 63 percent margin, fell far short of the 79 percent vote for mandatory anti-smoking controls aimed at adults and youth alike. "Students are much more willing to support a policy aimed at all age groups than they are to vote for one aimed just at their age group," Montana state chemical dependency chief Spencer Sartorius concluded.

Even given the negative wording of the referendum, 92 of 157 senior highs, 204 of 221 junior highs, and 46 of 56 counties ratified the anti-tobacco referendum. Montana adults were not so wise. In the 1990 general election, voters by a 59 percent margin rejected a modest 25-cent increase in the state's cigarette tax after the tobacco industry spent $1.4 million ($5 for each of Montana's 300,000 voters) to oppose it.

One clear trend in the divergence between adult and teen attitudes toward smoking showed up in the student balloting. At the time, Montana had no laws or ordinances against teenage smoking or tobacco purchases, except for the cities of Missoula, Billings, and Livingston. In those three Montana communities where local officials had pursued punitive fines and arrests against youthful tobacco users, senior high students (in contravention of their peers statewide) resoundingly voted "no" on tobacco controls, and even junior high students were muted in their support.[83]

The Clinton withdrawal

The weaknesses of Clinton smoking policy helped sabotage the most promising experiment in reducing tobacco use—Canada's $2 per pack cigarette tax enacted in the 1980s. Contrast the simplistic teen-blaming attitudes of U.S. officials with those of Canadian officials on youth smoking:

> "There's no magic bullet here," concluded Bill Maga, a senior policy analyst
> in the Health Ministry. "This is a complex social-psychological phenomenon that
> goes beyond just one element, be it price or advertising. It goes to a lot of factors
> —who your parents are, social backgrounds, friends."

David Sweanor, of Ottawa's Non-Smokers' Rights Association, argued that increased cigarette prices through higher taxation are the best means of reducing youth and adult smoking. In contrast, "the Clinton administration is focusing its anti-smoking campaign on teenagers, but it has not proposed upping prices with increased taxes."[84] The reason, of course, is that raised taxes annoy tobacco state lawmakers, the tobacco industry, and 50 million tobacco-addicted grownups.

Yet higher taxes seem to work, not just with adolescents but, more importantly, with their grownup role models. "Smoking among teenagers has dropped dramatically as the price of cigarettes has shot up over the past 15 years," Health and Welfare Canada reported. As the real prices of cigarettes rose by 150 percent from 1979 to 1991, smoking by Canadian teenagers dropped from 43 percent to 15 percent[85]—a bigger decline than in the U.S. Smoking among Canadian adults, once 20 percent higher than among American adults, declined to virtually the same level by the mid-1990s. Studies have also repeatedly linked past increases in U.S. cigarette taxes to large reductions in smoking, especially among teens.[86]

But by 1994, Canada's tobacco tax was in trouble and slated for rollback in major provinces, beginning with Quebec. Why? "Cigarette smuggling... between the United States and Canada," the Canadian health ministry noted. The worst influx was in illegal tax-free cigarettes from U.S. Native American reservations.[87] Gunplay between rival cross-border tobacco smugglers occurred, as for any dangerous drug required by a mass of addicts. To stem the scourge of illegal and increasingly violent enterprises dedicated to smuggling smokes, Canada threw in the towel. The failure of Clinton to pursue vigorously the 75-cent per pack cigarette tax he originally promised, as well as the failure to enforce laws against tax-free cigarette sales to non-Native Americans, is directly responsible for undermining Canada's tobacco tax.

For reasons of political popularity, decades of anti-smoking policies targeting both teens and adults have been replaced by Clinton's current rhetorical attack aimed solely at teenage smoking. The administration's new proposals—regulations on the format and color scheme of cigarette ads, the placement of vending machines, tobacco as a drug only as it applies to youths—are pointless and trivial. For example, the policy demands that tobacco ads in publications with youth readership be restricted to *black and white formats*. These kinds of strategies are winning cheers from anti-tobacco groups as revolutionary? And consider the disastrous trade-offs. The administration's endorsement of adult smoking as a reasonable choice, its support for millions of dollars in federal subsidies for tobacco growers, and its explicit recognition of the economic importance of the tobacco industry indicate these policies are not meant to work. The point is to blame an American health disaster, which adults practice, promote, and profit from, on the children and adolescents who suffer most from adult irresponsibility.

The minority of teens who smoke do so because of the widespread acceptance of smoking by adults. That acceptance is advertised by 50 million adult smokers. By a multi-billion-dollar legal industry selling them. By the cheap price of cigarettes in millions of outlets. By a media which profits from tobacco ads reinforcing smoking as mature. By a president who endorses the industry line that adult smoking is "a reasonable decision" and merits no further regulation. By lawmakers who subsidize tobacco growers and thrive on tobacco dollars. By health groups who countenance parents' smoking even when it harms children. And by official political charades that shrink from confronting tough issues like raising tobacco taxes but pass off berating teens and fiddling with ad colors as real policy. These are the multitude of ways nicotine addiction is advertised to American youths, ones which render cartoon Camels, Montana cowboys, and Virginia Slims to supporting roles.

The most effective mix of anti-smoking policies would yoke agency health promotions to the intense dislike American youth harbor for smoking to bring about vital change in the one-third of American adults of parenting age who continue to smoke. An unrecognized symbolic milestone in the tobacco-corrupted adult political world, the Montana Student Tobacco Referendum demonstrated that teenagers are the most staunch allies of the strongest anti-smoking measures health agencies want to advance. They are in a key position to affect smoking parents, as Maureen Bomactao and her age-mates did on their own initiative. All that they need is organizing support from the health lobbies who today remain preoccupied with justifying adult nicotine addiction while excoriating teenage motives and decisions.

6. Doped on Duplicity

Marijuana is a very dangerous drug that can well cause you to fight for your health and your very life in a hospital emergency room.

—Lee Brown, White House drug policy coordinator, 1995[1]

I often wonder what happened to the half-dozen hippies with whom I shared red wine, joints and acid tabs in idyllic Sypes Hot Springs one cold starry late spring night in 1969 twelve miles up the rugged Big Sur River trail. We did in fact solve all the problems the world had or ever contemplated before the sun glimmered through the redwoods. Then we strapped on our backpacks and set out into the 1970s to cause more of them.

I picture them now, still in granny glasses and ripped jeans, storming the local school board to demand just-say-no, zero-tolerance programs to suppress the "epidemic" of pot smoking among "children" (7 percent of whom were cited in the most recent survey to have ignited the killer weed within the past month).[2] I see my Sixties sulphur spring smokers, as I have seen so many of my age and background, 40-ish, in anger and fear, berating public authorities to punish their teenagers for taking drag, a smoke, a beer—lord help us, a tab or a bong. I meet ex-hippies running DARE programs, advising parents not to tell their kids about their '60s highs. An unfair image, I know. We can't all be as bad as Bill, Al, Newt, and Clarence, '60s ex-tokers who in 1995 endorsed mandated urine-testing of school students for drugs.

I inhaled, I turned on, I tuned in. Not a lot, but I enjoyed it. Then the Sixties ended. Some of us even knew it. I did mild hallucinogens when the occasion called, maybe a weekend or two a month at most, like the mass of Sixties kids who never were the inveterate druggies of legend. We did not journey to the center of our minds, touch the sky in Itchycoo Park, or beautify the streets of San Francisco. We just had a fine and miserable time, and the radicals among us still managed to roll out (red eyed and tongue parched) for the 1969 San Francisco Moratorium and the Vietnam Day sit-in. I was never more than what Frank Zappa derided as a "phony hippie" in the first place—maybe not as pathetic as those who had to "ask the Chamber of Commerce how to get to Haight Street" to "smoke an awful lot of dope" and sport "a psychedelic gleam in the eye at all times"[3]—but no claimant to counterculture stardom. I am privileged to have come of adolescence in what an excellent PBS documentary correctly termed a "dark time." But the Sixties are over, gone, even (can it be?) unlamented and repealed. In 20 years it's been a rare day when I've just said yes.

Rolling Stone revealed the extent of our new-found hypocrisy in a 1987 poll of 816 Americans age 18-44 by Peter D. Hart Research:

Forty-six percent said they have used drugs. Of those under age thirty-five, the figure was 50 percent. Marijuana had been used by twice as many respondents as speed, cocaine, and hash, which have each been tried by about 20 percent. More than one in ten have used psychedelic drugs like LSD. Those figures mean 40 million people in this generation have used drugs at some time in their lives. Almost 20 million still do.

But they are very clear on what their children should be taught about drugs. Seventy-four percent would disapprove if their own children experimented with drugs. (When only parents were asked, the figure was 94 percent). The generation that said yes to drugs now joins Nancy Reagan in telling its kids to just say no.

We ourselves, writing in *Rolling Stone*, assured us that our motives are noble:

> At first glance, this conservatism might seem hypocritical: "It was all right for us to try this, but you'd better not." Yet in the end, it may be less despicable than that. It's not so much that they want to deny the next generation the freedom to experiment. It's more that they acknowledge the high toll exacted for that experimentation.[4]

But it's not quite as drippy as that, is it? The poll showed only one fifth of the pot smokers, one fifth of the heavy drinkers, and one third of the hallucinogen and cocaine users regretted having used drugs as they did. Half of our drug contingent *still* uses drugs, and half of them as much as they ever did. That doesn't sound like a bedrock just-say-no ethic.

Nor does the draconian zero-tolerance, mandatory-test, mandatory-sentencing punitiveness toward drugs in the 1980s and '90s bespeak a tolerant generation willing to let its kids "experiment" but worried, as any parent would be, that they might go too far. Being expelled from school or imprisoned in the '90s for drug taking no worse than 40 million of us admitted doing in our growing-up is to inflict what leading addiction researcher Stanton Peele branded as a "'cure'... worse than the problem."[5] Once again, we're lucky our more traditional parents' attitudes toward us were more open-minded than ours toward our kids.

Yes, Baby Boomers did indeed suffer from drug abuse. The scary part, for us and our kids, is that it is not behind us. The worst drug abuse crisis among my '60s cohorts, as well as among the '50s generation (who used drugs far less in their youth) and '70s generation (who took dope even more than we did), is going on *right now*. Our current rage at even the most minimal and harmless marijuana use among youth, reflected in the extremism of public officials, has less to do with today's teenagers than with conscripting today's young to become casualties in the Baby Boom's war with ourselves.

Killer middle-agers on dope

In the 1990s, the United States has a genuine drug disaster on its hands, quite probably the worst in our history. It begins with tobacco (which kills 400,000 every year) and alcohol (100,000). All illegal drugs—counting all accidents, suicides, homicides, and chronic deaths attributed to drugs—dispatched at least 14,000 in 1993. At least one-fourth of these "drug deaths" are in conjunction with alcohol, and half involve pharmaceutical drugs that may be legally prescribed.

After a decade of the most intensive anti-drug "war" in American history, consuming hundreds of billions of dollars and effecting more than 10 million arrests, the results are as follows:

- A record 12,000 Americans died from drug overdoses and chronic drug abuse in 1993, the highest rate of drug fatality in this century and probably our history. The chief victims: Adults ages 30-54, particularly men. The chief killers: Medical drugs, cocaine/crack, and heroin.[6]

- Drug death rates, which had declined by 25 percent from 1970 to 1983, reversed and rose 50 percent from 1983 to 1993 as the drug war intensified (Figure 6.1).

- Drug-related murders tabulated by the Federal Bureau of Investigation,[7] which previously had been stable, rose from around 500 per year during the 1970s and early 1980s to 2,000 in 1993 (Figure 6.2).

- In the past five years in particular, drug abuse deaths among middle-aged adults of all races rose 150 percent, and drug-related emergency room visits involving middle-aged adults doubled. Today, a 40-year-old is 15 times more likely to die from drug abuse than is a high-school-age youth (Figure 6.3).

- In the last decade, 25,000 more Americans died from drug abuse and drug violence than if the low drug death rates of the early 1980s had prevailed.

- The War on Drugs was launched in 1983 specifically to eliminate drug abuse and crime. The results: From 1983 to 1993, drug abuse death rates doubled, and drug murder rates tripled.[8]

- Preliminary estimates by the National Safety Council for 1994 show another major increase in drug overdose deaths, up 25 percent from 1993.[9]

Today, Americans are more in danger from illegal drugs than ever before. There is no age group, race, or geographic region untouched by multiplying drug fatality. Given the massive, open-ended resources poured into it, the issue of whether the "war on drugs" caused some of the massive death increase, or failed to address the chief causes of drug malaise, is simply the same question asked two ways. The death toll among middle-aged adults, particularly men ages 30-55, from heroin, cocaine/crack, and medical drugs has been the most severe, more than doubling since 1980 and now claiming a record 7,000 lives every year.

Figures 6.1, 6.2, and 6.3 show the results of a decade of drug hypocrisy and self-serving politics among America's top health and policy officials. A sharp rise in drug deaths and drug murders among both teens and adults in the 1980s, reversing a 1970s pattern of stable or declining trends, is one officials are loathe to discuss and the media remains too timid to publicize.

Conscientious officials would frankly admit this alarming disaster and open the agenda to far-reaching reforms. Instead, the response of federal drug authorities to the mushrooming crisis of adult drug abuse, the tip of whose iceberg is revealed in growing thousands of deaths and hundreds of thousands of emergency room treatments every year, is not simply one of denial, but scapegoating and diversion.

In the face of a real and growing national drug tragedy, it may seem astoundingly perverse that federal health officials have frenzied themselves and saturated the ever-spongelike media with a barrage of hysteria over what Shalala deplored as "casual use, single-time use" of marijuana by teenagers. *Teenagers, marijuana,* and

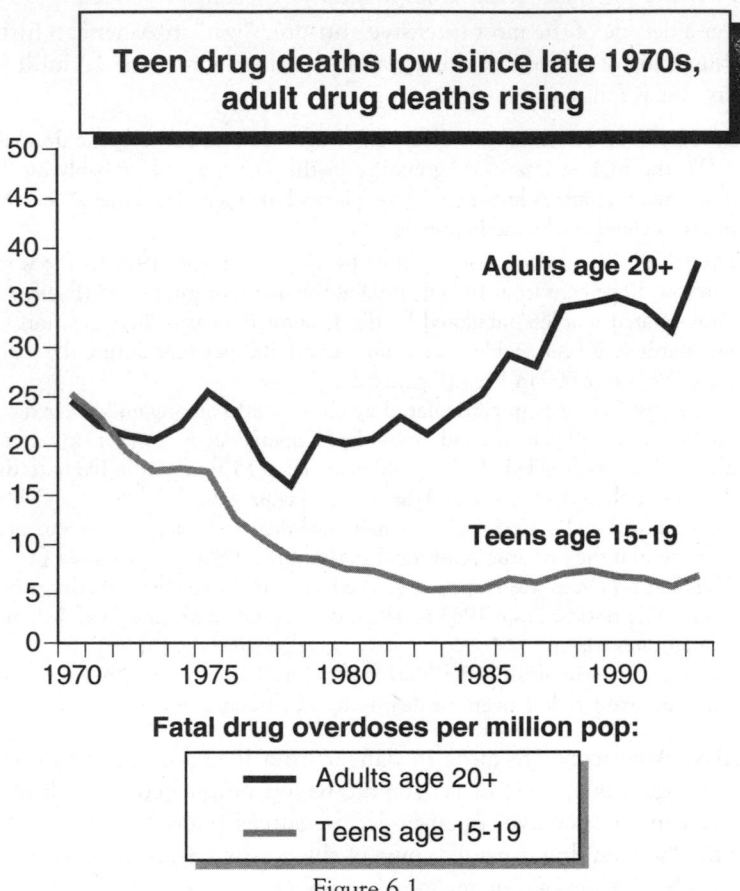

Figure 6.1
Source: National Center for Health Statistics (annual). *Vital Statistics of the United States*, 1970-1990, and advance data.
See Ref. 6.

casual or one-time use—exactly the age group, drug, and style of use *least* likely to produce difficulties now or in the future.

As with smoking, teenagers are blamed by officials and the media for the "drug crisis." As with smoking, they are the age group, other than pre-teen children, that has the least to do with it. In families and communities, children and youths appear to be suffering more coping with adults' drug abuse than with their own. Not only do teenagers suffer far fewer injuries and deaths from drug use than do adults, teens have not been a significant part of the nation's drug problem in nearly 20 years. As in the 1970s, when the National Institute on Drug Abuse fabricated a "teenage drinking crisis" to win more funding, today's drug agencies led by top administration officials and consultants cynically manipulate public and legislative attention with tales of teenage pot demise in a ploy to win hundreds of millions of dollars for drug war interests.

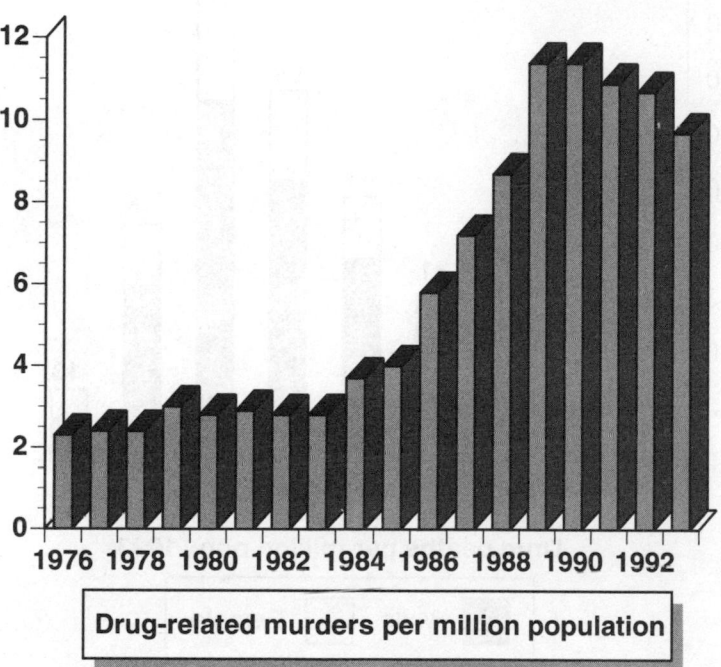

Drug-related murders skyrocketed during the War on Drugs

Drug-related murders per million population

Figure 6.2

Source: FBI (annual), *Uniform Crime Reports for the United States*, 1976-1993. See Ref. 7.

Hyping the phony "school drug crisis"

From December 1994 through September 1995, DHHS Secretary Donna Shalala, Education Secretary Richard Riley, White House drug control policy chief Lee Brown, and several academic consultants issued a barrage of near-hysterical press statements depicting the nation's chief drug menace as adolescents smoking marijuana. A June 1995 U.S. Supreme Court ruling initially affecting athletes effectively opened the door, the court majority announced, to the notion that just *being* a teenager constitutes reasonable cause for authorities to suspect drug abuse and demand urine samples.[10]

Shalala's December 12, 1994, multi-cabinet press conference, assisted by federal grantee and University of Michigan Institute for Social Policy surveyor Lloyd Johnston, was not an exercise in skillful media manipulation. That, at least, would have provided some excuse for the public circus that followed. Rather, the press splash incorporated a more troubling carnival silliness, one amply contradicted by information readily available to reporters. The result was a win-win situation: Officials got hero treatment in press accounts; the press got sensational statements

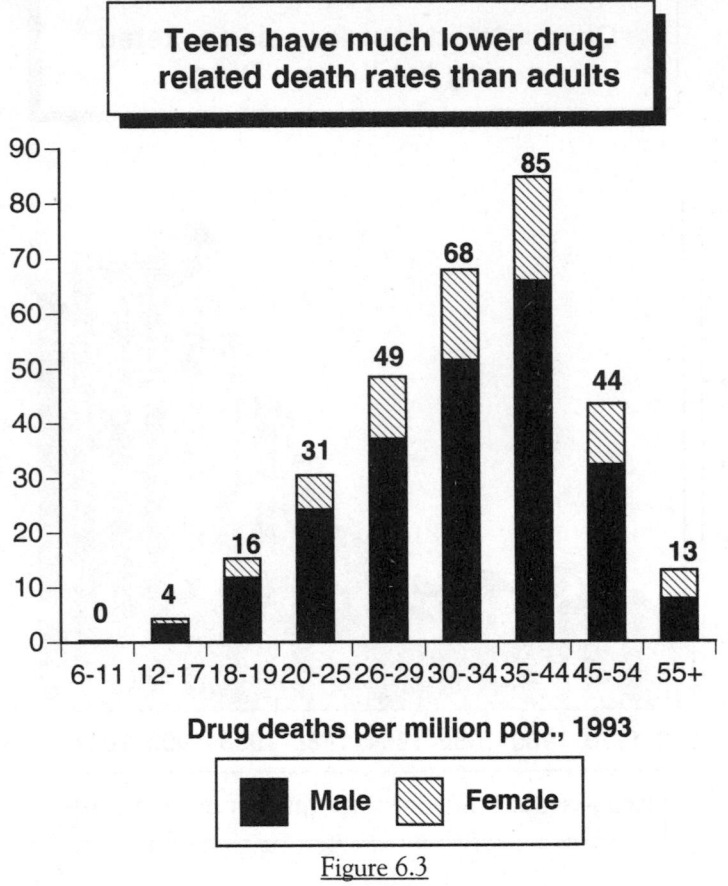

Teens have much lower drug-related death rates than adults

Drug deaths per million pop., 1993

Male   Female

Figure 6.3

Source: Drug Abuse Warning Network, *Annual Medical Examiner Data*, 1993. See Ref. 39.

and images to embellish.

What explanation did Shalala and Johnston provide for the "alarming" increase in teenage drug use shown in Johnston's Monitoring the Future survey? Rising youth poverty? Rising drug abuse by adults (their parents, perhaps)? Deteriorating urban schools? High youth unemployment? Sexual abuse of children? Not a word of it. Any serious explanation would throw the question right back to a decade of failed policy. No, as the secretary declared, "Let's not forget, we're talking about 13-year-olds!" That is, fun time.

The official "cause" of increasing teenage drug use: "There has emerged increasing glorification of marijuana and other drug use by a number of rock, grunge, and rap groups," Johnston declared.[11] Shalala paraded "t-shirts bearing pro-drug-use slogans and symbols" purchased right from her Georgetown clothiers, cited alleged pro-drug music influences, and announced: "Increasingly, drug glorification messages are creeping back into our popular culture."[12]

Here we go again. In 1956, experts blamed "horror comics" for teen depravity. In 1970, Vice-President-at-risk Spiro Agnew (speaking in Las Vegas!) blamed the

Beatles, Jefferson Airplane, and *Easy Rider* for "brainwashing" youth into the "drug culture:"

> Mr. Agnew said in a speech to 1,000 Republicans at the Space Center Auditorium of the Sahara Hotel that popular songs such as the Beatles' "With a Little Help From My Friends" or the Jefferson Airplane's "White Rabbit" were a message of drug use.
>
> ...Mr. Agnew said it was, like many rock songs, "a catchy tune, but until it was pointed out to me, I never realized that the 'friends' were assorted drugs."[13]

The acronymic import of Lucy in the Sky with Diamonds apparently eluded the vice president, who was soon to be defending his own morals, unsuccessfully, to prosecutors accusing him of bribe-taking. Agnew, at least, didn't pretend that a few rock tunes and cultural messages were the only reasons Sixties kids took drugs. He cited "pill popping parents" and "growing adult alcoholism" as influences on youth "to do some experimenting of their own." Not so Shalala and company, who regard adult drug and alcohol abuse as taboo topics.

For sophisticated 1995 reporters, who seem to view the press as a state-run news agency when it comes to official pronouncements on youth, officials' pop-message theme sealed a good story. Wrote *U.S. News & World Report*:

> For a while, the "just say no" campaigns of the 1980s worked: Most teens concluded drugs are for losers. But now the glamour is back. Young people have bought 3 million copies of a Dr. Dre rap album entitled "The Chronic"—slang for a marijuana strain that can be 20 times stronger than the grass of the past. The Black Crowes, popular Southern rockers, perform before a pro-marijuana sign. And caps and shirts adorned with the marijuana leaf are fashion mainstays in schools across the land.
>
> Thus the results of a new survey by researchers at the University of Michigan should come as no surprise: Marijuana use among high school students has almost doubled since 1991.[14]

The broadcast media's evening news (12 December 1994) was stoked on teen degeneration. Most made it the lead story. For *CNN*, the issue was clear-cut, open and shut: Pop culture "messages" produced teen drug use. *ABC News* jumped on the crusade with a lead story featuring reporter Carole Simpson and officials berating teenagers to "stop using drugs." Other news outlets were equally breathless.[15]

What exactly did this terrifying drug survey show? That 51 percent of the high school seniors, 57 percent of the 10th graders, and 65 percent of the eighth graders had *never* used an illegal drug *even once* in their lives. Of 1994 high school seniors (average age 17-18), 62 percent never used pot, 90 percent never tried acid, 95 percent never used mushrooms or mescaline, 82 percent never used inhalants. Two-thirds of high school seniors, three-fourths of the sophomores, and 87 percent of the 8th graders had not used marijuana even once in the past year; 94 percent of the seniors and larger proportions of younger students had refrained from LSD in the twelve months before the survey.[16]

Nor do federal surveys show an alarming increase. The Monitoring survey found drug use within the previous month among high school seniors in 1994 was 60 percent below the level of 1979 and 30 percent below the "just-say-no" year

Shalala praised, 1988. Similarly, DHHS's 1994 National Household Survey on Drug Abuse found a 54 percent decline in teenage use of illegal drugs (within the past month) since 1979. Teens, in fact, showed about the same decline as adults (Table 6.4).

Table 6.4

Teenage drug use is down 50%... Today, a whopping 8% use drugs, mostly pot:

Use of any illicit drug within the previous month, by year (percent):

Age group	1979	1985	1990	1993	1994	Change, 1979-94
12-17	17.6	14.9	8.1	6.6	8.2	-54
18-25	37.1	25.1	14.9	13.5	13.3	-64
26-34	18.5	20.4	9.8	8.5	8.5	-54
35+	2.5	3.6	2.8	2.8	3.2	+28
Total	13.7	11.6	6.4	5.6	6.0	-56

Source: U.S. Substance Abuse and Mental Health Services Administration (1995, September). *Preliminary Estimates from the 1994 National Household Survey on Drug Abuse.* Rockville, MD: U.S. Department of Health and Human Services, Table 2A.

Once again, the question as to whether self-reporting surveys reflect real behaviors accurately enough to permit any strong conclusions, let alone today's hysteria over every two-point up or down, should be considered (see Chapter 5). In any case, the 1994 survey showed that 8.2 percent of the 12-17-year-olds had used a drug within the previous month, only slightly higher than in 1990 and well below the 17.6 percent in 1979.

Eleven out of twelve students in 1994 had not used an illegal drug within the past month (or said they hadn't), a record considerably better than among young and middle-aged adults. Adults over age 35 actually showed a higher rate of (or greater willingness to admit to) drug use in 1994 than in 1979. Sergeant Pepper's and Doors nostalgia? Subliminal Rogaine t-shirts?

Teenage deaths from drug-related causes remain extraordinarily low, as they have since the late 1970s. Local reports also fail to document widespread student drug use so often asserted in the media. Drug-sniffing dogs brought in to conduct surprise searches in Southern California schools believed to harbor high levels of youth drug-taking similarly turned up nothing: "No drugs were found in sniff-searches of lockers, gym locker rooms, and parking lots," the large Newport-Mesa Unified School District had to admit after a series of random, surprise searches in 1994-95. In a district with 7,800 middle and senior high students, "the searches yielded just 10 'alerts' in which a dog signals that a locker might have contained drugs at one time."[17] The Supreme-Court-bound Vernonia, Oregon, school district randomly tested 500 students in four years and found only 12 positive[18] (is Congress that clean and sober?). The much-feared school drug abuse crisis seems to consist of little more than individual anecdotes and drastic imaginings among adults, and some youth, that "other students" must be engaged in rampant narcotics taking.

This is your brain on baloney

In July 1995, White House drug policy chief Lee Brown was in the news with a mission: "To change the drug's [marijuana's] image to that of an addictive killer," the Associated Press headlined.[19] Brown sought to paint marijuana as a life-threatening drug generating 4,300 hospital emergency room visits among teens age 12-17 in 1994—more than for "cocaine and heroin combined."

The report Brown cited showed that the reason for this is not that marijuana is maiming youths, but that teen hospital treatments for cocaine and heroin use are extraordinarily rare. More important, "emergency room visits" are extremely common events only rarely involving life-threatening emergencies. There are about 100 million hospital emergency room episodes in the U.S. every year[20]—two for every five Americans. Of these, DHHS's *Annual Emergency Room Data*[21] found only a tiny percentage involved teens and marijuana, and four-fifths of these involved marijuana in combination with other drugs, primarily alcohol, cocaine, heroin, and acetaminophen (Tylenol) (Table 6.5).

Table 6.5

Teen pot-smoking accounts for 4 of every 100,000 emergency room visits:

	Number	Proportion
Hospital emergency room visits	95,800,000	1.00
Number due to drug overdose	466,897	0.0049
Number due to marijuana/hashish (all ages)	29,166	0.00025
Number of teen emergency room visits due to marijuana/hashish	4,293	0.00004

Source: SAMSA (1994, December). *Preliminary Estimates of Drug-Related Emergency Department Episodes*. Advance Report No. 8. Washington, DC: U.S. Department of Health and Human Services.

Of 20,375 drugs cited in 8,541 deaths in 1993, 457 (or 2.2 percent) involved marijuana (nearly always in combination with other drugs), and just 26 of these (0.1 percent) involved teens.

However, the same DHHS hospital emergency room data report cited by Brown showed that aspirin and aspirin substitutes were *by far* the leading cause of drug-related episodes involving teens.[22] Of the drugs ranked, which accounted for 90 percent of all teen ER visits, such highly-publicized killers as heroin and crystal methamphetamine ("ice") didn't even show up as major sources of youthful ER trips. Table 6.6 reveals some surprises.

Tylenol, aspirin, Advil, Motrin, and similar over-the-counter substitutes accounted for *four times* more youthful emergency room trips than did all street

Table 6.6

The drug sending the most teens to emergency rooms is—Tylenol and aspirin

Drugs found in hospital emergency room visits, age 12-17, 1992

Acetaminophen (Tylenol)	10,053	
Aspirin	7,108	
Ibuprofen (Motrin, Advil)	<u>5,480</u>	
Total aspirin/aspirin substitute		22,641
Marijuana	3,116	
Cocaine	1,546	
LSD	<u>1,183</u>	
Total street drug		5,845
Alcohol in combination with drugs		5,138
Caffeine		1,189
<u>Pharmaceuticals (various)</u>		<u>7,438</u>
Total, top 15		42,251
All other drugs (various)		<u>4,571</u>
Total		46,822

Source: SAMSA (1994, March). *Annual Emergency Room Data, 1992.* DHHS Pub #SMA 94-2080. Rockville, MD: U.S. Department of Health and Human Services, Table 2.06c.

drugs *put together*. The reports indicate that aspirin and aspirin substitutes may show up in ER visits from two sources: Attempted suicides to get attention, and when taken as a pain killer for the injury that really occasioned the hospital visit. Funny that the official crusade against drugs has never gotten worked up over those produced by pharmaceutical giants.

Does marijuana kill? In the most recent year for which detailed national vital statistics are available, 1990, 8,381 drug overdose deaths are reported.[23] Of these, three were attributed to all hallucinogens (marijuana, hashish, LSD, mescaline, psilocybin, peyote, etc.) put together. More dangerous by far were salicylates (44 deaths), aromatic analgesics (65 deaths), non-narcotic analgesics (aspirin, Tylenol, etc., 88 deaths), and nearly all other drugs. These are much topped in the death category, of course, by prescription drugs, heroin, cocaine, methamphetamine, and amphetamine. Diuretic drugs were implicated in 112 deaths, yet no drug officials called press conferences to warn about "fighting for your life" in ER over gout medicine.

If marijuana kills, California (the nation's top drug-death state, accounting for one-fourth of all drug corpses nationally) should be littered with bodies reeking of sweet smoke. The toll: Zero marijuana/hallucinogen deaths in 1993, zero in 1992, zero in 1991, one in 1990, and two in 1989. A total of 88,882 Californians died from non-natural causes during the five-year 1989-93 period; 10,789 of these were from drug overdoses (accidental, intentional, everything in between)—and a whopping three involved that "addictive killer," marijuana (or possibly some other Carlos Castañeda mind-blower, taken as it usually is in combination with harder drugs such as booze or coke). One of these was, however, a teenager, back in 1990.[24]

Enter Joseph Califano Jr., former Carter administration health secretary and now chief of Columbia University's Center on Addiction and Substance Abuse, as to why we should be terrified of a kid with a joint: "The most frightening thing is that smoking marijuana is clearly a steppingstone to more serious problems. Children who smoke pot are 85 times more likely to use cocaine."[25]

Reporters could have glanced down at their surveys and doused that hype. The University of Michigan poll found five-sixths of the high school seniors who smoked pot had never tried cocaine. Ninety-seven percent had not used cocaine (and 97 percent had not used crystal methamphetamine and 99 percent had not used heroin) within the past year. Ninety-eight-plus percent had not used any of these harder drug within the past month. Even assuming that every single coke and heroin user once smoked marijuana, over 90 percent of marijuana users do not go on to use serious drugs.

But the low rate of teen marijuana smokers advancing to harder drugs is not the only flaw in Califano's "steppingstone" or "gateway" claim: There is scant evidence that use of one drug *causes* use of another drug. Pot use, in and of itself, appears to predict no future problem with the hard stuff, as Clinton, Gore, and Clarence Thomas notably denote—though it appears directly related to a surfeit of middle-aged hypocrisy.

Rather, there appears a fraction of individuals who use a variety of drugs by dint of personal, family and social predispositions and who display distinctly different characteristics and styles of drug use than do the large majority of casual experimenters and occasional drug users.[26] Note, from autopsy reports cited above, that the average 1993 overdose corpse had 2.4 different drugs measured in his or her system. These are not adolescent weekend pot smokers gone bad; they are a breed of drug-obsessives unto themselves.

Drug use vs. drug abuse
Longitudinal (long-term) studies have repeatedly shown that casual drug and alcohol use by youth does not lead to harder drugs or drug abuse in adulthood.[27] [28] [29] A recent long-term study of 600 teenagers by University of California at Los Angeles researchers found that while teens who seriously abuse drugs display ongo-

ing problems in adulthood, adolescents who use drugs infrequently (once a month or less) showed no long-term effects:

> The [negative] effects we have noted are not the result of experimental or infrequent drug use, but reflect a pattern of relatively heavy use during early and late adolescence. Thus, it is those teenagers who have developed a life-style of drug use who must be the focal point of prevention and treatment efforts. Heavy use, abuse, or misuse of drug substances by these teenagers, and not the occasional social use at a party or among friends, led to the problems noted.[30]

Abstinence or occasional use of mild drugs is exactly the pattern the surveys found among 95 percent or more of adolescents. Another long-term study of 101 youths, by Berkeley researchers, found that those who abused drugs suffered from "interpersonal alienation, poor impulse control, and manifest emotional distress." However, youths who abstained from drugs altogether were also screwed up: "relatively anxious, emotionally constricted, and lacking in social skills." The study found that those who used drugs and alcohol moderately "were the best adjusted."[31] It was not that moderate drug use caused better adjustment, but rather its reflection of an attitude of moderate experimentation healthy to most teenagers.

Repeatedly, drug researchers have argued for concentration on the relatively small number of easily identifiable, budding drug abusers—the 5 percent or so—while leaving the majority of casual young experimenters alone:

> The occasional use of beer or marijuana at a party cannot be considered abuse or problematic use and may be a natural consequence of teenage curiosity and experimentation. As such, it should not be overly pathologized because this is not the type of drug use that will create problems as the teenager matures into adulthood.[32]

Nor does the corollary—that an adolescent generation relatively free of drug use will mature into an adult generation free of drug problems—hold true. One of the age groups with the fastest-rising and highest rates of drug abuse death today is adults age 45-54, who in 1993 accounted for 1,199 drug deaths nationally (*six times* more than the 206 deaths that occurred among *all* persons under age 20). Virtually all of these older adults would have attended secondary school in the 1950s and early '60s, a time when "drug use by school-age children was negligible to nonexistent."[33] Forcing drug abstinence on teenagers, even assuming it could be accomplished, does not prevent serious, later drug abuse among grownups.

Top on the press's list of critics of the UCLA study was the University of Michigan's Lloyd Johnston, who argued that the best way to prevent drug abuse was to prevent all teens from ever using any drug. Officials' single-minded fixation with enforcing absolute teenage abstinence to the exclusion of facing the adult crisis is set forth by Califano:

> The President has his public health sights on precisely the right target. Virtually all individuals addicted to cigarettes and illegal drugs begin smoking nicotine or marijuana cigarettes or using drugs before they are 21. The way to reduce adult disease and death from smoking, alcohol and illegal drugs is to persuade children and teenagers not to start.[34]

And the way to persuade teenagers not to start is to stop adults from using drugs, tobacco, or alcohol etc., an equally impossible goal. Given their insistence that behavior by parents and adults has nothing to do with how youths act, it must be a shock to America's public health officials that children of English-speaking parents do indeed speak English.

The strategy pushed by Califano, Johnston, Shalala, and modern anti-drug campaigns is like arguing that if 5 percent of all church bingo players become compulsive gamblers, the best deterrent is to ignore the 5 percent who are addicts and to concentrate on shutting down all church bingo. That is the side that has prevailed in the political arena, or perhaps the arena prevailed on it. No agency, program, or school on the government's immense funding list may by federal law entertain any stance toward drug use other than absolute abstinence.[35] Seven years and millions of arrests later, Johnston and Califano (who still have never acknowledged the sharp rise in drug deaths under current drug policies) complained during the 1995 press-capades that teen drug use was a rising crisis and that the $100 billion-per-year government anti-drug army was being routed by t-shirts, pot-leaf caps, and Dr. Dre.

After months of relentless news stories on the "resurgence of drug abuse" among high school students, another coordinated round of headlines was due. In July 1995, Califano released a new study showing around four in ten high school students (after being subjected to months of media reports hyping drugs in schools, heavy publicity over a U.S. Supreme Court case on student drug testing, and a phone call to answer questions by "drug" surveyors) cited "drugs" as their schools' worst problem.[36]

It is difficult to discern any truth in the array of misstatements, wholesale exaggeration, and lack of any semblance of perspective by the administration and its consultants—or even any evidence that student safety is the main concern. Shalala and other drug-war officials assert that youths were safer from drugs in the "just say no" 1980s. Yet her own agency's reports show that emergency room episodes from drug use by 12-17-year-olds were much *higher* in 1988 than in 1993. From 1988 to 1993, teenage emergency room trips involving the real killers, cocaine and heroin, dropped 36 percent; and for all drugs (including aspirin), such visits decreased by 9 percent. Adolescents appear less likely to die or be injured by drugs today than at the height of the just-say-no era.[37] But such figures on drug abuse death and injury seem unimportant to drug warriors, because preventing drug abuse does not seem to be the priority of the anti-drug campaign.

Rather, the real purpose became evident in yet another multi-cabinet youth-drug press conference on 12 September 1995. Waving the 1994 National Household Survey—which showed 8 percent of the 12-17-year-olds had smoked marijuana in the month before the survey—Shalala blasted Congress for cutting $700 million from her budget and predicted dire results if the funds were not restored.[38]

Ignoring the real drug crisis: Adults

The reasons for the administration's ludicrous scare campaign over adolescents and pot are obvious. Any other tactic would require admitting that after a decade of the costliest, most intensive campaign against drug abuse and drug crime ever, the United States now has the highest levels of drug death and drug murder in its history. Worse than that: Drug deaths and crime, low and even declining prior to the early 1980s, have marched upward as the War on Drugs has escalated.

In 1993, DHHS's *Annual Medical Examiner Data*[39] reported details of 8,541 deaths from drug-related causes in 43 major metropolitan areas nationwide. These included all deaths, whether accident (including traffic accidents), suicide, or homicide, in which drugs were found in the deceased's system (Table 6.7).

Table 6.7

Middle-agers are *eight times* more likely than teenagers to die of drug abuse

U.S. drug deaths compiled by Drug Abuse Warning Network, 1993

Age	Drug deaths	Drug deaths/100,000 pop	% male
6-11	7	< 0.1	43
12-17	91	0.4	76
18-19	108	1.6	75
Total teen	199	0.7	75
20-25	697	3.1	79
26-29	798	4.9	76
30-34	1,517	6.8	75
35-44	3,386	8.5	78
45-54	1,199	4.4	74
55-older	698	1.3	60
Total adult	8,295	4.6	75
Total	8,541	3.7	75

Source: U.S. Substance Abuse and Mental Health Services Administration. *Annual Medical Examiner Data, 1993.* DHHS Report #95-3019, 1995, Tables 2.01, 2.02, 2.09.

Only 2.3 percent of the drug death toll was teens age 12-19. The teenage drug abuse death toll was vanishingly small: Children and teens comprised 17 of 3,885 cocaine/crack deaths, 12 of 3,789 heroin deaths, and 16 of 3,427 deaths from alcohol taken in combination with other drugs. The percentage of teen drug deaths that are male (75 percent) is the same as for adults.

National hospital emergency room figures compiled by DAWN, though less

Table 6.8

Adults account for 97% of all emergency room treatments for illegal drugs:

Drug emergency room visits compiled by Drug Abuse Warning Network, 1993

Age	Cocaine	Heroin	Marijuana	Total	Rate*
6-11	7	2	na	9	< 0.1
12-17	1,583	282	4,293	6,158	29.8
18-25	22,077	7,912	9,656	39,645	133.7
26-34	52,715	21,127	9,342	83,184	215.0
35-44	37,477	25,792	4,540	67,809	170.0
45-54	7,669	6,561	959	15,189	55.4
55+	1,789	1,289	376	3,454	6.5
Total	123,317	62,965	29,166	215,448	92.8

*Drug-related ER episodes per 100,000 population in each age group.
Source: SAMSA (1994, December). *Preliminary Estimates of Drug-Related Emergency Department Episodes*. Advance Report No. 8. Washington, DC: U.S. Department of Health and Human Services.

detailed, show the same pattern (Table 6.8).

Further confirmation of this pattern is found in a 1992 survey reported by the U.S. Bureau of Justice Statistics of drug-testing of persons arrested for crimes in 24 major cities. Consistently, teens age 15-20 were the least likely of any age group to test positive for drugs; middle-aged adult arrestees the most likely.[40]

Is *anything* we have been officially told about drug abuse in America true? Teenagers are relentlessly hyped. Occasionally the elderly are implicated. That teens account for only 3 percent of all drug emergencies and just 2 percent of all drug deaths, and the elderly comprise 2 percent of all drug emergencies and 8 percent of all drug deaths, is completely unexpected. That middle-agers are the biggest drug abusers by far is completely at odds with what drug policy makers, drug experts, and the media have told us.

Officials have argued that teenagers are at the highest risk of death and injury from drug use. It turns out they are among the least at risk. Perhaps logic might tell us that it takes a few years to nurture a really deadly drug habit, placing adults at higher risk. That's not the official image of "impetuous, risk-taking teens," and it doesn't explain how today's youths manage to avoid not only the coffin, but even the hospital, from what officials claim are their widespread abuse of today's array of lethal drugs.

Standing out like a mountain range in the figures Shalala and other health officials *failed* to emphasize is America's real drug crisis: Emergency room visits among middle-aged grownups for cocaine and heroin jumped 48 percent, part of a 50 percent rise in overall adult drug abuse injury and death during the last five years. Over 185,000 emergency room episodes involved cocaine or heroin (more than 99 percent of these were adults) in 1993. Today's teenagers of all races are coping with unprecedented levels of drug abuse among their parents and adult relatives.

What is the nature of today's middle-aged adult drug crisis, and where did it come from? National and California figures (the latter due to their excellent consistency, detail, and recency, and patterns that duplicate those nationally) paint a depressing picture. Baby Boom adults of all races, particularly men, appear to harbor serious, continuing problems with drug abuse, of which premature fatality is only one outcome. It is our middle-aged vulnerability to narcotics that seems to account for the unusual escapism and viciousness of modern "just say no," anti-marijuana anti-casual-use anti-adolescent campaigns waged by our official proxies of 1995.

Surprisingly, most adult drug deaths are unintentional overdoses—exactly the kinds of mistakes least expected among middle-agers—while most of the relatively small drug death toll among teens and the elderly are intentional (suicides) (Table 6.9).

Table 6.9

The enormous middle-aged drug toll is primarily accidental overdoses:

Drug overdose deaths by age, California, 1993:

	Accidents	Suicides	Total	Rate*
Child (age 0-12)	16	0	16	0.3
Teenager (age 13-19)	15	11	26	0.8
Young adult (age 20-34)	637	104	741	9.0
Middle-age adult (age 35-49)	1,094	230	1,324	21.1
Older adult (age 50-64)	189	99	288	8.2
Elderly adult (age 65+)	46	83	129	4.0
Total drug deaths	1,998	527	2,525	8.1

*per 100,000 population for each age group.
Source: Center for Health Statistics (1995). Microcomputer injury surveillance system (MISS). Sacramento, CA: California Department of Health Services (diskette).

This is a stranger pattern than it appears at first glance. Note that the minuscule drug toll among teens, and the somewhat higher number among the elderly, contain a high proportion of suicides. However, for young and middle-aged adults, nearly all of the enormous toll of drug deaths are accidental overdoses. This is exactly the kind of careless death that one would expect from supposedly accident-prone adolescents, not middle-agers who have had plenty of years to learn discretion. What is going on?

The bitter irony indicated by research is that today's drug abuse crisis heavily concentrated among middle-aged men is a continuing legacy of the four million sent to the Vietnam War. Writing in the February 13, 1987, *Journal of the American*

Medical Association, Centers for Disease Control researchers reported that veterans of Vietnam War combat were 2.5 times more likely to die from drug abuse than a comparable group of men not sent to Vietnam. In fact, while most of the unusually high post-service suicide, murder, and accident death toll among Vietnam veterans (which study authors attribute to "unusual stresses endured while stationed in a hostile fire zone") occurred within five years after the war's end, high and rising rates of drug death among veterans were continuing right up to the time the study was completed in the mid 1980s. That government war policy was and is a major factor in Americans' drug abuse is another matter 1990s anti-drug warriors don't seem eager to publicize.

It isn't that adolescents are immune to drug demise. As the early 1970s toll shows, groups (including teenagers) that harbor problems with drugs display high rates of death from drugs, and outright deaths are only the tip of the iceberg. For every drug death recorded in 1993, there were 100 emergency room visits—and even these do not tell the whole story. America's drug crisis lies in the progression of drug abuse among Baby Boomers and the age groups that flank us—and the effects the Baby Boom generation's intractable drug abuse has on today's young.

The worst drug problems among youths appears to be coping with drug abusing adults. The chief reason for foster placement of children today is neglect due to parents' drug and alcohol abuse. Two-thirds of all pre-school children in foster care were exposed to drugs before birth.[41] I have heard many examples from teenage mothers, school dropouts, and other "at-risk youths" of their parents' terrible drug (and even worse, alcohol) afflictions, resulting in beatings and other abuses and neglect to parents too debilitated to take care of their children, requiring teens to stay home from school to watch younger siblings. The role of parental drug abuse in a variety of teenage problems—especially in promoting early pregnancy, violence, and school dropout connected to adolescents' efforts to escape such households— has not been systematically assessed but is likely to be serious.

A major factor in drug and alcohol abuse is a history of sexual abuse and rape, which affects both males[42] and females. The 1992 *Rape in America* study found that the age at which a girl's first rape occurred was younger than the age at which she first became intoxicated on alcohol or used drugs. Serious drinking problems were twelve times higher, and serious drug abuse problems 25 times higher, in rape victims than in non-victims.[43] Though histories of rape and sexual abuse appear to be significant factors in teenage and adult drug and drinking problems, or part of the childhood environments in which such problems develop, they are rarely addressed in media or official pronouncements on teenage addiction.

Drug arrests target nonwhites and teens

Drug-related murders have also exploded since the early 1980s, reaching nearly 2,000 in 1993. American Society of Criminology past president Alfred Blumstein points out that criminalizing drug use is a major reason for "the use of guns in drug markets," which is linked to "the recent rise in the juvenile homicide rate."[44] (It is more accurate to say that rising poverty among young people has led to increased youth involvement in all manner of illegal and "shadow economy" activities, resulting in increase gun use and homicide). Bolstered by 1.1 million new arrests in 1993, 60 percent of the federal prisoners and 20 percent of all state prisoners are drug offenders.[45]

Drug laws and their selective enforcement represent the new Jim Crow laws. Writing in *Scientific American*, veteran drug researcher David J. Musto noted the "powerful theme in the American perception of drugs: Linkage between a drug and a feared or rejected group within society."[46] It is no surprise that anti-drug enforcement targets minority youth. A 1995 report by The Sentencing Project found 90 percent of those imprisoned for drug possession were black or Latino. In particular:

> African Americans constitute 13 percent of the monthly drug users, but represent 35 percent of arrests for drug possession, 55 percent of convictions, and 74 percent of prison sentences...
>
> Public policies ostensibly designed to control crime and drug abuse have in many respects contributed to the growing racial disparity in the criminal justice system, while having little impact on the problems they were aimed to address.

Blacks represented 42 percent of all teenage drug arrests and 39 percent of all adult drug arrests in 1993. Law enforcement officials have responded that drugs are "devastating" the black community. Yet national vital statistics figures show that only 15 percent of those who die from drug overdoses or suicides are blacks. A black teenager is only one-fifth as likely to die from drugs, but is ten times more likely to be arrested for drugs, than is a white adult.[47]

The Sentencing Project report—phrased in terms of racial disparity—drew a favorable reaction from White House drug chief Lee Brown as "exactly right."[48] This is the Lee Brown who three months earlier was instrumental in manufacturing the image of marijuana as a deadly drug and youth (which in practical terms means "nonwhite youth") as trapped in an urgent crisis of drug abuse requiring tough measures.

As usual, the political needs of the '96 election campaign won out. A week after lamenting "the disproportionate percentage" of young black men sent to prison, Clinton reversed himself and promised to sign a GOP-backed bill to maintain much harsher prison sentences for possessing small amounts of crack cocaine than for the expensive powdered cocaine favored by wealthier users. Under the bill, a person convicted of selling $225 worth of crack cocaine would get the same penalty as a person convicted of selling $50,000 worth of powdered cocaine. Most arrested for powdered cocaine are older, white and more affluent; 96 percent of those arrested for crack are blacks or Latinos, primarily in young age groups.[49]

Talkin' about degeneration

As with alcohol and tobacco, use of drugs by teenagers shows up throughout history. Until 1903, Coca-Cola contained cocaine in quantity and was ingested by minors and adults alike. Use of many drugs, including cocaine (legal until 1903), opiates (legal until 1909), and marijuana (grown in the Massachusetts Bay Colony beginning in 1611, recommended as a medicine in the Civil War era, and not outlawed until 1937), were used recreationally and medicinally in past centuries and were generally considered anything but social problems.[50]

Concern about drug abuse by youths, as opposed to anyone else's, first surged in the late 1930s with a series of government docu-dramas on "Reefer Madness" and "Cocaine Fiends." "Reefer Madness" depicts a school official declaring that in 1930, drug arrests among youth "scarcely filled a page; today [1939], they fill entire cabinets, with hundreds of new cases reported every day... Organized gangs distribute marijuana to every school in this city... A lawlessness we can scarcely imagine is flourishing in every community and hamlet in our nation." Teenage violence, promiscuity, deadly driving, doped students and athletes, suicide, and murder were attributed to marijuana. "Stamp out this frightful assassin of our youth," the film implored parents.

The teen dope scare of the early 1950s was also of particular note. In Oklahoma City, 300 upscale white teenagers were brought before a legislative investigating committee in 1953 to describe their drug use (typically marijuana, or morphine and paregoric mixed with alcohol) and drug suppliers, one of whom, age 16, murdered the state legislature's chief investigator in front of a police headquarters in 1952. (In Oklahoma City of 1990, police reported only 200 drug arrests among youths.)[51]

The U.S. Senate's 1953 investigation described teenage drug abuse as "epidemic." Descriptions, as today, were given of junior high youths spending lunch money on drugs, violence and theft among urban youth addicts, and the devastating effects of youth addiction. While the press—with its usual sensational attitude and lack of historical perspective—reported in 1990 that a 9-year-old arrested for drugs was believed to be the youngest ever, Youth In Danger (1956) reports 8-year-olds selling drugs at school.[52] Arrest records show youths under age 10 arrested for drugs every year back into the 1930s.

Drug use increased rapidly from 1965 to 1972, especially among youth. Law enforcement increased even more (Table 6.10).

From 1965 to 1975, drug arrest rates increased 1,400 percent for teenagers and 500 percent among adults. While teens and adults were about equally likely to be arrested in 1960, by 1975 teens were six times more arrest-prone. The rise in '60s drug (and alcohol) use was principally a teenage and young adult trend, but one in which adults also participated with relish.

Teenage drug mortality in the U.S. peaked in 1970, when 15-19-year-olds accounted for 650 overdose deaths (10 percent of all drug deaths nationally), a rate of 33.4 per million population. Though drug excess among a fraction of the population was serious, the Sixties was not a time of widespread junior or senior high school drug taking. In fact, most Sixties drug use began after high school. In 1972, the National Commission on Marihuana and Drug Abuse's surveys reported that 86 percent of 12-17-year-olds had never tried marijuana, 94 percent had never illegally used a medical drug or an inhalant, 95 percent had never used LSD, and 99 percent had never tried cocaine or heroin—in fact, 82 percent said they had never used any illegal drug at all.[53] Only 20 percent of high school seniors had used an illegal drug within the previous month. Why, then, were teen drug death tolls so high, approaching those of adults? Much of the drug mortality of the '60s appears to have

Table 6.10

Adults are far more at risk of drug abuse, but teens get arrested more:

	Number		Rate*	
U.S. drug arrests, 1960-94	Teens	Adults 20+	Teens	Adults 20+
1960	6,000	41,000	45	37
1965	15,000	50,000	90	42
1970	200,000	260,000	1052	206
1975	275,000	300,000	1297	208
1980	207,000	373,000	978	242
1985	194,000	633,000	1044	376
1990	191,000	932,000	1074	524
1994	285,000	1,090,000	1618	588

*Per 100,000 population age 15-19 and 20 and older.

Source: Federal Bureau of Investigation (1960-1994). *Uniform Crime Reports for the United States*. Washington, DC: U.S. Department of Justice (annual, arrest tables for years cited). Arrests are adjusted to reflect the population covered by each year's reporting agencies.

been teenage abuse of prescription drugs, especially barbiturates, similar to that found among '60s grownups.

Drug education programs implemented in the 1970s have since been criticized as too pharmacological (that is, focused on the chemical effects of drugs and drug overdose), as lacking in moral values, as increasing student interest in drugs, and therefore as failures.[54] Indeed, self-reports show student drug use rose rapidly during the 1970s. By 1983, 31 percent of high school seniors had used an illegal drug within the previous month, a large increase over 1970. Yet as student drug use was reportedly increasing, student drug deaths were declining—exactly the opposite of what policy makers would predict.

It may be that the 1970s' straightforward pharmacology—absent the "values" preaching that has plagued 1980s and '90s drug education—was exactly the right recipe. Drug use may have risen, but from 1972 to 1983, youthful drug deaths fell rapidly (Figure 6.1). In 1983, only 196 U.S. teens died from drug overdoses (3 percent of the national toll), a modern record-low rate of 10.2 per million population and a decline of 70 percent from 1970s levels. The plummet in teenage drug deaths during the 1970s, in the face of rising teenage drug use, remains a spectacularly encouraging development. It was all the more remarkable since adult drug fatalities were decreasing only moderately.

No one seems to know that it occurred, let alone why it occurred or what lessons it holds for modern drug education. Americans' continuing, deadly confusion over the difference between drug use and drug abuse propelled an official preoccupation with drug-use surveys to the exclusion of far more important and reliable indexes such as drug abuse injuries and deaths.[55] Once again, an unstudied teenage phenomenon appears to have occurred, drawing no one's interest as to what actually happened amid the zeal by agencies and programs to manipulate the issue for their own ends.

Partnership for a Truth-Free America

The 1980s and 1990s showed the high price of expedient official delusion and exploitation of drug abuse issues. The "War on Drugs," instituted in 1983 and expanded rapidly with billions in congressional appropriations in 1986, brought increasingly strident legal and behavior education mandates to prevent all drug use. No program qualifying for federal funding could present an alternative other than absolute abstinence.[56]

The first half of the drug war, through the late 1980s, brought rising arrests of adults. The second half, after 1990, has found rising arrests of teenagers and young adults, particularly nonwhites, which reached a record high level in 1994. This despite the fact that, as has been noted, teens are much less at risk of drug injury or death than are adults. Students (in self-reports) asserted reduced drug use: By 1988, only 21 percent of high school seniors admitted using an illicit drug within the previous month. Officials called press conferences to praise themselves for the "decline."

"The message is out, and America's young people have heard it," a beaming President Reagan announced in the election year 1988. Health and Human Services Secretary Otis Bowen credited the "just say no" campaign. The media gushed stories about "winning" the school drug battle.[57]

What officials didn't cite, and therefore the media didn't report, was that the teenage drug death toll climbed steadily from 1983 to 1989, then levelled off. By 1993, it stood at 280 deaths, or 16.5 per million population—a 60 percent increase since 1983 but still well below both 1970's drug death rate and that of adults. It is difficult to imagine a more crushing defeat. Whether the drug war actively converted an improving situation into today's crisis, or merely burned $10 million and 100 arrests every hour for ten years while utterly failing to address the true causes of drug malaise, is nothing any official presiding over the calamity seems eager to explain. The upshot was that despite all the slogans about "caring for kids," an increase in teenage drug deaths during a "war on drugs," which was heavily concentrated on teenagers, was not supposed to happen, and so officials displayed no interest in why it happened.

The surprising implication is that if self-reporting surveys are accurate, an *inverse* relationship exists between self-reported adolescent drug use and adolescent drug deaths over the past 25 years. That is, the more students who report using drugs, the fewer who die from drugs.[58] To "just say no" adherents, this pattern can't be true; it defies logic. However, such a pattern makes perfect, if tragically misunderstood, sense.

Rigid, punitive, "us vs. them" policies are exactly the ones that push marginal youths toward heavy drug-abusing peers and adults. They encourage students to be dishonest, to hide drug use on self-reporting surveys and from those who might counsel them alike. They turn drug treatment into a stigma and punishment rather than a safety valve. They make criminals of even the most "casual use, single-use" teens (to cite the drug style most pointedly criticized by Shalala). They increase the odds that borderline youth will gravitate toward permanent drug subcultures, "underworld use patterns that are not controlled by ordinary social mechanisms" as addictions researcher Stanton Peele terms them,[59] rather than toward the larger mass of moderate-using and non-using peers and adults. Identical patterns were observed among drinkers during Prohibition, when the great-grandparents of today's youth (including, by autobiographical admission, former President Reagan) were drunkenly defying the chief Drug Law of their day en masse.

The Drug War: We're hooked

The abysmal failure of the War on Drugs makes two issues clear. First, today's policy makers have no workable strategy to forestall drug abuse. Second, young people are forced to cope with the worst of misguided drug policy's failings.

America's teenage drug-abuse crisis of the late 1960s and early 1970s was essentially over by the end of the '70s decade. Despite temporary late-1980s increases in drug mortality, teenagers have not been a major part of America's very real drug abuse epidemic for nearly two decades, and they are not a significant part of it today.

If the anti-drug crusade rampant in Washington and the 50 states was seriously interested in preventing drug abuse, the reasons for youthful resistance to rising, epidemic adult drug abuse would be a topic of prime agency and media interest. The teenage counter-trend needs to be understood and reinforced so that today's youths may, as they age into adulthood, avoid emulating their elders. But a sober and honest evaluation of what has caused the marked increases and decreases in adolescent drug abuse and fatality during periods when they might be least expected is rendered impossible by the slavering of agencies to manufacture hysteria over, or grab credit for, every 2-point up or down in any of a half-dozen drug surveys. Real-world developments suggest profound changes in drug education, programming strategy, and public policies, directions radically different from the punitive, escapist, and often downright silly escapades now emanating from Washington.

What alternative strategy holds promise? The common-sense conclusions of decades of research focused on styles of drug use offer guidance: (a) De-emphasize measures taken against the large numbers (primarily teenagers) whose drug use is experimental, casual, occasional, and involves relatively low-risk drugs, and (b) Focus heavily on the smaller numbers of all ages (primarily adults) whose drug use is heavy, abusive, involves harder drugs, and is creating unmistakable consequences. A third strategy, indicated by today's unique pattern, is to determine why teens have charted a different, healthier path over the last two decades and to do our best to reinforce it.

The vituperation these self-evident suggestions engender among today's anti-drug officials and consultants is evidence that anti-drug wars, like all wars, generate a variety of rewards for the warriors (financial, political, personal). Thus defeats, even calamitous, only serve to generate increasing commitment built on escalating distortions of truth. Ten years of hundreds of billions of dollars lavished on a wild array of law enforcement, programming, education, and political care and feeding has produced the usual coalition of wartime interests (not the least of them cabinet-level) whose chief fear is cutback, de-escalation, and re-strategizing.[60]

However, the principle alternative now on the table—drug decriminalization for adults, as presently framed—is not a solution to the drug crisis and may exacerbate it. Legalizing drug use by adults while retaining criminal sanctions for youthful use[61] is not a challenge to, but an extension of, the thinking that plagues drug and other behavioral theory: That advocating tougher policing of teenagers somehow justifies tolerating egregious behaviors by adults. The practical effect of decriminalizing drug use for those over age 21 (as several state initiatives, such as Oregon's proposed) would further concentrate law enforcement on adolescents (particularly nonwhite youths), increasing the stigma, sanctions, and dangers to that age group. This is a singularly poor time to legislate more party time for grownups at the risk of more prison time for teenagers.

Current drug legalization initiatives miss a larger point. The root of the drug crisis lies not in widespread, casual, and typically short-lived drug experimentation by today's drug-abuse-resistant teenagers, but in the singularly unhealthy conduct of today's large, drug-enmeshed cohort in their 30s, 40s, and 50s. Any legalization scheme that promises to reduce drug problems would be one that focuses on style of drug use, not user age. Until American attitudes toward drugs evolve away from the current conundrum of strident public insistence on absolute abstinence combined with widespread private tolerance for severe drug abuse, drug legalization will simply place young nonwhites even more in the official crosshairs than they already are.

The most promising reforms continue to be drowned in a tide of emotionalism. For a century, the hypocrisy of American adult society toward drugs and alcohol, condemning them with one hand while abusing them with the other, has proven a serious impediment to the kinds of drug policy experiments emerging in Western Europe. Dutch addictions policy expert Govert van de Wijngaart exemplifies both the more rational premises and outcomes of his nation's flexible approach of decriminalizing marijuana and focusing on prevention and treatment of drug addiction rather than punishing moderate styles of drug use:

> It is generally recognized that experimenting with drugs does not automatically lead to regular or excessive use. The number of experimenters who subsequently give up the use of these substances, or the occasional users (so-called chippers) is several times greater than the number who ultimately become addicts. Consequently, preventing drug-related problems may receive more emphasis than preventing drug use.
>
> ...It has been shown that non-sensational drug/health education projects which have been embedded in the school curricula do have positive effects on the attitudes (knowledge, opinion, and concrete behavior) of school children... Nevertheless, one should not expect miracles from school-based education programs. The example set by parents and other role models in the social and cultural context has been found to be of greater influence.
>
> ...It is important to recognize that the criminal status of drug use is a major factor in causing problems for addicts and the community in general.

Van de Wijngaart points out that drug death rates are lower in the Netherlands than in comparable nations, and "statistics suggest these policies are relatively successful." There has been no increase in hard-drug use following decriminalization, repeated studies have shown. Overall, drug deaths have declined sharply and marijuana use is much lower among Dutch youths than among U.S. youths. The legal age for purchasing and smoking marijuana in the regulated Netherlands coffee shops that dispense the drug, U.S. drug-decriminalizers please note, is not absurdly high, but is sensibly set at 16. In an editorial deploring the political pressures sabotaging the Dutch drug-decriminalization experiment, the British international medical journal *The Lancet* declared:

> The smoking of cannabis, even long term, is not harmful to health. Yet this widely used substance... has become a political football, and one that governments continually duck. Like footballs, however, it bounces back. Sooner or later politicians will have to stop running scared and address the evidence: cannabis per se is not a hazard to society but driving it further underground is.[62]

With an eye to the irrational politics surrounding mild drugs, Van de Wijngaart aptly warns: "The Dutch context does not include other factors which seem to be important elements of the drug problem" in the United States. A major difficulty in implementing more flexible drug policy in the U.S., he points out, is America's "strong social polarities" and "lack of adequate welfare provisions."[63]

True enough. The U.S. has deployed its anti-drug measures primarily against poorer nonwhites and adolescents. Reform requires a major change in attitude not just toward drugs, but toward nonwhites, adolescents, and the maintenance of poverty. No such change appears on the horizon.

"We have tried moral exhortation," wrote crime and drug policy analyst Elliot Currie. "We have tried neglect. We have tried punishment. We have even, more grudgingly, tried treatment. We have tried everything but improving lives."[64] But Dutch law sociologist Hans van Mastrigt sardonically suggests that "alternatives which aim at providing relief for drug users, their direct social environment, and society as a whole, but fail to reckon with the needs and problems experienced by policy makers during their daily routines, may easily be set aside by those in power as impractical, unrealistic, theoretical, and therefore, irrelevant."[65] That is, the most realistic reforms to reduce drug addiction at the street level are not likely to foster, at the highest policy levels, the withdrawal of a large array of well-funded interests from their addiction to profitable drug-war myths.

For U.S. drug politics is frightening because it is not driven by the search for reasoned approaches toward drugs, but visceral fear. It is a fear anyone who has attended anti-drug conferences or workshops, or observed anti-drug crusaders in the media, can feel. It taps into a tragic paradox in our tradition: Americans publicly uphold absolute abstinence and morality, but privately we turn a blind eye toward out-of-control behaviors. It is no surprise that Shalala's, Califano's, Clinton's, and other public officials' fiercest anger should be directed at the concept of occasional or moderate drug use, or that the standard school anti-alcohol program will spend a great deal of time demeaning the concept of "moderate drinking." Alcoholics Anonymous labels such strident prohibitionism as characteristic of the "dry drunk:" The individual who substitutes addiction to a loudly-proclaimed absolutist morality for addiction to a chemical as a signal of vulnerability to both.

Modern American drug and alcohol policy is a dry-drunk crusade. The shrill anger at teenagers emanating from Washington in the guise of "concern" is exactly the kind of denial and scapegoating to be expected from an older generation that has not confronted the dimensions of our own drug tragedies. Yet for all the sound and fury in the Beltway, the neighborhood reality is that adolescents seem to be forming their own drug policy. The large majority of teenagers, for now and for unknown reasons, are resisting both the addicted examples of many of their elders and the histrionics of the official anti-drug crusade. The national turning away of American youths from drug abuse, which began two decades ago, now promises to produce not a drug-abstaining but a much more promising drug-managing generation.

7. Two-Fisted Double Standards

No society can reasonably expect to single out certain drugs or certain age groups for proscriptive or restrictive policies, while at the same time condoning (or even encouraging) the consumption of alcohol and other drugs in the rest of the population.

— Washington State University study team, 1988[1]

Our society considers the use of alcohol socially acceptable. It should not surprise us that the majority of our adolescent population consumes alcohol... usually motivated by the same reasons provided for most adult drinking.

— Gail Milgram, Rutgers Center for Alcohol Studies, 1982[2]

Don't try to do no thinkin'
Just go on with your drinkin'
Just have your fun you old son of a gun
Then drive home in your Lincoln.

— Frank Zappa, Mothers of Invention, 1967[3]

The high school survey results were in. It looked bad for the future of the motherland. More than 90 percent of the 13-18-year-olds reported drinking. A shocking 47 percent had downed alcoholic beverages within the week before the survey. One-third drank after school events, half drank on dates. One in six started drinking before age 11, and 79 percent were drinking by age 14. One in ten had a false i.d. to buy booze, one in three held teen parties where alcohol was served, and nearly all teen drinking took place on weekends.

Fifteen percent of the students mentioned problem behavior such as fights, accidents, property destruction, speeding, and sexual activity after drinking, and 16 percent had gotten sick from overimbibing. The survey authors concluded that "drinking reaches its peak at age 16" and that the "law has little relation to drinking of high school students."

But Donna Shalala didn't call an "urgent" press conference to wail, "We're talking about 13-year-olds!" and decry "a generation at risk." She was only 13 years old. That was her generation. The "first ever high school survey" of 1,000 suburban New York junior and senior high students was published in the March 1954 issue of *Better Homes and Gardens*.[4] Another report of that same year deplored:

> ... a youth element that ran rampant... One youth gang, crazed by sixty-cent-a-gallon wine spiked with alcohol, roamed the streets, knives in hand, stabbing indiscriminately everyone they met. This outburst of senseless savagery sent six persons to hospitals with serious injuries and resulted in the deaths of two others... High school students massed in a phalanx and swept through the trolleys, as ruthless and destructive as a tornado, literally tearing the cars apart, beating drivers and robbing their fares... a group of high school football players found a girl alone on a bus and shredded her clothes from her on the spot in a mass attempt at rape.[5]

According to prevailing alcohol theory, that level of teenage drinking should have produced a generation riddled with drunks and crippled by alcoholism. Instead, this is the Fifties traditional-values generation that in the troubled '90s holds itself up as a model for the rest of us. Yet any generation that was mostly drinking by seventh grade, half of whom was boozing every weekend, 90 percent of whom were defying underage drinking laws, was the definition of a "generation at risk," true? Shalala herself in her reign as president at the University of Wisconsin was wont to accompany Madison police to campus parties, where she would lecture 1988 students on the dangers of underage drinking.

Teenage drinking (and suicide and mental health, examined in the next chapter) represents a distinct break with the previous chapters. Up to this point, it has been argued that the foundation of anti-youth policies is the traditional issue of race and class discrimination. The heavy hand of anti-teen welfare reform, employment, drug, violence, pregnancy/motherhood, and smoking policies falls on minority and lower-class adolescents. In these cases, the issue of young age is largely one of poverty, primarily nonwhite poverty.

But 1990s America is not just anti-minority or anti-poor, but fundamentally anti-adolescent regardless of race or class. Evidence for this assertion is the intense and hostile official focus on such issues as teenage drinking and teenage suicide. The fundamental difference is found in simple arrest statistics (Table 7.1).

Table 7.1

Nonwhite youths get busted for drugs, whites for booze:

U.S. youth arrests for drug and drinking offenses, 1994

Offense*	White	Nonwhite	Percent nonwhite
Drugs	98,800	65,500	40%
Alcohol	135,400	13,900	9%

*Hispanics are included with whites. Drug offenses include possession and sale. Alcohol offenses include drunk driving, public drunkenness, and alcohol possession.
Source: FBI (1995). *Uniform Crime Reports for the United States, 1994*. Washington, DC: U.S. Department of Justice, Table 43.

In areas such as teen suicide and drinking, an enormous treatment industry has arisen, targeted primarily at middle-class and wealthier white families. The discrimination remains, of course, in the much stronger sentences given for drug violations than for alcohol violations. The pattern is that nonwhite youths are going to prison for drugs; white youths are serving a variety of more creative sentences for alcohol.

Alcohol policy in the United States is the classic example of the genesis, entrenchment, and perpetuation of modern anti-youth doctrine. It is the model for modern scapegoating of youth, the increasing tendency of American "sin" politics to evade confronting larger problems among adults by slapping more restrictions on adolescents. Its history is worth recounting.

Bombed on Main Street

Despite the popular image of Puritan austerity, "children were encouraged to drink... Drinking was common with students, adolescents, children, and even babies" in Colonial America.[6] According to 1990s alcoholism dogma, our revolutionaries and founding fathers should have been serious sots. Yet for all this permissiveness, there is no indication of any particular alcoholism problem, nor proscription directed at youth.[7] "What few regulations were developed during the [18th] and 19th centuries to restrict youthful drinking usually involved persons of relatively young ages, 16 or younger, never prohibited liquor outright, and usually honored parental discretion."[8]

Consumption of alcoholic beverages reached about four gallons per capita in 1760, 50 percent higher than in 1990. There are descriptions of severe and humiliating punishments meted out to habitual drunkards of the day, often involving stocks and overripe comestibles, as well as the enactment of laws in all thirteen colonies to regulate tavern hours and prohibit alcohol sale to servants, apprentices, slaves, Indians, debtors, habitual inebriates and like riffraff.

There are references to increasing drunkenness among 19th century youth along with that of adults, "particularly in colleges where students engaged in extremely heavy daily drinking, gambling, and disruptive delinquent behavior."[9] The reform movement prompted by this liquor-soaked climate of post-revolutionary America, when adolescents and adults drank in widespread number, with two fists, and in public as well as private, focused on the sins of all age groups.

The great Temperance crusades of the 18th and early 19th Centuries deplored the effect of parents' drunkenness on innocent children but did not single out youth as victimized by their own tippling. Sociologist Robert Chauncey's review of 19th and 20th century literature reveals that "scarcely a mention was made of youthful drinking" as a distinct social problem until well into the 20th century—when such distinction was discovered to serve adult purpose.[10]

Exploiting "teenage drinking" I: Prohibition

Mark Twain portrayed Tom Sawyer, around age 12 in the Missouri of 1847, as more tempted to drink and smoke after taking vows of temperance with the traveling crusade than when he was free to choose. There were no "drinking ages" in that time; these were soon to evolve as prohibitionist and booze purveyor alike discovered their respective interests served by taking dead aim at the young. The emotional imagery of the teenager swilling demon rum was exploited by both sides in the Temperance debates, a model for modern parlance.

"It was no accident that youths were chosen as a worthy group for symbolic prohibition," writes J.F. Mosher of the history of youth-drinking policy.[11] The first minimum drinking age laws of the late 19th and early 20th centuries "became an acceptable revocation of rights from a powerless minority group in order to appease the powerful Temperance Unionists, without placing an unbearable burden on the alcohol trade," write alcohol policy researchers Vingilis and De Genova.[12]

The pattern of the usefulness of adolescents to adult interest thus emerged in both sides of the prohibition battle: To reformers as an expedient stepping stone to larger goals, and to drinkers as an agency to divert troublesome reformers into a side alley where they could do no real damage. The difference between this first anti-youth drinking campaign and the similar one of today is the 19th century's absence of anger and selective imprecations directed at young people. One similarity, however, is that in the late 1800s, as in 1980 and 1990, efforts were underway to get youths out of the economy during business downturns. The economic retrenchment of the 1890s exerted pressures to clear younger workers out of industrial jobs to make room for adult workers, and it is no accident that the prevailing political view of adolescents, certified as adults during previous industrial expansions, shifted during this period to claims that they were innocent children requiring protection. The stagnant economy of the 1990s brought similar claims that teenagers are "children" and efforts to reduce their wages and restrict their employment (the latter to "protect" them from alcohol, described later in the chapter).

Youths of the 19th and early 20th century were not seen as causing any more problems with alcohol than adults, nor was absolute youth abstinence demanded. None of the laws of that era made it a crime for youths to drink, only for servers to provide it to them. The quaint concept of the "possession" arrest was far in the future. The temperance reforms won by the Antisaloon League in a number of states and localities, including bans on sales to minors, did not express anti-youth sentiment common today, but rather the practical goal of cutting various economic bases from under the saloon business. Frances Willard, founder of the Women's Christian Temperance Union, frankly declared that "whatever tends directly to this result [prohibition], viz. restricted hours of sale, Sunday closing, prohibition of sale to minors and drunkards, we will strongly favor."[13] Similar regulations banned saloons from providing gambling, prostitution, and sales near schools, universities, churches, and military posts.

These primitive measures did not seriously affect youthful imbibance outside or inside of saloons, particularly in their Western and city-slum manifestations. Many states continued to have no regulations against minors being served. Montana's turn-of-the-century law is typical; perhaps still smarting from the disastrous Battle of Little Big Horn, the state banned alcohol provision only to Indians and to soldiers on duty.

By 1916, twenty-three states had adopted prohibition for all age groups. In 1919, national Prohibition through the Eighteenth Amendment took effect. The radical temperance movement had won. For the purposes of this analysis, it had demonstrated that early 20th century society was willing to treat youths and adults alike when it came to drinking: No sauce for the goose, gander, or gosling.

Prohibition, while successful in reducing drinking and alcohol-related problems, created both an anti-personal-freedom ethic and dangerous enterprises dedicated to its subversion. Twelve thousand deaths from alcohol poisonings were recorded in 1927, many from chugging toxic industrial spirits. Lawbreaking was wholesale, from the streets of American cities where agents found the gap between liquor solicitation and sip averaged nineteen minutes, to Congress and the White House, where lawmakers and President Harding routinely patronized bootleggers.

My journalistic interviews with old-timers in southern Montana turned up amusing stories of high school students who volunteered to transport confiscated alcohol to the dump, of course diverting it to their own use, or kids who met secretly with the local bootlegger to obtain a pint for small but precious change. ("Money was the limiting factor" in teenage alcohol acquisition during Prohibition, one recalled.) The Park County, Montana, high school "kegger" of 1933 at a local hot springs (!) was said to be of particular legend. But youth were not seen as any unusual contributors to the national alcohol problem.

A popular 1931 lamentation, "This Moderate Drinking," from *Harper's Monthly*, denotes the disintegration of Prohibition and the evolving peculiarity of American adult attitudes toward drink. The author is as discreet as any modern teenager in remaining anonymous so as not to activate the zealous agents of a dying abstinent order. He declares his intention to give up tipple in this baffling new world in which "moderate drinking" is moderating its devotees into debauchery and asylum:

> In a generation we have changed... There is mighty little moderate drinking and... few if any moderate drinkers who have not gotten tight on occasion... In American homes, where there is no privacy, where young people and older people are jumbled up together, the children naturally see their parents and their parents' friends drinking. They see guests who have passed out. They wake up to hear a group of moderate drinkers coming home to have a sandwich and what is known as a few drinks. How many times have I heard stories of a mildly wild party being interrupted by the children waking up and going to find out what all the row was about... There was plenty of drinking twenty-five years ago, but there were at that time very few growing children who had seen their fathers lit, and practically none who had seen their mothers lit.[14]

Adult tolerance of drunkenness had degenerated to the point that "the critic is now the youngster—who looks on his elders' antics with pained disapproval."

Repeal and vacillation

The odd thinking of American adults is reflected in their vote for Prohibition as a moral imperative and their wholesale violation of it as a personal one. Prohibition was adopted by popular vote in seventeen states, approved by large majorities in Congress, and quickly ratified by legislators in 36 states with full support from President Harding. As Will Rogers observed, Oklahomans vote for Prohibition as long as they can stagger to the polls.

After its landslide approval in 1919, Prohibition was violated immediately and continuously by an estimated 60 percent of the American people, most of Congress, and by a president who publicly sang praises of the new temperance but whose private theme song was Ale to the Chief. In 1933, only fourteen years after overwhelmingly demanding their enactment, adults squashed the Volstead Act and Eighteenth Amendment by 3-1 margins in forty states. The Prohibition saga stands as neither the noble experiment nor the social disaster that it is so often dubbed today, but as a sad monument to the love-hate attitude toward drinking among American adults.

"The average American adult," Lena DiCiccio summed up, "drinks 'wet' and thinks 'dry.'"[15] Now that brew, spirits, and their devotees had proven themselves invulnerable to attack, it was time to find a new id for Americans' well-developed anti-drinking superego to repress. Fortunately, one was handy.

The chief repeal lobby, Americans Against the Prohibition Amendment, argued in part that Prohibition's era of lawlessness had "shocking effect" upon youth. The role of youths, newly discovered then and in full utility today, in maintaining adult alcohol hypocrisy, effecting adult political goals with respect to alcohol, and shifting the focus away from adult drinking excess is crucial to maintaining dangerous alcohol policy.

Prohibition's repeal in 1933 was tied to adoption in all states of the first true "drinking ages," usually 21 for liquor, with a dozen states allowing beer purchase at 18. The political failure of general Prohibition meant that American adults would increasingly focus justifications for alcohol policy less on the perils of drunkenness and more on the tenuous concept that adults can drink properly but youths cannot or should not. This argument contains an astonishing irony, for the Prohibition experience demonstrated not responsibility and moderation toward drinking on the part of American adults, but the extremes of their attraction for the very substance they voted to ban a few years prior. Ubiquitous law-breaking, dangerous home-brewing techniques, hundreds of thousands of cases of blindness and tens of thousands of deaths from drinking toxic industrial alcohols, and pervasive criminal violence dedicated to supplying a desperate American thirst for drink revealed an unrestrained hypocrisy. Further, the sharp rise in manifest drinking problems after repeal, in the form of skyrocketing drunken driving crashes, demonstrated a continuing American adult drinking problem. These contradictions in the national psyche would soon lead 1930s authorities to conjure up scapegoats. They turned out to be familiar ones: Minorities, teenagers, and marijuana.

A large part of the myth used to preserve unrestricted adult access to alcohol is the misrepresentation of Prohibition as a disaster to public safety. It was not, as the first few years after repeal proved. Poisoning from industrial alcohol substitutes (the beverage of necessity for millions of adults who evaded Prohibition) did decrease dramatically after repeal. But deaths due to cirrhosis of the liver, which had fallen sharply during the Prohibition era to an all-time low in 1923, began rising again after repeal and, by the mid-1940s, had returned to pre-Prohibition levels. Deaths from alcoholism (as measured by the disease "alcoholic psychosis," which is organic deterioration caused by chronic over-drinking) also increased.[16]

Although "National Prohibition did not put an end to drinking... Americans must have been drinking less than ever before during Prohibition, probably just under a gallon of absolute alcohol per capita annually," wrote researchers Lender and Martin in 1982.[17] By 1937, American drinking, in standard units of ethanol (pure alcohol, found in different quantities in different beverages), had boosted to around two gallons per capita, and the national party was back in full public swing.

The sharp rise in the rate of fatalities from alcohol-caused traffic wrecks following repeal of Prohibition brought the term into American nomenclature. "Drunk driving" is first indexed in *Reader's Guide* and written about in periodicals as a separate subject in 1935.[18] [19] "In view of the rise in accidents from this cause, we will concentrate on just one thing—drunk driving," the president of the Automobile Manufacturers' Association declared in announcing a $300,000 safety campaign in 1938. "Records show more drunken drivers are being arrested every year," *Literary Digest* reported, noting a 12 percent rise from 1935 to 1936 and a larger increase predicted for 1937.[20]

Compared to the average before repeal, traffic death rates rose 19 percent by 1934, and 28 percent by 1937. The four years following repeal of Prohibition show the highest traffic death rates in American history, even today.[21] The toll in 1937 (a year when fewer than one-fifth as many automobiles were on the highway as 1990) was the single highest death rate before or since, and its five-year increase was larger than any since. Nearly 30,000 more Americans died in traffic crashes in the four years after repeal than in the four years before (Table 7.2).

Only a part of that increase can be explained by increased driving or economic recovery. If simply more driving had caused this death increase, we would expect the rise to occur more or less evenly among all age groups and both sexes. This is

---

Table 7.2

Adult drunk driving deaths skyrocketed after repeal of Prohibition:

Prohibition, repeal, and traffic deaths by age

Motor vehicle deaths		Rate per 100,000 population			
Year	Number	10-14	15-19	>20	All
1929	26,662	9.9	18.8	26.6	21.9
1930	28,684	9.8	20.3	28.9	23.4
1931	29,658	9.1	20.5	29.5	23.9
1932	26,350	8.7	16.4	28.0	21.1
1929-32 (pre repeal)	111,354	9.4	19.0	28.0	22.6
1933 (repeal)	29,323	9.6	19.1	30.7	23.4
1934	33,980	10.6	21.5	35.9	26.9
1935	34,183	10.1	22.3	35.7	26.9
1936	35,761	10.7	24.2	36.8	27.9
1937	37,205	10.4	26.0	38.0	28.9
1934-37 (post-repeal)	141,129	10.5	23.5	36.6	27.7
Change, pre/post		+12%	+24%	+31%	+23%

Source: U.S. Bureau of the Census (1929-37). *Mortality Statistics.* Washington, DC: U.S. Department of Commerce, Table 7.

not the case. The traffic fatality increase was particularly pronounced among populations most likely to drink: men (up 39 percent, twice the rate of increase registered among less drunk-driving-prone women), drivers over age 20 (up 31 percent), and older teenagers (up 24 percent), though younger children were not spared (up 12 percent). Traffic deaths also rose sharply per motor vehicle registered and per mile driven in 1934 and were higher in the post-repeal than pre-repeal period.

Even if only half of the death increase was due to the increased public abuse of alcoholic beverages after 1933, several thousand additional traffic deaths (including 500 among adolescents and children) every year became one of the prices adult Americans were willing to pay, and to impose upon their children, to afford themselves legally available booze. Once again, the concern for youth well-being cited to repeal Prohibition, as in the campaign to enact it, evaporated once the adult goal was secured.

Youths joined in the burgeoning drinking climate of post-repeal, just as they had in every previous adult alcohol trend. However, now that Prohibition had been removed as an option, adults increasingly cited adolescent drinking to express dismay previously directed at adult drinking. The same kinds of anecdotes, testimonials, horror stories, and questionable science used to demonstrate alcohol's perils for all humankind in the 19th century were resurrected in the 20th, in almost identical form, to rail against teenage boozing.

"No question is more urgent with parents of young people today than what stand they should take on the matter of drinking," *Parents* magazine opined in 1937. The first appeals against youthful drinking in the mid-1930s focused on the powers, not vulnerabilities, of the young. In an imaginary "letter to my son" in that same magazine, widely reprinted, Dr. Charles Durfee admitted that parents could not prevent their teenage children from drinking. Efforts to do so, in fact, "give it all the charm of forbidden fruit." Instead, he offered a plaintive rationale for adult drinking and youthful abstinence that, were adults today so candid, might be recognized as closer to the real issue than today's pseudo-science.

"Old folks," Durfee confessed, need "a couple of cocktails" every night to "put a little pep" in the old rustbuckets. On the other hand, "youth should be intoxicated with life."[22]

Teenage drinking, 1945-1970

The wild revelries that greeted soldiers victorious after World War II observed no legal drinking ages. Tales of intrepid 16- and 17-year-old American pilots were legend, but soldiers under age 21 comprised a smaller fraction of the armed forces than in Vietnam. Unlike today, officials were not about to manifest the silliness of sending a soldier to war and arresting him as a veteran for drinking a beer upon his return. American Legion and other veterans' halls were private clubs to which legal drinking ages were not applied.

The first teenage drinking surveys in the late 1940s and early 1950s showed widespread alcohol consumption by junior high, senior high, and college students. It was greeted with adult yawns: No surprise. Teenagers had always drank and always would. Those who drank heavily tended to have heavy-drinking parents, the 1954

Better Homes & Gardens survey reported, also to no one's astonishment. Even multiplying FBI arrest statistics ten-fold to account for under-reporting, drinking age laws were not enforced in the 1950s to any appreciable extent.

The first drinking survey showed that by the standards of the day, most teens were "moderate drinkers ... only 2 percent drink intemperately." Intemperate drinking was then defined as downing twenty or more drinks per week,[23] a tolerance that would bring official apoplexy today. U.S. Senate investigations of 1953 turned up plenty of illegal drinking by minors, including widespread junior and senior high weekend partying and a fair amount of drinking in urban bars.[24] That drinking could be dangerous was noted not only in the survey but in the awareness of thousands of drunken driving deaths among youths and adults every year. But youths were not thought to be a special problem, and regular drinking by most of them was not thought to be of cataclysmic importance.

The early 1960s featured domination of the teenage population by younger 13-15-year-olds not as inclined to drink as older teens. General levels of drinking decreased for demographic reasons. Still, alcohol surveys noted that the average age of initiation was 13, around 4 percent drink daily, and one-fourth of all students get "high" from drinking once a week or more often.[25] Yet only 6 percent of the males and 1 percent of the females reported reaching late adolescence having experienced one or more serious incidents—an accident, injury, or criminal arrest and punishment—related to drinking, the same proportions found in surveys in the 1970s and 1980s. A national survey using the Jellinek method (which estimates alcoholism rates from cirrhosis deaths) found only 5 percent of the American population could be so classed in 1975.[26] Widespread teenage drinking is not linked to future adult alcoholism.

The prevailing adult attitude in the 1960s toward teenage drinking remained rational. The advice of Duke University medical sociologist George Maddox to secondary school educators in 1964 would be greeted with official outrage today:

> Drinking or abstinence among adolescents, then, seems best understood as an integral aspect of growing up, of becoming an adult as they understand what adulthood means. For the majority, adulthood means some drinking; for a persistent minority, it does not... insofar as drinking remains a culturally defined and institutionalized aspect of adult behavior, the adolescent who is learning what it means to be an adult is likely to continue to drink in spite of any risks which may be involved, just as the adults he observes do. The adolescent, like the adult, is typically aware not only of what alcohol may do to him but also of what it can do for him, and he behaves accordingly.[27]

What? Teenagers can think? That adolescents are so stupid that a Coors shirt or a Near Beer display could tip them over the precipice into besottedness had not been discovered.

As Sixties Baby-Boom youth matured, the number drinking increased. By the late 1960s, surveys continued to show widespread drinking by youth, with more than 60 percent reporting regular use. The legal drinking age, 21 in nearly all states, continued to have little effect on teenage drinking even with 86,000 underage drinking arrests in 1960, rising to 170,000 by 1965. Yet in the midst of the most widespread drug abuse up to that point in American history, which arrived in the 1968-72 period along with larger demographic and sociological change, adults did not panic. Drinking ages were lowered in the early 1970s, and 18-year-olds were temporarily welcomed into adulthood's inner sanctum.

Teen enfranchisement: 1970-1975

From 1970 through 1975, nearly all states lowered their legal ages of adulthood, thirty including their legal drinking ages, usually from 21 to 18. This reform was largely in recognition of the unfairness of sending teenage draftees to Vietnam who could not exercise most adult rights. Despite the immense attention given the legal drinking age, it is clear such laws do not have dramatic effects on teenage drinking or alcohol mishaps. Effects are so small, in fact, that arguments over drinking age effects on teenage drinking and drunken driving have become increasing exercises in hair-splitting in the literature and wild exaggeration in the political arena.

It would be expected that allowing greater teenage use of alcohol in public would increase drinking and drunken driving mishap among that minority of youth, as among that minority of adults, whose misbehavior would be stimulated by greater availability. As we have seen, repeal of Prohibition in 1933 was followed by a doubling in per capita consumption of alcohol, a 31 percent increase in motor vehicle deaths among adults (including a 39 percent increase among men), a 24 percent traffic death rise among teens, and sharp rises in cirrhosis and alcoholism deaths. Examining these social costs in the same manner that the social costs of teenage drinking are examined, there is little argument to be made that adults can handle legal alcohol responsibly while teenagers cannot. Rather, adults are willing overlook their own misbehaviors, pay an enormous societal price, and impose a share of that price on youth in order to maintain legal alcohol availability for grownup convenience.

Logically, we would expect disproportionate effects from removing prohibition (however previously ineffective) on older teenagers just as we saw among adults from repealing Prohibition. The surprising thing is how small the effects, if any, turned out to be. In fact, contrary to the current near-hysteria on the subject, several measures show that the experiment in legal drinking turned out to be one of the least important influences on teenage traffic deaths.

Most of the many analyses of drinking age effects (including some dubious contributions by this author) ignore the fact that teenage highway fatalities had been increasing for sixty years before drinking ages were lowered. From 1915 to the present, teenagers have shown an increased rate of highway deaths not shared by other age groups. This effect resulted from decreasing driving ages, the increase in driving by youths relative to adults, and increased employment among teens. The only respites in this steady increase coincided with (a) more rapidly rising drunken driving fatalities among adults than teens following repeal of Prohibition in 1933, and (b) more rapidly falling declines in teen than adult drunken driving fatalities coinciding with falling numbers of teenage licensed drivers during the 1980s.

Some of this teenage fatality rise in the 1960s and 1970s was due to huge numbers of postwar Baby Boomers reaching driving age. In 1960, non-driving 13- and 14-year-olds dominated the teen population. From 1960 to 1976, the older, more driving-prone and drinking-prone 18-19-year-old component rose by 55 percent. By 1976, the two largest teenage groups were 18 and 19, the ages that account for two-thirds of all teenage drunken driving deaths. Thus long-term highway fatality trends, demographics, adult trends, and the Sixties revolution—all of which produced significant increases in teenage drinking and in highway fatalities *prior* to drinking ages being lowered—were of paramount importance, confounding and dwarfing whatever effects occurred from teen alcohol enfranchisement.

In 1969, for example, only about 25 percent of the nation's 18- and 19-year-olds could legally purchase some form of alcohol, usually beer. In 1975, after thirty states lowered their legal drinking ages, 70 percent of all 18- and 19-year-olds could legally buy alcohol, usually in all forms. In 1989, after the national drinking age of 21 was finalized in all states, no 18- and 19-year-olds could buy booze in any form. Thus the fluctuation in the legality of alcohol purchase by older teens, from 25 percent (mostly for beer) in 1969 to 70 percent (mostly for all beverages) in 1975 to 0 percent in 1989, has been enormous.

Yet drunkenness arrests and highway deaths among teens showed only small changes over that period. The fatality effects of teen alcohol enfranchisement in the early 1970s which, due to the unavailability of drunken driving figures themselves, are compared for total highway fatalities among teens and adults (Table 7.3).

Note that teenagers have higher traffic death rates than adults age 20-44, who

Table 7.3

Legal drinking did not lead to teenage traffic carnage:

Teen and adult traffic death rates during teen alcohol enfranchisement, 1969-75

Motor vehicle deaths		Rate per 100,000 population			
Year	Total	Age: 10-14	15-19	20-44	All
1969	55,791	9.3	47.1	35.7	27.5
1970	54,633	9.6	43.6	33.9	26.7
1971	54,381	9.9	43.1	33.3	26.3
1972	56,278	10.2	45.3	33.6	27.0
1973	55,511	9.6	44.8	33.4	26.4
1974	46,402	8.0	38.7	28.2	21.9
1975	45,853	7.7	38.0	27.8	21.3
Change, 1969-75		-17%	-19%	-22%	-23%

Source: National Center for Health Statistics (1969-1975). *Vital Statistics of the United States.* Part B, Mortality. Washington, DC: U.S. Department of Health and Human Services, Table 7-5.

in turn have higher death rates than drivers over age 45. While this fact is incessantly cited to buttress claims that adolescents are naturally reckless, in fact it appears more a function of driving inexperience in a youth population dominated by novice drivers. It is a bigger question why 20-24-year-olds have much higher traffic death rates than teens, and 25-29-year-old similar levels, given their greater experience. A comprehensive examination of violent deaths by age in the next chapter shows that teens are less at risk of traffic deaths than drivers age 20-24 and are less at risk for all types of accidental and deliberately-caused fatality than many adult age groups (See Table 8.3, Chapter 8).

For the purpose of examining the dangers of legal drinking on teens, the effect, if any, is small. From 1969 to 1975, when some four million teens were stepping up to bars and state liquor store counters legally for the first time, the highway death rate among teens *decreased* by 19 percent. Legal alcohol purchase did not, of course, cause this decrease. Lower highway speeds and higher gasoline prices brought down tolls among all age groups, particularly among adult drivers whose disproportionately high rates of interstate and highway deaths were most reduced by the gas-saving 55-mph speed limit implemented in 1973. Note that the traffic fatality decrease among 20-44-year-olds, nearly all of whom could drink legally throughout, was only slightly greater, at 22 percent.

Analysis of the massive teenage enfranchisement from 1969 to 1975 is hampered because precise drunken driving tolls are not available for this period. Some researchers found the teenage highway death decrease somewhat weaker in states that lowered their drinking ages, on the order of 5 percent to 7 percent in more comprehensive studies by the Insurance Institute for Highway Safety[29] and University of North Carolina researchers.[30]

Other analyses, particularly those that examined highway death changes prior to the 1970s, found no unusual trend. A 1977 review found studies on the issue badly flawed and "little agreement at the present time concerning the effects of the changes."[31] A 1984 review of studies of states that lowered their drinking ages during the 1970-75 period found that "the results have been mixed."[32] Even assuming the worst, repealing Prohibition in 1933 was followed by an increase in teenage highway deaths several times higher than anything attributed to lowered drinking ages in 1970-75, as well as a large increase in adult fatalities. The question is not the legal availability of alcohol to teenagers, but its availability period.

Studies found increases in teenage drinking in bars, primarily reflected in increased draft beer sales. This effect was later reported in tones of disapproval, leading to puzzlement over just what adults thought the effect of teen enfranchisement would be. Given that surveys do not show any general increase in teenage drinking during the early 1970s, this measure indicates only a shift in location of use.[33] The chief effect of legal drinking appears to have been an increase in the number of teens drinking in public rather than at private parties and "keggers," producing more public arrests relative to adults. Surveys show no increase in teens getting drunk during this period, indicating that enfranchisement simply brought teenage drinking out in the open.

There was thus no carnage or crisis of drunken binges to motivate drastic removal of teenage rights. The large majority of teenagers proved that legal alcohol availability did not lead to dire results. In fact, they remained less inclined to drunken behavior in public than were young and middle-aged adults. Yet the public has been led to believe that enfranchising adolescents led to a blood-soaked carnage. The campaign to create this misimpression was manufactured via a questionable, self-interested campaign masked as "concern for teenage safety"—which later evolved into failure masked as success.

Exploiting teenage drinking II: A new "social problem"

Although virtually every headline-hunting agency and program over the past two decades has asserted dramatic increases in teenage drinking at younger ages, these claims appear to be myth. Surveys of the 1970s showed drinking by youths similar to that of the 1950s and before. In 1977 the Research Triangle Institute surveyed 5,000 students during the height of American leniency about "teenage" drinking and found about the same patterns as in 1952 and the 1960s (Table 7.5).

The 1977 survey found that 87 percent of the students drank, 27 percent drank once a week or more often, 85 percent were drinking by tenth grade, and 13 percent reported problems such as drinking and driving, or trouble with family, friends, teachers, or police, at least twice in the previous year. Fewer than 5 percent reported serious outcomes, such as an accident or criminal arrest. The survey classed 14 percent of the students as "weekly heavy drinkers" who consumed an average of 16 drinks per week. The 1978 survey contacted only senior high students and used a lower measure of heavy drinking than the 1952 survey, which included junior high students. The surveys show that overall teenage alcohol habits changed little between 1952 and 1978.[34]

Similarly, a 1977 review of some 1,100 documents on youthful drinking from 1951 to 1974 by researchers Howard Blane and Linda Hewitt for the National Institute on Alcohol Abuse and Alcoholism (NIAAA) concluded that "there has been no significant shift over the last twenty-five years in the age at which youngsters consume their first drink." Their survey found the average age of drinking initiation was 13.5 in 1951-65 and 13.3 in 1966-75 and that there was a moderate increase in both college and high school drinking from the early 1940s to the 1960s and none thereafter.[35] Blane and Hewitt's calming findings were initially reported by the NIAAA to Congress in 1978, then vanished from the official literature in 1981.[36]

Instead, in the 1970s, for the first time in any country or in any time in history, at a time when teenage drunkenness arrests and traffic accidents were decreasing, the apocalyptic perils of "teenage drinking" were suddenly discovered in the U.S. The campaign to ban teens from drinking assumed frantic proportions over the next two decades, backed by regression to the rhetoric of the Washingtonians and Temperance crusaders—but this time cloaked in reference only to teenagers. The foundations of today's anti-teen-drinking crusade are not logic, science, teenage safety, or responsibility with alcohol—none of which it has furthered—but the needs of the modern adult to which adolescents have proven useful.

The first—a new one, which accounts for today's shrillness on the issue—is profit and advancement of agencies and programs that arose in the 1970s and 1980s to address alcohol, safety, and youth issues. As sociologist Robert Chauncey's extensive 1981 analysis of the federal government's entry into the alcohol and drug fields points out, the National Institute on Alcohol Abuse and Alcoholism, created in 1971, wasted little time in publicizing the horrors of "teenage drinking."[37]

In 1974, a *Time* magazine cover story quoted NIAAA director Morris Chafetz as warning, "the switch is on... youths are moving from a wide range of other drugs to the most devastating drug—the one most widely misused of all—alcohol."[38] Similar reports appeared widely in other media. "Across the nation, more teenagers—and even preteenagers—are drinking than ever before," NIAAA announced in 1975. "Teenage alcoholics" sprouted from television screens and P.T.A. podia, creating the modern image of adolescent drunkard-turned-crusading-teetotaller.

In 1976, the U.S. Senate Committee on Appropriations (based on assertions by the NIAAA) noted "with chagrin that the problem of teenage alcoholism continues to rise." It provided $83 million to the NIAAA "to develop a comprehensive public education and information dissemination program dealing specifically with teenage alcoholism." The NIAAA obliged with redoubled propaganda in 1977. "This wave of alarm over youthful alcohol abuse has no precedent in U.S. history," Chauncey wrote of the NIAAA-manufactured campaign. A Gallup Poll showed that for the first time, Americans considered alcohol a serious youth problem.[39]

"Two possibilities emerge," wrote Chauncey:

> Either the extent of the problems associated with teenage drinking had grown dramatically in recent years and the diligence of the newly created NIAAA served to publicize this burgeoning problem heretofore clouded by misinformation and blithe ignorance; or the NIAAA, in an effort to sustain itself, has seized on an emotionally charged topic certain to generate demands for a variety of educational and treatment programs.[40]

As Blane and Hewitt's review found, teenage drinking and alcohol problems had not increased. But calming findings were not what the NIAAA wanted to publicize. The agency preferred to argue, via director Chafetz, with all the breathlessness of a Temperance pulpiteer:

> Arrests of young people for public drunkenness are occurring in larger numbers and at younger ages. Alcoholics Anonymous groups for alcoholic teenagers are springing up around the country, where there were none before 1970. Even among pre-teens—children between 9 and 12 years old—alcoholism is becoming more and more common.

As Chauncey pointed out, "all of these perceptions are easily disputed." The FBI's *Uniform Crime Reports* show a 7 percent decrease in public drunkenness arrest rates for teenagers from 1970 to 1975, with a particularly large decrease in drunkenness arrests of juveniles under age 15. A 1975 Alcoholics Anonymous membership survey found "no discernible trend regarding either young or older members." Nor did the NIAAA present any evidence of an increase in teenage alcoholism, which its own researchers had found to be rare.[41]

"Twenty-three percent of all students, including 36 percent of the male high school seniors, report getting drunk at least four times a year—a frequency that some experts, including myself, believe is indicative of a developing alcoholism problem," Chafetz declared in 1974. Note that this level is almost identical to the weekly levels of teens who reported getting "high" from drinking once a week in 1950s and 1960s surveys.

In positing a future of alcoholism for as many as one-third of the nation's teenage males based on their getting drunk four times a year, the advice to Chafetz and other experts would be the same given to a weather reporter lamenting showers during blue skies: Open the window and look outside. Teenage drinking from Colonial times to the 1950s had been as heavy or heavier than at present. Yet no one was arguing that one-third of the nation's men had turned out to be alcoholics.

Interestingly, Chafetz himself was to dispute his own campaign only a year later. In 1975, he lamented to *The Alcoholism Report* that the media have "gone the usual route," "blown it (teenage drinking) out of proportion," and may "intensify the problem."[42]

Chafetz's successor as NIAAA director, Ernest Noble, resurrected the campaign, calling teenage drinking a "devastating problem" at "epidemic proportion" in 1977. "Every indication points to the conclusion that the teenagers in our country are not only drinking more, but that they are drinking earlier and experiencing more problems with alcohol," Noble testified in 1978, again turning on its head the findings of NIAAA's own comprehensive review of several decades of literature. Chauncey's conclusion:

> The NIAAA, as a young bureaucracy, faces stiff competition for funds from older, better established, and more insulated bureaucracies... The manipulation of teenage drinking as a public and political issue by the NIAAA offers self-preservation as a dominant motive behind the campaign.[43]

Jack Mendelson and Nancy K. Mello, editors of the *Journal of Studies on Alcohol*, agreed: The evidence "did not suggest a growing teenage drinking problem."[44]

The NIAAA campaign on teenage drinking consisted of fabrication of a new "social problem" (what sociologists call "moral entrepreneurship"), and it fit into a growing official scheme to promote public health through imprecation rather than information. As University of Virginia law professor Richard Bonnie pointed out of growing government "health" advocacy in 1981;

> Recent regulatory and legislative initiatives strongly suggest that... the declared government policy appears to be shifting away from an 'informed choice' model and toward the public health model—reducing aggregate consumption of alcohol and discouraging its use by target groups... I predict, then, a transition from information to persuasion—or, as the industry might say, to propaganda.[45]

It was an apt forecast. The accuracy or falsity of information released by agencies on health issues has become of less importance in the 1980s and 1990s than its usefulness in pursuing a public health goal.

In a crasser sense, other adult interests such as the Hotel and Restaurant

Employees and Bartenders union, facing increased competition from teenage bar employees after drinking ages were lowered, supported returning to the 21 drinking age to eliminate job competition from 18-20-year-old applicants. Yet simple agency, program, and economic self-interest could not have succeeded without the changing motivation of post-Sixties adults.

If it is accepted that political agencies will engage in public relations efforts, often including the manufacture of nonexistent crises, in order to win attention and funding, why did the NIAAA target teenagers? Why did the agency not seek to exploit the much larger, more lucrative "market" of adult drinking problems? Or, if a scapegoat was being sought, why not the drinking problems of minority groups? On its face, an attack on white teenagers (the group that drank the most) might have seemed risky, liable to provoke a negative reaction from white parents whose sons and daughters were mass-accused of being the new town drunks—or at least the kind of so-what indifference that similar teen drinking revelations of the 1930s, 1950s, and 1960s had engendered.

Whether consciously or not, the NIAAA perceived that adolescents were the new scapegoats. Part of the isolation and vulnerability of youths to political attack was brought on by the sharp rise in family breakup, led by a doubling in divorce from 1965 to 1975. By 1975, one in two marriages had ended in, or was headed for, divorce. Mushrooming family stresses suddenly had made children and teenagers a liability, a vexation to parents at odds with each other, a control problem for rising numbers of single-parent households. Increasingly fragile families turned to government, laws, programs, and professionals to fill in where parents were opting out. The NIAAA was the first to exploit this period of rising household turmoil with a fear campaign and rescue plan. Its spectacular success—in winning funding and favorable media, not in effecting healthier teenagers—served as a model for an avalanche of 1980s duplication and duplicity.

Adult motivators in teen prohibition
The manufacture of the "teenage drinking crisis" and the subsequent campaign after 1975 to raise the drinking age back to 21 did not result from any of the motives commonly given for it, although some of its advocates may have believed them. It was not motivated by a massive teenage highway carnage resulting from lower drinking ages, nor a national desire to protect the young, nor any genuine increase in alcohol damage in general.

Nor did raising drinking ages produce noteworthy benefit in any of these areas. The principle benefits accrued: Adult economic advantage, public moralizing while privately protecting adult alcohol access, and invoking government controls on the young to make up for rising family instability. It is clear that any effects of lowered drinking ages were small and overwhelmed by other risks to which society deliberately exposes the young—including those from adult drinking.

If the adult motive in removing teen drinking rights was a benign one to protect youth, as many advocates claimed, it is curious that it did not extend into areas such as military combat, where youth disenfranchisement might have resulted in increased adult risk exposure and obligation. For one such topical risk, 25,000 under-21 soldiers died in the Vietnam War during the 1965-74 period, and thousands more stateside from war-related traumas. The coming national fervor for protecting youths from expanded rights, such as legal drinking, did not extend to protecting them from expanded adult obligations. This we-don't-care contradiction was most evident in the fury expressed by Candy Lightner, witness for Mothers Against Drunk Driving (MADD), who told lawmakers she was "sick and tired" of hearing the complaint that youths were old enough to be sent to war but not to drink.

Lightner, motivated to organize MADD because her daughter was killed by an adult drunk driver in 1980, turned out to be a case study in activists whose crusades end up focusing their hostility against teenagers. In the early 1980s, when I was a member of MADD and lobbied for stricter anti-drunk driving laws in Montana, I noticed Lightner's MADD newsletter would only print the ages of drunk drivers when they were under 21. In 1994, Lightner wound up on the payroll of the brewery industry opposing efforts to toughen state laws against adult drunk driving.[46]

Another risk, by conservative estimate, is the 4,000 teenagers and children killed every year by drunken adults—including 2,000 youths killed by drinking adult drivers and an equal number who die in other accidents and homicides in which adult drinking is a factor. These tolls do not include birth defects caused by parental alcohol abuse. If prohibition on teenage alcohol use is as dramatically successful in saving teenage lives as officials claim, then imposing it upon adults would save the lives of many young people every year, including small children, who are now victims of adult intemperance.

In terms of effective remedies, alcohol "tax policy is more potent than drinking age policy in reducing mortality," a comprehensive literature review by Berkeley research psychologist Joel Moskowitz concludes.[47] Yet taxes have not been raised for the purpose of "protecting young people" or adults. Similarly, states have not moved to restrict liquor-by-the-drink sale even though it is associated with a significant increase in alcohol-related traffic accidents.[48]

"Protecting young people," then, is a dubious motivator in the campaign to stop teenage drinking. Adults are unwilling to reduce the exposure of teenagers to wartime combat, raise the age of parental obligation to protect youth, raise taxes on alcohol, or reduce adult access to alcohol (or even the form it is served in). If the concern was over growing realization of the alarming damage caused by alcohol in American society, it was curious that the New Prohibition campaign stopped with adolescents. The effect of lowered drinking ages, if any, was insignificant compared to the 100,000 annual deaths Americans accept among all age groups as a price for general alcohol availability and use.

Teenage and adult drinking and driving

The often-cited "unacceptable level" of teenage drunken driving mishap represents wholesale manipulation of statistics which show that in fact, it is legal-drinking *adult* drunk drivers we should be the most worried about. Since no level of drunken driving death can be considered acceptable, efforts to attack it require careful analysis rather than age-based prejudice.

Who's driving drunk? While teenagers hog the media and presidential atten-

Table 7.4

Adults in their 20s and 30s, not teens, are worst for drunken fatality:

U.S. drunk drivers and pedestrians in fatal traffic crashes, 1993*

Age group	Drunk drivers*	Drunk pedestrians*	Total	Rate
16-20	1,210	90	1,300	7.6
21-24	2,020	150	2,170	14.1
25-34	3,820	500	4,320	10.4
35-44	2,360	460	2,820	6.9
45-64	1,470	370	1,840	3.7
65-older	330	130	460	1.4
Men	9,580	1,460	11,040	11.6
Women	1,620	250	1,870	1.9
All	11,200	1,700	12,900	6.6

*Blood alcohol content of .10 or greater. Rate is per 100,000 population for each age.
Source: National Highway Traffic Safety Administration (1995). *Traffic Safety Facts, 1993*. Washington, DC: U.S. Department of Transportation, Tables 3 and 5.

tion, adults are committing 90 percent of the intoxicated motorway damage. The National Highway Traffic Safety Administration's most recent *Traffic Safety Facts 1993,* shows grownups in their 20s and 30s—and especially men—deserve much more limelight (Table 7.4).

If age is to be a sole criterion, drivers age 21-34 account for more than half of all fatal drunken traffic mishaps—a per-person rate 50 percent higher than teens. Nearly 30 percent of all deadly drivers age 21-34 are drunk. In fact, all age groups under 45 have higher than average drunk driving tolls. The vaunted safety record of adult drivers (at least those under age 45) is a myth. The huge number of elder drivers with low death tolls dilute the accident-prone record of young and middle-aged adults.

If the most-offending arbitrary group is to be singled out for the sins of a fraction of its members, drunken driving deaths are overwhelmingly a male problem rather than a youth problem. Men display alcohol-related death rates (11.6 per 100,000 population in 1993) 50 percent higher than do teenagers and six times higher than women. In 1993, 24 percent of the male drivers in fatal wrecks were drunk, compared to only 16 percent of teen drivers. Men account for 86 percent of all traffic fatalities involving drinking—just about the same percentage men occupy in legislatures and editorial staffs, which is why nothing is said or done about the "male drinking and driving carnage."

Not only are these legal-drinking adult age groups much more likely to be drunk when in fatal wrecks than are teens, they are drunker drunks when they are (average adult blood alcohol content of 0.22, compared to 0.17 for teens).[49] But when was the last time you witnessed a politician speech or news special on the twenty-thirtysomething male drunk driving mayhem?

But more drunk driving is "mature"...

The campaign to force teenage abstinence did not altogether ignore the inconsistency that if safety was truly the goal, adult drinking presented even more of a hazard and should face greater Carry Nation axwork. Rather than wrestle with that thorny problem, officials switched the measures used to analyze drunken driving. Two of the biasing measures are described here, both amusing were they not used to such serious ends.

In 1982, National Highway Traffic Safety Administration (NHTSA) statisticians, whose figures showed that teenagers had fewer drunken accidents per person than adults in their 20s and 30s, changed the measure to drunken crashes per million miles driven.[50] (Even this analysis showed that alcohol-related fatalities peaked not among teenagers, but at age 21, which did not receive much publicity). Normally, such "risk exposure" logic would be good. The more one drives, the more one is "at risk" of being in a wreck.

As a measure of *drunk driving*, however, the per-mile measure is ludicrous. In order to be "at risk" of being in a drunk driving wreck, one has to drive drunk. NHTSA's re-analysis first conceded (without expressly stating as much) that adults in their 20s and 30s drive many *more* miles while *drunk* than do teenagers. It further found that adults that age were *more* likely to cause drunken fatal traffic accidents than teens. The only measure that would make adults look safer than teens is an absurdity: That adults experience fewer deadly crashes *per mile driven drunk*. In other words, a person who drives drunk 1,000 miles a year and causes 10 crashes is safer—100 times safer per mile driven drunk, in fact—than a person who drives drunk one mile a year and gets into one crash. This measure (not drunk driving fatality rate, not drunk driving risk- taking), one which turns the concept of public safety upside down by rewarding more drunken driving, became the standard used to downplay adult drunken driving while building a public perception of out-of-control inebriated teen slaughter.

This Red Queen logic was hyped nationwide in bulletins by insurance companies eager to justify their discriminatorily high rates charged to teenage drivers. The figures were also widely quoted in the popular media, which trumpeted the myth that teenagers were three or five or ten times (or whatever the numbers du jour turned out to be) more likely to commit drunken motorway murder than clean-living grownups.

A second meaningless statistical concept involved intensive publicity that drunk driving is "the leading cause of death among teenagers." Not true: Sober driving is. Other than not being true, the other problem with the oft-repeated declaration is that it is pointless. While creating the wrong impression that teenagers are unusually dangerous, the only fact it really communicates is that teens are far less likely to succumb to the leading causes of death for adults: Cancer and cardiovascular disease.

Often an agency's own statistics were ignored. In arguing for the 21 drinking age as a measure to reduce "teenage alcoholism," the NIAAA ignored its 1981 report showing alcoholism and alcohol-related death rates significantly higher in states with long-term drinking ages of 21 than in states with lower drinking ages. Interestingly, this higher rate of alcohol abuse in more conservative states occurred even though their per-capita drinking rates among adults and adolescents were lower than the national average.[51]

Adolescents thus became the first group to which Bonnie's 1981 warning of the outcome of government health propaganda has applied. As addiction researcher Stanton Peele wrote: "Any regulatory approach whose ultimate aim is to orchestrate changes in mass behavior implies a significant sacrifice in human freedom... not only by changing attitudes toward substance consumption, but also toward human liberty itself."[52] Even with teenage "freedom" considered an irrelevant issue, teenagers have not proven amenable to behavioral modification as a separate group.

Effects of teen prohibition

The failure of teen-prohibition has not been for want of trying. Adult enthusiasm in pursuing the goal achieved the on-paper blueprint of a coordinated law-enforcement-school-community-program-agency prevention-intervention-treatment offensive of multi-billion-dollar proportions. Its popularity among adults has been overwhelming; its funding lavish; its publicity laced with the frightening pronouncements; its coordination among public and private sector incestuous; and its endorsement by virtually every interested adult entity, from Baptist to boozer, unanimous.

The result: Teen drunken driving crashes show no change relative to adults for 20 years. Teen drinking is the same today as in 1952 and 1978. In forty years (and probably far longer than surveys go back), through enormous variations in adult opinions and efforts to change teenage drinking, the only influence on youthful alcohol practices has remained adult alcohol practices (Table 7.5).

Table 7.5

1950s, 1970s, and 1990s teens drink the same amount...

Grades 7-12	1952	1978	1991
Ever had a drink	90%	87%	90%
Drinks weekly	47%	46%	48%
Reports problems with drinking	16%	16%	15%
Average age of first drink	12	12	12

Sources: Lomask M (1954, March). First report on high school drinking, *Better Homes & Gardens*, pp 72-75; Lowman C (1981/82, Winter). Facts for planning no 1: Prevalence of alcohol use among U.S. senior high school students. *Alcohol Health & Research World* 6, pp 41-46; comparable high school surveys compiled by the author from Montana, Oklahoma, California, 1991.

But the chief public issue was not what was really going on, but the political utility of teenagers to adult needs. In the mid-1970s, the war was over, and it was time to start stamping out adolescent rights won in the wake of the Sixties and thousands of teen Vietnam War deaths. States began to raise their drinking ages again in 1976. Cries of success were immediate.

A number of individual state studies in the late 1970s claimed that raised drinking ages resulted in huge decreases in adolescent drunken driving deaths. Claims of crash reductions of 47 percent in New Jersey, 31 percent in Michigan, and 27 percent in Illinois were typical. These studies left out a few variables: Stronger anti-drunken driving laws aimed at all age groups (which reduced fatalities among teens more than adults), post Baby-Boom teenage population declines (which meant fewer teenagers on the roads to get into accidents), and the fact that states that kept low drinking ages also showed teen fatality drops (which meant that legal drinking status was not leading to more deaths). And the studies were selective. The experiences of states such as Iowa, Maine, Montana, and New Hampshire, where raised drinking ages were followed by *higher* adolescent drunken driving tolls, didn't get studied or press. Despite their flaws, these studies won breathless media attention in the early 1980s but are not now given much credence.

Earlier predictions of huge benefits from the 21 drinking age—for example, 1,250 lives saved annually, forecast by the National Transportation Safety Board in 1983—dwindled in later studies. Even the NTSB reduced its estimate to 600 lives saved a year later, indicating how accurate the process was.[53]

An Insurance Institute for Highway Safety study in 1983 reported a decrease of 28 percent in the ratio of nighttime to daytime fatal crashes among the teen age groups banned from drinking in states that raised their drinking ages.[54] The measure chosen was a poor one, so unstable that its effects did not show up using other measures and quickly disappeared. Still, the study quickly became the most widely cited study in the press and Congressional debates.

In 1986, the Insurance Institute released a new and much improved study pegging the traffic death decrease among teens banished from alcohol at 13 percent for nighttime crashes and 9 percent for all accidents through 1984.[55] This was less than half the previous estimate. Most studies of the mid-1980s suggested overall crash decreases of 5 percent to 10 percent, with the percentage diminishing with each new study.

The consensus of the more recent, better-done studies was that the effects of raising the drinking age to 21 were small. If accepted at face value (and, as will be noted, some counter-research found all that was really accomplished was redistributing fatalities to other time periods and older age groups, not saving lives), the much-touted 21 drinking age might have reduced the national traffic toll by 1 percent to 2 percent. For the immense political effort put into it, more lives could have been saved by virtually any other highway safety strategy (such as increased use of seat belts, or stronger anti-drunk driving law enforcement) targeting all age groups.

Its effects were practically nil compared to the 20 percent surplus in traffic deaths Americans had accepted as the price for legal adult drinking in the 1930s. Thus the larger issue remains: American grownups are willing to accept substantially higher death tolls (including among children and teens killed by drunken adults) to preserve adult drinking rights but profess extreme concern over "saving lives" when it comes to adolescents' right to drink.

Adult drunks, teen drunks

In 1975, federal data compilers, through the newly formed Fatal Accident Reporting System (FARS), first made available fatal accidents by driver involved and time of day. This measure brought some uniformity and precision to drunken driving analysis among various states and over different time periods in which inconsistency had previously been the rule.

Table 7.6 shows the pattern of teenage and adult drunken driving deaths by five-year period from 1975 through 1994 by time of crash. Night-time fatal traffic accidents (a large majority of which involve drinking), are shown separately from daytime fatal crashes (most of which do not involve drinking), along with total crashes. Rates of teenage (age 15-20) fatal accidents are compared to those of two adult age groups, 21-24 and all age 21 and older, who could legally drink throughout the entire 20-year period. The top half of the table shows the absolute change in teen and adult fatal crash rates, and the bottom half shows the change in teen crashes relative to adults, by time of crash. The intent is to see whether raising drinking ages to 21 during the 1976-1988 period is connected with any unusual decline in teenage traffic deaths that did not occur among adults.

None can be glimpsed. As we have seen in other behaviors, the trends in traffic deaths for teens and adults are astonishingly similar. As the net changes shown at the bottom of the table show, over the 20-year period in which 8 million teenagers were banned from legal drinking, the rate of teenage fatal traffic accidents varied by less than 1 percent relative to those among drivers over age 21, who were able to drink legally throughout the period. Year to year trends among teens and adults are likewise parallel (Figure 7.7).

Note that daytime fatal traffic accidents among teens rose relative to adults. This is an unexpected result, since a lower proportion of teens were licensed to drive in 1994 than in 1975. Thus raising the drinking age to 21 nationwide did not save lives. The most plausible conclusion is that banning teens from bars and nighttime entertainment simply shifted a small proportion of teen fatalities away from nighttime and toward daytime hours, with a "seesaw effect" (slight decline in nighttime deaths offset by a slight rise in daytime deaths) most pronounced when teen-driver trends are compared to those of drivers age 21-24. Note, finally, that while teens have traffic death rates about 50 percent higher than drivers over age 21 as a whole (whose tolls are diluted by the large number of elder drivers who cause few deaths), teens are safer than drivers age 21-24—whose legal right to drink no one has challenged.

Note that there was a period, in the early 1980s when nearly all studies of the effects of raising the drinking age were done, when some small effects could be claimed—especially if, as nearly all studies did, traffic crashes among under-21 drivers were compared to those age 21-24. From 1975-85, nighttime traffic deaths among under-21 drivers fell by 9 percent relative to those age 21-24—which some researchers believe was due more to a rise in fatalities among 21-24-year-olds than a

Table 7.6

Raised drinking ages did not reduce teen traffic deaths relative to adults':

Fatal traffic crashes per 100,000 population, by age and time of crash:

Age:	Nighttime fatal crashes* (8pm-4am)			Daytime fatal crashes (4am-8pm)			All fatal crashes (all hours)		
	15-20	21-24	21+	15-20	21-24	21+	15-20	21-24	21+
1975	23.8	27.5	11.6	24.4	30.3	20.0	48.3	57.8	31.6
1980	27.7	32.8	13.7	24.4	29.8	19.5	52.1	62.6	33.2
1985	20.5	26.0	10.2	24.0	28.3	18.9	44.5	54.4	29.1
1990	19.8	23.0	9.6	23.6	25.4	18.9	43.3	48.5	28.5
1994	15.4	18.7	7.6	23.7	24.4	17.9	39.1	43.0	25.4

Absolute change (percent)

	15-20	21-24	21+	15-20	21-24	21+	15-20	21-24	21+
'75-85	-14.1	-5.1	-12.3	-1.7	-6.4	-5.4	-7.8	-5.8	-7.9
'85-94	-24.7	-28.3	-25.9	-1.3	-14.1	-5.5	-12.0	-20.9	-12.6
'75-94	-35.3	-31.9	-35.0	-3.0	-19.6	-10.6	-18.9	-25.5	-19.5

Net teen (age 15-20) traffic death rates versus adult traffic death rates:

Teens vs:	Nighttime fatal crashes*		Daytime fatal crashes		All fatal crashes	
	age 21-24	21+	age 21-24	21+	age 21-24	21+
1975	0.87	2.05	0.81	1.22	0.84	1.53
1980	0.85	2.03	0.82	1.25	0.83	1.57
1985	0.79	2.01	0.85	1.27	0.82	1.53
1990	0.86	2.05	0.93	1.25	0.89	1.52
1994	0.83	2.04	0.97	1.32	0.91	1.54

Net change in teen traffic deaths (percent):

	age 21-24	21+	age 21-24	21+	age 21-24	21+
'75-85	-9.4	-2.1	+5.0	+3.9	-2.1	+0.1
'85-94	+5.0	+1.6	+14.9	+4.5	+11.2	+0.7
'75-94	-4.9	-0.5	+20.7	+8.5	+8.8	+0.7

*Nighttime crashes are the most likely to involve drinking.
Source: Fatal Accident Reporting System (1975-1994). Drivers Involved in All Fatal Accidents and in Nighttime Fatal Accidents by State, Age. Washington, DC: National Highway Traffic Safety Administration, 1975-94 (annual printout, 1975-1994).

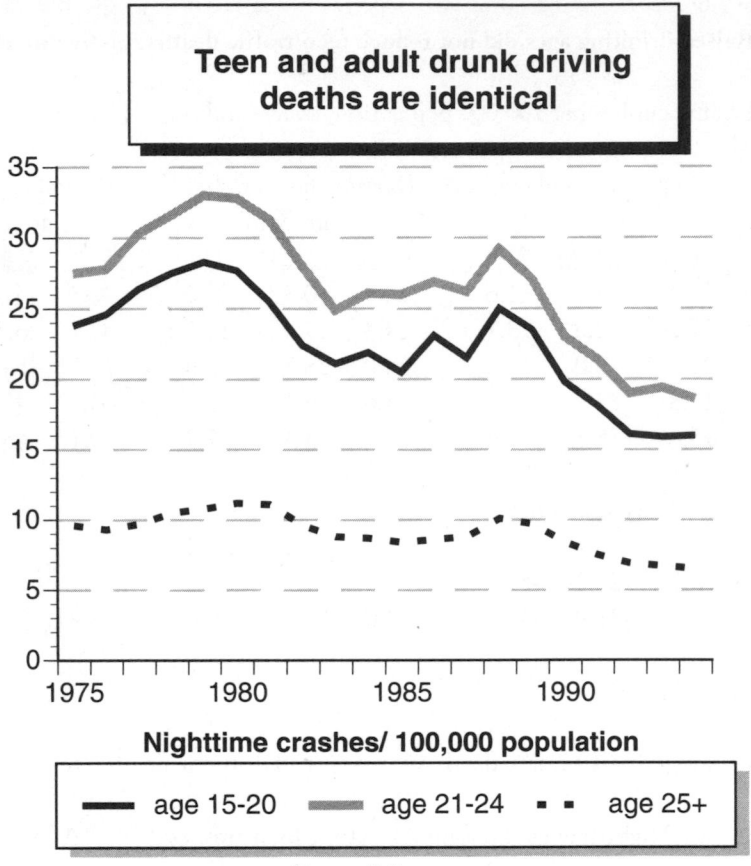

Figure 7.7

Source: Fatal Accident Reporting System (annual, 1975-1994). Drivers involved in Fatal Crashes, Nighttime, 8pm-4am (printout). Washington, DC: National Highway Traffic Safety Administration.

fall among younger drivers (discussed later). But these effects reversed from 1985 to 1994. Today, the 21 drinking age appears to have no discernible effect—at least, not a positive one, if the category "all fatal crashes" is examined. The most salient effect of the 21 drinking age that can be glimpsed, if any, is a shift in teenage traffic deaths from nighttime to daytime hours. All the furor over the drinking age, and the hundreds of thousands of arrests for underage alcohol possession, appear to have yielded naught in terms of saving lives on the highways.

It is encouraging that the drunk driving situation is improving among all ages. The sharp reduction in nighttime accidents—those most likely to involve drinking—occurred among both teens and older drivers. A major part of the alcohol-wreck decrease may have been the early 1990s recession, which reduced booze and bar patronage.

Drinking age doubts

The official response to raised drinking ages and other teen-targeted prohibition measures was enthusiastic. These policies were popular because they did not affect adult drinking. As a result, analysis of them has been glossy.

Policy makers have continued to cite the Insurance Institute study even though it is now a decade out of date. Or rather, officials have mis-cited it. Where the study itself found only a 9 percent decline in age 18-20 traffic deaths accompanying raised drinking ages through 1984, NHTSA officials applied the larger 13 percent figure which the Institute found only for nighttime fatalities. Large exaggerations ensued.

In its 1993 report, the NHTSA claims "minimum drinking age laws have saved 13,968 lives since 1975."[56] The press has reprinted this figure regularly even though it is absurd. Note from Tables 7.4 and 7.6 that this purported life-saving effect would be the equivalent of *eliminating for ten years the entire 1993 drunken driving death toll among all persons under age 21*! One would think that 14,000 saved lives among the teen age group would show up as a massive anomaly in the two decades of trends shown in Table 7.6 and Figure 7.7 (which, if it occurred, would constitute an irrefutable argument for banning alcohol use by adults in order to save literally hundreds of thousands of lives). But none of this huge life-saving effect can be glimpsed in the traffic death rates for the 1975-94 period, which remain virtually parallel throughout for teens and adults. Such wildly exaggerated statistical claims, absent connection to real-life statistics, can be expected when government agencies become staunch advocates for government policies aimed at unpopular groups.

In fact, the issue of whether higher legal drinking ages "save lives" is many times more complex than the mistakenly-calculated sum generated by officials for consumption by an uncritical media. If we examine what might succeed in reducing teenage alcohol mishaps, a curious and forgotten period is worth examining. From 1979 to 1982, drunken driving fatality rates decreased among teenage drivers (down 21 percent) at an impressive clip, much faster than the decrease among drivers over age 21 (down 13 percent). The decrease in drunken deaths among teenage drivers began before the decrease among adult drivers.

This improved safety was short-lived. The decrease levelled off after 1982 and began to reverse in 1985. By 1988 (following a five-year period in which states rushed to meet the Congressionally-mandated deadline to enact a drinking age of 21), the rate of drunken driving crashes among high school drivers had *risen* by 18 percent over its 1983 level, slightly larger than the adult rise. This is the reverse of the pattern officials pushing higher drinking ages predicted.

What caused teenage drivers to experience their unique decline in drunken driving during the 1979-82 period? This was years before the greatest impact of laws, enforcement, and education connected with the "war on drugs" and youthful drinking—all associated with deleterious, not beneficial, effects in any case. But for some reason not explained by adult theory of uncontrolled teenage boozing, many fewer teens were in drunk driving wrecks during this four-year period. Homicides, many of which are alcohol-related, also declined among teens.

Not only were teenage drunken driving fatalities in sharp decline well before most states began to raise their drinking ages and step up efforts to ban youths from drinking, teenage drunken driving tolls also declined in nearly all states which did *not* raise their drinking ages. For example, the rates of alcohol-related fatal crashes among teens declined by 18 percent in Indiana, 28 percent in Pennsylvania, 30 percent in Louisiana, 31 percent in Vermont, and 54 percent in Oregon in the late 1970s and early 1980s without changes in the drinking age.[57] It appeared that teenage drivers responded earlier, and more forcefully, than adults to campaigns against drunken driving and were reducing their traffic tolls without mandated prohibition.

A body of recent counter-research on the drinking-age issue suggested that studies affirming its benefits may have addressed the wrong issues. Three detailed studies in 1983, 1984, and 1985 of Massachusetts' raised drinking age found that the chief effect was not to reduce frequency or amount drank by the 500 teenagers studied, nor driving after heavy drinking, but only to change the drinking locale to clandestine settings.[58]

An early study on Maine, which had a particularly dismal experience with boosting its drinking age from 18 to 20 in 1977, found an increase in daytime drinking and accidents among teens after prohibition on their bar drinking.[59] Note that in Table 7.6, while most measures of nighttime and total crash rates are consistent for teens and adults, the rate of daytime traffic deaths among teenagers increased (up 8 percent) relative to those of adults (and 21 percent relative to young adults age 21-24) over the period in which drinking ages were raised.

A 1985 study of several thousand youths by Boston University researchers found "no evidence that raising the drinking age will produce beneficial reductions in teenage homicides, suicides, or non-traffic accident deaths. Inexplicably, teenage murder actually increased in Massachusetts after it raised its drinking age." That state's higher drinking age brought higher rates of murder, suicide, and non-traffic deaths among teens compared to nearby New York, whose drinking age stayed at 18.[60]

That raising the drinking age—because it does nothing about the underlying problems that lead to alcohol abuse—might simply change the time and nature of alcohol-related deaths was an issue not examined by most researchers. Yet in my initial 1986 study published in the *Journal of Legal Studies*, I had found a clear effect: Banning 18-20-year-olds from drinking leads to increased drunken deaths among drivers age 21-24.

The pattern was consistent: Whether a state set its legal drinking age at 18, 19, 20, or 21, that was the same age at which the most traffic deaths occurred. My preliminary analysis found that 18-year-olds were 5 percent more at risk of traffic death in states with a drinking age of 18 compared to 18-year-olds in other states; 19-year-olds had a similarly higher risk when the drinking age was 19; 20-year-olds were 9 percent more likely to die when the drinking age was 20; and 21-year-olds were 12 percent more at risk in states where the drinking age was 21 than in states with lower drinking ages.

The first year of legal drinking was hazardous no matter when it occurred—and it appeared to be more hazardous the higher it was set. Thus a drinking age of 21 only meant that a few less 18-year-olds would die, offset by a few more dead 21-year-olds. The net result was a wash.[61] That finding was later ridiculed by Insurance Institute researchers.

Yet two subsequent Rutgers University studies of the effects of the drinking age on *both older and younger drivers*—not just younger drivers—examined my findings "in detail" under what authors politely termed "more demanding methodological criteria:"

> If one looks exclusively at young drivers (those directly affected by all changes in U.S. drinking age laws during the past two decades) and ignores the issue of drinking experience, safety effects of the laws may well be observed. The findings above suggest inclusion of experience measures, or equivalently, the examination of cohorts as they attain the new (higher) drinking age, may point to a different conclusion about the impact of these laws.

After measuring the offsetting effects of reduced deaths among 18-year-olds balanced by more deaths among 21-year-olds, the Rutgers researchers, Peter Asch and David Levy, found the same lack of effect of raised drinking ages that I had:

> Our findings suggest that minimum legal drinking age is not a significant— or even a perceptible—factor in the fatality experience of all drivers or of young drivers. Inexperience in drinking offers a more likely candidate to explain the peculiar fatality risk of young drivers... the evidence is accumulating in such a way that the claims for the traffic safety benefits of higher drinking ages ought to be viewed with serious skepticism. Such claims very probably have been oversold.
> ...The current legal environment, in which consumption of alcohol is prohibited until attainment of an arbitrarily specified age and permitted from that moment on, may itself create heavy costs in terms of driving risk.[62]

In other words, a rigid "drinking age" of the American type is a hazardous way to initiate the young into drinking. "A rigid, proscriptive control system," another Rutgers University study found, is "associated with less drinking among those youth; yet it also was associated with more rebellious or problem drinking than would be evidenced in more prescriptive drinking contexts."[63] Adult policy has little effect on teenage behavior except to change the setting of teenage drinking from supervised settings (with adults) to unsupervised ones where heavier drinking is more likely to be the rule.[64]

Yet another effect of the raised drinking age was to cut 18-20-year-olds out of several million entry-level jobs in establishments that serve and handle alcohol. At the same time 1970s and 1980s laws were reducing the legal age (usually from 21 to 18) above which parents were no longer required to support their children, states were removing youths from a major economic sector that provided jobs they needed to support themselves. There are indications that preventing teenagers from competing in the job market was an unstated reason for raising the drinking age. In 1991, Surgeon General Antonia Novello urged businesses—including grocery and convenience stores—that sell alcohol to personally "control" persons under age 21 (another way of saying, "don't hire them") to prevent "children" from getting alcohol.[65]

Protecting adult alcohol abuse

The teen-teetotalling campaign now emphasizes placing barriers between youth and adult use of alcohol. The campaign is naturally well received because it subtly flatters adults for our "responsibility" and ability to handle a dangerous drug while invoking the need for controls on immature youths.[66] It enabled the peculiar American habit of publicly proclaiming high standards of anti-drinking morality while quietly leaving high rates of alcohol abuse among adults untouched. It allowed the alcohol industry to present "public service" ads claiming in sappy piety that they want to "stamp out underage drinking before it starts."[67]

Prohibitionist sentiment selectively aimed at teenagers is in full bloom. The National Commission Against Drunk Driving's 1988 *Youth Driving Without Impairment* report featured a coordinated "community challenge" plan that emphasized expanded legislation, law enforcement, adjudication, supervision, school, extra-curricular, work-based, and community-based measures to be brought to bear against youth. As in anti-smoking salvos, parents were not urged to change their own habits, but to serve as agents of the government campaign to enforce abstinence upon adolescents. These were exactly the types of approaches that have failed because they ignored the pivotal factor of adult behavior in influencing youth behavior.

That report is remarkable for its illustration of the extremism to which age-based obsession leads. The commission recommended shifting drunk driving enforcement toward "the hours when most impaired driving offenses by youths occur," and focusing on "patrolling parties, parks, school events, and other locations where young people tend to gather"—which by definition means shifting attention away from adult drunk drivers. As indicated by the figures in Table 7.4, any shift away from policing areas and hours in which legal-drinking adults in their 20s and 30s imbibe would entail a higher net risk to public safety. Yet, amazingly, participants in preparing the report of a commission set up specifically to reduce drinking and driving *were uncomfortable even declaring that parents and other adults should not drink and drive!* The commission wound up making no recommendations regarding the drinking behaviors by parents or other grownups.[68]

Age thus became the only criterion applied. I participated in scores of school drug and alcohol policy meetings during the 1980s and aroused intense anger whenever I advocated that adult and youthful alcohol abuse be treated in equivalent fashion. "We don't talk about adult drinking at all," one renowned alcohol program designer admonished me. "It alienates adults in the community." A popular regional alcohol and drug program consulting firm, Community Intervention, told schools and communities to base their drinking policies "on age alone." That firm advised schools to suspend students who were discovered to have drunk alcohol, even moderately and on their own time, for weeks or months, while teachers or administrators caught drunk at school were to receive a few days' paid leave "to seek counseling." At another conference, a visibly furious high school vice-principal pounded the podium and declared that he took no action against a large number of loud and drunken adults at the recent school graduation. "When kids complained that we punish students who drink even a little, I told them: 'You see a double standard? Damn right there's a double standard!'" The audience, consisting of numerous drug and alcohol programmers, erupted in applause.

None of these popular, lucrative programs was able to produce rigorous scientific evaluations showing their effectiveness in reducing teenage drinking problems.

What they did produce were dubious testimonials of the 19th century patent-medi-cine model. The "recovering" teens who participated in these conferences were learning the rules of American alcohol hypocrisy fast. From the lectern they recounted their odysseys from demon rum to program-produced sobriety while grownup conferees laughed sympathetically, clapped, and cheered. On nearly every occasion in which I inquired privately afterward, the students freely admitted they continued to drink or use drugs—and their sponsors knew it. "Shit, I was bombed last weekend," one girl told me after her temperance testimonial, inhaling one ciga-rette after another. "I tell them what they want to hear," joked a long-haired high school junior in the hallway after his poignantly humorous (and heavily embell-ished) tale of seventh grade pot, whiskey, and cocaine mayhem and rescue by tough-love school anti-drug programs. "Then I do what I want."

I did encounter counselors and programs who helped students and families with drug and alcohol abuse problems. But as a rule, they were quiet, modest, serene, and tolerant. "Ninety-five percent of the kids I see for possession don't have a drinking or drug problem," one Montana counselor, a recovering alcoholic, told me. "So I tell them: Next time, don't be so stupid. Drink if you want, but stay put. Be discreet." The most effective counselors I worked with were those who had licked their own drinking or drug problems and didn't hallucinate addiction in every adolescent they saw.

Nonetheless, the strident situations above, which are more typical, are reflect-ed in even more extreme legal double standards. Adults with ten drunken driving convictions are allowed to resume legal drinking as soon as they are off probation, while a 17-year-old with no history of alcohol abuse is subject to severe punish-ments for drinking a single lite beer. The danger inherent in the noisy campaign against teenage drinking is that it has come at the expense of quietly ignoring the much larger threat to public safety posed by adult drinking.

In 1988, Surgeon General Everett Koop endorsed reducing the blood alcohol content necessary to prove driver drunkenness from the current .10 percent (.08 percent in a few states) to .04 percent for adult drivers over age 21 and .00 percent for those under 21. Yet, while Koop's recommendation to get tough on youths under age 21 was enthusiastically embraced by legislators, his recommendation to reduce the blood alcohol standard for adults to .04 (still a fairly lenient standard) went nowhere. No safety rationale, certainly not the reality of millions of traffic accidents and thousands of deaths caused by adult drivers who had been drinking "moderate-ly" could justify official endorsement of "moderate" adult drinking and driving. "Moderate drinking and driving," like "moderate drinking and airline piloting" or "moderate drinking and oil tanker captainship," is not the same thing as "moderate drinking." Safety officials, of all people, should be in the forefront of pointing out that alcohol use and the operation of vehicles is incompatible. The willingness of adults to demand the same tough standard of no drinking and driving from their own age group would have done more to impress the young than the moralistic fin-ger-pointing of modern anti-youth policy.

In a blast at the hypocrisy of demanding absolutist standards from teens while tolerating adult license, the *Salt Lake Tribune* took Utah lawmakers to task:

If it's wrong and obviously dangerous for teenagers to drive with no more than a trace of alcohol in their bloodstreams, then it's equally wrong and dangerous for adults to be so impaired.

...The pending new statute's admirers would require people in that younger age group to surrender their driver's licenses for 90 days when found to harbor the slightest trace of alcohol while simultaneously driving. A second such offense would cause the license to be lost for a year. But this new, distinct class of drinking drivers is being created in contradiction and hypocrisy.

...Currently used methods for testing blood or breath alcohol content can detect .001 grams. So while Utah law says it's presumed someone old enough to be licensed for driving is dangerous if he or she tests at the .08 level, the pending adolescent scapegoating law directly contradicts that declaration.

Which is it, .08 or .001? And if it is .001, then that should apply to adults as well as teenagers.

...The plain political fact is that legislators won't dare hold voting adults to the same harsh, difficult-to-rationalize exactions as teenagers because they know adults are far more likely to register their justified anger at the polls. The willingness, then, to terrorize youngsters is as hypocritical as it is unreasonable.

...Teenagers aren't the sole source of the problem; they surely haven't earned a heavier, more arbitrary, and costly burden for the solution.[69]

Indeed they have not. The National Highway Traffic Safety Administration's 1992 report showed that legal-drinking adult drivers sporting a "legal" blood alcohol content of .01 to .09 were involved in 12,500 fatal crashes that year, more even than the 9,800 additional adult drivers in fatal wrecks who were outright drunk.[70]

Did the nation's top highway traffic safety authorities and President Clinton speak out forcefully against the previous year's "unacceptable" fatal carnage by drinking and drunk adult drivers? Did those charged with protecting the public recommend tougher standards targeting adult drunken driving so that the U.S. would not continue to harbor the most lenient drunken driving standards in the industrial world?

They have not. Instead, Clinton, in a June 1995 radio address, recommended imposing tougher laws to enforce a "zero tolerance" standard on teenagers. The president called on Congress to force states "to punish drivers younger than 21 who are caught driving with a blood-alcohol-level of .02 or more. On average, a .02 level would occur after drinking a single beer, wine cooler or shot of alcohol."[71] Clinton didn't mention that most states allow an adult to drive legally after downing a six-pack of beer, a quart of wine, or six shots of whisky in two hours. Nor did he mention that an adult driving with a "legal" blood alcohol content of .09 is six times more likely to cause a traffic crash than a sober driver.[72]

The president emotionally deplored that "hundreds of our young people are dying because hundreds and hundreds of our young people are drinking and driving." He did not mention the deadly fatal crashes perpetrated by more than 20,000 boozing adults who kill not only themselves and other adults, but also more than 500 children and teens, every year. He did not mention that every day in the U.S., 25 people are killed by drunken adult drivers, and an even larger number, 35 per day, are killed by over-21 drivers with "legal" amounts of alcohol in their systems. The drinking-grownup threat to public safety is many times greater than that imposed by teenagers.

Much-touted get-tough-on-teens policies too often accompany ones to go-easy-on-grownups. Law enforcement efforts to force total youth abstinence have risen while states and localities have abolished and deemphasized public drunkenness laws. Ninety percent of all public drunkenness arrestees are adults over age 21. From 1975 to 1993, arrests of persons under age 21 for simple possession of alcohol rose by 70 percent while arrests of adults for public drunkenness decreased by 50 percent.[73] In a common pattern, laws and law enforcement are increasingly turning toward punishing younger and younger drinkers for lesser and lesser offenses.

The price of leniency toward grownups is the growing body count caused by repeat offenders. In 1993, adults with previous drunken driving convictions were involved in 2,000 fatal crashes involving alcohol.[74] Yet the evasive strategies of modern health officials reveal a particular reluctance to adopt common-sense strategies to prevent those who abuse alcohol (regardless of age) from drinking and leave the remainder who drink moderately (regardless of age) alone. The stronger standards adopted in Canada's Saskatchewan and other provinces, providing that convicted drunk drivers must (in addition to other legal punishments) abstain from drinking alcohol for a lengthy period after conviction and provide witnesses to their sobriety,[75] correctly focus the drunk driving issue on individual alcohol abuse in ways Americans seem fearful to contemplate.

Enforcing alcohol abstinence on teens is not a strategy to prevent drinking problems later in life. Several long-term studies have found that problem drinking in adulthood does not necessarily stem from problem drinking in teen years, nor does alcohol abuse as a teen predict alcohol abuse in adult years.[76] In any case, school anti-drinking programs have not proven effective in reducing student alcohol abuse in real life,[77] though paper-and-pencil surveys are often brandished to claim success.

In the American environment of tolerance for widespread drinking and prescription narcotic use by adults, "any effort to teach youngsters abstinence from these substances is a little like trying to promote chastity in a brothel," Washington State University researchers concluded.[78] In 1987, I studied the Montana school district, Great Falls, that had enforced the most punitive zero-tolerance anti-drinking policy during the 1980s, forcing hundreds of students into alcohol and drug treatment, thereby winning several national awards. Yet drunk driving statistics showed that Great Falls had the state's highest drunk driving accident and fatality rate among high school students. One of its school principals later reported to the legislature many more serious alcohol-related incidents among students than in districts in similar cities that took a more relaxed stance.[79]

The mechanisms by which other societies have transmitted moderate drinking values to youth are summarized by consistent research and were even officially recognized in the United States before the 1970s: (a) Early use of alcohol by children in family contexts, (b) Use of beverages containing low amounts of alcohol, (c) Drinking with meals, (d) Adult modeling of moderate drinking, (e) Non-association of drinking with virtue, sin, masculinity, or (note well) adulthood, (f) Social acceptance for refusing alcohol, (g) Social rejection of drunkenness, and (h) Broad societal agreement on strict "ground rules" for drinking.[80] As Princeton University senior psychiatric researcher and addictions expert Stanton Peele points out, those societies with the lowest alcohol abuse problems are those "where the young drink mild alcoholic beverages in the company of parents and older relatives," drinking is incorporated "in a low-key way in a family context," and disapproval of overdrinking is applied by both family and society.[81] "As a rule," the Texas Council on Alcoholism pointed out, "societies which don't have problems with adult drinking don't have problems with teenage drinking."[82] Whether in 1790, 1880, 1950, or 1995, the norm remains: "It has been documented that patterns of drinking among teenagers closely reflect the alcohol consumption behaviors of adults in the same sociocultural context", with "heavier drinking parents... more likely than other parents to have adolescents who were also heavier drinkers," studies by Gail Milgram of the Rutgers Center on Alcohol Studies pointed out.[83]

"Many of the 'problems' of teenage problem drinking stem from the legal status of underage use," Chauncey writes, "making it difficult to distinguish between teenagers whose excessive drinking has led to personal problems and teenagers whose problems stem not from alcohol but from the illegality of drinking it."[84] Observes Peele:

> Control policies toward both alcohol and drugs have not shown they can prevent young people from consuming these substances. It may be that we have arrived at a 'worst-of-both-worlds' situation in the United States where, in the absence of a capacity actually to eliminate the use of powerful psychoactive substances, we succeed mainly in exacerbating the fear of such substances that marks heavy use and addiction. That is, we actively attack the belief in and the capacity for self-management that remain the strongest prophylactics against substance abuse and addiction.[85]

The unacknowledged pattern

Adolescents are severely punished not only for using alcohol, but even more when they force adults to recognize that youth, like adults, consume a substance about which great confusion and anxiety exist. Like temperance audiences of a century ago, adults prefer to hear about alcoholic disaster and abstinence salvation (today in youthful mode only), and media and program have responded accordingly.

In fact, "teenage drinking" is another fabricated issue. There is no separate behavior definable as "teenage drinking" in the United States, any more than "blue-eyed persons' drinking" or "40-age drinking" exists. There are individuals within all age groups and social classes who harbor drinking problems. But the danger is that attempts to isolate teenagers from adults have and will produce higher rates of alcohol abuse among both groups.

Alcohol, cigarettes, and illicit drug abuse present three illustrations of this development over the past twenty years. For substances and time periods in which teenagers are treated the same as adults, adolescents display decision making similar to that of adults. When general safety campaigns are inaugurated, teenagers respond more quickly and vigorously than adults, displaying declining abuse rates in response to measures aimed at all age groups. These trends are evident in the earlier, stronger reductions in teenage smoking, drug fatality, and drunken driving during the 1970s and early 1980s. These eras are noteworthy in that they found adults demanding increasing responsibility from adults, not just from teens—policies to which teens responded even more positively.

After initial successes, public safety advocates typically encounter resistance and suffer defeats as adults balk at further changes in behavior. This adult resistance is most evident toward raising tobacco taxes or strengthening anti-drunk driving laws beyond the reforms achieved in the early 1980s. After such defeats, advocacy groups refocus their campaigns away from reforming the behavior of all age groups and toward punishing teenagers, who lack political resources to fight back. Successes (though often claimed) are few in reality. Youth behavior stubbornly continues to resemble adult behavior. Frustration rises, then anger. Demands for even more sweeping and punitive anti-youth policies ensue amid evidence that teenage behavior patterns are not responding and may even be worsening. It is at this point, where the mid-1990s finds us, that perspective is lost altogether. Adolescents become the only issue, draconian punishments aimed at teenagers—forced testing, forcible searches, heavy fines and jail or treatment mandates, dismissal from sports and other extra-curriculars even for trivial violations—are demanded. In tandem, similar or worse adult behaviors are excused or even defended.

Confident of media support, groups often make contradictory claims within brief periods. Shortly after the national drinking age of 21 took effect in the late 1980s, the Insurance Institute for Highway Safety declared that teenagers were the only age group to show an increase in drunken driving fatalities.[86] As detailed in previous chapters, complete success by anti-smoking forces in obtaining national mandates against youth smoking was followed by frantic claims in the early 1990s that youth smoking had reversed previous declines and was now rising. A decade of intensive teen-focused arrest, punishment, and behavior education by the War on Drugs culminated in a series of official press conferences declaring rising adolescent drug use. Aside from the obvious success-failure contradictions these declarations reveal, adolescents have become the 1980s and 1990s perpetual motion generator for agency and program self-promotion of which the media never seem to tire. The media seem not so much bamboozled by the avalanche of self-serving publicity by advocacy groups as it seems not to care whether its coverage of teenage issues meets even rudimentary standards of fairness and accuracy.

This is a cycle of futility and wholesale manipulation of basic facts, one which depicts the smallest adolescent problem as catastrophic and the worst adult problem as negligible. It is a syndrome modern public health advocacy groups would do well to grow out of instead of becoming ever angrier that they cannot educate or force teenagers, through demeaning assertions and punitive measures, to act better than the adults around them.

8. Growing Up Referred

The creation of adolescence as an age-based pathological condition contributes to the masking of factors that contribute to threats to health in a highly differentiated complex society... racism, the juvenilization of poverty, underemployment, inadequate education, and declining per-capita resources for dependent children and youth.

— Robert Hill, J. Dennis Fortenberry,
"Adolescence as a Culture-Bound Syndrome," 1992[1]

What're you trying to say?
That *I'm* crazy?
How can *I* be crazy?
When I went to *your* schools?
When I went to *your* churches?
When I went to *your* institutional learning facilities?
How can you say that *I'm CRAZY?!*

Suicidal Tendencies, "Institutionalized,"
BMG Music, 1983

Teenage suicide, teenage car wrecks, teenage violence, teenage pregnancy, deadly and injurious teenage insanity. The drumbeat of American news media and periodical reports of adolescent disaster invariably include various experts explaining them as the consequence of "innate" teenage immaturity, instability, rebelliousness, self-destructiveness, and impulsiveness—in sum, "high risk." So common are these assertions that few realize there is no such thing as "high risk adolescent behavior." Nor are there any innate teenage tendencies toward impulsive, irrational, or dangerous behavior. These notions are rooted in the same kind of social-non-science that has plagued analysis of race, gender, and ethnic issues.

Where did American social scientists get the idea that adolescents are intrinsically perilous? They *defined* it that way. As Robert Hill and J. Dennis Fortenberry, of the Department of Pediatrics at the University of Oklahoma Health Sciences Center, explain:

By creating adolescence as a developmental period defined by its problems, "adolescent health" becomes an oxymoron... "medicalized" into a condition that is inherently pathological... Adolescence per se is seen as the inevitable "risk" factor for these widespread problems as if the origin of these problems were innate to adolescents, rather than complex interactions of individual biology, personality, cultural preference, political expediency and social dysfunction.[2]

If adolescence is defined as a disease state, it must be cured. The major impetus for the development of psychological techniques in the late 1800s and early 1900s, writes historian Joseph Kett, was the "testing," "treating," and "controlling" of teenagers.[3]

The views of the psychological industry are cited constantly by the media as "objective" commentary on adolescents. That is akin to relying on the Christian Coalition for objective commentary on homosexual behavior. Several studies have documented the biases, many extreme, held by most mental and medical professionals against teenagers. In repeated studies, psychologists and doctors, when asked to project how normal adolescents would respond to a battery of tests for various neuroses, predicted levels of anxiety, hostility, depression, vulnerability, and other indicators of mental disturbance that were *two to three times higher* than not only normal, but disturbed, violent, and disabled teenagers rated themselves on the same tests![4] [5]

Where prejudice exists among scientists, as Stephen Jay Gould points out in *The Mismeasure of Man*, criteria are selected and evidence assembled to support it.[6] Theories of "innate" teenage instability and recklessness derive from a fundamental mistake in psychological research: The tendency of clinicians to make unwarranted assertions about all adolescents by generalizing from clinical or institutionalized populations. "Even though normal teenagers were not studied by clinical investigators," psychiatrist Daniel Offer and colleagues write of the earlier studies in which these stereotypes were fostered, all teens were simply assumed "to have the same basic conflicts as psychiatric patients or juvenile delinquents" that the researchers had captive to study.[7]

Yet the view of roiling teenage biology determining reckless teenage destiny clearly remains the mainstream view of the social and health scientists providing commentary to the media and to political authorities. It is the chief surviving atavism of biological determinism, a 19th century pseudo-science that sought to classify nonwhite racial and ethnic groups and women as *innately* inferior under precisely the same criteria now applied to adolescents. Modern psychology and human behavior disciplines have resurrected, when convenient, the extreme *Sturm und Drang* notions of adolescents asserted by early-1900s psychologist G. Stanley Hall.

Wrote Hall in 1904 on teenagehood:

> The momentum of heredity often seems insufficient to enable the child to achieve this great revolution and come to complete maturity, so that every step of the upward way is strewn with wreckage of body, mind, and morals. There is not only arrest, but perversion, at every stage, and hoodlumism, juvenile crime, and secret vice... Home, school, church fail to recognize its nature and needs and, perhaps most of all, its perils.[8]

This depiction of puberty as soul debilitation was based on the twisted adolescence of G. Stanley Hall, infused with mental and physical abuses by his father, more than any objective study of growing up. Similarly traditional psychodynamic theory viewed adolescence as a period of "disturbances of varying seriousness and crippling effects, transient or permanent."[9] Anna Freud wrote, "the upholding of a steady equilibrium during the adolescent process is itself abnormal."[10]

Were social scientists' declarations of "biological determinism"—the innate disadvantages of nonwhites and women, as detailed in Chapter 1—issued in a spirit of hostility? Not of the overt kind. It was with compassion and caring that the white man's burden to exercise greater control over impetuous, childlike, nonwhite races was invoked. Wrote one early-century scientist:

> Modern science [has] shown that races develop in the course of centuries as individuals do in years, and that an undeveloped race, which is incapable of self-government [is like]... an undeveloped child who is incapable of self-government.[11]

In modern nomenclature, nonwhite races were "high risk" and required a comprehensive prevention-intervention-treatment management strategy, which just happened to buttress a variety of early-century domestic and international political goals.

For those who emerged from hermetic theorism to study teenagers as they actually lived and breathed, Hall's dirisms were easily refuted. Despite "the widespread myth that every child is a changeling who at puberty comes forth as a different personality," psychologist Leta Hollingworth wrote in *The Psychology of the Adolescent* in 1928, adolescent development is characterized by a "gradualness" in which social mores played a far bigger role than biology.[12] Wrote anthropologist Margaret Mead in *Coming of Age in Samoa* that same year: "The stress is in [American] civilization, not in the physical changes through which our children pass."[13]

Gould's 1981 treatise, *The Mismeasure of Man*, explores the fallacies of labeling blacks and women as grownup "children" or "adolescents" subject to the control of innately superior white northern European men. This concept applies in equal and opposite fashion to today's efforts to resurrect the same stereotypes once inflicted on minorities and females to apply them against teenagers. Gould's opinion of biological determinism:

> I would rather label the whole enterprise of setting a biological value upon groups for what it is: irrelevant, intellectually unsound, and highly injurious... By what right, other than our own biases, can we... hold that science now operates independently of culture and class?[14]

Gould recounts sincere, outrageous, and amusing efforts by 19th century social scientists to shoehorn inconvenient findings into predetermined theory. Like yesteryear's discredited predecessors who demeaned females and minority groups of their day, social scientists aiming the same charges at today's teenage class insist objective science is on their side.

Yet modern pop science ignores the preponderance of literature findings on adolescence, such as the following exhaustive textbook review of dozens of studies:

> A few adolescents experience identity crises that are traumatic and totally preoccupying. However... for most, identity formation proceeds in very gradual, uneventful way... For most people, adolescence is not a period of intense emotional upheaval that brings with it an increased risk of adjustment difficulties, although it has often been thought of in this way. In fact, the incidence of serious psychological disturbance increases only slightly from childhood to adolescence (by about 2 percent), at which time the rate is about the same as it is in the adult population.[15]

Daniel Offer's studies of 30,000 youths from the 1960s through the 1980s reported "no support for adolescent turmoil" or instability theories. Three decades of surveys of a wide variety of adolescents found 85 percent were healthy and confident, 90 percent were concerned with the future and work, and 90 percent held attitudes and values similar to those of their parents.[16] From a cognitive, developmental, maturity, or behavior standpoint, there is no reason to view 16-year-olds as different from adults, Offer's lengthy studies concluded.[17]

"Few ideas in adolescent psychology are as accepted by *researchers* with such unanimity as the notion that parent-adolescent relations basically are not stressful," another 1980s review found.[18] The study authors emphasized "researchers" since the modern cult of pop psychologists and media mythmaking tends toward fear profiteering. Entire books, documentaries, news features, and talk show formats have geared themselves to terrifying parents of berserk and savage teenhood.

Larger examinations of the treatment of teenagers have pointed out that stereotyping is no accident. Historian Joseph Kett's definitive 1977 text, *Adolescence in America*, observed that the development of anti-teen stereotyping among social scientists is inherent in the term "adolescence" itself:

> To speak of the "invention of the adolescent" rather than of the discovery of adolescence underscores a related point: adolescence was essentially a conception of behavior imposed on youth rather than an empirical assessment of the way in which young people actually behaved... A biological process of maturation became the basis of the social definition of an entire age group.[19]

Thus modern social scientists who vehemently reject biological determinism as the basis of behavior for racial groups or women nevertheless continue to claim the "intrinsic" nature of violent or libidinous teenage actions (applied in practice mainly to the behavior of nonwhite teens). Gould sums up the damaging constriction of imposing the mass rigidity of "innateness" on behavior versus the broader realities of human potential evaluated according to individual and circumstance:

> Biological determinism... is fundamentally a theory about limits. It takes current ranges in modern environments as an expression of direct genetic programming, rather than a limited display of a much broader potential... [But] if... behavior is an expression of broad rules tied to specific circumstances, we anticipate a wide range of behaviors in different environments... This flexibility should not be obscured by the linguistic error of branding some common expressions "innate" because we can predict their occurrence in certain environments.[20]

If impoverished youth tend to be more violent, it is the condition of poverty that engenders it and not some violence "innate" to poorer youth—let alone to all youth.

The dissenters: Affirming adolescence

In the 1940s and 1950s, a reaction to perpetuation of the extreme views of Hall and his followers had set in. A minority of social scientists affirmed teenhood as a dynamic antidote to the sterility of an increasingly regimented adult world.

The famous Swiss psychologist Jean Piaget, whose revolutionary studies of child development found youths beginning at around age 11 were fully capable of the mature "formal operational" thinking of adulthood, declared that it is the "duty of the modern adolescent... to revolt against all imposed truth and to build up his intellectual and moral ideas as freely as he can."[21] The problem with teenagers was that they were not rebellious enough.

Similarly, sociologist Edgar Z. Friedenberg found in adolescence the salvation of an increasingly regimented, conforming, corporate-dominated society. America is "a society which has no purposes," he wrote in a series of essays including *The Vanishing Adolescent* (1959) and *The Dignity of Youth and Other Atavisms* (1964). Adults deploy high schools and psychologists in "sedative programs of guidance... to keep young hearts and minds in custody until they are without passion." The struggle between generations is like that between classes, with adults striving to prevent teenagers from defining themselves through conflict with society.

Friedenberg correctly predicted the increasing anger against teenagers of coming decades. "Fear of disorder, and loss of control; fear of aging, and envy of the life not yet squandered—these lie at the root of much adult hostility to adolescence."[22] The society of facelifts, Grecian formula, and Rogaine evidences one that oppresses teenagers to mask its contempt for the old. Modern America seeks to "infantilize adolescence"[23] by exploiting teenagers as a projective device for adult inadequacies:

> Adults read their own hopes and fears into the actions of adolescents, and project onto them their own conflicts, values, and anxieties. They take desperate measures to protect the young from imaginary menaces, which are in fact their own fantasies, and to guide them to imagined success, which is in fact surrender.[24]

Such affirmations of adolescence are rare among social scientists of the 1980s and 1990s. Many of today's much-publicized declarations on teenagers follow the conforming paths of adult interest Friedenberg forecast three decades ago would increasingly repress "the new adolescent minority" seen as "having no rights at all."

Dissenters, though rarer today, remain. In addition to Hill's and Fortenberry's argument that American negativism toward adolescents is the bogey of our own cultural creation, a 1990 review by Peter Aggleton and I. Warwick chastised colleagues for their political exploitation of youth and the AIDS epidemic, concluding: "Dominant ideologies... appear to have more to do with shoring up popular prejudices about young people than examining their unequal statuses in a differentiated society."[25]

Are teenagers "high risk"?

A particularly thorough justification of the "innate risk" theory of adolescence occurs in the Winter 1990 issue of *New Directions in Child Development*. In assessing teenagers' risk-taking with regard to AIDS, authors William Gardner and Janna Herman first declare the consensus among social scientists that "there is abundant evidence that adolescents take serious risks with their health, as compared with both adults and younger children."[26]

AIDS is one of the most common areas in which to assert "adolescent risk-taking behavior." But it is a peculiar illustration. As noted in Chapter 2, nearly all sexually-contracted adolescent AIDS appears to result from relations with adults. Except in cases of outright adult exploitation resulting from extreme power differences or rape, this indicates a shared risk-taking behavior. Even ignoring that salient issue and adopting the most extreme view possible—that *all* AIDS cases diagnosed among persons age 20-29 were acquired as HIV in adolescence, and that teenagers *only* have sex with other teens—teenagers are still not the most "at risk" group to contract HIV (Table 8.1).

Table 8.1

Adults in their 20s and 30s, not teens, are most "at risk" of HIV and AIDS:

U.S. AIDS diagnoses through September 1993,
under worst-case assumptions for teens:

HIV acquired at age:	AIDS diagnosed at age:	Rate/1000 pop.
13-19	20-29	2.25
20-29	30-39	3.62
30-39	40-49	2.43

Source: Centers for Disease Control (1993, October). *HIV/AIDS Surveillance Report.* Atlanta, GA, Table 8. Rates calculated by author.

Using the authors' own example of HIV/AIDS infection, adolescents are not more likely to take health risks than adults.

Still, unlike most who so assert, Gardner and Herman buttress the claim of innate adolescent risk-taking not as an article of faith, but as the product of empirical evidence:

1.   "The primary causes of mortality among 15-24-year-olds were accidents (54 percent), suicides (14 percent), and homicides (11 percent), events that either result from or are closely related to behavioral choices... Young people also experience more accidents than adults, of which motor vehicle accidents are the best understood because they can be clearly linked to specific risk-taking behaviors."

2.   "Adolescents and young adults are also more likely to participate in and be the victims of violent crimes. Although the level of crime varies as a function of gender, historical period, ethnic group, and many other variables, the overrepresentation of adolescents and young adults is a remarkable constant."

3.   "The typical adolescent will score higher than an adult on personality measures associated with risk taking, such as the psychopathic deviance score of the Minnesota Multiphasic Personality Inventory or measures of sensation seeking."[27]

Let us take these claims one by one. First, the assertion that violence is the *leading* cause of death for adolescents, and therefore teens are a "high risk" group, contains a fundamental fallacy. What it really reflects is a positive fact: Teenagers have much lower death rates than adults because they are far less likely to die from major natural causes, especially cancer and heart disease. Further, violence is the leading cause of death for adults age 20-29 (groups with violent death rates higher than those of teens), and trends among teens and adults display an almost identical pattern over the last 40 years (Figure 8.2).[28] As has been discussed, the recent rise in

U.S. teen and adult violent death trends are similar over time

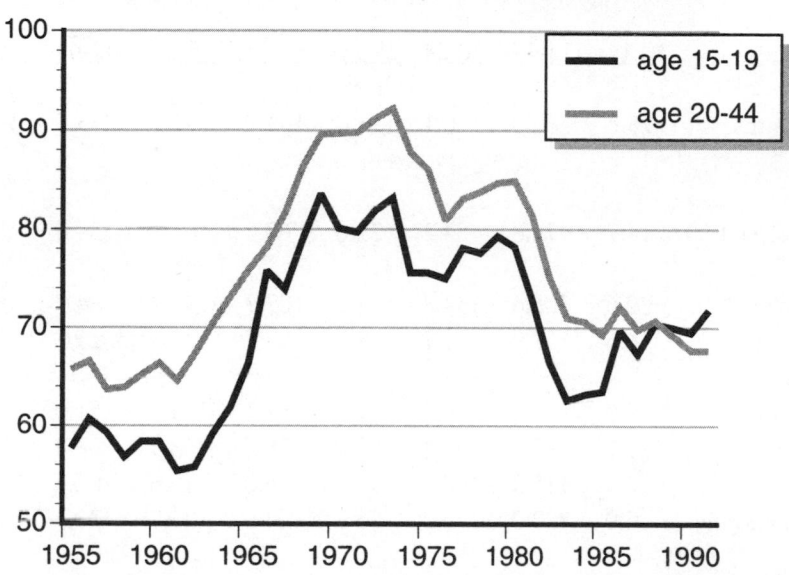

Figure 8.2

Source: National Center Health (annual) Vital Statistics of the United States, 1955-1991. Volume II, Part A, Mortality. Washington, DC: U.S. Department of Health and Human Services. See Table 8.3.

teen violent deaths (which still have not reached levels found among Baby Boom adolescents in the Sixties) is due to homicide increases. This trend, in turn, is close-ly related not to intrinsic youthful violence, but to the unique rise in teenage pover-ty since the 1970s. The death rates for whites, Hispanics, blacks, and other non-whites by age and sex for each major cause for adolescent, young adult, and middle-aged adult groups are shown in Table 8.3. Professing that a characteristic is "innate" to a group necessarily entails arguing that it makes members of that group behave more like each other, and less like those outside the group. Under this concept, teens should act more like teens of other races and of the opposite sex, and unlike adults of their own race and gender.

This is not the case. Even when examining the indexes chosen by those who claim risk-taking is intrinsic to adolescents—suicide, homicide, accidents, and espe-cially motor vehicle accidents—no innate pattern is evident. The variation in teenage behavior is substantial when analyzed separately by sex, race, and cause of death. Overall, adolescents display no more risks than adult age groups. For all types of violent fatality, young adolescents age 10-14 are less at risk than every adult age group, and older adolescents (15-19) are less at risk than adults in their 20s.

Race and gender are much more dominant than age in predicting violent

Table 8.3

Teens are not the age group most likely to die from violence:

Deaths per 100,000 population by age, race, and sex, 1991

All races	10-14	15-19	20-24	25-29	30-34	35-39	40-44	45-49
All deaths	25.8	89.0	110.1	123.0	154.1	197.7	253.6	380.5
All violent deaths	14.7	71.8	84.2	71.6	67.2	61.1	54.6	54.2
Males	20.6	108.6	134.8	114.2	107.9	95.2	84.7	81.4
Females	8.6	32.9	31.7	28.7	28.7	27.5	25.1	28.0
White	9.9	58.7	69.9	57.3	57.1	54.7	51.0	50.8
Hispanic	17.7	83.6	87.4	82.0	76.2	68.5	58.7	53.6
Black	22.8	115.3	160.7	136.8	126.0	115.6	106.6	87.5
Asian/other	5.0	23.0	26.0	25.7	24.6	23.7	23.3	24.9
All accidents	11.1	41.2	44.4	36.6	35.3	32.9	30.3	29.4
Auto accidents	6.1	31.2	32.8	23.3	19.3	16.2	14.2	14.6
All other acc.	4.8	9.1	10.7	12.1	14.3	14.8	14.6	13.7
Suicide	1.4	11.0	14.9	14.9	15.5	15.1	14.3	15.7
Homicide	2.2	19.6	25.0	20.1	16.4	13.1	10.0	9.1

Source: National Center for Health Statistics (1995). *Vital Statistics of the United States* 1991. Mortality, Part B. Washington, DC: U.S. Department of Health and Human Services, Table 8-5. Hispanic and white totals apportioned from 1990 national and California ethnicity breakdowns.

death. Asian teens (focusing on 15-19-year-olds), for example, are less at risk than every adult age group regardless of race. White teens are less at risk of violent death than every adult age group of blacks, and of all Hispanic adult groups up to age 40. For all races, the risk is less in teen years than at ages 20-24. Teen violent death patterns most resemble those of persons age 25-34 of their respective races.

Even for motor vehicle crashes, teenagers of all races rank second in risk behind 20-24-year-olds. Black teenagers are less likely to suffer a fatal motor vehicle accident than black adults under age 40, but white and Asian teens are second only to 20-24-year-olds. Adding in gender makes the situation even more chaotic. White and Asian female teens are riskier drivers than any other female age group of their race, but black females are less at risk than black adult women under age 35. White male teens have fatal crash rates second only to 20-24-year-old white men. Asian male teen drivers are safer than Asian adult males under age 30, and black males are less likely to die in a traffic mishap than black adults males under age 50! This is far from a clear picture of a teenage group at unique and extreme risk.

Note that motor vehicle crashes—the index chosen by most authors to rank behavior risk by age—happens to be the one least favorable to teenagers and most favorable to adults over age 25. As pointed out in the last chapter, the high risk of teenagers is an artifact of the high proportion of novice drivers among adolescents; inexperience, not immaturity or intrinsic recklessness, is the chief culprit.

Further evidence for this is that teenagers are much less at risk of other types of violent death than are adults. A ranking based on all other accidental deaths produces dramatically the opposite result: Teenagers as a group, and of every race, are much less likely to die from mishaps other than traffic accidents than are adults under age 50. For the two largest non-traffic accident causes, falls and drug deaths, teenagers are far less at risk of fatality than are adults in every older age group. Thus, if viewed according to the reasonable standard of drug poisonings or falls, which are mostly self-inflicted deaths reflecting behavioral choice and causing thousands of fatalities annually, adolescents would be judged uniquely invulnerable to premature demise.

Despite the assertions to be found in morning papers and news broadcasts on any typical day, teenagers are not the most at risk of dying from homicide. Adults age 20-29 are (see Table 4.5). Major gender and race qualifiers apply here as well. Female teens display less vulnerability to murder than women age 20-34 and about equal risk as women age 35-39. Male teens are less likely to be murdered than adult men age 20-29 and have the same risk as men age 30-34. Asian teenage females are less likely to be murdered than Asian women ages 20-49, while Asian male teens are about equally at risk as Asian men ages 20-49—which is to say, hardly at all. The most likely group to be murdered are black men ages 20-24. Black men ages 45-49 are 12 times more likely to be murdered than are Asian teens and twelve times more likely to die in homicides than are white non-Hispanic teens.

A second argument against the "intrinsic risk" theory of adolescent behavior emerges from the close similarities between the violent death patterns of teens and of adults of their gender and race. Teenage males are about 3.5 times more likely to die violently than are teenage females, a ratio similar to that between adult men and adult women age 20-44. Blacks at all age levels, from 15-19 to 45-49, are about four times more likely to die from violent causes than are Asians, and 1.5 times more likely to die violently than are whites, of corresponding age groups. In fact, as Table 8.3 shows, adolescents' deaths appears to conform to the adult mortality patterns of their race and sex. Arguing that risk is synonymous with adolescence, while popular, is not supported by the evidence.

Finally, note that the numbers involved for all age groups are very small. In 1991, 1,399 of every 1,400 teens age 15-19 did *not* die from violent means, compared to 1,299 of 1,300 persons in their 20s and 1,549 of 1550 persons in their 30s. Assertions about the characteristics of a group should be based on the behavior of its *majority*, not what happens to one in a thousand.

For adolescents, assertions about risk are repeatedly made with regard to the behavior of a small number of youth, a "collective guilt" standard not applied to adults. Note that if stigma is to be applied on a group basis, males at every age level experience much higher rates of violent death than do teenagers. As Table 8.3 shows, the demographic group represented by President Clinton, men age 45-49, is 13 percent more likely to die from violent causes than is a teenager.

At the risk of repetition, the divergences in fatality by age and race, particularly for homicides, turn much more on the factor of poverty than that of adolescent age. Adolescents are greatly overrepresented among poverty populations of all races (Table 8.4).

Table 8.4

For every race, adolescents are much poorer than adults

Percent of population living in poverty, by race and age, U.S. 1993

	Age <18	Age 18-64	Age 65+	Total	Number
White (non Hispanic)	13.0%	8.2%	10.1%	9.6%	188,340
Black	46.1	26.2	28.0	33.1	32,910
Hispanic	40.9	25.2	21.4	30.6	26,559
Asian and other	24.1	15.3	16.5	18.9	11,469
Total	22.7	12.4	12.2	15.1	259,278
Number (thousands)	69,292	159,208	30,779	259,278	

Source: U.S. Bureau of the Census (1995). *Poverty, Income, and Valuation of Noncash Benefits 1993.* Washington, DC: U.S. Department of Commerce, Table 8.

The same erroneous logic governs interpretation of teenage versus adult responses to standard psychological tests. Teenagers do indeed score higher on risk-taking scales. So, to an even larger degree, do minority men. Black adult men score so high on anti-social personality disorder scales of the MMPI that separate scales for evaluation have been adopted. Are black men, therefore, "intrinsically" prone to unhealthy behaviors? Few social scientists (Charles Murray aficionados excepted) would so declare today. Rather, an array of discriminatory social conditions such as racism and poverty are typically cited as reasons for the discrepancy. Yet as a rule, social scientists have been unwilling to accept that teenagers, whose populations are much more heavily nonwhite and whose poverty rates exceed those of adults by 60 percent or more for every racial group, might be displaying attitudes and behaviors related to imposed social conditions rather than "innate" defects.

When researched directly rather than simply asserted in popular media forums, risk-taking and delusions of immortality are no more features of American adolescents than American adults. University of California at San Francisco psychologist

Nancy Adler studied adolescents (average age 15) and their parents (average age 43) and found the two groups expressed very similar perceptions of risk. Society has "overestimated how much adolescents feel invulnerable," she concluded. Other research found that illusions of invulnerability were "no more pronounced for adolescents than for adults." In fact, teenagers tended to see themselves as more vulnerable to some risks than their parents.[29]

"Researchers suggested it may even be a myth that adolescents intentionally take more risks than adults do," an April 1993 summary of recent findings in the American Psychological Association *Monitor* concluded. In fact, it may be adults who have more delusions of immortality:

> "Although evidence of perceived invulnerability among adolescents is sparse, studies with adults have consistently shown" that adults feel invulnerable, they [researchers] wrote. Adults think they are more likely than other adults to have positive as opposed to negative experiences in many areas, from business transactions to natural disasters to social events.[30]

To their credit, the "innate risk" authors Gardner and Herman, cited above, eventually acknowledge the primacy of social conditions, sort of:

> Risk taking may be intrinsic to adolescence and youth, but... we may notice that we are creating a future for our young that is uncertain, impoverished, and dangerous.[31]

Wait a minute! Stable, healthy, well-adjusted, low-risk adults do not create impoverished and dangerous environments for their young. Enumerating the even higher risk behaviors among adults would lend the myth of "high risk adolescents" some much needed perspective. Points out an 18-year-old writer in the *Toronto Star*:

> North American culture both craves and denigrates its youth... We are tired of being held responsible for all that is wrong... We didn't ask for things like poverty and racism that push people to crime... As for lack of respect for others, poor nutrition, sluggish lifestyle and ignorance, well, we might ask to see our role models in the adult world... The examples teenagers have had have not been good.[32]

Is there a teen suicide "epidemic"?

The most dramatic assertion for the allegedly rising self-destruction of modern teens is the claim that the rate of teen suicide has quadrupled since 1950, including a doubling since 1970.[33] Suicide is a pure indicator of high risk behavior, of self-destructive intent. By definition, suicide is always self-inflicted, always fatal, contains no element of mere "bad luck," inexperience, or "being in the wrong place at the wrong time," and is the only crime for which the characteristics of the victim are identical to those of the perpetrator.

Even if taken at face value, the scary-sounding claim of "epidemic" teen suicide amounts to a lot less when a never-mentioned fact (easily seen in the tables above and below) is considered: For both sexes and all races, teenagers experience the *lowest* suicide rates of any age group except pre-teens.[34] In 1992, about 1 in

12,000 teens ages 13-19 committed suicide, compared to one in 6,000 young and middle-aged adults and 1 in 5,000 older adults. If suicide were adopted as the standard, teenagers would be judged uniquely immune to self-destruction.

A quadrupling in teen suicide since 1950 would represent a change in behavior by approximately 1 in 10,000 teens age 15-19. That is far from a widespread trend sufficient to support the kinds of dire assertions about adolescent mental health that have accompanied it. Further, as will be seen, it is unlikely that teen suicide has increased as claimed.

Puzzlement over why a few teenagers—about one in a sizeable high school of 2,000 students every five or six years—commit suicide has become mired in just such generalized speculations about the mental health of adolescents. When suicidal teens are studied directly, some clear differences emerge. These are not "average" youths. The reasons for their suicidal feelings often are not comfortable for adults to contemplate.

One of the biggest is a history of sexual abuse. In a 1992 study of 276 low-income pregnant teenagers, a California pediatrics team found histories of physical and sexual abuse increased the risk of suicide four-fold.[35] Similarly, a 1993 survey of 5,000 exemplars by Who's Who Among American High School Students found that the one in seven girls who had been sexually assaulted were four times more likely to have attempted suicide (17 percent versus 4 percent) than students who had not been assaulted.[36] The 1992 *Rape in America* study of 4,000 women found one-third of rape victims had contemplated suicide and that 13 percent had attempted suicide. In contrast, suicide attempts were practically non-existent (only 1 percent reported having tried) among females who had not been raped. Of those raped, 62 percent had been victimized prior to age 18.[37]

In addition to sexual abuse, key factors in suicide incidence are maleness, homosexuality, economic stress, childhood neglect and violence, and individual biochemistry.[38] Most of these factors cannot be changed by the affected individual, but they can be changed by changes in social environments and attitudes. For example, child abuse and neglect and negative attitudes toward homosexuality can be addressed by changes in policies and attitudes controlled by adults.

These changes are not easy to accomplish and require sacrifices and long-term commitments harder to bring about than mere quick-fix salvos aimed at "teen suicide." Former Secretary of Health and Human Services Louis Sullivan, illustrating how political prejudices remain part of the nation's health problem, repudiated a portion of a January 1989 HHS report urging a more positive stance toward homosexuality as a way of reducing high suicide rates among gay youth, drawing criticism from the American Psychological Association and the American Association of Suicidology.[39]

As on other troubling issues, federal health authorities have avoided unsettling questions and instead have lent the impression that suicide means there is just something wrong with teenagers. A 1995 CDC report stated that suicide among 10-14-year-olds has "soared" since 1980. When the numbers were examined, the "soaring" consisted of the fact that 1 in 60,000 youths age 10-14 committed suicide in 1992, compared to 1 in 125,000 in 1980. Nor did the CDC mention that the most recent suicide figures show 10-14-year-olds are only one-tenth as likely to commit suicide as are adults.[40] The report blamed gun availability, childhood drug abuse, aggression, family problems (which authorities typically blame on unstable youths), and stress. The image of teen suicide as a technical challenge, curable by legal adjustments, programs, and treatments aimed at youths continues to be the official-recommended diagnosis and remedy.[41]

Perceptions of youth suicide and its causes seem to depend on prevailing beliefs about the young, death, the state of society. Teenage suicide, like adult suicide, was almost certainly higher in a number of past eras in the United States than today—the most recent being the early 1900s, the Depression years, and the early 1970s. Today's is not America's first wave of panic over the young taking their own lives. Nor has our understanding of youth suicide advanced much over that of eighty years ago, when assertions of "epidemic child suicide" gripped Europe, Russia, and the United States.

Teen suicide, 1920: Feminism and moral decay

American authorities, even in an era when many states did not report deaths to the Bureau of the Census registry, found a rapidly rising rate of youths taking their own lives. In 1915, there were 395 youth suicides reported among the two-thirds of all reporting states, leading to an estimate of 600 for the entire nation.[42] Three thousand additional teenage deaths from firearms, poisonings, and drownings (all leading methods of suicide) were ruled as "accidents" that year. The media described the toll as "staggering." Famed Stanford University child psychologist Lewis Terman lamented:

> Suicides, like all forms of crime, are becoming more and more precocious. In these days children leave their marbles and tops to commit suicide, tired of life almost before they have tasted it.[43]

"Nothing should cause more real alarm than the suicide of children," the newly formed Save-a-Life League declared in 1920, noting that teen suicides were projected at 100 more than in 1919. The "appalling rate of child suicide," wrote *Literary Digest*'s editors in 1921, "is a frightful indictment of our Christian civilization... the average age of boys is sixteen years and girls fifteen."[44]

Based on European rates and rates among American adults, Terman estimated the true level of youth suicide in early 20th century America at 2,000 per year—if accurate, a rate double that of today. "The official [suicide] figures are certainly below the actual facts, because of the well-known tendency of relatives to assign the cause of death to accident," Terman wrote. Just as today, it was not clear that teen suicides were rising so much as being better reported and distinguished from fatal accidents, perhaps even exaggerated. Just as today, the detail that a youth suicide epidemic might not exist did not stop pundits of 1920 from citing the "youth suicide epidemic" as proof of whatever evil the commentator most deplored.

The *Catholic Universe* blamed utilitarianism, "refined paganism," and a production-obsessed society. "Our children are not so clean and innocent as those of an earlier generation," the church contended. "The men and women of to-day [1921] have not the moral strength of their ancestors."[45] The *Baltimore American* blamed feminists' "steadily insidious propaganda to stir up hostility between the sexes" for pressuring young women to assert their "superiority." Young women were committing suicide in record numbers in despair of Suffragette messages that "they were the coming mistresses of civilization; men were back numbers; marriage was a relation of convenience; the world had been made a mess by the ignoramuses now in control."[46]

Terman cited severe schooling, parental harshness, family disgraces, excessive ambitions placed on the young, "cheap theatres, pessimistic literature, sensational stories, the newspaper publicity given to crime and suicides, and the dangerous suggestive effect of the suicide of relatives or comrades—in other words, contagion, in the broad sense," as well as alcoholism, venereal disease, heredity, illegitimacy, divorce, and just plain "morbid impulse." Although schools were blamed for rising youth suicide, "education may make just the difference" in suicide prevention as well, he added.[47]

Divorce, congested living conditions, and Prohibition (apparently some youth were thought to prefer death to drought) were accused by various sources. High suicide rates were also found among those of "wealth and social position," the League observed. Noting that boys most often used guns and girls poison, just as today, the League (eight decades before the CDC) called for "strictly enforced laws to suppress the sale of all poisons and firearms."[48]

Another panic ensued in 1927 when a "wave of suicides" was reported among college students. Terms such as "terrifying" and "epidemic" were common in the popular press again, along with contention that rising cynicism and materialism among youth were at fault.[49] However, in 1932, Arthur Beeley of the University of Utah presented figures showing that although there had been great publicity attached to the suicides of 26 students from prominent families, there had been no unusual rise in youth suicides that year. "Writers who assumed the alleged 'wave' to be fact and understood to point out its causes and suggest a cure" for the "epidemic" contributed to the hysteria, Beeley declared.[50] But on it marched. In 1937, *Science News Letter* reported that kids "as young as six to 13" were being treated in hospitals for suicide attempts and preoccupation with death.[51]

Examining teenage suicide trends in historical context produces an astonishing fact: Certified suicide rates among teenage girls are 30 percent *lower* in the 1990s than in 1915, while suicide rates among teenage boys are alleged to have risen fourfold! Coroners of 1915 were particularly inclined to find deliberate intent in firearms and poisoning deaths among teenage girls, ruling 57 percent as suicides—three times more than among boys (Table 8.5).

Note that the overall teenage death rate from firearms and poisonings is virtually the same today as it was 75 years ago. Note also that fatality rates from these mostly self-inflicted deaths, including suicides, have dropped considerably for girls. What has changed is that the *proportion* of male deaths ruled as suicides has risen dramatically. The official judgment of suicidal intentions of boy-mind versus girl-mind has arrived at a bizarre kind of gender equality. It is not that more boys are dying, but that their deaths are much more likely to be classified as suicides today.

To take literally the past records of teen suicide is to introduce anomaly after anomaly. Such rulings appear to have as much to do with prevailing public and

Table 8.5

How statistics manufacture an epidemic:
Teen girls' suicides are plummeting, boys' suicides skyrocketing?

U.S. teen deaths, 1915*	Males 10-19	Females 10-19
Total firearms and poisoning deaths	661	279
Ruled as suicides	126	160
Percent ruled suicide	19%	57%
Firearms/poisoning deaths/100,000 teens	10.2	4.3
Total suicides/100,000 teens	2.7	3.4
U.S. teen deaths, 1990		
Total firearms and poisoning deaths	2,058	420
Ruled as suicides	1,394	311
Percent ruled suicide	68%	74%
Firearms/poisoning deaths/100,000 teens	11.5	2.5
Total suicide rate/100,000 teens	10.3	2.3
Change, 1915-1990:		
Firearms/poisoning deaths/100,000 teens	+12.7%	-41.9%
Total suicide rate/100,000 teens	+281.5%	-32.4%

*Death registration area covered 67.5 percent of U.S. population.
Sources: National Center for Health Statistics (1995). *Vital Statistics of the United States* 1990. Mortality, Part A. Washington, DC: U.S. Department of Health and Human Services, Table 1-27; U.S. Bureau of the Census (1915). *Mortality Satistics.* Washington, DC: U.S. Department of Commerce, Table 7.

coroner attitudes and prejudices toward the age, sex, and race of the deceased, and their assumed generic tendencies to "suicides" or "accidents," than to consistent analysis of the circumstances of similar types of death. Commentators of the first four decades of the 1900s left little more to be said, shouted, blamed, pushed, or debunked on the subject of teenage suicide.

Today's teen suicides vs. yesterday's "accidents"

On February 8, 1953, the Associated Press reported that the self-inflicted gun-shot death of a 12-year-old New Jersey boy, originally ruled an accident, was re-certified as a suicide when a note was found in his pocket on the way to the cemetery. Coroners of 1953 were not inclined to rule deaths of 12-year-olds, even when self-inflicted under suspicious circumstances, as suicides. Fewer than a dozen were so classified that year. Only about 180 teenage firearms deaths in the whole country were labeled as suicides. Coroners often refused to do so unless there were suicide notes.

A 1957 study reported that notes were found in only 15 percent of all suicides. "Many committed suicides go unreported" due to "evasion, denial, concealment, and even direct suppression of evidence (such as relatives deliberately destroying suicide notes)," it found.[52] However, adults in that era were willing to believe teenagers could have fatal accidents. In 1953, some 650 teenagers died from mostly self-inflicted gunshot "accidents," one third of the nation's firearms accident toll and a rate double that of adults. Even this "accident" level was an improvement over the 1930s, when teens accounted for nearly 40 percent of all accidental firearms mortality.

We move ahead 37 years to the most recent for which comprehensive figures are available, 1990. That year, in a youth population double that of 1953's, 1,474 teenage firearms deaths were classed as suicides—an apparent 500 percent increase in the rate. But only 520 firearms deaths among teens were ruled accidents or undetermined—a decrease of 65 percent. The overall teenage firearms mortality rate was little higher in 1990 than in 1953; only the way deaths were ruled had changed.

The supposed "increase" in teen suicide is largely boils down to changes in the classification of firearms deaths among teenage boys. Prior to around 1960, fewer than one in five firearms deaths among teenage boys were classified as suicides. After 1960, this percentage steadily rose, so that by 1986 three-fourths of all firearms deaths among teenage boys were ruled suicides. This shift in firearms death classifications among boys accounts for three-fourths of the purported "rise" in teen suicide. No one has offered explanation as to why teenage boys should, in a 30-year period, become radically more suicide-prone and radically less accident-prone with firearms than was any other age group with any other instrument. The official theory that "gun availability" is to blame for teenage deaths does not explain such a large decrease in gunshot accidents. Since the decrease in adolescent firearms accidents did not serve any official theory, it—like other important youth behaviors—was simply ignored.

A few experts, most notably epidemiologist Paul Holinger in 1979, raised the question of whether a "selective certification artifact" might be lending the appearance of a rising teen suicide rate not occurring in reality.[53] In 1989, a study by Richard Gist and Q.B. Welch of the Kansas City Health Department documented the correspondence between the "rise" in teen "suicides" and the "fall" in teen "accidents."

Gist and Welch argued that the artifact of death certification changes are "the primary factor influencing suicide rates" among teenagers from firearms from 1955 through 1966, and that certification changes continued to influence reported teen suicide rates from 1967 through 1979. A large share of the apparent increase in teen suicide results, they argued, from increased willingness to certify equivocal teen firearms deaths as suicides and a corresponding "strongly consistent" decline in certifications of such deaths as accidents. In particular, "youthful suicides may historically have been subject to greater levels of misreporting."[54] By the time Gist and Welch first provided empirical evidence of a "primarily artifactual epidemic" of teen suicide, publicity over its "skyrocketing" rate had been raging for a decade.

Yet anomalies stood out everywhere. If suicides among teenagers increased both significantly and uniquely over the past 35 years, we would expect to see a sharp rise in total (suicide + accident + undetermined) deaths from firearms and poisonings not shared by other age groups. My historical analysis of death tabulations by age from *Vital Statistics of the United States* shows this is not the case.[55]

Figure 2 shows the trends for teenagers age 15-19 versus adults age 20-44 from 1953 to 1990 for certified suicides plus those types of mostly self-inflicted "accidental" deaths (firearms and poisonings) most likely to be ruled suicides. The trends are parallel, with adult death rates substantially higher than those of teenagers. This close similarity in overall self-inflicted death trends over time between the two age groups argues strongly that there has been no unique increase in adolescent self-destruction.[56]

As Figure 8.6 shows, for both teens and adults, total deaths from firearms and poisonings, suicides and accidents (excluding homicides) were stable from the 1950s to the early 1960s, rose sharply during the mid- and late 1960s, peaked during the early 1970s, and declined slightly through the 1980s. But while certified suicides comprise a consistent proportion of total firearms-poisoning deaths for 20-44-year-olds for the entire period, certified suicides comprise a steadily rising (and certified accidents a steadily falling) proportion of total firearms-poisoning deaths for 15-19-year-olds.

The result, if the official view of rising teen suicide is valid, is that from 1970 to 1990, the rate of teen suicide *rose* by 50 percent while the overall rate of deaths from the two causes, which account for three-fourths of all teen suicides, *decreased* by 60 percent. This implausibly large decrease in teen accidental deaths from firearms and poisonings in just 20 years—which occurred among no other age groups and within no accident categories not connected with suicide—would be required to account for the above "suicide increase." If true, it would be an equally dramatic counter-trend!

Evidence of artifact is indicated in another area as well. In 1969, coroners ruled 434 deaths among teens age 15-19, including 300 firearms and poisoning deaths, as "undetermined whether accidentally or purposely inflicted." This number was equivalent to more than 40 percent of the teen suicide toll that year. In 1987, only 149 teen deaths were ruled as undetermined as to intent, including only 97 firearms and poisoning deaths—a number equivalent to only 8 percent of the teen suicide toll. The evidence is compelling: Coroners are becoming more adept at distinguishing teenage suicides from teenage self-inflicted "accidents."

The results of this analysis indicate three apparent facts:

(a)   A significant past undercount of youth suicides is likely,

(b)   Whatever change in youth suicide has occurred is not unique but a trend shared with adults, and

(c)   Any youth suicide increase that did occur took place prior to 1972 and is not a modern phenomenon.

Yet agencies and official panels continue to overlook the certification question. In 1989, the Secretary of Health and Human Services' Task Force on Youth

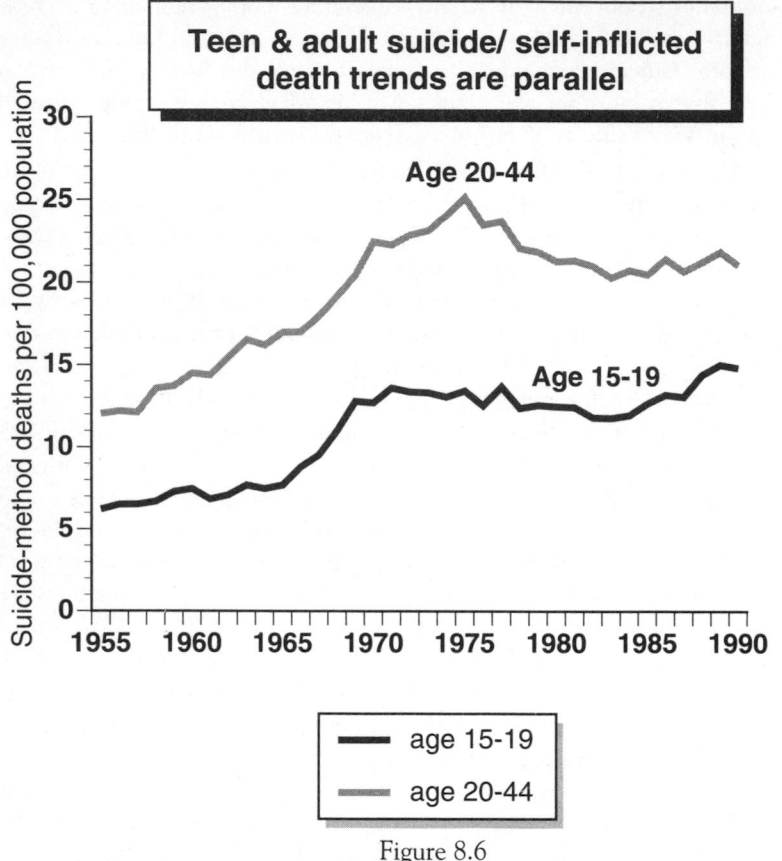

Figure 8.6

Source: National Center for Health Statistics. *Vital Statistics of the United States*, 1995-91. See Figure 8.2 and Table 8.7.

Suicide summarized the issue in its most inflammatory terms:

> The suicide rate for young people between ages 15 and 24 almost tripled during the past 30 years... The sharp increase in suicide rates in one segment of the population, especially when most other causes of death were decreasing in the United States... has critical implications for public health priorities.[57]

So enrutted is the nature of youth suicide analysis that authorities do not consider any alternative explanations—especially as indicated by the closely parallel nature of trends in similar types of teen and adult deaths (the example highly relevant to suicide is shown in Figure 8.6) and the "seesaw" nature of teenage deaths ruled as accidents and as suicides in recent decades.

Worse still, Centers for Disease Control officials suggest that the true number of teen suicides could be double that now certified. This claim has been convincingly refuted by the Florida State University's Gary Kleck.[58] The only way the teen suicide rate could be higher is if the teen accidental death rate was lower—where else would the extra suicides come from? But if the teen suicide rate is twice as high, there would be very few deaths left over to classify as fatal accidents! Authorities would then have to explain why modern teenagers do not have fatal "accidents," while adults do. (Or at least, they would have to explain it among themselves, for such a surprising elimination of teenage accidents would not be discussed publicly until some major interest could be trotted out to take credit for it).

In many measures, statistics of the past are not reliably comparable to those of the present. Suicide certification—a definitive judgment demanding rigorous evidence as to perpetrator intent when the perpetrator is no longer around to question—requires complex investigation dependent upon coroner technique, training, and attitude. Most people who commit suicide do not leave notes. The question of whether today's teen suicide "epidemic" is not a real trend, but largely an artifact of improvement in the death classification process and awareness, is one that should have been thoroughly examined and disposed of before dire alarms were sent out to the public about unprecedented and terrifying adolescent self-annihilation.

Questioning the teenage "death wish"

The alarm among parents, professionals, schools, and youths themselves regarding the reported, inexplicably mushrooming incidence of young people taking their own lives has raised questions about adolescent mental health and led to extensive interventions aimed at stopping their purported self-destruction. The Centers for Disease Control's 1986 *Youth Suicide Surveillance* is characteristic, stating that, "in the past 30 years, the suicide rate among youth of the United States has increased dramatically," with 15-24-year-olds said to represent "a high risk group" for suicide. Youth suicide has risen sharply "while the rate for the remainder of the population remained stable," the C.D.C states.[59] These assertions are so common that few realize their dubious nature.

Teen suicide is considerably rarer than adult suicide. As Table 8.7 indicates, the puzzling aspect of suicide is not its teenage incidence, but its high rate among young and middle-aged white male adults, who should be experiencing a time of greatest opportunity.

Like other youth behaviors, suicide is patterned after cultural norms. Adult men age 20-44 commit suicide 4.5 times more than women that age; teenage boys commit suicide 4.5 times more than teenage girls. Young and middle-aged white adults are 1.6 times more likely to kill themselves than corresponding nonwhite adults, and white teens are 1.5 times more suicidal than nonwhite teens.

Massachusetts and Alaska, respectively, consistently display the nation's lowest and highest adult suicide rates, and also the nation's lowest and highest teen suicide rates. In 1990, firearms, poisons, and hangings accounted for 61 percent, 18 percent, and 10 percent of all adult suicides, respectively; and 66 percent, 10 percent, and 21 percent of all teen suicides. Women's suicides are five times more likely to involve drug overdoses than men's suicides; and teenage girls' suicides are seven times more likely to involve drug overdoses than those of teenage boys.

Homosexuals account for an estimated one-third of all adult suicides, and 30 percent of all adolescent suicides. Youths whose parent committed suicide are several times more likely to commit suicide themselves.[60] Despite correlations so consistent they can only be called overwhelming, links between youth and adult suicide

Table 8.7

Teens are much less likely than adults to commit suicide

U.S. suicides per 100,000 persons of each age group, sex, and race, 1991

Age group	Total	Male	Female	White	Nonwhite
10-14	1.5	2.3	0.7	1.6	1.0
15-19	11.0	17.6	3.7	11.8	7.8
All 10-19	6.2	10.0	2.2	6.7	4.4
20-24	14.9	25.4	3.9	13.6	11.3
25-34	15.2	25.0	5.4	16.0	11.3
35-44	14.7	24.0	6.5	15.9	8.1
All 20-44	14.9	24.7	5.5	15.5	9.9
45-64	15.5	24.4	7.1	16.6	7.9
Over 65	19.7	40.2	6.0	21.0	8.4
All ages >10	14.4	23.9	5.6	15.5	8.4

Source: National Center for Health Statistics (1995). *Vital Statistics of the United States 1991*. Mortality, Volume I, Part B. Washington, DC: U.S. Department of Health and Human Services, Table 8-5.

are rarely mentioned in the scientific literature and never in media treatments of the "epidemic."

As with the case of drunken driving and drug abuse, when teenage behaviors turn out to be less alarming in reality than officials and programmers want to depict, the measures are changed. It has become standard for psychiatric lobbies (as shown later) and agencies to lump the much higher suicide tolls among 20-24-year-olds with those of teens, produce a total of "5,000 to 6,000 per year," and then label this exaggerated number as "teenage suicides"—a figure popular in the media as well.[61] And rather than talk about the comparatively low teenage suicide death toll, most discussions of teen suicide have switched the measure to much murkier and uninterpretable self-reported behaviors such as self-reported "suicide ideation" or "suicide attempts."

Questioning teen suicide "attempts" and "contagion"

The punk band Suicidal Tendencies rants in "Suicidal Failure" (in which the inept narrator employs guns, pills, jumping off a bridge, lye, hanging, heroin overdose, driving off a cliff, and poison: "BUT I'M STILL NOT DEAD!") that the human body can prove difficult to dispatch. Still, suicide is a deliberate and calculated act. We would not expect that a truly suicide-bound individual would accidentally survive many attempts given the efficacy of readily available instruments. I recalled four teenage suicides I had reported on in my ten years as a Bozeman, Montana, journalist. Three shootings and one hanging from one girl and three boys ages 13, 14, 17, and 18—no ambivalence, no ineptness, no failures on their part.

Yet we are told by health officials and psychiatric authorities that hundreds of thousands, even millions, of teenagers "attempt suicide" every year but somehow don't die. The CDC estimates that about 3.5 million 9-12 grade students have "suicide ideation," 2 million have made "specific suicide plans," and over 1 million have made "suicide attempts."[62] Other self-reporting surveys estimate 500,000 teenage "suicide attempts" every year ("one every minute of every day," in the language of today's hype). As in the case of eighth grade boys' reports of sexual achievement, experts have taken these reports of adolescent "suicide ideation," "suicide plans," and "suicide attempts" at face value, which is manifestly silly, rather than considering the alternatives.

For example, is it possible that what is being reported are thoughts such as the following 14-year-old's?

> It seemed to him that life was but a trouble, at best... It must be very peaceful, he thought, to lie and slumber and dream forever and ever, with the wind whispering through the trees and caressing the grass and the flowers over the grave, and nothing to bother and grieve about, ever any more. If he only had a clean Sunday-school record, he could be willing to go, and be done with it all.

If Hannibal, Missouri, of Mark Twain times had self-reporting surveys, thoughts like those would have scored ideation, perhaps even plans. Yet Tom Sawyer hardly seems the profile of the suicidal teen. Is it possible that "suicide attempts," particularly given the fact that these are so disproportionately found among sexually abused girls, are efforts to get attention and help from a previously oblivious adult society?

In 1987, a week after the suicide of a popular 13-year-old girl in a Montana mountain town, I interviewed a dozen of her best friends, ages 13 to 15, alone and for an hour or more each, on their thoughts of suicide. All "said they had seriously contemplated suicide at one time or another in their lives. All said they are no longer considering the idea now." Perhaps their elaborations illuminate what adolescents mean by the boxes they check on self-reporting surveys.

Suicide ideation:

> "I could get away from my problems. I wouldn't have to change the sheets or do my homework," an eighth grade girl said. "It's like a video game—you die, you're out of the game, the problem is over. You get to start again.
> "But now I think, 'You die, but your problems are still there. Killing yourself is like staying in a hole forever.'"
> ... "Yes, I thought seriously about killing myself," another 14-year-old said, poking moodily at a sandwich in her kitchen. "I didn't wear clean clothes, my bedroom wasn't clean, I had a poor self-image. I didn't think I was popular."

Plans:

"Once I thought about killing myself when I was really upset about the way people were treating me," another 14-year-old said, sitting in her living room and scribbling absently in a notebook.

Memories of being sexually abused when she was younger kept "popping up in my mind," the girl said.

"I thought about taking pills or cutting my wrists. But my friends talked me out of it," she said.

... "I talked to them, and the problem began to go away. If I killed myself, my mom and my friends would take it very hard. It's not the easiest way out, it's the hardest way."

An attempt:

"I tried to kill myself when I was 13, but mainly I wanted attention," a girl said, chewing on a taco at a fast-food restaurant.

"I wanted people to notice me. I wanted my mom to look at me. She was really sleeping around with everybody then, a regular town whore.

"I got a razor and made a cut on my wrist in the bathroom. I was really upset that day. I got attention, all right.

"My best friend came in the bathroom and saw the blood and started screaming.

"I started thinking, 'My dad really loves me, my sister looks up to me, plus if I don't stay around, my best friend will wind up going out with some sleazebag.'

"And plus I thought, 'Wait a minute, this hurts.'"

In none of the hours-long interviews with these distressed eighth and ninth graders, a week after one of their closest friends shot herself with a .357 magnum, did I encounter the purported illusions of invulnerability, lack of appreciation of the finality of death, self-preoccupation, or glamorizing of suicide that authorities so often attribute to adolescents.

What I found instead was a biting realism. "Suicide is stupid, idiotic," said one 15-year-old of her best friend's demise. "You only really get that attention for a day. Then it starts to fade away." "What she did was wrong," another told me. "She hurt us a lot." What the dead cheerleader candidate's friends did the night after her death would send experts into apoplexy. They acquired a copious supply of alcohol and pot, sat up the night together in an empty house talking about their friend and suicide—and made a pact with each other to talk more openly about their despair.

"Lots of kids see no hope for the future, but we're not going to do that [kill ourselves]," one eighth grader told me. Another 14-year-old summed up the wake: "You've got to talk about your problems, not let them eat and eat and eat at you. If she had, she wouldn't be dead."[63] If more sane attitudes toward suicide have been articulated, I haven't encountered them.

How can experts get this so wrong? If 500,000 teens attempt suicide annually, and only 2,000 succeed, this represents an astonishing failure rate of 250 to one. Modern girls (considered the scheming sex in 1915) must be especially inept. While 10 percent of teen females are reported to have attempted suicide, only one in every 5,000 girls actually kills herself during her entire adolescence through age 19. That's 500 failed attempts for every suicide.

Either suicidal adolescents are a lot stupider than we think, the methods at hand are not really that deadly, or these are not true "suicide attempts." A "suicide attempt" is a deliberate effort to die. It fails only due to unanticipated inadequacy of the method or intervention of a rescuer. The tendency of adolescents (and to a lesser extent, adults) to use suicide "attempts" to gain attention is not new. As Finch and Poznanski pointed out twenty years ago, adolescents report some 120 suicide "attempts" for every completion; adults eight for one.[64] It is evident that the vast majority of what are called "suicide attempts" are not true efforts to die, but to use the attention-grabbing drama of attempted suicide to gain some other goal.

Similarly, the alleged contagiousness of teen suicide—whereby one suicide initiates "copycat" suicides—is rarely put in perspective appropriate to the panic raised in communities where a teen suicide has occurred. Columbia and Emory University researchers analyzed teen suicide "contagion" in 1988 and found that "cluster suicides account for approximately 1-5 percent of all teenage suicides."[65] Suicide contagion merits concern and response, but not the level of fear raised in the media and by psychological experts, which has, in any case, done nothing tangible to reduce the chances of imitators.

The myths of the generic nature of teen suicide are reflected in the well-meaning, and widely circulated, list of traits suicidal adolescents supposedly display. These include giving away prized possessions, engaging in violent arguments, remaining depressed over a period of time, suddenly changing eating or sleeping patterns, talking about death, abusing drugs or alcohol, or threatening suicide. These traits are easy to list but hard to pin down in practice, as they show up at various times in millions of individuals. It is important to understand that profiles of suicidal individuals are "unfortunately nonspecific and... weak," with "little empirical consensus" showing their validity in predicting suicide.[66] Non-suicidal teens (and suicidal and non-suicidal adults) also display many of these same behaviors, and more than a few teens have been shipped off to treatment based on over-reliance on such profiles.

Prevention programs aimed at teen suicide have shown little effectiveness.[67] Some argue, though not convincingly, that prevention efforts may actually increase teen suicide.[68] The six-fold increase in teenage psychiatric hospitalizations since 1970 cannot be shown to have reduced teen suicide either on a societal level or among the individuals in question. The failure of current efforts can be tied directly to the attempt to single out teen suicide for special attention rather than recognizing the pivotal links between general and specific adolescent and adult suicide patterns.

Beyond teen suicide myths

A couple of years ago I had an eye-opening conversation during a long bus ride with a 19-year-old West Texas rancher's daughter whose unhappy home life (mother divorced five times, molested by mom's "boyfriends" and a policeman) had led her to seriously contemplate killing herself. This young woman's searing real-life experiences contrasted starkly with the popular hype on how movies and rock 'n' roll songs cause teen suicide. Of the four Montana teen suicides I'd reported on, friends told me two had listened to classical music and jazz, one to Top-40 rock, and the fourth idolized the saccharine "Lean on Me," which is distinctly not about killing oneself. I asked this young woman if she had a favorite song that made her think of suicide. She replied, yes: "Fade to Black." Red flag. The very Metallica song singled out by Tipper's Parents Music Resource Center for promoting kids' self-dispatch. Maybe I had a case right here, if you overlook (as the PMRC does) minor details such as a childhood of rape, molestation, and parental anarchy. "I wouldn't go so far as to say that song saved my life," she said, "but hearing someone felt the way I did made me feel a lot better."

Parents can sue Judas Priest for marketing albums they claim "caused" teenage suicides, insisting that four-minute rock songs are more important than their kids' backgrounds of beatings and abandonment by alcohol-abusing parents, and win accolades and mass media attention. But youths do not kill themselves because of rock songs. There is, in reality, no such distinct phenomenon as "teen suicide." Its only distinguishing characteristic is that it is significantly lower than suicide among adults. In all other respects, it is as tragic and baffling as suicide among apparently healthy grownups.

As we have seen, teenagers commit suicide in the same patterns, by the same methods, and under the same circumstances as adults of their gender, era, and socioeconomic background. In particular, a startling and unpublicized "counter trend"—the large and unique decline in suicide among coastal California teenagers and adults over the last 25 years—is discussed in the concluding chapter.

Despite its dubious origin, the myth of the teen suicide "epidemic" is an essential argument in convincing parents that families are unable to cope with the self-destructiveness of today's youth. An American Psychological Association task force notes that claims of rising teen suicide are persuasive in winning increased commitments of marginally troubled youth to expensive psychiatric treatment, a point discussed next.

Youth as commodity

Given the circular logic that adolescence itself is a disease, it is not surprising that "distinctive professional cultures have arisen to provide the culture-specific ideology and technology for diagnosis and treatment" of its "intrinsic" pathology.[69] The concept of "adolescence itself as a disease state"[70] is invoked by American social scientists, in circular fashion, to blame "high-risk adolescent behavior" rather than to engage in conscientious analysis of troubling issues surrounding race, poverty, and individual experiences such as abuse and rape.

Gould raises a better question than any of the youth-fixing profiteers:

> Shall we concentrate upon an unfounded speculation... that follows the determinist philosophy of blaming the victim—or shall we try to eliminate the oppression that builds ghettos and saps the spirit of their unemployed in the first place?[71]

But eliminating oppression, ghettos, poverty, and unemployment costs money and requires adult sacrifices. The utility of locating the problem *within youth* instead, subject to fixing by myriad interests, is many-fold: For profit, to support prevailing prejudices, to win support for the authors' programmatic approaches, and—to a large degree—to sweep aside those troubling (and costly) social and environmental attritions that just happen to explain the behaviors authors deplore. The campaign ranges from the mundane to the highest levels.

A psychologist announces on one weekday talk show that the two worst things that can happen to a family are the death of a spouse or the presence of a teenager. Psychiatrists and doctors declare to *Newsweek* and *Journal of the American Medical Association* readers that teenagers are "high risk" and "especially vulnerable" for suicide, even though (as we have seen) the opposite is the case. A distinguished blue-ribbon commission established in 1990 by the American Medical Association and the National Association of State Boards of Education under the auspices of the Centers for Disease Control—after dismissing such inconsequential matters as "the complex and troubling societal issues of poverty, family instability, and discrimination, as well as housing and neighborhoods" *and* child abuse as "beyond the scope of this report"—states its plan to address the "crisis" they postulate in youth behavior: More behavior education programs and more medical interventions.[72]

The American Psychological Association (1993) recommends more psychological interventions to forestall the "aggression" and "anti-social behavior" they connect to "the developmental crises of adolescence."[73] The National Association of Private Psychiatric Hospitals recommends more teenagers shipped to psychiatric wards to treat the "severe psychological problems" of adolescents.[74] Psychiatrists' invention of new malaise such as "oppositional defiant disorder," "conduct disorder," and "transitional disorder," ensconced in their *Diagnostic and Statistical Manual,* have been applied as catch-alls to stigmatize and "treat" tens of thousands of youths as mentally disturbed.

Despite glowing press accounts often planted by the treatment industries themselves, youths have not been the beneficiaries of this trend. Teenage problems of the type treatment is supposed to alleviate, from drug and alcohol mortality to violence to suicide, were decreasing in the 1970s prior to the advent of 1980s mass youth therapy campaigns. All are now increasing. This failure is cited by the industry, and its agency allies, as pointing to the need for more of the same.

"Conduct Disorder": *Sturm und Drang* returns

Nineteenth century physician S.A. Cartwright postulated psychological disorders of slaves: "Dysesthesia" (the disease of sabotaging Master's orders) or "drapetomania" (the disease of trying to escape slavery). These would have allowed the new enterprise of psychology to insert itself into the presumably profitable field of treating and readjusting slaves to their conditions of servitude had not political systems rendered slavery obsolete.

Efforts to classify screwed-up kids according to objective criteria were pioneered by Richard Jenkins and his colleagues in the 1940s. Diagnosis of the disorder was based on the way a youth acted—aggressive stealing, running away, cruelty, obscenity—and his or her reaction to adult authority. Ignored were family and environmental influences.[75]

Psychologists today continue the bad habit of theorizing about individuals and classes of potential patients in isolation from, rather than in relation to, their conditions. Consider now the invention by psychiatric authorities of two new diseases of adolescence in the 1970s. They have proven instant hits. Two-thirds of all juvenile psychiatric inpatients today enter treatment under diagnoses of conduct disorder (CD) or oppositional-defiant disorder (ODD).[76]

The definition of ODD in the psychiatric industry's *Diagnostic and Statistical Manual of Mental Disorders* (version III-R) is as follows:

> Oppositional defiant disorder is "a pattern of negativistic, hostile, and defiant behavior without the more serious violations of the basic rights of others that are seen in Conduct Disorder." Its diagnostic criteria are: "A disturbance of at least six months during which at least five of the following are present:
>
> 1. Often loses temper
> 2   Often argues with adults
> 3. Often actively defies or refuses adult requests or rules
> 4. Often deliberately does things that annoy other people
> 5. Often blames others for his or her own mistakes
> 6. Is often touchy or easily annoyed by others
> 7. Is often angry and resentful
> 8. Is often spiteful or vindictive
> 9. Often swears or uses obscene language."[77]

Given no information, we have no idea why the youth in question might be angry, argumentative, defiant, annoying, blaming, touchy, angry (again), resentful, spiteful, vindictive, or swearing (!). Stamping one's foot (criteria 1, 2, 3, 4, 6, and 7) and hollering "fuck you" (criterion 9) a couple of times in six months more than earns an ODD badge. It's no surprise that girls get tagged with ODD much more than boys, for whom the above conduct is considered less "negativistic, hostile, and defiant." No one would accuse the psychiatric industry of blazing new ground in gender equality.

Conduct disorder (CD), nearly always diagnosed in boys, is a stepped-up form of ODD:

> Conduct disorder is "a persistent pattern of conduct in which the basic rights of others and major age-appropriate societal norms or rules are violated. The behavior pattern typically is present in the home, at school, with peers, and in the community. The conduct problems are more serious than those seen in Oppositional Defiant Disorder." Its diagnostic criteria are: "A disturbance of conduct lasting at least six months in which at least three of the following have been present:
>
> 1. Has stolen without confrontation of the victim on more than one occasion
> 2. Has run away from home at least twice while living in parental or surrogate home
> 3. Often lies
> 4. Has deliberately engaged in fire setting
> 5. Is often truant from school
> 6. Has broken into someone else's house, building, or car
> 7. Has deliberately destroyed others' property
> 8. Has been physically cruel to animals
> 9. Has forced someone to have sexual activity with him or her
> 10. Has used a weapon in more than one fight

11.   Often initiates physical fights
12.   Has stolen with confrontation of a victim
13.   Has been physically cruel to people."[78]

Now this is bad stuff. We don't want this kid running loose. But the law already has means to deal with this list of behaviors. The criminal codes call them: Burglary (criterion 1), incorrigibility (2), arson (4), truancy (5), trespassing (6), vandalism (7), cruelty to animals (8), rape (9), aggravated assault (10), assault (11), robbery (12), and more assault (13). We might wonder why psychologists rather than the criminal justice system are handling it. The reason turns out to be that wealthier parents can park their annoying kids in a facility that is not a jail or prison.

How do kids catch the disease of CD and ODD? Whether a consequence of nature or nurturing, the overwhelming majority of youth in inpatient treatment have "serious problems with relationships with their parents."[79] It is a beautifully circular process: "All major psychological theories of the origins of conduct problems in children state that parent and family functioning play key etiological roles."[80]

Three simple insights can be sifted out of the research on ODD and CD, beginning with a profound yet pithy statement of the etiology of the disordered child:

Insight No. 1: Screwed-up kids have even more screwed-up parents.

Horne and Sayger point out that often the youth seemed normal, but the parent trying to get him or her committed was messed up:

> Many children referred for treatment could not be differentiated from non-clinic children based on their behaviors, but... 90 percent of the clinic children and 90 percent of the nonclinic children could be correctly classified on the basis of the negativism and commanding behavior of the parent.[81]

Lewis et al (1984) found that youths diagnosed with conduct disorder had parents who had been in a psychiatric hospital (35.3 percent of the cases), in trouble with the law (17.7 percent), alcoholic (47.1 percent) or drug-addicted (30.0 percent), and one-third of the youth had been physically abused. But 100 percent of the parents controlled the purse strings, so lock up the kid. We move on to what might be called the functional mechanism by which kids become disordered:

Insight No. 2: Screwed-up parents often beat, abuse, abandon, serve as rotten models for, and otherwise mistreat their kids, producing screwed-up kids.

Horne and Sayger's review consistently refutes the popular and news media notion that all kids are natural candidates for padded walls:

> The common belief that oppositional or conduct problems on the part of a child or young adolescent represent a form of rebellion against an otherwise well-functioning family does not hold up under scrutiny... Aggression is generally not isolated within one individual family member but is a family characteristic.[82]

These authors also report that "conduct-disordered and abused children... are often the same."[83] The American Psychiatric Association adds that teenagers who misbehave typically have suffered rejection by parents, harsh discipline, an absent father, frequent shifting of parental figures, and parents who are alcoholics or drug addicts.

The Psychiatric Association notes that kids infected with the "disease" of CD or ODD often act perfectly normal. But the hospital admissions staff shouldn't be fooled:

> Typically, symptoms of the disorder are more evident in interaction with adults or peers whom the child knows well. Thus, children with the disorder are likely to show little or no signs of the disorder when examined clinically.[84]

CD and ODD kids may not be troubling anyone else with their disorder, but they are seriously ticking off the screwed-up parents who played a big part in causing it. One might call that justice, not mental disease.

Horne and Sayger (1990) point out that running away from home, one criterion for diagnosing CD, may represent a youth's "chronically maladaptive reaction," or "fundamentally healthy reaction to a pathological environment."[85] Even DSM-III-R admits that lying by a child "to avoid physical or sexual abuse" is exempted from the diagnostic criterion of "often lies."[86] Is it really a "disorder" for a youth to react negatively to violent, disturbed, alcoholic, addicted, and/or abusive grownups?

The highest professional and legal authorities agree that it is—or, more correctly, that we don't need to trouble ourselves whether it is or not. Instilling in youths the notion that violence or addiction is an acceptable part of adulthood is a temporary expedient likely to be regretted later on. Here we find that the problem is much larger than blaming screwed-up parents for screwed-up kids. Screwing up kids is a cooperative, top-to-bottom enterprise.

At the urging of psychiatric lobbies, forced, unreviewable juvenile commitments based on little more than medical industry self-interest were authorized by the U.S. Supreme Court in yet another of its modern rulings that youths have no rights worth inconveniencing adults to respect. Admitting that parents trying to get their children committed to a psychiatric facility are not necessarily objective, the Court allowed designation of a "neutral fact finder" to make the decision. The neutral fact-finder, the Court said, may be the "admissions staffs of the hospitals," to whose coffers the youth's admission would grace with $16,000 or more in income over the next 30 days.

Dismissing the notion of requiring the same kinds of agency hearings required for adult psychiatric commitments, the Court held that allowing the hospital authority to decide whether to admit a profitable patient "must be left to the judgment of physicians in each case."[87] The result of the Court's indifference to the rights of adolescents, as will be shown, was a flood of tens of thousands of youths forced into inappropriate psychiatric commitment under vague diagnoses[88] at immense profit to hospitals and inestimable damage to adolescents wrongly branded as mentally disturbed.

We finally arrive at the very troubling probabilistic assessment of objective outcome measures to be expected from today's management of ODD and CD:

Insight No. 3: When screwed-up therapists and screwed-up governmental authority consort with screwed-up parents in beating up on a youth all have played a part in screwing up, the result is likely to be a dangerously screwed-up kid.

Epidemic KID (Kid-with-Insurance Disorder)

Experts tell us CD (conduct disorder) and ODD (oppositional defiant disorder) are rampant in the young. Approximately 9 percent of male children and 2 percent of all female children are estimated to have CD. A 1989 Duke University study found 5.2 percent of all children diagnosed with CD, 6.6 percent with ODD.[89] Thus estimates indicate these disorders may affect 7.5 million children, 12 percent of the child/youth population. If they can get to all of them, treatment facilities would take in $225 billion per month.

The Supreme Court unbarred the gates. The psychiatric industry was ready and eager to receive a mob of crazy kids. Medical hospitals had been drastically overbuilt during the 1970s, leaving many in serious financial straits. Clinical patients weren't filling the beds as expected. A new market to rescue the industry from its own poor planning was needed. The industry squared its shoulders and went after it.

Private hospital spokespersons, such as Dr. Frank Rafferty, vice president for medical affairs of the Health Care International psychiatric hospital chain, publicized the idea that "minor problems" such as running away, truancy, or stealing are in reality "extreme behaviors... a sign of serious mental illness" that "can require hospitalization."[90] Yet the industry would have to move quickly. Professional studies typically conclude that most childhood disorders cure themselves.

An example from the *New York Times* illustrates the "headline hype" versus research reality: "As many as one in five children suffer from psychiatric problems serious enough to impair their lives in some way, according to the surprising findings of several new surveys of the mental health of children," the article began. However, details of the surveys noted that 20 percent of all 10-year-old boys display CD (declining to 7 percent by age 17), as do 10 percent of all 15-year-old girls (declining to 1 percent by age 17). What is called "conduct disorder" was "found to cool spontaneously," the studies found.[91] Bad news.

So hospitals' advertising and public statements pinpointed exactly those emotional issues most likely to arouse suburban parents. Private psychiatric hospitals all over the country displayed "sensationalistic and frightening ads" designed to convince parents that only inpatient treatment lies between their disturbed child and suicide or violence. Such ads have included scenes of teenagers putting guns to their heads and parents visiting graveyards.[92] Representative George Miller (D-California), chairman of the U.S. House of Representatives' Select Committee on Children, Youth, and Families, noted:

> As it appears on the TV screen, the message is to bring your child in and we'll take him. It's sort of like getting your car repaired. No fuss, no muss. Show up at the care unit if you have insurance or means to pay. It's almost as if the only diagnosis you need is that the parent says, "I want my child placed here."[93]

In 1987, a task force of the American Psychological Association (not the same as the Psychiatric Association) led by Brian Wilcox reported that hospitals had filled their vacant wards with "troubled teens." The hospitals' increased advertising and marketing for disturbed adolescents "have led to the flux of adolescent admissions. 'There were an awful lot of empty beds out there before they started pushing for teenagers,' Wilcox said."[94]

A 1985 investigation by the House's Select Committee on Children, Youth, and Families found that juvenile admissions to *just a sample* of inpatient private psychiatric hospitals rose from 10,764 in 1980 to 48,375 in 1984. The number of youth confined in locked psychiatric wards rose from 6,452 in 1970 to 16,735 in 1980 and to over 36,000 by 1986—up six-fold in 15 years. Nearly all were committed under catch-all diagnoses such as CD, ODD, "transitional disorder," or "adolescent adjustment disorder" (the latter two of which are particularly incomprehensible maladies).[95]

What kids were the hospitals recruiting? Objectively, we would expect more ODD and CD kids to come from poorer households. Adults, including parents, react to the stresses of poverty much the same as youths do. Abuse, violence, addiction, and child neglect are found more often in low-income families. Fighting, assault, disobeying laws and rules, and school difficulties—supposedly the signatures of CD and ODD—are common in low-income neighborhoods, where arrest rates among all age groups for violent and anti-social offenses are many times higher than average.

Diagnostically, that is the case. When researchers apply the CD and ODD diagnoses to general populations, they find that a large surplus of nonwhite youths display this teenage "disease."[96] Only their parents don't seem to want to get rid of them. Youths in public treatment programs are typically referred by courts, public agencies, schools—not parents.[97] Nevertheless, we would expect that the psychiatric hospitals, so eager to open their doors to troubled kids, would teem with the children of the impoverished.

Not so. Regardless of how they might be psychiatrically "diagnosed" if they ever met a psychiatrist, low-income, primarily minority, youth are much more likely to be declared delinquent and channeled into the criminal justice system. In the mid-1980s, the Select Committee on Children, Youth, and Families pointed out that for the first time, a majority of youth incarcerated in detention centers (jails and prisons) were nonwhite.[98] Today, that figure has rocketed to over two-thirds.

But poor kids were not who the private psychiatric hospitals wanted. Instead, professional treaters targeted parents who had insurance coverage and thereupon tapped into a surprising 1970s and 1980s phenomenon: A large and growing mass of yuppie parents who *wanted* an extended vacation from their kids. While the overwhelming majority of youths confined in public facilities are low-income, the diametric opposite is the case for the private hospitals that now handle a large majority of youth cases. Private-facility diagnoses of ODD and CD are *much higher among middle and upper-middle income youth*.

Pandemic Not-Getting-Along-With-Affluent-Parents Disorder erupted coast to coast. "A growing number of children are being placed in mental hospitals by frustrated parents who are either unable or unwilling to cope with problems that have traditionally been handled at home or by mental health professionals in their offices," the Psychological Association task force found. Nearly all private placements are requested by parents rather than by courts or agencies.[99]

Inpatient treatment often costs $16,000 per month, or more, which is the limit most insurance policies will pay. "You get some pretty rapid cures when the insurance runs out," noted Ira S. Lourie, M.D., director of child and adolescent services at the National Institute of Mental Health.[100]

Defending its members' admissions policies as based on "appropriate assessment" and "fully implemented quality assurance," the National Association of Private Psychiatric Hospitals assured Congress that profiteering was not the reason for the rising juvenile clientele:

> Child and adolescent admissions to psychiatric facilities are increasing because more of them are seriously psychologically disturbed. The most recent President's Commission on Mental Health Report (1979), estimated that 1.4 to 2.0 million adolescents have severe psychological problems. More current objective studies confirm these figures. Tragically, these severe psychological problems often manifest themselves in suicide. An American teenager takes his or her own life once every 90 minutes, and this year, an estimated two million young people between 15 and 19 will attempt suicide. Suicide is now the third leading cause of death among young Americans.
>
> Fortunately, the American public is becoming increasingly aware of the problem and increasingly accepting of the need for appropriate treatment. Public education campaigns have contributed to this heightened awareness of the growing numbers of troubled youth.[101]

The NAPPH's prepared statement does not inspire confidence that the public campaign to increase juvenile psychiatric admissions was based on calm, clinical evidence rather than scare tactics and overblown promises. NAPPH's claim that a teenager commits suicide "every 90 minutes" yields an annual toll of 5,840, three times the true annual toll (1,849 in 1985). The estimate that "two million young people between 15 and 19 will attempt suicide" per year is four to eight times that predicted by even the highest survey estimates. NAPPH's claim that adolescent psychological problems "often manifest themselves in suicide" is dubious: By their own figures, only one in 1,000 adolescents with "severe psychological problems" takes his or her own life.

Further, there is no evidence that more teenagers are "seriously psychologically disturbed" today. The rate of teens diagnosed with more clinically defined, serious mental disorders, such as schizophrenia and manic depression, has remained stable. The recent increase is due to "minor and family problems" often diagnosed as "conduct disorder" or other vague disorders: Kids not getting along with their parents. "There is no great reason to believe that adolescents have more serious problems today than they once did," the American Psychological Association's Wilcox concluded after the task force study.[102]

Fortunately, a major player was becoming surly. The insurance industry, fed up with paying heavy reimbursements for the derelictions of the Supreme Court and mental health professionals, undertook its own investigation. Studies by Blue Cross and other insurers found that "at least 50 percent of the admissions in this inpatient psych and CD programs for juveniles were inappropriate." Public interest groups found the complaints were more than just insurance industry moaning. Ira Schwartz, director of the University of Minnesota's Center for the Study of Youth and Policy, agreed the percentage of inappropriate youth commitments was "probably higher."[103] Studies by the Children's Defense Fund and the above-mentioned American Psychological Association task force reached similar conclusions of substantial over-commitment of youths based on vague diagnoses of ODD and CD.[104]

Schwartz argued from extended study of juvenile psychiatric admissions that the chief admitting criteria for private facilities is not behavior, but insurance coverage or other evidence of ability to pay. A study of California youth psychiatric admissions showed youths with insurance were held in treatment twice as long as uninsured youth.[105] Youths were held in private treatment facilities twice as long as adults with similar disorders despite the lack of clinical evidence showing that "juveniles are twice as sick or that it takes twice as long to cure them." Schwartz found that even though youths are admitted for "far less serious problems" than are adults, children spend an average of 55.8 days, and adolescents 48.6 days, in psychiatric wards, compared to 25.5 days for adults.[106]

The growth in private psychiatric confinement of the young paralleled the decrease in youth in detention and public facilities. The number of non-delinquent youth held in detention facilities declined from 199,341 in 1969 to 22,833 in 1981, while those in residential care declined from 155,905 to 131,419 (nearly all such youths were minor status offenders). By virtue of vague criteria, an "open-door policy in terms of admissions," financial abuses, and inappropriate treatment, psychiatric care had become "a hidden system of juvenile control," Schwartz testified.[107] Within this "hidden system," there appear two sharply differing standards of "conduct disorder" based on socio-economic status:

(a)   A specific standard of violent behavior applied by courts and agency professionals to low-income youth, who are sent to punitive detentional dispositions or public treatment centers;

(b)   A vague standard of parent-annoying behavior applied by self-interested parents and diagnosticians to middle and upper income youth, who are forcibly incarcerated in private treatment facilities—often for longer periods than minority teens received for criminal convictions.

In neither case do the punishments/treatments afforded serve the interests of the youth so much as adult complainants and profiteers. In neither case can they be shown to have rehabilitative effect.

For low-income youth, the replacement of jail time with ward time circumvents federal reforms designed to channel mildly delinquent youth away from detentive measures. Middle and upper class youth are often hospitalized for being a "pain in the ass" to their higher-income parents.[108] Troubled and rebellious non-delinquent adolescents are increasingly diagnosed as the "locus of the problem" for their difficulties in coping with families and societies that are themselves troubled and disordered.

"The intent of the Juvenile Justice and Delinquency Prevention Act [of 1974] was not to have status offenders removed from institutions in the justice system only to have them incarcerated" for even longer "terms" in psychiatric facilities under open-ended "sentences," Schwartz notes. But that was viewing the matter in terms of the interests of the youth. There were bigger interests to consider. Only 10 percent of the mental health facilities surveyed in 1973 were operated for profit. Four years later, that percentage had grown to 50 percent, many involving multi-facility chains.[109] Kid fixing had become big business.

Iatrogenics: Manufacturing mental illness

Forcing youth into psychiatric treatment when they are not disturbed can turn an imaginary problem into the genuine article. Reviews are not simply pessimistic regarding the ineffectiveness of institutional, residential, educational, and pharmacological approaches to treating CD and ODD.[110] A massive 1992 textbook review found that wrong-headed treatment may worsen any anti-social tendencies present in CD-diagnosed youth:

> By and large, our society tends to take a punitive, rather than rehabilitative, attitude toward an antisocial, aggressive youth. Thus the emphasis is on punishment and on "teaching the child a lesson." Such "treatment," however, appears to intensify rather than correct the behavior. Where treatment is unsuccessful, the end product is likely to be an antisocial personality with aggressive behavior.[111]

An initial evaluation and follow-up of 53 adolescent girls hospitalized for conduct disorder found the outcomes "poor; 6 percent had died a violent death, the majority had dropped out of school, one-third were pregnant before the age of 17 years, half were re-arrested, and many suffered traumatic injuries."[112]

Why doesn't institutional treatment for such modern adolescent afflictions as Not-Getting-Along-With-Parents Disease in conjunction with Kid-With-Insurance Disorder work? Because most private treatments rely on ineffective behavior modification and drugs. CD and ODD are, with few exceptions, rooted in parent, family, and chronic community malaise. Therefore, "therapy for the conduct-disordered child is likely to be ineffective unless some means can be found for modifying the child's environment."[113] Whether we are talking about the "delinquent" minority youth or the "disordered" white teenager, the crux of the issue inevitably spins back to the same conclusion: Fix environments, and most kids will fix themselves.

I witnessed a 16-year-old girl committed to inpatient psychiatric treatment (essentially for police- and parent-annoying curfew violations) for 30 days, at a cost of $24,000 to the insurer, return to the home of her drunken psychotic mother and resume her old misbehaviors within one weekend of release. It was perfectly predictable. When the girl, at age 17, moved to a nearby college community to live with her older sister, the change of environment worked wonders. She got her GED and enrolled in vocational school. Some especially searing, detailed descriptions of mis-treated young, relentlessly punished by the system for the crime of being child abuse victims, can be found in Louise Armstrong's Of 'Sluts' and 'Bastards.'[114] Inpatient therapy is not for the annoying, but for the severely disturbed, applied upon an independent, objective review.

The examples of the costly failure of hospital greed preying on disordered parents are not only individual, but large scale. In the early 1970s, Minnesota pioneered laws requiring insurance companies to provide coverage for mental health and chemical dependency treatment. Minnesota's effort is an example of how apparently progressive health coverage legislation backfires into a repressive nightmare in a climate of punitive attitudes toward an unpopular and unprotected group—in this case, the young. In practice, Minnesota's new law created "an enormous potential for the growth of these programs as well as the potential for abuse."[115]

Abuses forthcame. In 1984, 3,047 juveniles, a number equal to nearly 1 percent of the 13-17-year-olds in Minnesota (a high-income state with extraordinarily low rates of juvenile crime and violence), were committed to psychiatric hospitals in the Minneapolis-St. Paul area. That year, they spent a total of 83,000 patient days in treatment. This admission level, more than triple the rate of 1976 and a 50 percent rise from 1983, does not include all hospitals, nor juveniles admitted to drug and alcohol or other treatment facilities. Minnesota youth were being psychiatrically managed at levels three to five times higher than youth elsewhere in the nation.

Minnesota thus provides a laboratory for the study of the effectiveness of mass treatment of youth compared to measures treatment is supposed to affect. If psychiatric diagnosis and treatment is accurately targeted and is effective in reducing youth disorders, we would expect to see significant reductions in suicide, unwed birth, violent death, violent crime, and other crime among Minnesota youth compared to youth nationally. These are the major complications of conduct disorders and the consequences private psychiatric treatment center advertising vigorously claims to deter.

Recently, I measured six key Conduct Disorder-related indices—violent crime arrests, property crime arrests, suicides, violent accidental deaths, nighttime fatal traffic crashes (a standard index of drunken driving), and unwed births—over the 1970-1989 period. Minnesota youth generally fared worse than did youth nationally. Of these indexes, only accidental deaths showed a larger net decline among Minnesota youth than youth nationally. Violent crime (including rapes and homicides), property crime, suicides, nighttime fatal crashes, and unwed births among Minnesota youth showed net increases compared to youth nationally.

The treatment industry has based its advertising and scientific justification for more juvenile admissions on claims that treatment reduces just such problems. These claims cannot be demonstrated for individual programs, nor can they be shown for general outcomes such as those of Minnesota's heavily treated youth population.

Affirming opposition and defiance

Adolescent antagonism to adult behavior and the prevailing order is a critical factor in societal evolution. It is neither to be fawningly lionized nor angrily punished as a mental illness, but evaluated on the merits of the challenges it makes to the legitimacy of the adult authority against which it rebels. In this regard, conduct disorders can usually be seen not solely as youth diseases, but as symptomatic of a constellation of familial (and often social) breakdown:

> When we take a look at the underlying vulnerabilities, we are almost
> invariably faced with such a variety of intrinsic problems (e.g., psychotic, organic,
> psychoeducational) and such a dearth of external family and institutional sup-
> ports that we may wish that we had never looked so carefully at the youngster in
> the first place.[116]

When we do look, we find a product of the adult society that raised the youth.
The treatment involves less what is done to fix the young target, which is of little
use in any case, than what is done to fix his or her larger environment. Adverse
environmental circumstances are not a problem that can be solved by mental health
professionals; "the problem is one for our entire society."[117] Too often, psychiatric
disciplines have served as agents to force or coerce unpopular groups to adjust to
intolerable conditions, unfortunately profitably but fortunately unsuccessfully. It is a
traditional role of mental health industries that has long been in need of reconsideration.

If suicide, in particular, is a complex response to hopelessness (based on an
individual's reasoned analysis) rather than to depression (a clinical state based on
feelings and, in some cases, chemistry), then it cannot be alleviated by injections of
programs, classes, and treatments. Adolescents do not need to be taught to be hopeful. They typically display low rates of suicide and depression. In attacking their self-
efficacy as so many laws, publicity, and prevention and forced treatment programs
inadvertently do, we attack their biggest defense against self-destruction. The myths
of adolescent suicide and the responses engendered by those myths, as in other areas
of teenage behavior, hamper the societal changes necessary to make America a
more hopeful place for the young to grow up.

9. Generation Y

There can be no adolescence in *1984*.

— Edgar Friedenberg, 1959

Mr. America try to hide
The product of your savage pride
The youthful minds that it denied
The day you shrugged and stepped aside
    The left-behinds
    Of the Great Society

— Frank Zappa, "Hungry Freaks," 1966

My gang will get you
Scenes of rape in the arroyo
Seductions in cars, abandoned buildings
Fights at the food stand...
Dreams watching each other narrowly...
We could plan a murder
Or start a religion.

— Jim Morrison, *An American Prayer*, 1970

What better way to pay tribute to the ingenuity of the younger generation than by making sure they will need it?

— David Brower

Five thousand youths crammed into a state fair Quonset warehouse cheer violently as Billy Corgan screams:

"*I fucking hate the U.S.A.!!*"

The kids jump up and down and toss about their compadres they have elevated over their heads. It is not a kindly sound, no fulsome ode to the ghost of parents past reverberating in the giant metal arch. "Welcome to the *cowbarn*," Corgan taunts. "Here we are, one *big happy family* in the *cowbarn*."

Corgan is leader of a bitter alternative band, Smashing Pumpkins, that seems to have spent its professional life in therapy. Ridiculing his "white trash" childhood of divorce, chaos, and abandonment, Corgan rants: "Why the fuck did you have me if you didn't want me?... Why was I raised to lose?"

These are as they appear: Thousands of down-and-out kids of pre-militia-bombed Oklahoma City, white trash capital of the Milky Way. My descendants by race, class, and heritage, 1994's version of early Sixties inner northside kids. The age is 12 to 20 late on an April school night, dope smoke and redeye in the air. Tipper Gore metaphor alert: Through the haze I see a girl who couldn't be more than eleven in spandex and a t-shirt proclaiming, "Don't be a pussy." The mood is understated savage. Earlier thousands, including me, were forced to squat prostrate in gravel as reactivated brownshirts brandishing metal detectors combed for guns and shivs. They paid $15 and are now crushed into a dirt-floored livestock arena without a single seat and only one restroom.

Mournful alternative-radio songs take on a brutal edge. "The killer in me is the killer in you..." Corgan snarls as the crowd slows its back-and-forth lurching to savor the animosity.

A week earlier, in late March 1994, bespectacled 78-year-old industrial-emeritus Lee Iacocca, "dressed like a million bucks... stood and delivered like an NFL linebacker" much the same message to 3,000 "middle-aged business men and women" in the shimmering ballroom of the Civic Center downtown. "Iacocca swung a broadsword at the older generation," reported the ultra-conservative *Daily Oklahoman*:

> "I'm ashamed to say that this is probably the most irresponsible and selfish generation that this country has ever produced.
> "Remember, now, I'm not talking about the younger generation. I'm talking about most of us in this building.
> "There's talk of a generation war coming. Hell, if I were 25 years old and really understood the debt burden I was being forced to carry—for the rest of my life—I think I'd be mad enough to go to war with the old geezers who did this to us.
> "...The most damning thing we can say about ourselves as Americans is that we're pushing this big load off on our kids. And we're doing it with our eyes wide open."[1]

Integrated zones

Madness, says 18-year-old Stephen Bruner of the summer of 1992 that led to spending his ninth grade year in Oklahoma juvenile lockup. He won't talk about what he and his gang Panic Zone did in that place of "confusion," where the rural black community of Spencer intersects the southeast Oklahoma City suburb of Midwest City.

He rattles off the names of a dozen gangs—Hoover Street, Westside, Candlewood, 6-0—that inhabit the district. "It's meaningless," said Bruner of the violence. "The things I did, things I had done to me... madness."

Wayne Thompson, who employs Bruner as an intern in his office at the Oklahoma Health Care Project in Founder's Tower overlooking the city's opulent northwest side, has had 25 more years to reflect on *madness*. Thompson spent three years in prison at Terminal Island and Lompoc in the 1970s for armed bank robbery on behalf of the San Francisco Black Panthers' military wing. "The Black Panthers' level of armed struggle was more than the community could support then. We were"—he pauses—"premature."

Madness, as Thompson phrases it in more erudite terms, is "the natural, predictable reaction" of young people to form alternative social organizations against the "larger, hostile adult culture that is anti-youth, particularly anti-African American youth." Twenty thousand more Oklahoma City-area children and teenagers live in poverty than a quarter century ago. "These kids are at risk of extinction if they depend upon adults to protect them," Thompson declares. It is not just parents who fail them, but an adult society increasingly angry and punishing toward its youth. "That is the perception of the young people who are being ground up in this culture and the grinder of the juvenile justice system."

"Their perception of their situation," says Thompson, "is very correct."

As youth poverty mushrooms and the attitudes of larger society become harsher, the traditional markers of race and class are sliding toward new realignments. "There's still a racial element, sure," says Thompson. "But this has gone beyond race now. There's a larger madness. This culture is engaged in harming its kids. There is a youth subculture growing in response to that rejection, and if we don't learn how to respect it and deal with it, they're going to send this America we spent 200 years building up in flames."

Bruner recounts the harassment of white police in Midwest City under the array of new anti-gang laws. But black officers, he quickly adds, are just as hostile: "The black cops act like, 'trust us, we're just like you.' Then they burn your ass. It took us a while to catch on."

And "gangs are integrated, too," Bruner says. "It surprises me to think about it now, because we just took it like it was. There are white kids in black gangs, blacks in Mexican gangs, Mexicans in white gangs, blacks in white gangs, Asians in everyone's gangs. It isn't a race thing. It's who's in the 'hood.'"

The 1995 Oklahoma Kids Count *Factbook* reported 47,000 impoverished children and adolescents in metropolitan Oklahoma City in 1990—21,000 whites, 13,500 blacks, 4,500 Native Americans, 3,000 Asians, 5,000 Latinos—and projected that the number has grown rapidly since then. In a November 1995 series on the metropolis's exploding poverty, the *Daily Oklahoman* reported that the city's poor are increasingly isolated, jammed together in a chain of destitute neighborhoods ringing downtown and extending eastward to the suburbs. New networks form in these neighborhoods, ones beyond race. "You go to school with them, people ask about this guy you know, 'Is he okay with you, 'cause if he's okay with you, he's okay with me,'" says Bruner.

Integrated police battling integrated gangs is not the white-and-black-walking-together that Martin Luther King dreamed of. Interracial gang loyalties forged by school associations is a permutation *Brown vs. Topeka*, the 1964 Civil Rights Act, and busing advocates never anticipated.

For teenagers forced into poverty, marking by the system is permanent. "There's a history to this city," Bruner says. "If you're in a subcultural group, it's no different in society's eyes whether you're in a gang or not. Kids had no choice but to hang with us." The marking is personal as well. "My last name is famous with the police," he says, referring to siblings, cousins, family members well acquainted with law enforcement and wardens. "Racism is here. You can't run away from it. [But] racism is not just black or white." Nonwhite youths, white youths on the wrong side, "we are all targets."

Once in, the system does not gently turn loose. One day after he emerged from a year in youth prison and returned to his sophomore year in school, the principal called Bruner to the office. A uniformed police officer was there. "They waved $200 in front of my face and told me I could have it if I'd tell them who had guns."

Bruner had never seen a gun at school. "You know it happens. But we're stereotyped as it is. We'd be doing them a favor by taking a gun to school."

Bruner decided the incident was a ploy by school and law enforcement authorities to keep him trapped in the prison system. He dropped out of school. "When you're in the system, you can't do enough in your lifetime to get out," he says. "I believe they want to keep me and every other black male and minority male and poor kid in the system permanently, send us all to the penitentiary."

Bruner is training in office management and in television production and editing through Thompson's program. Enough of his friends remained trapped in the justice system. Bruner sees that as surrender. "They didn't get out like I did, now they're up for murder one. Those that don't get involved with the system at all were smarter than the ones like me who did."

In recent years, twice as many Oklahoma youths have been placed in the adult prison system as in the juvenile system. Youths can be tried as adults at age 14 now, and legislators want to push it down to 13. Oklahoma imprisons more of its citizens than any other state except Texas, and youths serve sentences longer than adults for the same crimes. Oklahoma juvenile prisons won nationwide attention for their brutality, including regular beatings, hogtyings, excessive drug and isolation punishments, and sexual assaults, in a 1978 lawsuit filed by Oklahoma Legal Aid and in a Pulitzer Prize-winning 1982 Gannett News Service series, "Oklahoma Shame."

For two decades, Oklahoma has done what get-tough advocates want. If forcing youths into the adult prisons at earlier ages, enforcing longer sentences, and administering harsh punishment is the remedy, Oklahoma should be a paradise of peace. Yet arrest figures over the last fifteen years show Oklahoma's juvenile violence growing at twice the national pace. That contrary to predictions, redirecting public efforts toward putting more people in prison coincides with more, not less, crime outside of prison still hasn't registered with officials or the public, Oklahoma Legal Aid's Gary Taylor said.

Of a state whose lawmakers and law enforcers now want the U.S. Supreme Court to allow them to execute 14- and 15-year-olds (and lost only on a 5-4 vote), Thompson catches the drift: "Society wants to kill these kids. The death penalty. Shooting them in the street. If it can't do that, then killing their spirit."

Those most responsive to his message of breaking two cycles—rescuing youths and families their from poverty and powerlessness, rescuing the political system from its self-destructive prison binge—are in the business community, Republicans more than Democrats, Thompson says. "That's frightening. The social services, academia, are bound like serfs to the status quo."

When he talks to Oklahoma City's business groups, Thompson finds growing concern over the costs of more prisons and "alarm in the white community because the gangs are becoming more integrated." He doesn't push charity or altruism, but self interest. "I tell them, 'You're going to die in 15 or 20 years, and you have grandchildren. They're going to have to live with the environment you've created. And you've created a hellacious environment.'"

Exposure to the wider world after his prison term clarified the nature of the struggle he wanted to continue, Thompson says, and gaining a larger perspective will do the same for gang and former gang kids who now think of themselves as engaging in *madness*. "This is not just some teenage rite-of-passage problem. The alienation of young people from the traditional institutions is profound. The schools are being replaced by the prisons as the primary agents of socialization. There's a culture growing, becoming more and more aware of its conditions. And this is the legacy we're leaving: Armed camps."

Lost then and now

We have lied about today's adolescents in every conceivable negative way to every conceivable profitable end. Moralized about them through our politicians and media to our smug satisfaction. Defunded their schools and sustenance to our temporary benefit. Truncated their larger futures the better to temporarily enrich our smaller ones.

And now, we expect Generation Y, in the poverty we have left behind, to pay our massive senior subsidies at the same time they pay off our bloated debts. We have bludgeoned our primitive antagonisms of race and ethnicity upon the young who must, for their own survival, negotiate and rebuild the diverse and divided world of post-millennium California and America.

Today's teens, we are told, are the worst ever. Compared to who? Well, we are incessantly reminded by today's sanctimonious elders, Dear Abby and Ann and their Depression cohort (the same seniors more exercised about their property taxes than about a future America it appalls them to contemplate), how their generation weathered tough times due to the fiber of moral, pull-together families and upstanding youths. Kids today, these elders claim, haven't got the high standards and grit of generations back then. A challenge well worth examining.

Today's popular image of the tranquility of 1930s youth is summed up in the much-publicized "study" of the "Top Ten School Problems" of that era (gum-chewing, hair-pulling, giggling, talking in class) compared to the "Top Ten School Problems" of today (violence, suicide, pregnancy, dope). My efforts to locate that study proved fruitless. It was a hoax, falsely attributed to the California Department of Education and to *Phi Delta Kappan* magazine among others, apparently derived from a few random comments made at a 1987 California teacher's conference.[2] The fact that no study existed didn't prevent it from being cited profusely by an adult generation of the '90s in a lather to praise itself and damn its own children. "We got thousands and thousands of calls about it," a spokesman for the Fullerton, California, police told me after his agency was identified as the "study's" source.

In fact, today's crop of senior citizens was once considered pretty appalling itself. Younger generations can extract ample revenge on sermonizing grayhairs by researching what *their* elders said about *them*. A scan of the media of the 1930s demolishes the upright image of teens of that day. It also provides a crucial lesson in how different adult treatment of the young, even amid denunciations and dire laments no different in 1935 than in 1995, produced much more benign results than today's.

Latter-day angelification stands in stark contrast to contemporaneous image of 1930s teenagers, who horrified grownups of the day. In fact, the top school problem of the 1930s was that half of all teens were not even *in* high school. If you took a public high school of 1995, kicked out three fourths of the nonwhites and low-income students, and warehoused all the pregnant, handicapped, and learning-disabled youths out of sight, you'd have a pretty good approximation of a public high school of 1940.

There was alarmism about drugs. "Organized gangs are distributing drugs to every school in this city... dope peddlers infest our high schools... in every community and hamlet in our country," a government-backed docu-drama harangued in 1937. "Hundreds of new (drug) cases involving our youth come in every day... Drug-crazed teens have murdered entire families."

The famous "Reefer Madness" was one of a series of official anti-drug manifestos (another was "Cocaine Fiends") designed to alert parents to skyrocketing drug use by 1930s teens and attendant violence, promiscuity, intoxicated driving, doped athletes and students, and suicide. As in the 1990s drug scare, the alarms over a relatively mild "teen pot" crisis coincided with a mushrooming rate of drug abuse mortality among adults—in this case, a 40 percent increase in drunken driving deaths among men following the repeal of Prohibition. And as in later decades, an idle bureaucracy proved the devil's workshop. Agencies whose lively roles enforcing Prohibition had ended with the Volstead Act's repeal in 1933 were casting about for new villains to justify their budgets. Suddenly a "drug crisis" was discovered. Marijuana was outlawed in 1937. Then as now, pot-smoking kids, Mexican immigrants, and blacks became a new national terror to replace white drinkers.[3]

"Youth Gone Loco: Villain is Marijuana," another magazine of the day trumpeted.[4] But youth malaise was deeper than mere drugs. Tabbed the "lost generation" by Washington journalist Maxine Davis, who travelled 10,000 miles around the country looking for it, Thirties adolescents were described by adult observers as passive and melancholic, "confused, disillusioned, and disenchanted," in a listless mental state "rapidly approaching a psychosis." Lamented Davis in her 1936 work:

> Dixie's youth of today would never fire on Fort Sumter. British tea and King George's taxes would be unloaded without protest by the young men of Massachusetts and Vermont... Today's younger generation accepts whatever happens to it with sheep-like apathy.[5]

Scholars George Leighton and Richard Hellman warned in 1935 of high school kids who "can't get work" roaming the land "armed" and "out for what they can get, while it lasts." The authors forecast the motherland at gravebrink by mid-century:

> When a generation, numbering in the millions, has gone so far in decay that it acts without thought of social responsibility, the name for this condition is not socialism but collective anarchy. Assuming the unmitigated demoralization of these people, American society may find itself in the throes of this pathology within another generation. The lost generation is even now rotting before our eyes.[6]

No matter how much beneficent welfare was dumped on the 1930s young, the underclass still lacked personal responsibility. In cities, fertile young mothers wallowed on the dole of 6.97 cents per person per meal, "allowing these people to breed in idleness... The slum grows, its borders expand in both town and country, and in this slum the delinquent children hasten toward their criminal maturity." Nineties welfare reformers are fortunate these authors are not extant and armed with copyright infringement lawyers.

American Magazine, after receiving "literally thousands of letters from people of all ages bearing on this problem," published a treatise by journalist emeritus I.F. Marcosson on "Our Muddled Youth" in September 1936. Muddled wasn't the half of it. The article declared that 75 percent of the 100,000 young men studied by the American Youth Commission "were suffering from some health defect induced mainly by mental anxiety."[7] (That, at least, is improving; only 40 percent of the teens age 12-17 were rated as in "fair or poor" emotional health in a 1988 Department of Health and Human Services report). "The average age of criminals was nineteen" the FBI reported in 1936, meaning the modal age—and we can be sure police agencies of the day were much less efficient at making arrests than now. Imagine what the Carnegie Council would have trumpeted about that teen mob on the trolley to hell.

In 1937, *Vital Statistics of the United States* reported 11,000 violent deaths among teenagers in a teen population much smaller than today's. Five thousand teens were in fatal motor vehicle crashes. Thirteen hundred teens died in suicides and homicides, included in the 1,600 killed by firearms, that year. It was an unhealthy, violent time to grow up, and many deaths in the chaotic Depression environment may not have been recorded with today's efficiency. And as usual, it wasn't just teens. The whole nation was in an uproar. Suicide jumped 40 percent from 1925 to 1931, reaching levels 30 percent higher than today's. Homicide rocketed upward; the record murder rates of the Depression years stood for six decades and were not eclipsed until 1991. Twelve teenagers were executed for criminal offenses in 1937, *eleven of them black.*[8]

There was teen sex. Writers of the day, more honest than today's, readily admitted a large share of it was with adults. *American Mercury*'s April 1936 issue primly lamented "the drinking bouts in which high school and college students frequently indulge, and which result in promiscuous relations."[9] More than 300,000 teenage girls gave birth and hundreds of thousands more had miscarriages and abortions in 1937, a teen pregnancy "epidemic" surpassing today's. Nine in 10 of the fathers in births among teen girls that year were over age 20; one-third were over age 25. In his 1936 *Abortions, Spontaneous and Induced*, gynecologist Frederick Taussig estimated 681,600 illegal abortions annually. A.J. Rongy, writing in *American Medicine* in July 1931, placed the total at one million,[10] indicating 200,000 to 300,000 among teens, in the United States every year.

Duke University sociology professor Hornel Hart and writer Ella Hart, in 1941, noted that the number of women who had premarital sex rose from 10 percent for those born in 1880 to 60 percent for those born after 1910; among men, from 50 percent to 80 percent. The authors astutely predicted that virginity at marriage would be extinct for men by 1950 and for women by 1965. Accompanying the rising immorality of the day were increases of 30 percent per decade in "illegitimate births" (popularized by dancer Isadora Duncan's scandalous public search for an inseminator and George Bernard Shaw's famous rejoinder). Divorce rates had quadrupled, from five per 100 marriages in 1885 to 21 per 100 in 1935. Forty-five percent of 1,000 college men surveyed in 1938 were rated as "sexually promiscuous," but only 12 percent of the women, the latter evidently very busy indeed.[11] The shame and stigma over extra-marital sex that today's commentators attribute to the past was not keeping Lost Generation hormones from being found.

Venereal disease, by best report, infected several hundred thousand teenagers annually during the 1930s, with many thousands more discreetly unreported by private physicians and clinics. The U.S. Public Health Service estimated more than one million new syphilis cases and three million new gonorrhea cases among all age groups in 1935.[12] Skyrocketing rates of these deadly, brain-crippling, highly infectious maladies—reflected in a growing street population of shambling lunatics—led to passage of the National Venereal Disease Control Act in 1938 and a wave of school sex education initiatives. A lot has been forgotten by those who postulate generational deterioration from the 1930s to the 1990s.

And there was radical politics. Adults who decried Thirties youth apathy waxed apoplectic about youth activism. The chief source of grownup ire was the American Student Union, "a left-wing student organization whose bogeys are capitalism and war" (American Magazine). In 1936, a year predictive of the upheavals of 1968, half a million students demonstrated against American economic and foreign policy. Youth humor akin to Sixties Yippies and their porcine presidential nominee surfaced in Thirties satirical student chapters: "Veterans of Future Wars" (Princeton), "Future Gold Star Mothers" (Vassar), "Profiteers of Future Wars" (Rensselaer Polytechnic Institute), and "Gold-Diggers Auxiliary" (Russell Sage College for Women).[13]

Displaying a self-fixation to become epidemic among American adults later in the century, it seemed to occur to few of these 1930s critics of the young that there was a Depression going on that might be affecting adolescent as well as elder. The solution, then, to rescue a generation at risk? Values education! Columbia University president Nicholas Murray Butler's 1935 address, "The Perpetual Youth Problem," warned:

> Day by day the newspapers report to us one grave crime after another, one moral delinquency after another and one dereliction of duty after another... there can be nothing worthy to be called education which is not based upon moral... discipline.[14]

In a fairness not found among today's ephebiphobes, Dr. Butler also found the same "shocking contempt of, and disregard for, fundamental principle whether moral or political" in Congress (academic toadying to win federal research grants was still far in the future). Others (the forebears of Chicago columnist and draft-'em-all teen-basher Mike Royko) said: Get tough! The universal youth service now championed as an innovative antidote to youth apathy was first proposed in School and Society to redirect aimless adolescent loiterers of 1938.[15] Of course, the schools of the 1930s, busy with their top problems of gum-chewing and talking in class, couldn't be expected to notice 100 teenage deaths, 2,000 teenage pregnancies, and three dozen teenage homicides, suicides, firearms deaths, and other violent deaths occurring *every day*.

Lost and hedonist as the violent, drugged, rotting, mentally deficient, promiscuous, apathetic, Bolshevik youth of the Great Depression were held up to be, it took only a few short years into the next generation for the last one to look like model teens. Two psychologists warned—in 1945—of "the seriousness and extent of adolescent problems of adjustment... at this time, as probably never before."[16]

No doubt about it. The Lost Generation was the epitome of youth-at-risk. We can see the terrible scars of their troubled teenhoods reflected in their preoccupation with their own welfare today.[17] It must have dawned on more than a few of the five million youths wandering the country in the early 1930s, riding the rails in legendary Woody Guthrie mode in search of work, that "the old bastards have run off with the store and cut us adrift." Neither President Roosevelt nor Congress would approve the $3 billion American Youth Act proposed by the most radical students to fund academic and jobs initiatives.

But in the end, FDR came through. Not with finger-pointing, budget cuts, therapies, and prisons, but with empathy, jobs, education, and bucks. Imagine a president today declaring what Roosevelt did to 5,000 youths crowded in the Baltimore armory on a spring night in 1936:

> The world in which the millions of you who have come of age is not the set old world of your fathers. Some of yesterday's certainties have vanished; many of yesterday's certainties are questioned... The facts and needs of civilization have changed more greatly in this generation than in the century that preceded us.
>
> ...You are measuring the present state of the world out of your own experiences. You have felt the rough hand of the depression. You have walked the streets looking for jobs that never turned up. Out of this has come physical hardship and, more serious, the scars of disillusionment.
>
> The temper of our youth has become more restless, more critical, more challenging... Youth comes to us and wants to know what we propose to do about a society that hurts so many of them. There is much to justify in the inquiring attitude of youth... It is clear that many of the old answers are not the right answers. No answer, new or old, is fit for your thought unless it is framed in terms of what you face and what you desire—unless it carries some definite prospect of a practical down-to-earth solution of your problems.
>
> ...Many older people seem to take unmerited pride in the mere fact that they are adults... And the tragedy is that so many young people do... grow up, and in growing up, they grow away from their enthusiasms and their ideals. That is one reason why the world into which they go gets better so slowly.[18]

What? A president invoking government to solve the employment and deteriorating social conditions of the young, instead of blaming the Depression on teenage moms and urban gangs? Praising adolescents as part of the solution to a mess made by grownups rather than recommending programs to force kids to adjust? This was not simply rhetorical sentiment. Billions of dollars were invested in new employment programs for the Lost Generation, putting millions of young people to work and subsidizing their training and education... through the welfare state, in short.

A huge welfare state. That same year, 1936, *Literary Digest* surveyed the first three years of New Deal programs and reported a major miracle:

> Searching aimlessly for a job, a place in the world, or an escape from a stul- ·
> tifying home life, 1,500,000 restless boys and girls flowed out over the nation
> when the depression struck... "Jungles" and hobo camps grew to unbelievable pro-
> portions...an enormous increase appeared in petty crime...
> ...Last week this flood of wandering youth had dwindled to 50,000... the
> normal crop of youngsters that summer always brings.

What caused this massive reversal? *Literary Digest* ticked off just a few of the
national investments aimed at the young, unheard of in scope and expense before or
since:

- 280 centers and 312 camps funded under the Federal Emergency Recovery Act
  from 1933 to 1935 "to provide food, shelter, recreation, education, and work for
  the wanderers."
- The Civilian Conservation Corps, employing 1.5 million youths and young adults
  at 24 to 30 hours per week for expenses and $1 to $3 per week in pay, and establishing 145,000 permanent jobs by 1935. Cost through that year: $1.25 billion, of
  which $600 million was returned in the form of the appraised value of the work
  done, and $250 million was sent home by CCC youths to their families.
- The National Youth Administration, set up in 1935 to establish employment programs and to provide college and high school students cash aid, which in its first
  year granted $50 million to 628,000 youths. The projected NYA college and high
  school grant budget grew to $71 million in 1936 [Note: the 1936 grant total
  would have paid full annual tuitions at the University of California that year for
  1.4 million students].
- So successful were these employment programs that statistician Louis Dublin's
  national survey found that "the chances of the average youth of twenty getting a
  job are four out of five, even during the depression period."[19]

Would that jobs were that available in south central Los Angeles today. What,
then, reversed the violence, disordered minds, and other sagging fortunes of the Lost
Generation? It could have been that good things just naturally accrue to clean living, morally superior, wholesome cherubs whose chief sin was pulling pigtails in
class. Or it could have been a government willing to invest massive confidence and
resources in its poorest young—young whom the president agreed were right to be
disillusioned and disaffected—through dynamic, experimental multi-billion dollar
initiatives to which youths responded admirably. And behind that, an adult attitude
of that day profoundly more generous, more absorbed with the future of its young,
than are today's adults. Let the reader decide.

In the 1930s, the total federal budget was $5 billion to $8 billion per year. In
1995, $1.5 trillion. Imagine the generosity of that investment by American adults
toward their adolescents during a skeletal Depression economy. A government
youth program in 1995, funded at 1935 levels for the CCC and NYA, would expend
well over $200 billion on youth employment and provide $15 billion in free grants
to low-income college students every year. Yet Clinton's AmeriCorps program, costing a tiny fraction of that much, is already slated for abolition after only two years
and employment of a few thousand youths in summer work. Federal Pell grants, at

$6.3 billion in 1995[20] and due for sharp cuts, would pay the equivalent of full University of California tuitions for fewer students in 1995 than were funded for America's much smaller college-bound population in 1935.

Modern youth-punishing policies continue even to the day this sentence is written, October 29, 1995, when the papers reported Congressional and administration studies that the newly-passed Republican budget will levy half its cuts on the poorest fifth of the population and another 25 percent on the second poorest fifth. "At the same time, the richest 5 percent of the population would benefit from tax breaks that, on average, are almost as large as the reductions in income and health benefits facing families with children," the Office of Management and Budget reported. Republicans did not dispute Democrats' estimates: "There was remarkably little disagreement over the question of whether the Republican budget cuts are concentrated on those at the bottom of the income scale."[21]

As noted, Clinton has ambivalently signalled his willingness to accept lesser, but sharp, cuts in family welfare that would add 1 million children to poverty rolls[22] and has backed substantial reductions in student aid.[23] The most fundamental impact of 1995 policy is to continue the enormous shift of resources from young to old (quickly under the GOP plan, more slowly under Clinton's) that has characterized the last quarter century. Forty percent of the nation's poor are children even before the new budget's impacts add to that total; a majority are under age 25. Four fifths of the nation's richest 5 percent are over 40 years old.[24]

Today's senior generation is small, rapidly playing through its 18th hole and retiring to the great clubhouse. The crucial question is what will happen as the Baby Boomers step up to the tee and assume our three decades of control. Not only do we have no plans to cushion our impact on younger generations, we stand ready to block any efforts to obtain more money (even for our own later benefit) from the largest and richest mob of middle-agers ever. Reads a Washington report on October 19, 1995:

> For all the partisan acrimony and special-interest *angst* over the GOP's Medicare reform plans, even the most far-reaching proposal—set for House passage today—would only postpone a financial crisis likely to make the current stakes seem like child's play.
>
> ...In the view of experts, unless far more drastic actions are taken than those now being contemplated, Medicare could collapse under a 20-year wave of baby boomers entering the federal health insurance program for seniors, starting in 2010.
>
> "The problem with Medicare isn't in the next seven years. The problem with Medicare is when all the baby boomers retire," Sen. Bob Kerry (D-Neb.) said...
>
> And that time bomb, experts say, can be averted only by draconian measures that are now barely hinted at by most politicians: tax hikes, service cuts, higher payments by the wealthy...[25]

Suggestions which, the story continued, generate "white hot" controversy. "No new taxes" might well be the Baby Boom's creed and epitaph.

To our own foolish advantage, we forget: Much, if not virtually all, of the phenomenal economic success of today's senior and Baby Boom generations owes itself to the support of prior generations, including government employment, education, housing, and welfare subsidy programs. Like so much else, today's adults say to the young: "Welfare was okay for us, not for you." Much of the economic throes of today's young are founded in the steady withdrawal of public and private support by elder from younger over the past two decades. It isn't the quality of American youth that has deteriorated over the last half century; it is the attitudes and policies of adults toward the young.

Beyond the boomer bust

If the shot marking the beginning of the modern generation war could be traced, it might be the 1966 decision by President Lyndon Johnson to maximize support for the Vietnam War by easing its impact on older citizens. First, the war would be fought not by trained army reservists and National Guard, but mostly by draftees—that is, low-income teenagers. Second, the president's "guns and butter" policy largely avoided raising taxes and invoking wartime sacrifices, but at the cost of increasing debt. It was a precedent for later, more deliberate political decisions to divide old from young by increasingly generous policies favoring the former at the expense of the latter. In Johnson's case, no doubt, one reason was to punish growing youth demonstrations against the war.

Not long ago I asked a recalcitrant radical who, like me, graduated from high school in 1968 as the Vietnam War was rapidly escalating, what his vision of adults was at that time. "I thought they were trying to kill me," he said. "I honestly thought adults hated me." I remember the same feelings. I couldn't understand why grown Americans were gambling my life on a war even minimal investigation showed was lunacy.

But in 1968, these anti-adult sentiments were tempered by the visible participation of older age groups in antiwar and radical reform groups of the time. Most prominent among these was Martin Luther King Jr., whose sermon to 3,000 at New York City's Riverside Church on April 4, 1967, one year to the day before his assassination, stands as a singularly courageous identification with the young and poor of all races not equalled by any prominent American since. King laid the million war dead, "mostly children," at Washington's door, denounced a then-popular war as "dishonorable and unjust" and declared: "If America's soul becomes poisoned, part of the autopsy must read Vietnam... A nation that continues year after year to spend more money on military defense than on programs of social uplift is approaching spiritual death."[26]

Perhaps, like conservatives, I believe we have deteriorated drastically—but at the top, not the bottom. I cannot imagine any major American political figure of King's stature taking such a bitterly forthright stand shoulder to shoulder with the beaten-down young, in contravention to polls, handlers, and media monoliths, today. Not in a 1990s world in which children and youths—from Iraqi toddlers murdered in the Gulf War to mundane adolescent sufferers of American adults' drug and nicotine addictions to the one million or two million children to be further impoverished and locked away under the alternating motifs of "welfare reform" and prison buildups pitched by '96-posturing politicians—are so manifestly unimportant.

But perhaps mine is memory reconstituted. My instamatics of the November 1969 Vietnam War Moratorium in San Francisco show the 200,000 marchers from many angles, and older faces are only a sprinkling. The activist anti-war movement was heavily young. Counterculture radicals who proclaimed, "don't trust anyone over 30," had identified what many of us, too facilely, thought was the enemy.

Post-Sixties Stress Syndrome or otherwise, why has the Baby Boom proven so willing to buy, even to initiate, scare campaigns against our own adolescents? Here was a generation of now-adults ideally suited to sidling up to our kids' thrash-metal planes-crashing-slowly tunes and nodding: "Sounds like a Hendrix riff, maybe the interlude to 'And the Wind Cries Mary'" (at this point our astonished 13-year-old would yelp—"Shit, Dad! 'Metal Week' says Hendrix is GOD!"). Or nostalgically comparing a modern gig with creamsicle-suited Frank Zappa and the Mothers of Invention's "announcements" to the disastrous 1969 Atlantic City Pop Festival about not swallowing the tabs with the blue Mickey Mouse—"It's bad acid, kids. Love your Mothers and don't take it"? No finer moment than accompanying burned-out adolescents to a Utah New Wave concert and hearing conventionally weird Echo & the Bunnymen break into "Light My Fire" and "People Are Strange" as an auditorium of mid-1980s 17-year-olds erupted in cheering and stomping (of quite different tone than in 1994 Oklahoma City). Or to see the top "drug song" voted by 1994 kids in a poll by an ultra-hip California "alternative rock" station turn out to be the Jefferson Airplane's "White Rabbit"? Bitchen, kids: "Feed your head..."

Other than being chagrined for a younger set that can't write its own dope ditties, how could we *not* like them? If ever there was a generation trained by its own upbringings to get down and dirty with its own teenagers' angst, drugs, and rock'n'roll, it was the Baby Boom. Like the perma-hippie parents in *Valley Girls*, we should be kicking our kids for being too conservative. In individual households, of course, teens and parents could be at each other's throats, much like the parents were battling their significant others with whom we lingered an average of 84 months (what we Boomers called "marriages;" "relationships" were more expedited). But as a generation, we should delight in our adolescents.

Yet America's fury at teenagers has mounted year by year as Baby Boom parents have bumpily lurched into the role of raising teens. We seemed to divide into three groups with distinct attitudes toward reproduction. A record number of us so-called adults, admitting our self-indulgences, decided to postpone adulthood until late middle age and wisely chose not to have kids. A minority of us so-called adults, having had kids, rearranged our lifestyles more or less radically to raise them more or less responsibly. Both sets deserve admiration; it is as much maturity from us as you're going to get.[27]

The third and fairly large cohort, however, seems to have reproduced with little or no clue as to what the monumental task of child-raising really entailed. The revelation that children demand parents who give up addictions, petty inabilities to get along, and general lifelong self-indulgence was bitterly unwelcome news—especially since the carefree condominium lifestyle of childless yuppie, particularly those with double incomes, no kids, super-opulence was abundantly flaunted before their eyes in the 1970s and '80s. These are the so-called parents who angrily, indignantly, as if nature and the universe had let them down, demanded that higher authorities raise their kids. There have always been parents less mature than their children, of course, but the Baby Boom sprouted them in job lots—and affluent enough to demand services.

The services, quickly established in the 1970s to meet this new demand brought on by seven-year marriages and doubled divorce rates, were establishing a life of their own in the 1980s. In combination with new federal agencies champing to do good and professionals with open appointments and bed spaces to fill, the mushrooming consumer market these quasi-parents created for self-interested and self-perpetuating "kid-fixing" utilities has generated an industry now extending its territory by spreading all-kids-are-killers propaganda. Its rationalizations for adult behavior are part and parcel of moral entrepreneurs out to flatter their client-supplying parents.

National leaders have stepped forward to endorse, not in so many words, the parenting style justifiably ridiculed in the past as Do As I Say Not As I Do. Confronted on his extramarital affairs, divorce, and failure to support his children, House Speaker Newt Gingrich asserted "a clear distinction between my private life" and his public championing of absolutist moral standards for others to follow.[28] Confronted by the press and daughter Chelsea on the bad example his cigar smoking set for his anti-youth-smoking crusade, Clinton replied, "I don't think that's the point. The issue is whether children are smoking cigarettes."[29] Personal responsibility, our leaders affirm, is kids' stuff: We have a *right* to demand that the young act better than we do.

This third parenting group seems to be garnering an inordinate amount of attention. Parents who hate their kids (and therefore, all kids) grace the "My Turn" column of *Newsweek* and letters to the editor. The most popular "family counselors" dispensing advice on the lecture circuit seem to be characterized by messed up families and kids they despise. And of course, the talk shows, which would wither without kid-loathing parents. These are parents amply willing to demean the children they raised, *in public and by name*, as drug-addicted, lying, promiscuous, value-free, leeching, immature sluts, with audiences openly invited to sympathize with the unfairness of it all. Whatever anger parents must have always felt at their kids, the modern phenomenon of taking it to the nation is a new kind of bitterness and cruelty. In years of working with families, I rarely met a screwed-up kid who didn't have an even more screwed-up parent—and it was the more affluent parents who seemed most anxious to farm out their kids. "They-locked-me-in-an-institution-they-said-it-was-the-only-solution-to-get-me-the-needed-professional-help-to-save-me-from-the-enemy-in-myself," as Suicidal Tendencies staccato-screeched (on a 1982 album specifically deplored by Tipper Gore), distinctly uncured. In the style of modern adulthood, Gore and the PMRC's cohort of Washington wives did not dedicate their apparently copious free time and influence to address the growing deficiencies of 1980s and '90s grownups, but to demand that Suicidal Tendencies be warning-tagged and censored.

The kid-fixing paradox

As the youth-rehab industry erupted in the 1970s and 1980s, a great deal of the agency/professional scare campaign against teenagers was deployed to overcome a fundamental economic paradox cited in the previous chapter: Programs and agencies want to treat youths whose parents can pay; to specialize in "diseases of the rich," as satirist Tom Lehrer put it. Yet nearly all of the behaviors most bewailed at the highest political levels—crime, violence, unwed motherhood, being on welfare—are those which are, and always have been, concentrated among the poor, where parents can't afford $800-per-day therapy bins.

The new array of interests doesn't want to address the *environments* of teens victimized by severe poverty and unfair treatment. To *study* poverty environments, certainly. (As Northwestern University professor Adolph Reed points out, hundreds of millions of dollars have been paid to a few major research centers for "endlessly cooking and rehashing data to fine-tune minute interpretations of aggregate statistical relationships in a self-consciously depoliticized way [as] alternatives to clear and direct arguments about inequality"[30].) But not to actually *do* anything about poverty. Doing something about youth poverty that works, as Europe does, would cost public money, bestowed directly on poorer populations and not to the benefit of large academic and institutional interests. Screw that New Deal stuff. The Nineties-preferred solution is to imprison young swarthy males in large numbers at huge public expense while private interests benefit from extracting similarly large sums from the insurance companies of the childed affluent.

The major thrust of the billowing post-1975 scare campaign has been dedicated to persuading Americans that *all* youth are at risk. *Especially* youths from families with wherewithal. Officials, programs, and agencies seeking attention and funding infusions from public and private sources have teamed up to perpetuate the image that every teenager is a suicide, homicide, pregnancy, and AIDS case in the making, a kinetic calamity manifest in the tiniest of signs: a mood change, a falling grade, an outburst, a quietude, sadness, exuberance, unexpected behavior or emotion, unexpected stability and calm, *just being an adolescent*. Unlike past eras, the large market of Baby Boom quasi-parents is ready to believe anything bad about their kids. Of course Baby Boomers are terrified of their teenagers, libertarian satirist P.J. O'Rourke said recently: "We know who raised them."

Roger Rosenblatt's *New York Times Magazine* piece, "The Society that Pretends to Love Children," illustrates the process by which frightening *general statistics* describing ghetto youth are blended with deplorable *individual anecdotes* about higher income youth to manufacture an image of *all* youth run wild. General inner-city youth statistics—such as, "since 1988 American teenage boys are more likely to die from gunshot wounds than from all natural causes combined"—are juxtaposed with the following suburban-kid misbehaviors over the last six years afforded breathless hype by newspapers and broadcasters alike:

> In Williamson County, Tenn., the richest county in the state, a boy driving the new car that his parents had just bought him shot and killed a horse in a field—for the fun of it. High school kids go on destructive binges in Montana and Vermont. In 1989, ABC's television news program, "20/20," ran a piece on high-

living teen-agers in wealthy Pacific Palisades, Calif., who were lost to drugs and drink. Last year, the network news shows broadcast a video of middle-class teen-agers in Florida on a rampage. They tore apart elegant homes, tortured a dog and cooked a goldfish in the microwave. The teen-agers made the video themselves.[31]

I don't mean to demean the viciousness involved in torturing, murdering, and microwaving dogs, horses, and goldfish. These are some sick kids (though anyone who confuses Montana and Vermont with rich states is sadly mistaken). The crimes of the wealthy should be of more concern because, as Will Rogers pointed out, more anti-social acts are accomplished with the point of a pen than the point of a gun. But confronting affluent criminality is not what these media treatments of mild and occasional suburban youth mayhem are concerned with. Instead, the press can be counted upon to hype occasional suburban youth murders or rapists, as in the pitiful Lakewood Spur Posse whose villainy reverberated through the major media like a grenade as a few suburbanite youth seemed bent on deadly excess to live up to their national stardom. We have to ask why news outlets are sensationalizing these kind of singular events as if they somehow equated with the enormous toll of inner-city life.

There is a reason for the seemingly puzzling obsession with painting middle-class and affluent suburban kids as mass-demented. The illusion of vast millions of teens at random and unpredictable risk has been manufactured in menacing but vaguely-stated terms. Nearly half of all youth do indeed live in poverty or near-poverty and suffer from defunded public services and schools, increased societal isolation, and attendant increases in serious problems. But that is not really who the youth-fixing lobbies exist to help, at least not by means of Rooseveltian investments whose largesse might actually find its way into the hands of the young and poor. Rather, the real money must be channeled into behavior-changing *programs* targeting upscale Everyteen. The American Medical Association declares that "in *every* neighborhood, we are seeing significant numbers of young people with serious social and emotional problems."[32] The Carnegie Foundation declares that "countless poignant examples exist of troubled, self-destructive, even violent behavior in the ten-to-fourteen age group, *among rich and poor alike*"[33] (emphasis added). Helpful media, such as *Rolling Stone* and *Utne Reader* as much as *Newsweek* and CNN, announce that "the disease is adolescence."

What information is communicated by these scary sentences? Nothing useful. On every block, we are seeing serious emotional problems and significantly troubled behaviors among psychologists, doctors, educators, journalists, politicians, agency personnel, academicians, school administrators, social workers, social scientists, foundation board members, parents, yuppie magazine writers, and authors of annoying books. By the absolutist criteria applied by agency and institute reports to adolescents, most adults—including two-thirds of all Baby Boomers and especially this one—are equally "at risk." (A recent, deplorable example: University of Chicago sociologist Jeffrey Arnett's widely-quoted recent study branding adolescent males as "high risk" because many reported driving over 80 miles an hour on occasion was trumped in startling fashion by many aging male lawmakers and highway officials, who *legalized* such life- and fuel-squandering speeds in the wake of the December 1995 repeal of the national 55 mile-per-hour speed limit!) Whatever can be said about 1990s adolescents can be said with similar or shriller urgency about 1990s "grownup disease."

Teen-scare campaigns exploit the image of disadvantaged-teen mayhem to penetrate the affluent-teen market. It has worked. The treatment industry, dominated by national chains such as National Medical Enterprises, which own 85 percent of all facilities, declares that 3 million teenagers nationwide need psychiatric therapies because "parents and children alike are no longer able to deal with ordinary growing pains."[34] As detailed in previous chapters, the prison industry has likewise exploded.[35] A double crime has thus ensued: The fear-invoking behaviors of poorer (mostly nonwhite) teens have been attributed in similar measure to higher income (mostly white) youths to provoke greater parental anxiety and demand for management services. At the same time, nonwhite youths have remained ignored, benignly or hostilely, until such time as the predictably negative reactions of many of their number ensure disposal in mushrooming prison systems.

The profit-driven scare campaign against adolescents is a political, media, and professional lie. It is a dangerous lie. It has exploited teenagers as scapegoats for the complex ills of society that have mounted as the Baby Boom aged. It has divorced youth from parent generation by its relentless diversion of public attention and resources into unworkable curative schemes. It has obscured worsening poverty and other genuine social origins of youthful malaise. As a result, it has pushed society to the point where, at best, future generations will survive in antagonistic indigence in abandoned cities and rural ghettos while older, richer age groups and their privileged progeny migrate further upslope behind barricades and gates.

Parents might be expected to take affront that the recommendations of programming interests they invoked are now busy reducing them to the minor role of agents in enforcing absolutists' official goals on adolescents—and when these fail, there are costlier professionals to call in. Parents with like resolve can return the programmatic interests to what they should be doing—helping to treat a very small number of individuals whose problems are serious and of personal rather than social origin.

It is time for American parents to reclaim their kids, and kids their parents, from the myriad of scaremongers. Both generations are troubled by the same things and for similar reasons. A large measure of that trouble is the imposed, unnatural, adversary role of parent and teenager which has no precedent (at least, not in the extremes to which we have taken it) and certainly no future. Roosevelt, in a measure of grownup humility justified by the manifest grownup-made mess all around, harnessed the healthy tension between generations to motivate the young to help solve it—and gave them the *opportunity* to do so.

Unreality bites

If an essential element of abandonment is the refusal to listen, the clearest examples are growing efforts to suppress adolescent speech in forums in which youth exercise some measure of control. Particularly when teenagers challenge adult stereotypes of youths or themselves, censorship has been invoked. The adult-controlled mainstream press has proven adept at collaring teenage quotes for whatever official hypothesis is being promoted. Several reporters have told me on various occasions that it is routine for journalists, when covering a topic like violence or drugs in the schools, to pitch for student quotes that will make the issue as dire as possible and to exclude those that might be calming. Student speakers for conferences are chosen from treatment populations guaranteed to support the program's abstinence agenda, not (for example) from the larger population who might, if allowed to speak freely, affirm moderate drug or alcohol use. We don't want our myths tampered with.

As a reporter in 1988, I covered the controversy over the U.S. Supreme Court's decision to allow school principals unlimited authority to censor school newspapers.[36] I found high school journalists who had been censored and threatened with removal for publishing articles investigating the basketball coach's favoritism for playing sons of school board members, a vice principal's conflict of interest in using school forums to promote his private for-profit sports clinic, the nutritional quality of food in the school cafeteria, and questionable uses of funds by student government. In the Hazelwood, Missouri, case that led to the Court ruling, the high school's *Spectrum* was censored from publishing 1983 interviews with pregnant students that presented them as less of a calamity than the official view, and comments by youths whose parents were divorced.

On the surface, the case concerned the non-issues of student privacy (unlike many articles on teen sex and pregnancy publicized by adult media outlets, students interviewed had given permission and were anonymous) and the "inappropriateness" of the school's youngest students (age 14) reading about "pregnancy." But a continuing theme throughout the case and the commentary on it was that the student *views* offended authorities and might provoke negative community reactions. The issue of adult control over teenagers was repeatedly cited. A report on a 1994 study of 234 schools by Freedom Foundation, an international journalism foundation, concluded:

> School administrators, the report found, have interpreted the 1988 ruling as supporting them in sharply limiting the freedoms of high school journalists.
> In a study of 270 high school newspaper advisors, 37 percent said school principals had rejected newspaper articles or required changes...
> "High school newspapers are dying a slow death," Judith Hines, who helped organize the report, said in an interview. Youngsters are discouraged from becoming journalists, she said, and they are discouraged from becoming newspaper readers because of skepticism they learn firsthand in high school about the independence of newspapers.[37]

High school journalism was "mainly flourishing in the nation's wealthiest suburbs" where "the majority of student journalists were relatively wealthy and white" and seldom cover "issues important to minority students in their schools," the report said.

As a seventh grader in 1962, I was permanently barred from the high school newspaper because of an editorial I wrote supporting desegregation of Oklahoma City schools. The advisor told me my punditry (which, ironically, praised the 1954 Supreme Court school desegregation decision and asked why city schools were not following it) was contrary to school board policy. The same arguments about appropriateness and creating discord were used, but the real issue was adolescents having the temerity to enter into the debate (on such issues as teen pregnancy and school integration!) which local powers had already decided. The solution was censorship and dismissal. There is nothing, adults from my 1962 high school advisor to the 1988 Supreme Court declared, to be learned from listening to adolescents, other than those whose views are channeled through the authorities first.

Anti-kids

If the abandonment of youth which has progressed from the 1970s to today were simply an element of the nation's growing political conservatism, hope could be extended for a new coalition of poor, minority, and young to forge a New Millennium Deal. But it is society's most liberal elements who have proven most vulnerable to simplistic kid-bashing and condescension on the very issues for which adult identification with adolescents would be most expected.

A recent example was the baffling and depressing acclaim of liberals for the 1995 movie "Kids." The film concerned 15-year-old "virgin surgeon" Telly, a New York whiteboy spreading AIDS among junior high girls amid a pubescent culture of wanton screwing, stoning, stealing, boozing, bragging, seducing, racism, homophobia, skateboard battering, and a plethora of public urination. Director Larry Clark meant to convey that young adolescents are akin to uncaged barbarians, a species he told the *Village Voice* that he frankly admires.[38]

So enamored was Clark of his perception of recklessness as the defining feature of adolescence that "Kids" depicted them as conventionally stereotyped, one-dimensional risk machines. The film's characters were utterly unoriginal, though inadvertent, caricatures of the 1959 film *Blue Denim* (Schlitz-sneaking prego kids then, pot-scarfing HIV kids now). Boys were single-minded, brutal testosterone ignition systems. Girls were burbling pushover morons. Little of the diversity or dynamic of early adolescent life was presented; only an emotionally flat, stoned, hypersexed, second-to-second hedonism. Adults were wise, responsible, and failing only in their lack of get-tough herd-riding on a youth generation inexplicably gone berserk. "Kids" was the consummate American grownup hate movie against its teenagers.

Clark claimed "Kids" was "what's going on out there." But realistic was exactly what "Kids" was not. It abjectly evaded the realisms of poverty, sexual abuse, rape, sexual liaison, and AIDS inflicted upon younger teens by adults. It produced little more than an NC-17 adult fantasy of junior high sex—a point amply made by those who deal with real street kids rather than filmmakers' fetishes.[39] If a director made a movie, "Blacks," stocked with rapist-killer Willie Hortons and crackhead welfare sluts, liberal outrage would have been swift and sure. Lancing of "Kids" by more progressive reviewers as America's most dishonest film of a dishonest time should have been a foregone conclusion.

Just the opposite occurred. *The New Yorker* and Pat Dowell of *In These Times* saw through the voyeuristic viciousness of Clark and 21-year-old writer Harmony Korine. The rest of the liberal press was awestruck. "Uncompromisingly authentic ...

a wake-up call to the world," breathed Janet Maslin in *The New York Times*. "The real movie event of the summer," lauded Peter Travers of *Rolling Stone*. "Insanely beautiful... a masterpiece," gushed Manohla Dargis of *L.A. Weekly*. "Street real," proclaimed the *San Francisco Chronicle*. The *Village Voice* afforded two laudatory reviews of "the reality adult America wants to shove out of our sight." Only one of them disgorged an honest sentence: "I hated the little monsters from beginning to end." Now that's authentic.

How do these grayed and graying liberal commentators *know* what the reality of 1995 junior high sex is? Do their kids, or grandkids, act like the kids in "Kids"? (...No). Like the Yellow Peril, the arch-villain adolescents are the menacing unknown: *Someone else's kids*. The same Bad Seeds we reject as we vote down school bond issues, support welfare reform that dumps a million more of *them* on poverty rolls, and resolve to leave this terrifying generation of *someone else's kids* to boil in its own evils. Agencies, programs, filmmakers such as Clark, and the media know not to confront the issue directly by depicting the "kids" we fear as black and brown and poor. The fictional junior high Darth Vader of Just Say No anti-drug announcements and celluloid degeneracy is white. His co-degenerates in "Kids" are a Rainbow Coalition of pubescents draped in drunken and drugged multi-hued, semi-nude sex-stupor on what could be any American floor. The message is less subtle than a train wreck and not missed by breathless reviewers: *Someone else's kids* are *all of them*. The danger of a movie like "Kids" is that it reinforces a building 1990s adult belief that we are justified in casting such a hopeless mass of vicious brats adrift. The ultimate exploitative absurdity was the NC-17 rating threatened by motion picture judges, meaning that adolescents would never legally be able to see a movie adults were touting as a realistic portrayal of teenage life.

Where, then, do these notions of adolescents that make sophisticated adults proclaim "realism!" at the most malicious stereotypes come from? They are manufactured. Three months later the theme of "Kids" was re-issued in book form by the Carnegie Corporation, whose Council on Adolescent Development embodied like escapism in its report declaring half of America's 10-14-year-olds "at risk" due to their bad behaviors. It is a well-worn theme not original to either film or academic exercise. It is a common fiction of adult self-flattery that underlies the public policies that endanger America's future.

The kid-bashers have accomplished their purpose. Studies of professionals, cited in previous chapters, reveal drastically exaggerated imaginings of teenage mental illness.[40] Polls of the public have revealed majority perceptions that youths account for over 40 percent of the nation's violent crime, three times more than they actually do.[41] At a personal level, American adults really believe adolescents are crazy. In 1993, I surveyed a diverse sample of adults, from University of Oklahoma School of Public Health graduate students to University of California at Santa Cruz undergrads, on their attitudes toward adolescents. On virtually every question, respondents liberal and conservative, younger and older adult alike, believed teenage behaviors much worse than objective measures show they are. For example, 72 percent mistakenly thought teenagers had higher suicide rates than adults, 63 percent mistakenly thought most teen births are fathered by teens, and 87 percent mistakenly thought teen drug death rates were higher than those of grownups. Adults' estimates of levels of anxiety, hostility, depression, impulsiveness, and other mental disturbances among adolescents, as predicted by adult respondents on standard psychological tests, were *three to four times* higher than these tests have actually found among adolescents—even disturbed ones![42] Agencies and the press have sharply distorted Americans' views of their own youth and show little interest in correcting their misportrayal.

This is the insight, far from profound, that is critical to salvaging two imperiled generations: Teenagers are the normal children of today's adults. They act in much the same ways as we adults who raised them, and for much the same reasons. They are not the best-acting group in society; neither are they the worst. In light of the rapidly deteriorating social conditions to which modern youth are subjected, most adolescents act better than we have a right to expect. If adults don't like the way teenagers act, the solution is not to turn a generation over to the professional treaters and imprisoners who have markedly worsened matters over the last decade, but to change our behaviors and the conditions in which youth are raised. In short, to reclaim them as our own.

Ceasefire in the generation war

The single biggest imperative is to reduce child, teen, and young-family poverty. It is the font from which the worst adult and adolescent destructions arise, an environment whose survival rules demand skills inimical (and understandably so) to larger society. It is not simply poverty, but America's enormous income disparities (the largest of any industrial nation, a 1995 Organization for Economic Cooperation and Development study found) which are most concentrated in high-income high-poverty states such as California and New York, that lead to social detachment and violence.[43] Reducing poverty and income disparity is an achievable, and elsewhere achieved, goal.

A kind of Marshall Plan for young families, teenagers, and children could be presented in these pages. We know what it would consist of: Massive redistribution of wealth away from a variety of affluent elder personal and corporate interests back to young families and the schools, universities, and transitional services upon which they depend. The imbalance in wealth between America's poorest and richest fifths of the population, already the most pronounced in the industrial world by a wide margin, is widening further: Today, the nation's 400 richest Americans have combined assets of $500 billion, 25 times more than paid in AFDC to 16 million needy children.[44] Increasingly, vast wealth is a matter of inheritance, not earning; of California's 45 richest citizens, 60 percent, including three-fourths of those under age 60, inherited their immense wherewithal.[45] Redistribution just of the hundreds of billions of dollars in added income concentration that has occurred in the last 20 years is an essential stratagem in requiring and enabling older generations, as a matter of "personal responsibility," to pay back the debts we generated to allow future generations to start off with a cleaner slate and expanded opportunities—as our parents allowed for us.

Such a plan to reduce child poverty is well within our fiscal abilities. Largely through the welfare system, we successfully reduced elder poverty by two-thirds over the past 35 years. We had cut child poverty rates in half in the 1960s, before selective anti-welfare sentiment (that is, opposition to welfare not benefitting older, wealthier interests) reversed the progress. Europe employs its social insurance system to ensure that few youths grow up impoverished. We were not afraid to levy hundreds of billions of dollars in taxes upon younger groups to pay for elder welfare. The process should now be reversed. Yet despite the enormous imbalances in wealth between old and young that have resulted not from private initiative but from our public allocation systems, *U.S. News & World Report* declared in November 1995 that "reducing child poverty, much less eradicating it, is no longer a paramount priority for either political party."[46]

Founders of the anti-deficit "Concord Coalition" such as former U.S. Commerce Secretary Pete Peterson and former Senators Paul Tsongas and Warren Rudman have presented detailed strategies to redistribute wealth from older to younger age groups.[47] Their critics reject any plans that might entail cutting or means-testing of elder benefits, which they argue would "stigmatize" the welfare the elderly receive, as young-family welfare is now. Instead, they propose higher taxes on corporations and the wealthy, including an end to the regressive mortgage interest tax deduction which overwhelmingly subsidizes wealthy homeowners (who are nearly all middle-agers and elderly).[48]

Liberals have argued, plausibly, that if benefits are means-tested and the rich are cut off Social Security, the wealthy will withdraw their support for providing aid to poorer seniors.[49] If that is true (and it probably is), would we then propose that all 70 million children, including those in Beverly Hills and Scarsdale, receive an AFDC check of, say, $700 per month (what we now pay the average Social Security recipient) in order to avoid "stigmatizing" poorer kids who get AFDC? Plus full-ride health insurance? The defenders of elder-welfare that now provides 30 million elderly retirees with $350 billion in benefits have not made a clearcut argument for a similarly universal income maintenance and Medicare program for families with children, which would cost around $750 billion per year to fund at similar levels. Again and again, advocates for children encounter double standards: The old should not be stigmatized for needing welfare, but the young can tough it out. The old must be provided for immediately and non-negotiably, but the young can wait for their fair share until that one fine day when swords are beaten into plowshares and the rich are fairly taxed to support the poor. When challenged on this cynical stance, the oft-repeated realism is cited: Seniors vote, children don't.

The stumbling block in the path to a universal income maintenance and medical insurance plan for young families is that America's middle-agers and elders would have to *pay* megabucks for extending the style of benefits to which they have or plan to become accustomed, and they would have to render such benefits to children and youths. The 40-plus generations appear adamantly opposed to that social-contract notion, which, in turn, illuminates the issue that liberal reformers seem to have difficulty engaging: America's elder welfare system is not a "universal insurance" program on the European model, but the opposite of one. It heavily taxes young workers (including the siphoning of of 7.65 percent from the incomes of 11 million young households earning less than $25,000 per year) to support older retirees, most of whom have had a quarter-century of high incomes and property accumulation sufficient to support themselves. It distributes benefits in regressive fashion, providing an average of $1,200 per month to seniors with cash incomes of over $60,000, versus just $550 to seniors with incomes of below $11,000.[50] No other nation's social insurance program is so wealth promoting, and no other nation has an elder poverty rate as high as the U.S.'s.

In a booming postwar economy in which each younger generation was larger and richer than the elders before it (and in which elders generously supported the young), such an inefficient, maldistributed elder welfare system could function, despite its flaws, to dramatically reduce the unconscionable pre-1960 level of elder poverty. It is a far different world today.

Liberals in particular have not faced the unprecedented fact that the past era of larger, richer, younger generations succeeding smaller, poorer, older ones has ended with a bang. Poorer younger workers are now being asked to shoulder massive welfare costs for richer, larger elder generations. Social Security status-quo defenders continue to paint rosy pictures (in which leftists sound like Laffer-curve supply-siders forecasting that "economic growth" will deliver the funds painlessly to finance their otherwise untenable schemes). But the harsh economic realities are that America faces a succession of smaller and not just poorer, but *much poorer*, coming generations than today's Baby Boomers and seniors.

The solutions to this generation-splitting fiscal crunch that are proposed by leftists—slashing defense spending, taxing corporations and the wealthy more heavily, and ending subsidies to the rich such as the home/business mortgage deduction and corporate tax breaks and subsidies—are reasonable, especially in light of the public policies that diverted hundreds of billions of dollars in new largesse toward wealthier interests in the past 20 years. Where they fall short is in their failure to account for the extreme *political* damage wrought by selective social insurance schemes such as Social Security.

To build the kind of support for universal social insurance programs now found in Europe, coverage must truly be universal. A fascinating study of the differences between the U.S. and other industrial nations' social welfare programs is found in The Urban Institute Press's 1988 collection, *The Vulnerable*. A comparison of policies toward children and the elderly in eight Western nations, led by Vanderbilt University's Timothy Smeeding, found that the U.S.'s excessive child poverty levels were not caused by greater numbers of children, more minority groups, more single parents, or differing systems of measurement. Rather:

> The income transfer system for families with children in the United States seems to be the main reason for these high poverty rates. It relies on categorical means-tested programs much more than do other countries (with the exception of Australia) to provide benefits to poor children. Despite their presumably more effective targeting, countries that rely on means testing seem politically unable or unwilling to raise benefits high enough to be as effective in moving children out of poverty as universal and social insurance approaches.
>
> ... The lack of U.S. commitment (through the transfer system) to securing minimum decent standards for poor children stands in sharp contrast to the commitment of other countries studied here. Although the U.S. public safety net does an average-to-above-average job for the otherwise needy elderly, many poor

families with children in the United States are largely excluded from the safety net, and those who are not excluded receive inadequate benefits... The situation of American children is comparatively bleak.[51]

America's attitude toward children sucks. Or as these authors phrase it more conventionally: "The social welfare programs of each country can be seen as a reflection of its social philosophy." Since the 1987 Luxembourg study on which the above analysis was based, America's support for its children has deteriorated further—and we still have the pending 1995 "welfare reform" measures that provide alternative menus for adding 1.2 million (Senate version) or 2.1 million (House version) *more* children to poverty rolls.[52]

Thus defenders of Social Security appear justified in their assumption that means-testing would jeopardize political support for the program. Although most nations with universal social insurance plans funded by taxing employers and employees do provide additional subsidies to low-income seniors (Britain provides low-income housing benefits, for example), these other Western nations regard public aid as "a right of the beneficiaries" or "a right of all citizens" rather than as "a favor (means tested)" as in the U.S.[53] The reform most needed to America's system, then, is not means-testing. It is to redirect Social Security from a regressive system favoring high-income seniors to one that reduces America's continuing high elder poverty rates (12 percent in 1994) by equalizing benefits paid to rich and poor, perhaps by greater taxing of higher-income elderly. This equalized approach would be in line with the concept of the European model. But it would not be a total policy. A worse problem looms.

What liberal defenders of the current American elder welfare scheme have failed to consider is their own logical argument about what happens when a benefits system is not truly universal. Just as cutting the wealthy out of Social Security would undermine its support, so selectively benefitting the elderly has removed the aged from the coalitions seeking to win similar benefits for other needy groups in society. If a full-ride social insurance program is provided to only one segment of the population, that segment may become the enemy—a well-financed, powerful enemy—of extending like benefits to other groups. This is exactly what has taken place with elder welfare and elder attitudes.

Over the past quarter century, as seniors have become increasingly well taken care of and comfortable, they have turned to defending their growing wealth against that of younger generations. As documented time and again in these pages, elderly voters, who in the past formed a major constituency for social reform, are now at the forefront of measures to cut taxes, punish immigrant groups, defund schools and other social services, build prisons, and elect candidates who promise to continue economic and social attrition against young families on their behalf.

In addition to the demands created by the growth of special interests designed to address the striking difficulty Baby Boom parents have had raising children, a second reason for the dangerous escalation of the generation war might be termed today's "imbalance of dependency." While younger generations remain dependent on the generosity of the old for funding numerous public services and education, older generations are (or believe themselves to be) increasingly financially independent of the good graces of the young. Part of this illusion of elder independence is widespread subscription to the myth that Social Security and Medicare represent paybacks for money seniors previously invested in the system. In fact, these elder entitlements are welfare funded on a pay-as-you-go basis by younger employees and employers at many times the level aged recipients ever paid for. How well seniors live is likely to depend on how well younger workers are doing, a fact politicians and the media have not driven home.

As a result of this perceived "imbalance of dependency," older voters and their representatives seem to operate on the unspoken theory that dismantling benefits for the young, under such guises as "welfare reform," government "downsizing," and "cutting the fat" from schools and universities, can be undertaken without risking benefits to which the old believe themselves entitled. It is becoming a standard pattern today that voters under 30 are locked in a battle to cancel the votes of middle-aged and older voters on education, welfare, taxation, treatment of immigrants, and civil rights. In the 1992 general election, a vicious California ballot issue backed by Governor Pete Wilson (R) to lop up to 23 percent from welfare payments, two-thirds of whose victims would have been children, was narrowly defeated. But seniors heavily favored it, the *Los Angeles Times* Poll of 1,100 voters found in an old-young, rich-poor, white-nonwhite electoral split that occurs today on practically every generational issue:

> People over age 65 favored it, but voters in their 20s were opposed. Affluent people supported it, but those on low incomes objected. Anglos leaned in favor, but minorities were against.[54]

The battle is bitter. California voters, led by the aged, have slammed the young again and again. Proposition 13 in 1978 slashed property taxes and the social services, schools, and medical care they funded for the state's families. In 1992, voters for the first time in recent memory rejected university construction bonds, eliminating spaces for hundreds of thousands of students. In 1994, voters lashed "illegal immigrants," particularly immigrant children in school, through Proposition 187. Elders' overwhelming votes to chop welfare for young families and children was particularly reprehensible, given seniors' own dependence on welfare footed by the same younger workers. Today's seniors and middle-agers have provoked a generation war that their apologists, including many liberals, are now trying to blame on younger-generation advocates engaging in belated protest.

California is an egregious example, more advanced in its splits over generational wealth and politics than other states. But it is not the only example. New York and Florida display the same discouraging trends. Florida is similarly experiencing uniquely large income discrepancies between its wealthier-than-average white retiree population (10.8 percent of whom lived in poverty in 1990, below the national mean) and a poorer than average, increasingly nonwhite youth population (18.3 percent in poverty). Florida's older middle-agers, approaching retirement, are richer still.

Florida thus joins California and New York in evidencing that greater affluence among older age groups does not produce benign generosity toward the young, but greater detachment. Like California, Florida ranks above average in elder wealth but well in the bottom half in youth poverty and per-student expenditures on schools. Florida Kids Count bluntly declares in its 1993 report:

> While our state ranks 19th in per capita income, our kids rank 45th on key indicators of health and well-being. Poor states may have an excuse for the dismal plight of their kids; they can't afford better. But Florida's leaders have no valid alibi for the neglect of our kids. We're not a poor state, we just treat our children poorly.[55]

More disturbing attitudes than those of seniors are found among the even more comfortable Baby Boomers heading toward what appears to be our publicly well-taken-care-of retirements. Moral arguments have been invented: The young don't deserve our help because they are "personally irresponsible." This dictum could be applied in spades to cut off aid for aging and aged beneficiaries who continue irresponsible habits such as smoking, drinking heavily, and failing to save for old age.

It is not the cost of the old, but the politics of the old, that is the problem. It is probably no coincidence that the Concord Coalition is comprised of *former* officials, or that most of their critics are unelected leftists. Those in power in Washington have sidestepped the issue. The reason is that the formulas (whether executed through the welfare system in the form of fewer benefits for the affluent and for corporations, or through the tax system in terms of higher taxes on the same) add up to the same politically unpalatable result: Today's elders and Baby Boomers must live more modestly—much more modestly—so that our society, in the form of its young, can survive at all.

Reversing rejuvenilization

The second, related, aspect of reform would be to move away from the growing avalanche of age-based laws that unfairly restrict adolescent opportunity, employment, and freedom. As the comparisons in this book indicate, there is no significant disparity between teenage behavior and adult behavior, certainly not one large enough to mandate absolute abstinence from alcohol, tobacco, or gun ownership, or severe restrictions upon employment, speech, sexual behavior, hours during which one can be present in public, driving, access to books, films, and works of art, or other rights while permitting adults a wide range of nearly-absolute freedoms.

Wildly exaggerated claims for the "safety value" of such laws and policies only prove that if blanket restrictions on behavior to promote safety are considered more important than individual freedoms, such restrictions on teenagers should apply in like measure to adults. Officials are not willing to advocate greater restrictions on adult behavior even where safety benefits would be large, and so it is clear that safety is not the chief consideration behind the growing array of absolutist legal shackles imposed on adolescents. Objective evidence of disparities in maturity and behavior between teens and adults is insufficient to justify the enormous and widening gap in rights afforded the two age groups; adult-teen sex is just one particularly embarrassing example of the similarity in grownup and adolescent conduct.

The mounting trend to resolve thorny public safety controversies by slapping another restriction on teens ultimately endangers the public, including children and youths, by diverting attention from the paramount issue of adult misbehavior. In particular, the behavior of adult men is many times worse, on nearly every count examined, than that of teenagers. Yet while authorities claim adolescence is a risk factor meriting restrictions, maleness continues to be cited as an *excuse* for dangerous conduct. When researchers pointed out the abnormally high rate of suicide among middle-aged doctors and psychiatrists and that many such deaths resulted from "impulsive or immature behavior,"[56] the profession responded that most members were men, and men normally have high suicide rates. When the *Orange County Register* found that California legislators crashed their state-owned vehicles at more than twice the rate of other citizens, (120 lawmakers had 163 crash claims in four years, costing taxpayers half a million dollars in insurance payments),[57] it was pointed out that most lawmakers are men, and men normally have more car wrecks.

When it is to adult benefit, teenagers are certified as adults at surprisingly young ages. It is a telling commentary on age-based laws that measures against sexual relations between adults and adolescents carry low age limits for "consent" of the younger partner and are rarely enforced. A society that freely allows its adults to have sexual intercourse with adolescents is engaging in rank dishonesty when it piously prevents adolescents from buying explicit magazines or attending R-rated and NC-17-rated movies to "protect" them. When adults want to have sex with teenagers, the law finds no "maturity gap" between a 30-year-old and a 16-year-old. While there may not be a maturity gap between these two ages in reality, there is a state-sanctioned power imbalance. The most hopeful reform in this area is to shift statutory rape laws away from the issue of age alone and toward the issue of the power discrepancy between the parties (of which age difference forms only a part), a concept similar to that embodied in sexual harassment laws.

The rising tolerance for adult, particularly male, immaturity has detoured health policy into a peculiar philosophy that at first sounds sensible: "If you want to change behavior, focus on the young." Authorities throughout history have fantasized about the power inherent in dictating input into young minds. I can't count the number of times over the past two decades that I heard anti-drug, anti-alcohol, anti-smoking, anti-teen-sex, anti-suicide, and anti-violence programmers (as well as the alcohol and tobacco industries) declare: "We have to stop underage _____ before it begins."

A particular manifestation of this theory has been anti-drug and anti-drinking programs such as DARE (Drug Abuse Resistance Education, implemented for a decade nationwide at a cost of $750 million per year). These programs have organized cadres of enthusiastic elementary school students to rally and sign pledges promising absolute abstinence. Yet evaluations, including a three-year $300,000 U.S. Department of Justice study released in 1994, have repeatedly shown that the effectiveness of DARE and similar programs fades to nothingness as these same students mature into very different attitudes toward drugs and drinking as they reach adolescence—attitudes that reflect those of the adult culture around them.[58] "Abstinence" and "values" programs may succeed in fibbing to fifth graders that American adults' attitudes toward dope, booze, smoking, extramarital sex, and other sins are just-say-no, but adolescents quickly perceive what the true values of American grownups are.

Whether for evil or good, regimes have never succeeded in educating, propa-
gandizing, or forcing *adolescents to behave differently from the adults around them*. This
continuity, when recognized and harnessed, is a particular strength of *healthy* societies. As is amply documented, the last two decades (if not all of human history)
show that kid-fixing approaches are badly flawed. The reason is that drugs, alcohol,
smoking, and other behaviors do not *begin* with adolescents. They are complex
products of adult behaviors within the society in which the youth grows up. This is
why the modern concept of youth-targeted "prevention" has not worked and is
unlikely ever to work—though politically-driven evaluations increasingly separated
from reality may make them appear temporarily successful.

When teenagers do act differently from their parents, it seems to be a matter of
unpredictability, happening when least expected. It is ironic that the biggest and
most unexpected improvements in teenage health—such as the dramatic declines in
youth smoking and drug deaths during the mid and late 1970s, or the decline in
teen births from 1958 to 1986—did *not* occur in the context of intensive prevention
programming, but changes in social conditions. Because no interest group could
claim credit, these improvements are not talked about. Further, the evident failure
of teen-targeted prevention efforts has obscured its more dangerous corollary: Easing
up on efforts to change destructive adult behaviors.

Investing in strident efforts to stop teenagers from acting like the adults
around them has obscured the much more difficult, but far more promising, challenge of promoting measures that will prevent unhealthy behaviors by all in society
(such as higher cigarette taxes, more stringent drunken driving laws, lower speed
limits, etc.). In a larger sense, we should worry less about the behaviors of demographic groups (whether the categorizing factor is age, race, ethnicity, or gender)
and worry a great deal more about the relatively few individuals who are manifestly
troubled. Adolescents deserve the same opportunities as adults to participate in the
economy and larger society without arbitrary restrictions selectively rationalized on
the basis of misdeeds by a fraction of their number.

The results of denying them that opportunity are found in the increasing
detachment of teenagers from adults which has taken place in recent decades.[59] If a
drinking age of 21 marginally decreases the chances that an adolescent will go to a
bar at night and subsequently drink and drive (as its backers claim), it also prevents
persons under age 21 from access to the several million entry-level jobs in bars or
liquor stores, increasing their unemployment and adding to the chances that they
will eventually give up on the closed opportunities of the mainstream economy and
join up with more dangerous shadow enterprises. (This is not an idle point: The
Surgeon General has urged not just bars, but groceries and convenience stores, to
restrict teenagers from the millions of jobs involving the sale of alcohol,[60] and ciga-
rette-sales positions will no doubt follow). Allowing employers to underpay teenage
workers through a "subminimum training wage," first enacted in 1990 as part of a
liberal-conservative compromise to obtain an increased minimum wage for adults,
likewise makes shadow-economy employment that much more attractive. Other
youth-penalizing and "barrier policies" cumulate in similar ways to isolate and
exclude teenagers from mainstream society. These increase the odds that adolescents, often as a matter of survival in a society in which adult financial support

legally ends at age 18 (and practically may end before that), will abandon the larger economy and seek enterprises where no such arbitrary barriers exist. Few countries in the world impose as many legal restrictions on their youth, especially those over age 16 or 18, while allowing such unlimited freedoms for adults.

But no matter what class or generational redistribution policy is proposed, it has little chance of success in today's climate for the same reason that economic and social attrition against younger age groups has proven popular in the first place. There is at present no constituency for reforms aimed at reducing the poverty and discrimination directed at youth. In fact, the impetus to punish young age is increasing.

Remedial measures are difficult to identify because it is difficult to fully explain modern American adults' hostility against teenagers. Factors can be listed. Some observers, such as 1950s social scientist Edgar Friedenberg and youth historian Joseph Kett, postulate an anti-adolescent trait in Americans' ambivalent character that leads us to fear the challenging and unpredictable qualities we identify with adolescence, which surfaces in ugly retribution during uncertain times. And these are times uncertain. The Sixties turmoil included open generational hostility over Vietnam and racial issues. Baby Boom parents experienced serious difficulties maintaining intact families and raising children, especially teenagers. A wealth of public and private interests have arisen, ostensibly to help but increasingly to terrify, modern parents and policy makers.

In the last fifteen years, these interests have come to dominate Americans' image of adolescents. Agency and program self-promotion has rested in publicizing assertions about the young that are dire, lacking in context, and to an increasing extent, utterly false. The attack by public, private, and political interests has in turn fed back into a dislike and fear of teenagers on the part of many adults. This attack has blended with the economic stake of a wealthier, largely white, aging America against a poorer, increasingly nonwhite, younger America with which it no longer identifies. Divorce, family dissolution, and the increasing financial independence of older generations (to the point that many elderly have come to believe that they are guaranteed support by a government system that has replaced voluntary support from younger generations in the past), seems to have diminished the "shared fate" older and younger generations within a society typically feel. Special youth-management interest groups and general aging-adult personal interests have combined in an escalating war against adolescents that is dangerous, unbounded, and extreme, both in its own right and compared to other societies and America's past.

The growing economic split between generations is exacerbated by the growing divergence in the racial/ethnic character of older versus younger age groups. It may be that elder groups, out of subtle unease more than overt racism, do not accept today's adolescents and children (beyond their own immediate progeny) as "theirs" and have thus proven amenable to political-interest campaigns attacking the young. If elder and Baby Boom generations do not accept that fact that the near-term future of California, as well as that of many other states and the nation itself within a few decades, will no longer be dominated by the mostly-white groups that have heretofore held sway, then our implicit attitude is a bleak one: America ends with us. Perhaps that is the reason for our rage at the polls, our disillusion with each party in alternating sequence because they cannot deliver on our unrealistic demands: To give us assurance that America's future remains in the hands of narrowly-identified "people like *us*," to continue *our* prerogatives built up and nurtured over the past quarter century, to preserve low taxes for *us*, to maintain beneficent government services for *us*, even if the price is a sizeable charge-card bill which someone somewhere over the rainbow will suffer due as we raise a tall one at that Nineteenth Hole in the Sky.

If that is what we expect, then the evolution will become wrenching. The age war, the generation war now reaching crisis proportions in California and similarly situated locales, tells us a great deal about how Americans will manage the coming transition. The news, from areas of the country where the generation split is most pronounced, is bad.

It has been easy to blame 1990s parents and adults for the officially-sanctioned mayhem inflicted on adolescents. There is a catch: Today's adults have never been presented with an alternative view of modern youth amid a monolithic agency-program disinformation cacophony faithfully reflected by the press. And this fact, in and of itself, is radicalizing. Look at the cardinal sources of information cited in the references section. They are hardly classified documents obtained under Freedom of Information Act stricture and re-interpreted with arcane and complex statistical techniques, nor are they far-left treatises espousing mind-blowing radical deconstructions and startling new post-modern discourse. Rather, the basic sources cited are straightforward tables from standard, easily available documents: *Vital Statistics of the United States*, *Statistical Abstract of the United States*, *FBI Uniform Crime Reports*, *Sourcebook of Criminal Justice Statistics*, *Drug Abuse Warning Network Annual Reports*, *HIV/AIDS Surveillance Reports*, and U.S. Bureau of the Census reports such as *Poverty in the United States*, *Social and Economic Characteristics of the Population*, and *Historical Statistics of the United States*. Mundane stuff.

We can be sure, then, that political officials, top experts, and most national lobbying interests are aware of these same documents; their sinecures authored them. We can be sure that officials are not suffering from ignorance when they present information and implications about adolescents that directly contradict what is shown in their own references. When we are told (or led to believe) that teenagers are the most dangerous groups in society for suicide or drug abuse or unwed parenthood or drunken driving, it is due to distortion of basic facts by authorities who know better and who are protecting interests deserving none. If facts crucial to understanding adolescent behaviors, such as poverty or victimization or racism, are omitted from official explanations, it is because of deliberate decisions not to let these facts intrude on their anti-youth doctrines. Well-intentioned sources normally disagree over the shadings, interpretations, or relative importance of what is known, but the assertions currently circulated on adolescents are so contorted that nuance is no longer the issue. If the information presented in this book is not widely known, and especially if it comes as a shock, it is because the leading spokespersons who inform us on youth issues are misleading us for their own purposes.

It is, however, a very different matter to suggest that local officials, or school personnel, or parents, or adults, whose sources of information about youths in general are the news media and official statements, are acting out of similar rancorous indifference toward the young. The barrage of negative information about teenagers is widespread, relentless, and monolithic. If misinformation is the problem, as a number of commenters who dissent from my criticism of the attitudes of older generations have suggested, then I hope this volume can play some small part in reducing misperception. My pessimism that the problem is deeper, one tied to modern American adult attitudes, is a point on which I would be delighted to be proven wrong.

Serfs' up

As a result of exploding child poverty, California and other urban states are engaged in a cutting-edge experiment. We are now seeing what happens when 1980s Golden State children raised with poverty rates of 15-20 percent—1.3 million poor youngsters—grow into teenagers.

California is not happy with the results of the experiment we never admitted was occurring. In 1994, 1,100 California youths age 10-19 were arrested for murder, 35,000 were arrested for other felony violence, 100,000 were arrested for non-violent felonies, and 200,000 were arrested for misdemeanors. Most of these are records or near-record peaks. The state now opens a new 2,000-bed prison every eight months to manage the violence of the youth and young adult cohort and fills the same to double capacity within a few weeks. It has been a long time since I heard any elder express any happiness or optimism about the new generation.

And if we are not happy now, let us contemplate the newer, more radical experiment coming of age: Greater numbers, by the hundreds of thousands, of 1990s California Generation Y children raised with even higher poverty rates of 25-30 percent. In elementary school, some 2.2 million impoverished California kids, numbers still rising at most recent count, set to enter adolescence as the 1990s come to a close. Although it is popular to blame this trend on recent immigration, the proportion of California's population that is foreign born is actually lower today than in the first half of the century.

Rather, the accelerating growth of child and youth poverty, the withdrawal of tax support and relentless deterioration of public schools, and the explosion of the prisons as the school infrastructure deteriorates, depicted graphically in the first pages, are the statistics of Baby Boom and elder California's abandonment of Generation Y (Table 9.1). They sum up this book.

For every child living in poverty, there are one or more adult parents living in poverty as well. Poverty places much the same stresses on adults as it does on adolescents. It sharply increases the odds of violence, family instability, and a variety of self-destructive behaviors such as smoking, drug and alcohol addiction, and risky sexual conduct that become influences on the next generation. For that reason, it is simplistic to blame teenage behavior solely on parental behavior. A more accurate framework is that both are responses to the stresses inherent in social conditions. The deterioration in public support for families with children, a direct result of declining tax revenue and school funding, reverberates across generations.

Veteran California capital journalist, political author, and *Sacramento Bee* editor Dan Walters pointed out that rising law enforcement budgets were taken

Table 9.1

The explosion of California child poverty:

Percentage of California children living in poverty (58 counties)

Number of counties with child poverty rates:	1970	1980	1990	1995*
Less than 20%	52	52	35	20
More than 20%	6	6	23	38
More than 30%			4	18
More than 40%				4

*Projections for counties for 1995 by author, from Children Now figures.
Sources: U.S. Bureau of the Census (1970-90). California. *Social and Economic Characteristics of the Population.* Washington, DC: U.S. Department of Commerce; Children Now (1995). California: *The State of Our Children 1995.* Supplement. Sacramento, CA: Children Now.

"almost directly from education, as younger voters who would favor education are being overruled by the older majority:"

> Fund revenue has been virtually a flat line for the last five years. There's been a direct shift from higher education to prisons, reflecting the priorities of aging, white voters who say that personal protection is No. 1.
> ... The priorities of the voters are being met. They may not be the priorities of the population as a whole, but they are the priorities of the voters.[61]

California prisons continue their land-office business: 18,000 guests in 1975, 125,000 in 1994. In the 72-month 1989-94 period, California added 32,000 new prison spaces—15 every day—at a cost of $2 billion, plus $600 million per year to operate.

At triple capacity, they would cage 100,000.[62] Not enough. Not nearly enough, even if adult violence is ignored and adolescent violence becomes the only target. During that same 72-month period, 2.2 million California teenagers were arrested, 865,000 for felonies; 200,000 of the latter violent felonies.[63]

Aging adult Californians are doing fine. We have cut our state and local tax burdens by 25 percent since the 1970s. Support for schools has plummeted in this affluent state, from $1.20 in state funding for every dollar spent in other states in 1970 to 80 cents today. Education and prison spending compete in the state's discretionary budget, and the winner has been declared.

Isolation of the new generation is not just a warped California futurism. Even those who witnessed the 1950s pre-civil-rights era's open racism and indifference to child poverty are profoundly fearful of this new '90s detachment. As Jonathan Kozol, a tireless voice for impoverished children since *Death at an Early Age* appeared in 1963, recently declared, a "pogrom mentality" consigns growing legions of children and youths to "the sickest, most diseased part of the city" because affluent adults do not want to see the results of our national failure of "will to act on what we know."[64] Abandonment of a younger generation signals a declaration by the older that survival of the society beyond our corporate and corporeal occupation of it is a matter of indifference. Concludes Kozol in *Amazing Grace*, his 1995 testament to South Bronx's poor children: "I have never lived through a time as cold as this in the United States."[65]

When they don't act like us

We might also look at California's experiment in reverse. Drug deaths, a key measure of self destruction cited earlier, provide insight. As P.J. O'Rourke points out, modern drug policy seems designed less to attack drug abuse than to express adult society's "strong subconscious wish to be rid of its young people."[66] And so it is in returning to the amazing patterns of drug demise over the last quarter century that we see a harbinger of larger social currents (Table 9.2).

Table 9.2

Teenagers are becoming less drug-destructive, adults more so...

California accidental drug overdose deaths, by generation

California	1970	1980	1994	1970-1994 Rate change*
Youth: age 10-19	134	25	14	-90%
Parent: age 30-54	284	290	1,431	+ 180%

*Rate per 100,000 population, accidents only, excluding suicides.
Source: California Center for Health Statistics. *Vital Statistics of California* (annual through 1992) and Microcomputer Injury Surveillance System files (1994). Sacramento: Department of Health Services.

In 1970, youths were nearly as likely than their parents to die from drugs. By 1980, the teenage drug fatality had mostly disappeared from California, and parent-age drug death rates were decreasing. By 1993, teen drug deaths were all but history, but parent drug deaths had exploded to record heights.

Drug overdose is not the signature of a generation. But it is an indicator of what is going on in the larger cultures from which the extreme cases are drawn, an iceberg tip revealing tens of thousands of lives crippled not just by drug and alcohol dependence, but by the misery that produced it and follow with it.

The trend away from self-destruction is not confined to drugs. Populous Los Angeles County, whose 880,000 teens age 13-19 in 1993 are as many as live in the entire state of Michigan, reflects the most extreme of California's youth evolution. Table 9.3 and Figure 9.4, in turn, summarize the shift among the most extreme of their number.

Over the past quarter century, L.A.'s nonwhite population grew rapidly, to the point that one writer dubbed it "capital of the Third World." The city added

Table 9.3

Los Angeles teenagers are no longer self-destructive, now aiming outward...

Los Angeles County, age 13-19	1970	1994	Rate change*
Population	860,000	880,000	+2
Percent nonwhite	34%	73%	+115
Number living in poverty	110,000	230,000	
Percent in poverty	13%	26%	+104
Self-destructive deaths			
Suicides	106	46	-58
Drug deaths(acc. + suic.)	113	6	-95
Other fatal accidents	273	161	-42
Total self-destructive deaths	435	207	-53
Total other-destructive deaths			
Homicide deaths	70	371	+418
Homicide arrests	81	459	+454
Total violent deaths	505	578	+12

* Change in deaths per 100,000 teens.
Source: California Center for Health Statistics. *Vital Statistics of California* (annual through 1992) and Microcomputer Injury Surveillance System files (1992-94). Sacramento: Department of Health Services.

120,000 teens to its poverty rolls. Yet the chances of a teenager dying violently increased only moderately (up 12 percent), surprising given that poverty populations usually have substantially higher mortality. The notion of uncontrolled, skyrocketing teenage demise is a myth.

What changed dramatically is *which teenagers died* and the *way they died*. In 1970, five out of six teenage deaths were self-dispatch: Suicides plus fatal accidents (mostly traffic wrecks, drug overdoses, drownings, and falls). Drug overdoses, the quintessential self-destructive "accident" since it is nearly always self-inflicted, are shown separately and display a particularly large decline. These were white Sixties kids, dying by their own hand by the score.

But not today. In 1994, two-thirds of all teenage deaths were "other-destructive"—that is, they were murdered. Homicide arrests are a better gauge, and their increase is even more dramatic. These are Nineties nonwhite kids. Those teenagers bent on taking a life have shifted dramatically from self to other destruction. In 1994, not one L.A. teenager died from an accidental drug overdose.

When the magnifying effect of these trends—in injuries and violent crime, in ripples throughout the population whose behaviors do not result in loss of life—are added, it is evident that the most volatile of L.A.'s teenage population is coming to very different conclusions about who is to blame for its unhappiness than did

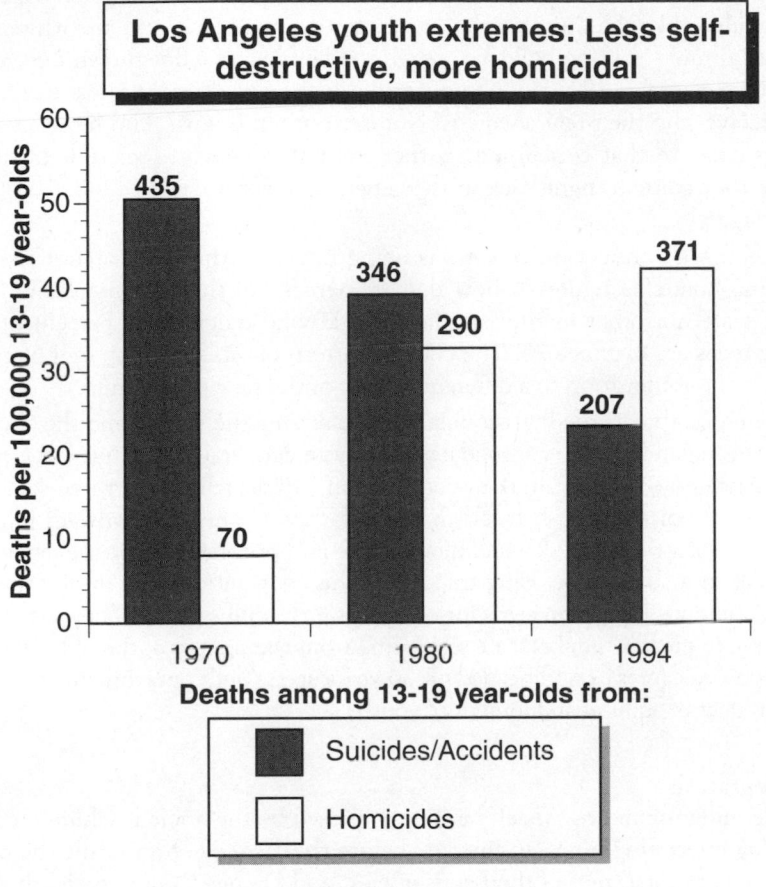

Los Angeles youth extremes: Less self-destructive, more homicidal

Figure 9.4

Source: See Table 9.3

teenagers of the Sixties. The hand of death was once aimed inward by one class and era of teens; today, it reaches outward by another.

Where once destruction was personal and solitary, claiming 435 L.A. adolescents in 1970 versus only 70 teen murders, now it is external and collective. Self-destructive youthful deaths fell by 50 percent to only 207 in 1994, but teen murders rose 450 percent to claim a staggering 371 lives.

As dramatic as these mega-trends are, the more astonishing fact (in this information age characterized by microanalysis of youth behavior) is that *they are not talked about.* The diverging trends—in poverty, in drug demise, in violence—expose aging adults at our extreme, scapegoating the next generation for our own malaise, making them repositories for the anger generated by our unresolved war with ourselves. But scapegoats have limits. We are provoking a reaction, all right, and it is spinning further and further from our control.

As the numbers of impoverished youth grow up in a state seriously considering education "rationing,"[67] systematically shutting off every opportunity to participate in larger society, when is a critical mass reached? When do today's teenagers and young adults—like the three youths, one Hispanic, one black, and one white, teaming up to throw a parking bollock through the window of a downtown Los Angeles bank in a memorable 1992 riot photo—arrive at the same conclusion as Lee Iacocca and perceive who their real enemy is? Not each other, but us? And if certain young activists come to that conclusion, as they must if American society is to survive, how are they going to fight back in the generation war we elders ignited a quarter-century ago?

Perhaps a connection of sorts is being made. Although it is not reported, California homicide figures[68] show that 60 percent of the victims of murders by teenagers are not other teens, but adults age 20 and older. Forty percent of those slain by teens are over age 25. The current pattern of violence may well be temporary, part of the transition to a different society of the new millennium.

It may be that as shadow economies grow among the young, and the "frontier" nature of gangland culture consolidates into more cooperative ventures, the murder and violence now inherent in their competition will decrease. The three-strikes and law'n'order lobbies will rush to claim credit for every annual downward blip with the same breath that they demand more police and prisons to combat every upward one.[69] Yet in a stark sense, gang truces and the cooperation seen during the 1992 riots are ominous long-term signs for contemporary adult culture. They suggest that the young, in greater numbers, are separating from the society of the old, a development Roosevelt foresaw and headed off 60 years ago. Youth detachment from adults is the product of adult abandonment of youth.

Re-integration

Pre-millennium Los Angeles is amply blessed by the ancient Chinese curse of occupying interesting times. In the days before the 1994 election, while the college campuses were quiet, tens of thousands of L.A. and Orange County high school students poured into the streets to protest Proposition 187, the virulent anti-immigrant ballot issue. In California's tradition of state-of-the-art reaction, Proposition 187 (like the government-dismantling Proposition 13 in 1979 and the anti-minority Rumford Fair Housing Act of 1964) succinctly focused cutting-edge popular bigotries for the nation to behold.

Proposition 187's sole substantive addition to law: Kick the children of illegal immigrants out of school. Beautiful. What better vehicle to deliver the majority-white sentiment to the newly-arrived (whether by reason of young age or foreign origin) in no uncertain terms: Picking artichokes, swabbing swimming pools, assembling Rodeo Drive garments in sweatshops, mired forever in subminimum wage jobs for our convenience—Yes. But earning a high school diploma, using public health services, enrolling in universities, dreaming of real futures?—No. You, the newly-arrived, are here for *us*. We are not here for you. Sayonara, kids. The train is pulling out.

Young students, especially Latinos but also a surprising contingent of whites and other races, got the message and joined the walkouts. "It's hard to recall another issue in recent years that has galvanized so many high school students throughout

California," the *Los Angeles Times* reported. "We are not illegal aliens, we are human beings,"[70] protesting students declared in a voice that hit to the essence of the multi-front war by today's established adults against the *new*.

"Thanks to the narrow minds behind Proposition 187, we may be witnessing the politicization of a new generation of Californians," *Times* columnist Robin Abcarian wrote. Six days later, the narrow minds would turn out to be two-thirds of the state's aging voters who dominated the election. "The opposite of an adolescent is, in this sense, a politician."[71] She was right. The Times Poll showed whites and voters over age 40 heavily favored 187; nonwhites and voters under age 30, even in a poor turnout, heavily rejected it.[72]

The polls on 187 revealed not simply an age, income, and race/ethnicity chasm of major proportions, but a "like we care" gap. The majoritarian proponents of Proposition 187 did not deny opponents' contentions that the initiative would wreak severe damage on the newly immigrant school-age young who had no choice about being "illegal." More ominously, 187's backers told pollsters they didn't *care* if it did.[73] A new, multicultural California is emerging into a harsh and violent world forged by parental hostility, rejection, and indifference to its future.

More success accrued to San Francisco's Youth Uprising Coalition, whose organizing contributed to the November 1995 electoral defeats of a citywide curfew for teens and a proposal to rename a street named after César Chávez. In an opinion column denouncing stepped-up police harassment against minorities, teenagers, and the homeless under the city's conservative mayoral regime (also ousted in the election), high school students Raquel Moreño and José Luis Pavón challenged voters to reject "scapegoating policy" and instead to "allow youths to be part of making the decisions that affect them."[74]

Our adolescents are not a cadre of idealistic angels. They are an equally derailed cohort of young who hold genuine potential to finish the obliteration of American society that we began. American elders of the 1990s seem to think teenagers landed on a meteorite or arrived like an unwelcome gift from Bloomingdale's. It seems not to dawn on our aging consciousness that the young do not come with 30-day free home demonstration and option to return. We cannot get a refund on the next generation, nor can we keep putting its future on plastic. It is ours. We bred it—or it came to America from abroad with its parents, much like we did and for the same reasons. They are very much like us. The wiser among them are striving to be less so.

The path back to intergenerational cooperation would be difficult at this advanced stage of deterioration even if a consensus existed among aging Americans to try. It lies in ending the futile efforts to "rejuvenilize" adolescents and, instead, inviting adolescents into adult society, where every sign over the last six decades suggests they belong. This is a modest proposal to fix two wayward generations together: Sixties and Nineties kids, at odds with each other's worst stereotypes.

What is needed is not a revolution of fiscal policy or remedial plan, but one of fundamental attitude. Nothing good will happen until elder America gazes down from our hillside and condominium perch and identifies the young—darker in shade as a rule, feisty, lustful as we were, violent as we raised them to be, no different from us in any major respect—as our children. *All of them.*

Of all people, we alienated Sixties types ought to glimpse what they face. We inherited an America, even in the throes of the Vietnam War, many times more hopeful and resilient than we will leave them. We sold out en masse to yuppiedom and moralistic defenses. They don't have our options. They are second-generation, confused children who still need to extract from us the gift they most need: A pure Sixties-kid challenge-it-all mentality capped by our grudging admonition: *Do it right this time.*

More than once, I've caught young people quizzing me pointedly on The Sixties and felt the distinct unease that they were not rapt in admiration at our sadly mixed achievements, but were scrutinizing our mistakes to avoid repeating them. We know firsthand what trouble the young can cause for the old when the old have it coming, and now we are the Establishment. Sixties counterculturists told us not to trust anyone over thirty. They were right. They were talking about *us.*

Notes

Chapter 1: Impounding the Future

1   Friedenberg EZ (1959). *The Vanishing Adolescent*. Boston: Beacon Press, p 115.

2   Demos J (1979). Images of the American family, then and now. In Tufte V, Meyerhoft B (eds). *The Changing American Family*. New Haven: Yale University Press, pp 43-60.

3   Gibbs N (1990, 8 October). Shameful bequests to the next generation. *Time*, pp 42-46.

4   National Commission on the Role of the School and Community in Improving Adolescent Health (1990). *Code blue: Uniting for healthier youth*. Alexandria, VA: National Association of State Boards of Education, p 1.

5   Rodriguez R (1993, 19 December). Who are our children? *Los Angeles Times*, pp M1, M6.

6   U.S. Bureau of the Census (1972). *General social and economic characteristics, California*. Washington, DC: U.S. Department of Commerce, Table 58.

7   Children Now (1995). *California: The state of our children*. Report card '95. Sacramento, CA: Children Now, p 5.

8   U.S. Department of Commerce (1995). *Statistical Abstract of the United States*. 1994 and previous annual.

9   Children Now (1995), *op cit*, p 18.

10   Morain D (1994, 16 October). California's proliferation of prisons. *Los Angeles Times*, pp A1, A20-A21.

11   Law Enforcement Information Center (1995). *Crime & delinquency in California*. Sacramento, CA: California Department of Justice, 1994 printout, and Table 33 (1993 and corresponding annual).

12   Law Enforcement Information Center (1995), *op cit*; California Department of Finance (1995). *Statistical Abstract of California, 1994*. Sacramento, CA: Tables F-1, N-2.

13   *Ibid*, pp 3, 11.

14   U.S. Bureau of the Census (1994). *Money income of households, families, and persons in the United States, 1992*. P60-184. Washington, DC: U.S. Department of Commerce, Table 1.

15   U.S. Bureau of the Census (1992). *Census of Population, 1990. California: General housing characteristics*. Washington, DC: U.S. Department of Commerce, Table 134.

16   California Department of Finance (1995), *op cit*, Table P-2.

17   Flanigan J (1994, 7 December). Debacle will cost every city, town in the nation. *Los Angeles Times*, pp D1-D2.

18   U.S. Bureau of the Census (1992). *Census of Population, 1990. California: General Population Characteristics*. Washington, DC: U.S. Department of Commerce.

19   Roosevelt FD (1936, April 20). Address to young Democrats. *Vital Speeches* II, pp 442-444.

20   Benac N (1994, 20 April). Clinton to youth: Believe in future. Washington: Associated Press.

21   Examine the trends tabulated by the U.S. Bureau of the Census in such periodic Population Series publications as *Poverty in the United States*; *Money income of households, families, and persons in the United States*; *Measuring the effects of benefits and taxes on income and poverty*; and *Social and Economic Characteristics* reports from the 1970, 1980, and 1990 censuses. Washington, DC: U.S. Department of Commerce.

22   Ostrow RJ (1993, 30 July). FBI nominee draws Senate panel acclaim. *Los Angeles Times*, p A15.

23   Ostrow RJ (1993, 20 October). War on drugs shifting its focus to hard-core addicts. *Los Angeles Times*, p A26.

24   DeParle J (1992, 22 March). Clinton target; Teen-age pregnancy. *New York Times*, p A11; DeParle J (1994, 10 June). Clinton to propose strategy to curb youth pregnancies. *New York Times*, pp A1, A9.

25   Whitmire R (1994, 13 December). Drug abuse rises among U.S. teens. Washington, DC: Gannett News Service. Ostrow RJ (1994, 13 December). Nearly 50 percent of 12th graders linked to drug use. *Los Angeles Times*, p A38.

26   Associated Press (1993, 14 November), Washington; Shogren E (1995, 11 June). Clinton seeks strict drunk driving laws. *Los Angeles Times*, p A24.

27   Jackson R, Hall J (1994, 21 October). Reno warns TV industry: Cut violence. *Los Angeles Times*, pp A1, A22.

28   See Currie E (1993). *Reckoning: Drugs, the cities, and the American future*. New York: Hill & Wang, p 327.

29   Smeeding TM (1990, Summer). Children and poverty: How U.S. stands. *Forum for Applied Research and Public Policy*, pp 65-70.

30   U.S. Bureau of the Census (1994). *Poverty in the United States, 1992*. P60-185. Washington, DC: U.S. Department of Commerce, Table 17.

31   See Hage D, Black RF (1995, 10 April). America's other welfare state; and Grant L, Black RF (1995, 10 April). Getting business of the dole. *U.S. News & World Report*, pp 34-38.

32   Calculations by author from data in, U.S. Bureau of the Census (1995). *Statistical Abstract of the United States, 1994*. Washington, DC: U.S. Department of Commerce, Table 607; and National Center for Health Statistics (1995). *Vital Statistics of the United States, 1990*. Volume I, Natality. Washington, DC: U.S. Department of Health and Human Services, Table 1-84.

33   Scheer R (1995, 3 October). As the world turns while watching O.J. *Los Angeles Times*, p B9.

34   California Center for Health Statistics (1995 and previous annual). California resident live births, by age of mother, age of father, marital status, race, county (printout, annual). Sacramento: Department of Health Services. California Law Enforcement Information Center (1995), op cit.

35   Besharov D (1994, 20 December). Orphanages aren't welfare reform. The New York Times, op-ed.

36   Calculations by author from data in California Center for Health Statistics (1995 and previous annual). Microcomputer injury surveillance system (MISS, annual data diskette); and birth report, op cit. Sacramento, CA: Department of Health Services.

37   Alan Guttmacher Institute (1994). Sex and America's teenagers. New York: AGI, p 70.

38   Calculations by author from data in U.S. Bureau of the Census (1994), op cit; National Center for Health Statistics (1995 and previous annual), op cit.

39   U.S. Bureau of the Census (1994). Poverty in the United States - 1992, op cit, Table 5.

40   The tendency of officials and experts to focus on trivial issues benefitting their narrow interests rather than larger social influences generating the problems they are supposed to be addressing.

41   California Center for Health Statistics (1995), birth report, op cit.

42   Barbour J (1990, 18 December). Shopping malls and teens: A love-hate relationship. Associated Press.

43   Johnson L, in Mosle S (1995, 11 September), op cit, p. 6.

44   See Peele S (1989). Diseasing of America. Lexington, MA: DC Heath & Co., p 275; Hill RF, Fortenberry JD (1992). Adolescence as a culture-bound syndrome. Social Science & Medicine 35, 73-80.

45   Jones MWM (1995, 3 April). Voting for local school taxes in California: How much do demographic variables such as race and age matter? San Francisco, CA: Paper presented to the Population Association of America annual meeting, p 7.

46   Mosle S (1995, 11 September). Dissed. The New Yorker, pp 5-6.   •

47   U.S. Department of Commerce and of Labor, in U.S. News & World Report (1995, 6 February 1995). A minimum wage hike? Don't bet on it, p 9. Growing together, growing apart, p 29.

48   See U.S. Bureau of the Census (1994), op cit.

49   McNamara RS (1995). In retrospect: The tragedy and lessons of Vietnam. New York: Random House, p 5.

50   Joint Committee on Higher Education (1968). The academic state. Sacramento, CA: California State Legislature, p 40.

51   Streisand B (1995, 18 September). Real-world troubles. U.S. News & World Report, pp 125-126, 128.

52   Rawls JJ, Bean W (1993). California: An interpretive history. Sixth edition. New York: McGraw Hill, pp 500-501.

53   Ibid, p 128.

54   Olen H (1995, May 30). Plan to cut university budget stirs admission policy debate in N.Y. Los Angeles Times, p A5.

55   Auster BB (1995, 27 November). Tantrums, taxes & tactics. U.S. News & World Report, p 38.

56   Chiem PX (1995, 9 January). Sudden rise in student loans now may mean problems later. The New University, Irvine, California, pp 8-9.

57   Council for Aid to Education (1995, 5 January). Investing in American higher education: An argument for restructuring. New York: CAE, p 13.

58   Tooley JA (1995, 25 September). A heavy loan burden. U.S. News & World Report, pp 81-84.

59   Furstenberg FF Jr, Hoffman SD, Shrestha L (1995, August). The effect of divorce on intergenerational transfers: New evidence. Demography 32, 319-333.

60   Whitehead BD (1993, April). Dan Quayle was right. The Atlantic, pp 47-84.

61   Flanigan J (1994), op cit, p D2.

62   Rabin JL (1995, 16 July). L.A. County mortgaged most major assets. Los Angeles Times, pp A1, A24.

63   Peterson P (1993). Facing up. New York: Simon & Schuster.

64   Glenn N (1993, July). Correspondence. The Atlantic, p 10.

65   From Greek (ephebe, or "young man"): Fear and loathing of adolescents. See Astroth K (1994, January), Beyond ephebiphobia: Problem adults or problem youths? Phi Delta Kappan, January 1994, pp. 411-413.

66   Clinton text, State of the Union (1994, 26 January). Los Angeles Times, p A19.

67   Boyer D, Fine D (1992). Sexual abuse as a factor in adolescent pregnancy and child maltreatment. Family Planning Perspectives 24, 4-11, 19.

68   Gershenson HP, Musick JS, Ruch-Ross H, et al (1989). The prevalence of coercive sexual experience among teenage mothers. Journal of Interpersonal Violence 4, 204-219.

69   Congressional Budget Office, Sources of support for adolescent mothers (1990), in Levin-Epstein J (1994, 27 July). Understanding the Clinton welfare bill. Teen pregnancy prevention and teen parents. Washington, DC; Center for Law and Social Policy, p 7.

70   The Alan Guttmacher Institute (1994), op cit; Moore KA, Nord CW, Peterson JL (1989). Nonvoluntary sexual activity among adolescents. Family Planning Perspectives 21, 110-114.

71   See Congressional Research Service, in Welch WM (1994, 9 February). Ending cycle of welfare hangs on the bottom line. USA Today, p 5A.

72   Shalala, in Brownstein R, Lauter D (1993, 12 December). Clinton aides find welfare vow easier said than done. *Los Angeles Times,* pp A1, A18.

73   Gallman V (1994, 4 December). Myths, facts of welfare sorted out. Washington: Knight-Ridder News Service.

74   Fellmeth RC (1995, 5 July). California: A society that cuts child welfare but boosts jails. *Los Angeles Times,* p B7.

75   Males M, Chew KS (1995, 8 April). The role of adult men in school-age fertility. Paper to Population Association of America, San Francisco, CA.

76   Whitman D, Cooper M (1994, 20 July). The end of welfare — sort of. *U.S. News & World Report,* pp 28-37.

77   Landry DL, Forrest JD (1995). How old are U.S. fathers? *Family Planning Perspectives* 27, 159-161, 165. See also Males M, Chew KS (1995, 8 April), *op cit.*

78   Cockburn A. (1994, 28 February). Beat the devil: Clinton and teen sex. *The Nation,* 259.

79   See the 1959 Philip Dunne film, *Blue Denim,* on "the shocking facts of teen pregnancy," featuring Carol Lynley and Brandon De Wilde, for example.

80   National Victim Center (1992, 23 April). *Rape in America.* Columbia, SC: Crime Victims Research and Treatment Center, pp 2-3.

81   Timnick L. (1985, 25 August). The Times Poll: 22 percent in survey were child abuse victims. *Los Angeles Times,* pp 1, 34.

82   Boyer D, Fine D (1992), *op cit.*

83   Gershenson HP, Musick JS, Ruch-Ross H, et al (1989), *op cit.*

84   Joyner K, Michael RT (1995, 8 April). Teenage sex and pregnancy. Harris School of Public Policy Studies, University of Chicago. San Francisco, CA: Paper presented to the Population Association of America.

85   Alan Guttmacher Institute (1994), *op cit,* pp 28, 73.

86   Vobejda B (1994, 7 June). Teens improve on prevention of pregnancy. *Washington Post,* pp A1, A9.

87   U.S. Centers for Disease Control (1994, November). *Facts about adolescents and HIV/AIDS.* HIV/AIDS prevention, draft. Atlanta, GA: CDC; See also Associated Press (1992, 10 April). Study shows one in five high schoolers run high AIDS risk. Atlanta, GA.

88   Lemp GF, Hirozawa AM, Givertz D, et al (1994, 10 August). Seroprevalence of HIV and risk behaviors among young homosexual and bisexual men. The San Francisco/Berkeley young men's survey. *Journal of the American Medical Association* 272, 449-454.

89   Centers for Disease Control (1993, October). *HIV/AIDS Surveillance Report* 5, Tables 5, 7.

90   Greene J (1994, 7 March). Sex between teens, adults growing factor in AIDS spread. Oakland (Michigan) *Press,* p A8.

91   Greene J (1994, 7 March), *op cit.*

92   All things considered (1995, 9 August). Washington, DC: National Public Radio.

93   Phillips L (1995, 31 August). Sex abuse: Silent factor in teen welfare equation. *USA Today,* p 6A.

94   National Center on Child Abuse and Neglect (1993, May). National child abuse and neglect data system. Working paper No. 2, 1991, summary data component. Washington, DC: U.S. Department of Health and Human Services. In U.S. Bureau of the Census (1994). *Statistical Abstract of the United States, 1993.* Washington, DC: U.S. Department of Commerce, Table 336.

95   Calculated by author from data in U.S. Bureau of the Census (1994), *op cit,* Table 5; and Federal Bureau of Investigation (1995). *Uniform crime reports for the United States, 1993.* Washington, DC: U.S. Department of Justice, Table 38.

96   FBI, *Uniform Crime Reports,* (1995 and previous annual), *op cit.*

97   U.S. Bureau of the Census. *Historical statistics of the United States.* Colonial times to 1970. Washington, DC: U.S. Department of Commerce, 1975, Series 971-986, p 414.

98   California Center for Health Statistics (1995). Microcomputer Injury Surveillance System, 1993, *op cit.*

99   U.S. Bureau of the Census (1990). Income and poverty status in 1989: 1990. *Summary, social and economic characteristics, California.* Washington, DC: U.S. Department of Commerce, Table 10.

100   Dodge KA, Bates JE, Pettit GS (1990, 21 December). Mechanisms in the cycle of violence. *Science* 250, 1678-1683.

101   American Humane Association (1989). National study on child neglect and abuse reporting. In *Statistical Abstract of the United States.* Washington, DC: U.S. Bureau of the Census, Table 291.

102   Dawson JM, Langan PA (1994, July). *Murder in families.* Special report. Washington, DC: U.S. Bureau of Justice Statistics, Table 2.

103   Rivera C (1995, 26 April). Child abuse in U.S. at crisis level, panel says. *Los Angeles Times,* pp A1, A23.

104   Whitmire R (1994, 13 December), *op cit.*

105   Ostrow RJ (1994, 13 December), *op cit.*

106   U.S. Drug Abuse Warning Network (1994, December). *1993 preliminary estimates of drug-related emergency department episodes.* Advance report No. 8. Washington, DC: U.S. Department of Health and Human Services, Appendix 4.

107   Neergard L (1995, 20 July). Marijuana use sends teens to hospital emergency rooms. Washington, DC: Associated Press.

108   Drug Abuse Warning Network (1995), *op cit*, Table 2.10.

109   Calculations by author from data in National Center for Health Statistics (1995), Mortality, *op cit.*, and FBI (1995), *op cit.*

110   Shedler J, Block J (1990). Adolescent drug use and psychological health. A longitudinal inquiry. *American Psychologist* 45, 612-630.

111   Newcomb MD, Bentler PM (1988). Impact of adolescent drug use and social support on problems of young adults: A longitudinal study. *Journal of Abnormal Psychology* 97, 64-75.

112   National Center for Health Statistics (1995 and previous annual). *Vital Statistics of the United States, 1990* (and previous annual). Volume II-A, Mortality. Washington, DC: U.S. Department of Health and Human Services, Table 1-27, 1990, and previous annual.

113   Richter P, Cimons M (1995, 4 August). Clinton to weigh plan to curb teen smoking. *Los Angeles Times*, p A14.

114   U.S. Substance Abuse and Mental Health Services Administration (1994, July). *Preliminary estimates from the 1993 Household Survey on Drug Abuse.* Advance report No. 7. Washington, DC: U.S. Department of Health and Human Services, Table 14-B; U.S. Public Health Service (1991, March). *Health in the United States—1990.* Washington, DC: U.S. Department of Health and Human Services, Table 57.

115   Office of Health and Environmental Assessment (1992, December). *Respiratory health effects of passive smoking: Lung cancer and other disorders.* Washington, DC: U.S. Environmental Protection Agency, p 1-1.

116   Office on Smoking and Health (1994). *Preventing tobacco use among young people: A report of the Surgeon General.* Washington, DC: U.S. Dept of Health and Human Services, pp 6-10, 28, 129-130.

117   Males M (1995). The influence of parental smoking on youth smoking: Is the recent downplaying justified? *Journal of School Health* 65, 228-231.

118   Office on Smoking and Health (revised 1989, October). Smoking tobacco & health, a fact book. DHHS publication no. 87-8397. Washington, DC: U.S. Department of Health and Human Services, p 7.

119   Office on Smoking and Health (1986). *The health consequences of involuntary smoking: A report of the Surgeon General.* Washington, DC: U.S. Department of Health and Human Services, p 91.

120   Devoy A (1995, 8 August). Clinton calls for tough — yet practical — program to combat teenage smoking. *Washington Post*, p A8.

121   Clinton WF (1995, 10 August). Washington: News conference. See excerpts in Protecting young people from the "awful dangers" of tobacco (1994, 11 August). *Washington Post*, p A14.

122   Fournier R (1995, 11 August). Analysis: Clinton hopes for political windfall. Washington: Associated Press.

123   Editorial (1995, 19 August). Kicking the teenage habit. *The Lancet*, 346, 453.

124   Bonnie R, in Mendelson J and Mello NK (1985). *Alcohol use and abuse in America.* Boston: Little Brown & Co, p 100.

125   U.S. Centers for Disease Control (1994, November) HIV/AIDS and adolescents, *op cit.*

126   U.S. Centers for Disease Control (1986). *Youth Suicide Surveillance.* Atlanta, GA; Associated Press (1995, 21 April). Child suicide rate on rise, CDC reports. *Los Angeles Times*, p A35.

127   Taylor P (1991, 12 September). Minimum drinking age laced with loopholes, Novello says. *Washington Post*, pp A1, A18.

128   Enright RD, Levy VM Jr, Harris D, Lapsley DK (1987). Do economic conditions influence how theorists view adolescents? *Journal of Youth and Adolescence* 16, 541-559.

129   Alter J. (1994, 12 December). The name of the game is shame. *Newsweek*, 15.

130   Sawyer D. (1995, 16 February). *ABC Prime Time Live*.

131   Rooney A, 60 minutes (1994, 17 April).

132   Burt M (1986). Estimating the public costs of teenage childbearing. *Family Planning Perspectives* 18, 221-226.

133   Goodman E (1992, 16 April). Welfare mothers with an attitude. Boston Globe Newspaper Co.

134   Goodman E (1995, 25 March). Teen victims of adult men. Boston Globe Newspaper Co; Sylvester K (1994, November). *Preventable calamity: Rolling back teen pregnancy.* Washington, DC: Progressive Policy Institute, Report No. 22, pp 20-22.

135   See Thomas C (1995, 7 February). Foster is Elders reincarnated. Los Angeles Times Syndicate; Charen M (1995, 10 August). Teenagers' sexual activity cause for deep concern. Creators Syndicate.

136   Walinski A (1995, July). The crisis of public order. *Atlantic*, pp 39-54.

137   Foster D (1993, 9 December). The disease is adolescence. *Rolling Stone*, p 55.

138   France K (1992, July/August). AIDS explodes among teens. *Utne Reader*, pp 30-31.

139   Males M (1990, December). Youth problem behaviors: Subcultural effect, or mirror of adult behavior? *Journal of School Health* 60, 505-508. See also later chapters for specific trends.

140   National Center for Health Statistics (1990 and previous annual). *Vital Statistics of the United States.* Washington, D.C.: U.S. Department of Health and Human Services (annual; refer to years cited). Tables cited are for 1987 and corresponding tables for prior years: Natality, table 1-6 (Total fertility rates and birth rates, by

age of mother and race of child: United States, specified years 1940-55 and each year 1960-87), Natality, table 1-59 (Live births by age of father, age of mother, sex of child, and race of child, United States), Natality, table 1-32 (Birth rates for unmarried women by age of mother and race of child: United States, specified years 1940-55 and each year 1960-87), General Mortality, table 1-25 (Deaths from 282 selected causes by 5-year age groups, race, and sex, United States, supplementary classification of external causes of injury and poisoning).

141   Chauncey RL (1980, Winter). New careers for moral entrepreneurs: Teenage drinking. *Journal of Drug Issues* 22, 45-55.

142   Centers for Disease Control (1986). *Youth suicide surveillance*. Washington, DC: U.S. Department of Health and Human Services, p 1.

143   Gist R, Welch QB (1989). Certification change versus actual behavior change in teenage suicide rates, 1955-1979. *Suicide & Life-Threatening Behavior* 19, 277-187.

144   Engs RC, Fors SW (1988). Drug abuse hysteria: The challenge of keeping perspective. *Journal of School Health* 58, 26-28.

145   Select Committee on Children, Youth, and Families (1985, June 6). Emerging trends in mental health care for adolescents. Washington, D.C.: U.S. House of Representatives, 99th Congress, first session, pp. 78-79.

146   Talan J (1988, 7 January). The hospitalization of America's troubled teenagers. *Newsday* 48, p 1.

147   National Commission on the Role of the School and Community in Improving Adolescent Health (1990). *Code blue: Uniting for healthier youth*. Alexandria, VA: National Association of State Boards of Education, p 2.

148   National Highway Traffic Safety Administration (1995). *Traffic safety facts 1993*. Washington, DC: U.S. Department of Transportation, Tables 3, 5.

149   Zill N, Nord CW (1994). *Running in place*. Washington, DC: Child Trends Inc, pp 29-41.

150   Carnegie Council on Adolescent Development (1995, October). *Great transitions: Preparing adolescents for a new century*. New York, Carnegie Corporation, p 103 and chapter 9.

151   National Commission on the Role of the School and Community in Improving Adolescent Health (1990), *op cit*.

152   Horne AM, Sayger TV (1990). *Treating conduct and oppositional defiant disorders in children*. New York: Pergamon Press.

153   Select Committee on Children, Youth and Families (1985, June 6). Emerging trends in mental health care for adolescents. Washington, DC: U.S. House of Representatives, 99th Congress, First Session, hearings transcript.

154   Harris R (1993, 22 August). A nation's children in lockup. *Los Angeles Times*, pp A1, A20-A21.

155   e.g., see O'Neil B, press release (1990, 10 December). Arlington, VA: Insurance Institute for Highway Safety.

156   Koontz S. (1995, March). The American family and the nostalgia trap. *Phi Delta Kappan*, pp K1-K20.

157   Roan S (1995, July 11). Having the first baby doesn't stop the cycle. *Los Angeles Times*, p E6.

158   Bean RB, and *American Medicine*, quoted in Gould SJ (1981), *op cit*, 80-81.

159   Le Bon G, cited in Gould SJ (1981), *op cit.*, 105.

160   Hall GS (1904). *Adolescence: Its psychology and its relation to physiology, anthropology, sociology, sex, crime, religion, and education*. New York: D Appleton, p xiv.

161   See Holmbeck G.N. & Hill J. P. (1988). Storm and stress beliefs about adolescence: Prevalence, self-reported antecedents, and effects of an undergraduate course. *Journal of Youth & Adolescence*, 17:285-306.

162   Scheingold L, Flint E (1987, March). Teen suicide. *The New Physician*, p 35.

163   Stolbert S (1995, 21 August). Joe Camel leads the pack in lighting up controversy. *The Los Angeles Times*, p A16.

164   Office on Smoking and Health (1989, October), *op cit*.

165   Gardner W, Herman J (1990, Winter). Adolescents' AIDS risk taking: A rational choice perspective. *New Directions in Child Development* 50, 17-34.

166   See Chapter 2, references.

167   Adelson J (1979, February). Adolescence and the generation gap. *Psychology Today*, p. 34.

168   Adler N, Matthews K (1994). Health psychology: Why do some people get sick and some stay well? *Annual Review of Psychology* 45, 246.

169   Offer et al (1981), *op cit*, 63, 65.

170   Offer D. (1987, June 26). In defense of adolescents. *Journal of the American Medical Association*, 257;24,3408.

171   Jessor R (1982). Problem behavior and developmental transition in adolescence. *Journal of School Health* 52, 296.

172   Males M (1990). Youth problem behavior: Subcultural effect, or mirror of adult behavior? *Journal of School Health* 60, 505-508.

173   Geismer LL, Wood, K (1986). *Family and delinquency*. New York: Human Sciences Press, Inc.

174   See Chapter 4, references.

175   See Chapters 2, 3, references.

176   See Chapter 8, references.

177   The correlations (r-values) between most adult and teenage behaviors exceed .80 and often top .90 (on a scale with a maximum of 1.00), with probability values well below .001 of such patterns occurring by chance.

178   Savage D (1995, 29 March). Justices consider school drug tests. *Los Angeles Times*, p A17.

179   U.S. Supreme Court (1989). Stanford v. Kentucky. 492 U.S. 361.

180   U.S. Supreme Court (1988). Thompson v. Oklahoma. 487 U.S. 815, 848.

181   U.S. Supreme Court (1984). Schall v. Martin. 104 S.Ct 2403.

182   House Select Committee (1985), *op. cit.*

183   U.S. Supreme Court (1977). Ingraham v. Wright. 430 U.S. 651.

184   U.S. Supreme Court (1969). Tinker v. Des Moines Independent Community School District. 393 U.S. 503.

185   U.S. Supreme Court (1988). Hazelwood School District v. Kuhlmeier. 484 U.S. 260.

186   U.S. Supreme Court (1986). Bethel School District v. Fraser. 478 U.S. 675.

187   U.S. Supreme Court (1981). Ralston v. Robinson, 454 U.S. 201.

188   U.S. Supreme Court (1966). Kent v. U.S., 383 U.S. 541. (1967). In re Gault, 387 U.S. 1.

189   U.S. Supreme Court (1984). Schall v. Martin, 467 U.S. 253.

190   U.S. Supreme Court (1987). United States v Salerno and Cafaro. 95 L Ed. 2d, 697.

191   California Department of Corrections, California Youth Authority, cited in Harris R (1993, 22 August). A nation's children in lockup. *Los Angeles Times*, p A20.

192   U.S. Supreme Court (1989). Stanford v. Kentucky, 492 U.S. 361.

193   U.S. Supreme Court (1981). Michael M. v. Sonoma County Superior Court, 450 U.S. 464.

194   U.S. Supreme Court (1990). Hodgson v. Minnesota, 497 U.S. 417.

195   U.S. Supreme Court (1995, June 26). Vernonia School District v. Acton, 94-590.

196   Savage DG (1995, 29 March). Justices consider school drug tests. *Los Angeles Times*, p A17.

197   U.S. Supreme Court (1995). Veronia School District v. Acton. 94-590.

198   Peterson P (1993). *Facing up.* New York: Simon & Schuster, p 106.

199   Skelton G (1992, 27 October). Voters evenly split over proposal to cut welfare. *Los Angeles Times*, pp A1, A18.

200   Times Poll (1994, 11 November). A look at the electorate. *The Los Angeles Times*, p A5.

201   Institute for Social Research (1995, January). Aging baby boomers could make schools go bust. *ISR Newsletter* 19, University of Michigan, p 11.

202   Petersen JE (1991, April). All Those goodies for the elderly, have they gone too far? *Governing the States and Localities* 4, 79.

203   Peterson P (1993), *op cit*, p 108.

204   Kaus M (1994, 5 December). They blew it. *The New Republic*, pp 17-18.

205   U.S. Bureau of the Census (1993, September). *Measuring the effects of benefits and taxes on income and poverty, 1992.* Washington, DC: U.S. Department of Commerce, Table J.

206   U.S. Bureau of the Census (1992). *Poverty in the United States 1990.* Washington, DC: U.S. Department of Commerce, Table 3.

207   *Ibid.*

208   Vinovskis MA. Institute for Social Research (1995), *op cit.*

209   Goodman, Ellen (1995, June 23). Boomers tell kids: Do as I say, not as I did. *Los Angeles Times*, B9.

210   National Commission on Marihuana and Drug Abuse (1973, March). *Drug use in America: Problem in perspective.* Second Report. Washington, DC: U.S. Government Printing Office.

211   Naughton JM (1970, 15 September). Agnew assails songs and films that promote a 'drug culture.' *New York Times*, p A15.

212   See Chapter 6, references.

213   Sheff D (1988, 5 May). Sex, drugs and rock & roll. *Rolling Stone*, pp 57-58.

214   Howe N, Strauss W (1992, December). The new generation gap. *The Atlantic 270*, p 79.

215   Roark AC (1992, 18 March). Most absent parents fail to pay child support. *Los Angeles Times*, pp A1, A20.

216   Associated Press (1995, 25 July). Study finds big gaps in savings for retirement. Washington, DC.

217   Furstenberg FF et al (1995, August), *op cit.*

218   Wilson P (1995, 7 January). Forging America's future. Inaugural address. Sacramento, CA: Office of the Governor.

219   Jones CT (1994, 25 March). Iacocca cuts through weighty issues. *Daily Oklahoman*, pp 23-24.

220   The Doors (1968). Five to one. *Waiting for the Sun.* New York: Elektra Records.

Chapter 2: Fertility Bites

1   Clinton H, in Mehren E (1995, 15 June). The First Lady's family values. *Los Angeles Times*, pp E1, E11.

2   Select Committee on Teenage Pregnancy (1995, 18 February). Teenage mothers and custodial care. Hearing, César Chávez High School, Santa Ana, CA. Sacramento, CA: California State Senate.

3   Males M, Chew KS (1995, 8 April). Adult involvement in school-age fertility. San Francisco, CA: Paper pre-

sented to Population Association of America, annual meeting.

4 Alan Guttmacher Institute (1994). *Sex and America's teenagers.* New York: AGI, pp 20-23.

5 See as one example of many, Hall M (1991, 19 November). Condoms in classrooms argued. *USA Today,* pp 1, 12A, 8D.

6 Alan Guttmacher Institute (1994). *Sex and America's teenagers.* New York: AGI, pp. 22-23.

7 Dryfoos JG (1988). *Putting the boys in the picture.* Santa Cruz, CA: ETR Associates.

8 Lauritsen JL, Swicegood CG (1995, 8 April). The consistency of self-report initiation of sexual activity: Longitudinal findings from the National Youth Survey. San Francisco, CA: Paper presented to the Population Association of America annual meeting.

9 Ventura SJ et al (1992, 16 November). Trends in pregnancies and pregnancy rates, United States, 1980-88. *Monthly Vital Statistics Report* 41, No. 6, Table 3.

10 Rosoff JI (1988, March/April). Not just teenagers. *Family Planning Perspectives* 20, 52.

11 California Center for Health Statistics (1992-95). Resident live births by age of mother, age of father, marital status, race, county, 1989-93. Sacramento, CA: Department of Health Services.

12 Horon IL (1995, 8 September). Paternal age for teen mothers less than 18 years of age. Baltimore: Maryland Department of Health and Mental Hygiene (printout).

13 Cockburn A (1994, 15 February). Clinton does a Quayle with facts of life. *Los Angeles Times,* p B7.

14 Landry DL, Forrest JD (1995, July/August). How old are U.S. fathers? *Family Planning Perspectives* 27, 159-161, 165.

15 U.S. Bureau of the Census (1994). *Statistical abstract of the United States, 1993.* Washington, DC: U.S. Department of Commerce, Table 132.

16 Spencer AG (1913, March). The age of consent and its significance. *The Forum* 49, 407.

17 Select Committee on Children, Youth, and Families (1992). *A decade of denial: Teens and AIDS in America.* Washington, DC: U.S. House of Representatives, 102nd Congress, Second Session.

18 Rosenberg P (1995, 24 November). Press statement, *Science.* In New study delineates toll of AIDS virus. Washington, DC: Associated Press.

19 Wendell DA et al (1992, January). Youth at risk. Sex, drugs, and human immunodeficiency virus. *American Journal of Diseases of Children* 146, 76-81.

20 Conway GA et al (1993, 9 June). Trends in HIV prevalence among disadvantaged youth. *Journal of the American Medical Association* 269, 2887-2889.

21 Sweeney P et al (1995, May). Teenagers at risk of human immunodeficiency virus Type 1 infection. *Archives of Pediatric and Adolescent Medicine* 149, 521-528.

22 Green J (1994, 7 March). Health crisis: Adults getting teens pregnant. Sex between teens, adults growing factor in AIDS spread. *Oakland Press,* pp A1, A8.

23 Lindegren ML et al (1994). Epidemiology of human immunodeficiency virus infection in adolescents, United States. *The Pediatric Infectious Disease Journal* 13, 525.

24 Sweeney et al (1995, May), *op cit,* p 521.

25 CDC (1992, 10 April). Selected behaviors that increase risk for HIV infection among high school students — United States, 1990. *Morbidity and Mortality Weekly Report* 41, 236-240.

26 CDC (1994, December). *Facts about adolescents and HIV/AIDS.* Atlanta, GA.

27 Knight S (1995, 25 September). What 'Kids' leaves out of the picture. *Los Angeles Times,* p F5.

28 Angelina PJ et al (1995, 17 November). The relationship of childhood sexual victimization to teenage pregnancy and STDs. Paper presented to the National Organization on Adolescent Pregnancy, Parenting and Prevention. Phoenix: Arizona Family Planning Council.

29 Wendell et al (1992, January), *op cit,* p 80.

30 Select Committee (1992), *op cit.* CDC (1994, November), *op cit,* p 2.

31 Centers for Disease Control (1994, November). Facts about adolescents and HIV/AIDS. Atlanta, GA: draft.

32 Rosenberg P (1995, 24 November), *op cit.*

33 Males M (1989, 19 November). Sex crimes and the courts: Judges getting tougher. *Bozeman Daily Chronicle,* pp A1, A8. Males M (1989, 22 November). Rape is a tough crime to prove. *Bozeman Daily Chronicle,* pp A1, A8.

34 National Victim Center (1992, 23 April). *Rape in America.* Arlington, VA: NVC, p 3.

35 Alan Guttmacher Institute (1994), *op cit,* p 73.

36 Gershenson HP et al (1989). The prevalence of coercive sexual experiences among teenage mothers. *Journal of Interpersonal Violence* 4, 204-219.

37 Boyer D, Fine D (1992). Sexual abuse as a factor in adolescent pregnancy and child maltreatment. *Family Planning Perspectives* 24, 4-11, 19.

38 Angelini PJ (1995, 17 November). The relationship of childhood sexual victimization to teenage pregnancy and STDs. Phoenix, AZ: Arizona Family Planning Council.

39 Okami P (1992, February). Child perpetrators of sexual abuse: The emergence of a problematic deviant category. *Journal of Sex Research* 29, 125-126.

40   Herrera R, Tafoya N (1995, 17 November). Teen sex — who's got the power? Workshop presented to the annu-
     al conference of the National Organization on Adolescent Pregnancy, Parenting, and Prevention, Phoenix, AZ.
     Las Cruces, NM: La Clinica de Familia Community Health Centers.

41   Weston B (1995, 29 May). Teen pregnancy has grown-up side. *The Orange County Register*, 1, 16.

42   American Association of University Women (1993). *Hostile Hallways*. Washington DC: AAUW Education
     Foundation.

43   Shakeshaft C, Cohan A (1995, March). Sexual abuse of students by school personnel. *Phi Delta Kappan*, 513-
     520.

44   Wishnietsky DH (1991). Reported and unreported teacher-student sexual harassment. *Journal of Educational
     Research* 3, 164-169.

45   Shakeshaft C, Cohan A, *op cit*, pp 514, 515, 516.

46   AAUW (1993), *op cit*, pp 8-9.

47   For those interested in statistical measures, the mathematical (Pearson r) correlations for these four teen and
     adult sexual outcome measures are as near to one-to-one as the figures indicate. The correlation between annual
     rates of teenage and of adult births (r = .928, 51 degrees of freedom), unwed births (r = .924, 51 df), abortions (r
     = .961, 16 df), and STD (r = .979, 36 df) are all significant (p < .0001). The coefficients of determination (r2)
     for each indicate that 85 percent to 96 percent of the differences in teenage sexual outcome trends over time are
     accounted for by the same factors that influence adult sexual outcome trends. Very little can be explained by
     any unique teenage influences or behaviors.

48   Alan Guttmacher Institute (1994), *op cit*, p 70.

49   The correlation between teen and adult birth rates by county is very close (r = .818, 22 df, p < .001).

50   Roan S (1995, 9 July). A sign of the times. *Los Angeles Times*, pp E1, E4-E5.

51   The correlation between poverty and teenage childbearing rates for California's 58 counties (r = .818, p < .0001)
     and for the United States' 50 states and District of Columbia (r = .812, p < .0001), both for 1990, indicates that
     poverty alone explains two-thirds of the differences in rate of teenage childbearing between various locations.

52   U.S. Bureau of the Census (1915-1936). *Birth, stillbirth, and infant mortality statistics*. Washington, DC: U.S.
     Department of Commerce. National Center for Health Statistics (1937-1992). *Vital statistics of the United States*.
     Natality, and advance figures. Washington, DC: U.S. Department of Health and Human Services.

53   Hayes C (editor), National Research Council (1987). *Risking the future: Adolescent sexuality, pregnancy, and child-
     bearing*. Washington, DC: National Academy Press, vol 1, p 1.

54   National Commission on the Role of the School and the Community in Improving Adolescent Health (1990).
     Code blue: Uniting for healthier youth. Alexandria, VA: National Association of State Boards of Education.

55   Morrison P (1988, September/October). Children having children. *Society* 25, 2-3.

56   Carnegie Council on Adolescent Development (1995, October). *Great transitions: Preparing adolescents for a new
     century*. New York: Carnegie Corporation.

57   Trussell J (1988). Teenage pregnancy in the United States. *Family Planning Perspectives* 20, 262-271.

58   Green J (1994, 7 March), *op cit*, p A8.

59   Kilpatrick W (1992). *Why Johnny can't tell right from wrong*. New York: Simon & Schuster.

60   Reynolds N (1991, 19 December). So-called San Marcos miracle actually may be just a myth. *San Diego Union*,
     1.

61   Focus on the Family (1993, 9 September). In defense of a little virginity. *Los Angeles Times*, p B4.

62   Roosa MW, Christopher FS (1990, October). Evaluation of an abstinence-only adolescent pregnancy preven-
     tion program: A replication. *Family Relations* 39:10, 363-367.

63   Savage BD (1987, November). *Child support and teen parents*. Washington, DC: Children's Defense Fund.

64   Burt MR (1986, September/October). Estimating the public costs of teenage childbearing. *Family Planning
     Perspectives* 18, 221-226.

65   Johnson JH (1991, 8 March and 24 April). Letters to author. New York: Alan Guttmacher Institute.

66   Green J (1994, March 7) *op cit*, p A8.

67   Rosoff JI, in Allen CL (1990, April). Teenage birth's new conceptions. *Insight*, 8-13.

68   Dixon-Mueller R (1993, September/October). The sexuality connection in reproductive health. *Studies in Family
     Planning* 24, 269-282.

69   Boyer D, Fine D (1992), *op cit*, p 11.

70   Boyer D, in Phillips L (1995, 31 August). Sex abuse: Silent factor in teen welfare equation. *USA Today*, 6A.

71   Landry, Forrest (1995), *op cit*, pp 161, 165.

72   Landry, Forrest (1995), *op cit*, p 161.

73   Clinton WF (1995, 9 August). All things considered. Washington: National Public Radio.

74   Sylvester K (1994, November). *Preventable calamity: Rolling back teen pregnancy*. Washington, DC: Progressive
     Policy Institute, policy report No. 22.

75   See Cutright P (1972). The teenage sexual revolution and the myth of an abstinent past. *Family Planning
     Perspectives* 4, 26.

76   Offer D (1987). In defense of adolescents. *Journal of the American Medical Association* 257, 3407-3408.

77   Whitman D (1989, 4 December). When pregnant girls face Mom and Dad: State laws requiring parental involvement don't stop teenage abortions. *U.S. News & World Report*, 25-26.

78   Cartoof VG, Klerman LV (1986). Parental consent for abortion: The impact of Massachusetts' law. *American Journal of Public Health* 76, 397-400.

79   Minnesota Department of Health (1990). Pregnancy outcomes and pregnancy rates by age of woman, Minnesota residents, 1980-1988. St. Paul: Center for Health Statistics (printout).

80   Blum RW, Resnick M, Stark T (1987). The impact of parental notification laws on adolescent abortion decision-making. *American Journal of Public Health* 77, 619-620.

81   Editors (1990). Factors associated with the use of court bypass by minors to obtain abortions. *Family Planning Perspectives* 22, 158-160.

82   Alsop D (1986). Hodgson v Minnesota, 648 FS up 756, Minnesota Digest.

83   U.S. Supreme Court (1990). Hodgson v Minnesota. 497 U.S. 417.

84   Rosoff JI (1990, August). The Supreme Court retreats another step on abortion. *Family Planning Perspectives* 22, 183.

85   O'Keefe J, Jones JM (1990, Fall). Easing restrictions on minors' abortion rights. *Issues in Science and Technology* 7, National Academy of Sciences, 1.

86   *Dateline NBC* (30 June 1992).

87   Rust ME (1988, March). Old enough to conceive, old enough to abort? *California Lawyer*, 35.

88   Alan Guttmacher Institute (1994). *Sex and America's teenagers.* New York: AGI.

89   Donovan P (1983). Judging teenagers: How minors fare when they seek court-authorized abortions. *Family Planning Perspectives* 15, 259-267.

90   U.S. Supreme Court (1981). H.L. v. Matheson. 450 U.S. 398.

91   For media reporting of sex survey, see Males M (1995, January/February). Sex survey's "warm oatmeal" sold as solid social science. *Extra!*, pp 24-26.

92   Laumann EO, Gagnon JH, Michael RT, Michaels S (1994). *The social organization of sexuality.* Chicago: University of Chicago Press, 1994, Table 12.8A.

93   U.S. National Center for Health Statistics (1993). *Monthly Vital Statistics Report*, Volume 41, Number 6, Supplement. See also U.S. Bureau of the Census (1994). *Statistical abstract of the United States, 1993.* Washington, DC: U.S. Department of Commerce, Tables 110, 112.

94   A very good review of this study, the type the press should have conducted before rushing to print, is in Wilson JK (1994, 28 October). Sexless in America? *Chicago Maroon* (University of Chicago), pp 2-3, 20.

95   See the popular companion volume by Michael RT, Gagnon JH, Laumann EO, Kolata G (1994). *Sex in America.* Boston: Little, Brown & Co., for major summaries.

96   Rosoff JI (1988, March/April), *op cit.*

97   Peterson KS (1995, 22-24 September). Birth rate drops for teens. *USA Today*, p 2D.

98   Palmer JL, Smeeding T, Torrey BB (eds, 1988). *The vulnerable.* Washington, DC: Urban Institute Press, p 113.

99   See Gold M, Kivisto P (1995, 17 November). Broad-based community assessment of attitudes and perceptions of teen sexuality and teen pregnancy in the heartland of Iowa. Phoenix, AZ: Research paper presented to the annual conference of the National Organization on Adolescent Pregnancy, Parenting, and Prevention; Alan Guttmacher Institute (1994), *op cit*, pp 33-37.

Chapter 3: Breeding Doomsday

1   Lord M (1993, 23 January). Pregnant — and now without a job. *U.S. News & World Report*, p 66.

2   Nakashima II, Camp BW (1984). Fathers of infants born to adolescent mothers. *American Journal of Diseases of Children* 138, 452-454.

3   Palmer JL, Smeeding T, Torrey BB (1988). *The vulnerable.* Washington, DC: Urban Institute Press, p 116.

4   Congressional Research Service, in Welch WM (1994, 9 February). Ending cycle of welfare hangs on the bottom line. *USA Today*, p 5A.

5   DeParle J (1994, 22 April). Idea of ending welfare is catching on. New York Times News Service.

6   National Center for Health Statistics (1995). *Vital statistics of the United States 1990.* Volume I, Natality. Washington, DC: U.S. Department of Health and Human Services, Table 1-77.

7   Murray C (1994, Spring). Does welfare bring more babies? *The Public Interest*, pp 20, 23.

8   Congressional Green Book (1995) in Welfare: House approves GOP plan 234-199. *Los Angeles Times* (1995, 25 March), p A26.

9   California Center for Health Statistics (1972-1995). *Vital statistics of California* (1970-1992). Births. Sacramento, CA: Department of Health Services.

10   The negative correlation between welfare benefits (higher) and birth rates (lower) among females ages 12-17 is r = -.452 for all teen births, r = -.387 for unwed teen births, 49 degrees of freedom, both significant at p < .01.

11   See Congressional Budget Office (1990). Sources of support for adolescent mothers. Washington, DC: 99th U.S. Congress, pp xvi, 52; Committee on Ways and Means (1994). *Overview of entitlement programs, 1994 Green Book*. Washington, DC: 103rd U.S. Congress, 2nd session, p 444.

12   Burt MR (1986, September/October). Estimating the public costs of teenage childbearing. *Family Planning Perspectives* 18, 221-226.

13   Shogren E (1995, 10 November), *op cit*.

14   U.S. Bureau of the Census (1994). *Statistical abstract of the United States, 1994*. Washington, DC: U.S. Department of Commerce, Table 590.

15   Kaus M (1994, 5 December). They blew it. *The New Republic*, pp 17-18.

16   Alan Guttmacher Institute (1994). *Sex and America's teenagers*. New York: AGI, p 70.

17   National Victim Center (1992, 23 April). *Rape in America*. Arlington, VA: NVC, Figures 9-11.

18   Congressional Green Book (1995, 25 March), *op cit*; Fellmeth RC (24 November 1995). Beyond the buzzwords, what welfare reform really means. *Los Angeles Times*, p B7.

19   Offner P (1994, 24 January). Target the kids. *The New Republic*, p 10.

20   Mosle S (1995, 11 September). Dissed. *The New Yorker*, pp 5-6.

21   Makinson C (1985, May/June). The health consequences of teenage fertility. *Family Planning Perspectives* 17, 132-139.

22   Kinard EM, Klerman LV, in McAnarney ER, editor (1983). *Premature adolescent pregnancy and parenthood*. New York: Grune & Stratton.

23   Makinson C (1985), *op cit*, p 138.

24   National Victim Center (1992, 23 April), *op cit*, Figure 9.

25   Makinson (1985), *op cit*, pp 138-139.

26   Herrnstein RJ, Murray C (1994). *The Bell Curve*. New York: The Free Press, pp 341-368.

27   DeParle J (1994, 22 March). Clinton target: Teen-age pregnancy. *New York Times*, p 11.

28   Brownstein R (1994, 27 March). Welfare reform plan seeks lid on aid to teens. *Los Angeles Times*, pp 1, 19.

29   Boyer D, Fine D (1992). Sexual abuse as a factor in adolescent pregnancy and child maltreatment. *Family Planning Perspectives* 24, 4-11, 19.

30   American Psychological Association (1994, October). Violence and teen pregnancy. *APA Monitor*, p 28.

31   Congressional Budget Office, *Sources of support for adolescent mothers* (1990), in Levin-Epstein J (1994, 27 July). Understanding the Clinton welfare bill. Teen pregnancy prevention and teen parents. Washington, DC; Center for Law and Social Policy, p 7.

32   *Ibid*.

33   DeParle J (1994, 10 June). Clinton to propose a strategy to curb youth pregnancies. *New York Times*, pp 1, 9.

34   Alan Guttmacher Institute (1994), *op cit*, pp 28, 73-74.

35   Brownstein R (1994, 20 February). New welfare limits could be aimed first at the young. *Los Angeles Times*, pp A1, A26.

36   California Law Enforcement Information Center (1995, 11 July). Sex and race/ethnic group of felony arrestees, 1994, by category, offense, and age. Sacramento, CA: California Department of Justice (printout).

37   Associated Press (1995, 3 January). Wisconsin puts time limits on welfare, getting a job. Madison, WI.

38   Whitman D, Shapiro J, et al (1995, 16 January). Welfare: The myth of reform. Welfare: The myths of charities. *U.S. News & World Report*, pp 30-40.

39   Hage D, Fischer D, Black RF, Grant L (1995, 10 April). America's other welfare state. Getting business off the dole. *U.S. News & World Report*, pp 34-38.

40   Males M (1994, August). In defense of teenaged mothers. *The Progressive*, 22-23.

41   Stiffman AR, Powell J, Earls F, Robins LN (1990). Pregnancies, childrearing, and mental health problems in adolescents. *Youth & Society* 21, 483-495.

42   Bayatpour M, Wells RD, Holford S (1992). Physical and sexual abuse as predictors of substance use and suicide among pregnant teenagers. *Journal of Adolescent Health* 13, 128-132.

43   National Center for Health Statistics (1995), *op cit*, Table 1-135.

44   Males M (1995, 9 January). Poor logic. *In These Times*, pp 12-15.

45   U.S. Bureau of the Census (1995). *Statistical Abstract of the United States, 1994*. Washington, DC: U.S. Department of Commerce, Tables 604, 605.

46   Owen SM (1995, 11 July). Tax agency to help collect child support. *Los Angeles Times*, pp B1, B5.

47   Warren J (1995, 29 September). Wilson signs bill aimed at deadbeat dads. *Los Angeles Times*, pp A3, A22.

48   Upchurch DM, McCarthy J (1989). Adolescent childbearing and high school completion in the 1980s: Have things changed? *Family Planning Perspectives* 21, 199.

49   National Center for Health Statistics (1960-1995), *op cit*, birth and unwed birth tables for year cited.

50   Harris KM, Furstenberg FF Jr (1995, 7 April). Divorce, fathers, and children: Patterns and effects of paternal involvement. San Francisco, CA: Paper presented to the Population Association of America annual conference.

51   Mehren E (1985, 2 October). Study disputes stereotype of the unwed teen father. *Los Angeles Times*, pp 1, 9.

52   Landry DJ, Forrest JD (1995, July/August). How old are U.S. fathers? *Family Planning Perspectives* 27, 165.

53   Lamb ME, Elster AB, Tavaré J (1986). Behavioral profiles of adolescent mothers and partners with varying intracouple age differences. *Journal of Adolescent Research* 1, 399-408.

54   Boyer D, Fine D (1992, January/February) *op cit*, Table 5.

55   Lamb ME et al (1986), *op cit*, p 406.

56   Brownstein R, Lauter D (1993, 12 December). Clinton aides find welfare vow easier said than done. *Los Angeles Times*, pp A1, A18.

57   Deavitt N (1991). Teenage pregnancy and educational opportunity. *Journal of the American Medical Association* 226, 2558-2559.

58   Willman D (1995, 18 September). Welfare provision faces veto threat. *Los Angeles Times*, p A11.

59   Lieberman J (1995, 6 September). *Congressional Record - Senate*, pp S12699-S12700.

60   Oldenburg A (1995, 17-19 November). Washington takes heat at debate over daytime talk TV. *USA Today*, p 1.

61   Will GF (1995, 14 September). A nasty twist to 'women and children first.' *Los Angeles Times*, p B11.

62   Gergen D (1995, 2 October). The 50 percent catastrophe. *U.S. News & World Report*, p 88.

63   Whitman D et al (1995, 6 November). Who speaks for the poor? *U.S. News & World Report*, pp 42-43.

64   Auster BB (1995, 27 November). Tantrums, taxes & tactics. *U.S. News & World Report*, p 38.

65   Shogren E (1995, 27 October). Welfare report clashes with Clinton, Senate. *Los Angeles Times*, pp A1, A14.

66   Shogren E (1995, 10 November). White House report assails welfare plan. *Los Angeles Times*, p A4.

67   Nelson J (1995, 7 November). Clinton reconsidering Senate welfare bill, aide says. *Los Angeles Times*, p A18.

68   Terry GP (1995, 22 October). Peter Digre. Trying to protect children enmeshed in welfare reform plans. *Los Angeles Times*, p M3.

Chapter 4: Wild in Deceit

1   Golding W (1954). *Lord of the Flies*. Jackson Heights, NY: Aeonian Press, 1975 edition, p 186.

2   Hendrickson RC, Cook FJ. *Youth in Danger*. New York: Harcourt, Brace & Company, 1956, pp 5, 193.

3   Commission for the Study of Youth Crime and Violence and Reform of the Juvenile Justice System (1994, June). *Preliminary Report to the Governor*. New York, NY, p 1.

4   U.S. Advisory Board on Child Abuse and Neglect (1995, April), *A nation's shame: Fatal child abuse and neglect in the United States*. Washington, DC: U.S. Congress. See also Rivera C (1995, 26 April). Child abuse in U.S. at crisis level, panel says. *Los Angeles Times*, pp A1, A23.

5   National Center on Child Abuse and Neglect (1995, April). National child abuse and neglect data system. *Child Maltreatment, 1993*. In U.S. Bureau of the Census (1993). *Statistical Abstract of the United States, 1995*. Washington, DC: U.S. Department of Commerce, Table 346.

6   Fremon C (1995, 15 October). Let no child be left behind. *Los Angeles Times Magazine*, pp 19, 20.

7   Moore DW (1994, September). Majority advocate death penalty for teenage killers. *Gallup Poll Monthly*, pp 2-4.

8   FBI (1994). *Uniform crime reports for the United States 1993*. Washington, DC: U.S. Department of Justice, Table 2.7.

9   Ostrow R (1993, March 10). Reno vows to attack crime by curbing home violence. *Los Angeles Times*, p A14.

10   Ostrow R (1993, July 30). FBI nominee Freeh draws Senate panel acclaim. *Los Angeles Times*, p A15.

11   Jackson R, Hall J (1994, 21 October). Reno warns TV industry: Cut violence. *Los Angeles Times*, pp A1, A22.

12   Males M (1989, 18 October). Youth crime tied to earlier abuse. *Bozeman Daily Chronicle*, p 3.

13   Liederman D (1995, 17 November). Does America really care about its teen parents? Phoenix, AZ: Address to the annual conference of the National Organization on Adolescent Pregnancy, Parenting, and Prevention. Washington, DC: Child Welfare League.

14   Bureau of Justice Statistics (1994, July). *Murder in Families*. Special Report, NCJ-143498. Washington, DC: U.S. Department of Justice, Tables 1, 2, 8.

15   Widom CS (1992, October). *The cycle of violence*. Washington, DC: U.S. Department of Justice, p 1.

16   Associated Press (1994, 14 November), Washington, DC.

17   FBI (1994), *op cit*, Table 38.

18   FBI (1955-1993, annual), *op cit*, Table 38 (1993) and previous annual tabulations of violent crime arrests by age.

19   See FBI (1951). *Uniform Crime Reports for the United States and Its Possessions, 1950*. Washington, DC: U.S. Department of Justice, Table 163.

20   Hendrickson RC, Cook FJ (1956), *op cit*, p 74.

21   National Commission on the Role of the School and the Community in Improving Adolescent Health (1990, July). *Code blue: Uniting for healthier youth*. Alexandria, VA: National Association of State Boards of Education, p 3.

22   FBI (1993), *op cit.*

23   Kantrowitz B (1995). Youth are increasingly violent. In Bender D, Leone B (1995) *Violence: Opposing viewpoints.* San Diego, CA: Greenhaven Press, pp 45-51.

24   Blumstein A (1995, August). Violence by young people: Why the deadly nexus? *National Institute of Justice Journal,* p 6.

25   U.S. Federal Bureau of Investigation (1994). *op cit,* Table 39 and previous annual, table of arrests by offense, age, gender.

26   Gibbs N (1994, 20 June). The vicious cycle. *Time,* pp 27-28.

27   Law Enforcement Information Center (1995). *Crime and Delinquency in California, 1993.* Sacramento, CA: California Department of Justice, Tables 33, 35.

28   Center for Health Statistics (1994). California resident live births, 1993, by age of father and mother, race (printout). Sacramento, CA: Department of Health Services.

29   Geronimus AT, Korenman S, Hillemeier MM (1994, September). Does young maternal age adversely affect child development? *Population and Development Review 20,* 585-609.

30   Boyer D, Fine D (1992). Sexual abuse as a factor in adolescent pregnancy and child maltreatment. *Family Planning Perspectives 24,* 4-11, 19.

31   Gershenson H et al (1989, June). The prevalence of coercive sexual experience among teenage mothers. *Journal of Interpersonal Violence 4,* 204.

32   Chesney-Lind M (1989, January). Girls' crime and women's place: Toward a feminist model of female delinquency. *Crime & Delinquency 35,* 5-29.

33   Sonkin DS, Durphy, M (1985). *Learning to live without violence: A handbook for men.* San Francisco, CA: Volcano Press.

34   See Blumstein (1995, August), *op cit,* pp 5-6.

35   Law Enforcement Information Center (1995), *op cit.*

36   Terry GP (1995, 22 October). Peter Digre: Trying to protect children enmeshed in the welfare-reform plans. *Los Angeles Times,* p M3.

37   Leighton GR, Hellman R (1935, August). Half slave, half free: Unemployment, the depression, and American young people. *Harper's Magazine 171,* pp 342-353.

38   U.S. Bureau of the Census (1975). *Historical statistics of the United States, colonial times to 1970.* Washington, DC: U.S. Department of Commerce, 1975, Series H 971-986, p 414.

39   For information on age, income, and generation issues, see U.S. Bureau of the Census (1994). *Money Income of Households, Families, and Persons in the United States: 1992.* Current Population Series, P60-184. Washington, DC: U.S. Department of Commerce. Peterson P (1993). *Facing Up.* New York: Simon & Schuster.

40   National Center for Health Statistics (1995). *Vital statistics of the United States 1990.* Volume II, Part A, Mortality. Washington, DC: U.S. Department of Health and Human Services, Table 1-27.

41   Prothrow-Smith D, Weissman M (1991). *Deadly consequences.* New York: Harper Collins, chapter 1.

42   Males M (1988, 16 October). Top cop candidates differ widely on crime theory. *Bozeman Daily Chronicle,* p 3.

43   U.S. Advisory Board on Child Abuse and Neglect (1995, April). In Rivera C (1995, 26 April), *op cit,* p 1.

44   Rivera C (1995, 26 April), *op cit,* p A23.

45   National Center on Child Abuse and Neglect (1995, April), *op cit.*

46   Timnick L (1985, 25 August). The Times Poll: 22 percent in survey were child abuse victims. *Los Angeles Times,* pp A1, A34.

47   American Humane Association (1989). In *U.S. Bureau of the Census, Statistical abstract of the United States.* In U.S. Bureau of the Census (1993). *Statistical Abstract of the United States, 1992.* Washington, DC: U.S. Department of Commerce, Table 301.

48   FBI (1993), *op cit,* Table 38. Estimates involving crime reports prorate tabulated arrests upward in ratio to population of U.S. versus population of crime reporting area.

49   Children often overlooked in crime reports (1994, November/December). *American Nurse,* 20. See also, National Victim Center (1992). *Rape in America.* Washington, DC, p 6.

50   Dodge KA, Bates JE, Pettit GS (1990, 20 December). Mechanisms in the cycle of violence. *Science 250,* 1678, 1683.

51   Straus MA (1985). Family training in crime and violence. In Straus MA, Lincoln AJ (1985). *Crime and the family.* Springfield, IL: Charles C Thomas, p 168.

52   Hutchings N (1988). *The violent family.* New York: Human Sciences Press, p 93.

53   Fulwood S III (1995, 15 October). Clinton urges men to pledge end to domestic violence. *Los Angeles Times,* p A23.

54   Becker M (1995, 5 October). Yearlong drive by anti-violence groups pays off. *Los Angeles Times,* A3.

55   Straus MA (1985), *op cit,* p 168; Straus MA, Gelles RJ (1988). In Kirkpatrick JT, Straus MA. *Family Abuse and its Consequences: New Directions in Research.* Newbury Park, CA: Sage.

56   Bureau of Justice Statistics (1994, June). *Child Rape Victims, 1992.* Crime Data Brief, NCJ 147001. Washington,

DC: U.S. Department of Justice.

57   Bureau of Justice Statistics (1994, July), *op cit*, Table 2.

58   FBI (1995), *op cit*, Table 2.27.

59   Giles-Sims J, Straus MA, Sugarman DB (1995). Child, maternal, and family characteristics associated with spanking. *Family Relations* (in press).

60   Straus MA, Mathur AK (1995, 7 April). Corporal punishment of adolescents and academic attainment. Paper presented to the annual meeting of the Pacific Sociological Association, San Francisco, p 3.

61   Straus MA, Kaufman Kantor G (1994). Corporal punishment by parents: A risk factor in the epidemiology of depression, suicide, alcohol abuse, child abuse, and wife beating. *Adolescence* 29, 114.

62   Turner H, Finkelhor D (1994). Corporal punishment and the stress process. In Donnelly M, Straus MA (editors). *Corporal punishment of children in theoretical perspectives*. New Brunswick, NJ: Transaction.

63   Straus MA, Gimpel HS (1994). Alienation and reduced income. *Beating the devil out of them: Corporal punishment in American families*. Lexington, MA: Lexington/Macmillan Books, chapter 9.

64   Kandel E (1991). *Physical punishment and the development of aggressive and violent behavior: A review*. Durham, NH: Family Research Laboratory, University of New Hampshire.

65   Larzelere RE (1986, March). Moderate spanking: Model or deterrent of children's aggression in the family. *Journal of Family Violence* 1, 27-36.

66   See summary of findings connecting criminal behavior to past child abuse, in Braun E, Lustgarten K (1994). *Breaking the Cycle of Child Abuse*. Woodland, CA: Childhelp, USA.

67   U.S. Supreme Court (1977). *Ingraham v. Wright*, 490 U.S. 651.

68   Johnson RN (1995, 4 August). Targeting of civilians is now the ugly norm. *Los Angeles Times*, p B9.

69   Alberto A, Chase R, Coté T, et al (1992, 24 September). Effect of the Gulf War on infant and child mortality in Iraq. *New England Journal of Medicine* 327, 931-936. See also Schwarz B (1993, 24 May). Perspective on war: Beware the call to righteousness. *Los Angeles Times*, p B7.

70   Cockburn A (1994, 1 March). Real wars, not war movies, spawn murder. *Los Angeles Times*, p B7.

71   Straus MA (1985), *op cit*, p 168.

72   *Ibid*.

73   Boyer D, Fine D (1992), *op cit*.

74   Braun E, Lustgarten K (1994), *op cit*.

75   See Miller A (1983). *For your own good: Hidden cruelty in child-rearing and the roots of violence*. New York: Farrar Straus & Giroux; Miller A (1990). *Banished knowledge: Facing childhood injuries*. New York: Doubleday.

76   Widom CS (1992, October). *op cit*, pp 1, 2.

77   Dodge KA, Bates JE, Pettit GS (1990, 20 December), *op cit*, pp 1681-1682.

78   Prothrow-Smith D, Weissman M (1991), *op cit*, p 104.

79   Chesney-Lind M (1989), *op cit*, pp 24-26.

80   Connie L et al (1993, 2 August). Girls will be girls. *Newsweek*, p 44.

81   National Commission on the Role of the School and Community in Improving Adolescent Health (1990), *op cit*, p 4.

82   Maguire K, Pastore AL, Flanagan TJ (1994). *Sourcebook of criminal justice statistics — 1993*. Washington, DC: U.S. Department of Justice, Table 3.69.

83   National Center for Education Statistics (1995). *The condition of education, 1995*. NCES 95-273. Washington, DC: U.S. Department of Education, p 134.

84   FBI (1955-1993), *op cit*, Table 38, 1993, and previous annual tabulations of arrests by offense and age. Calculations of annual rates by author.

85   Calculations by author from data in National Center for Health Statistics (annual, 1940-1989), *op cit*, Table 1-27, 1989, and corresponding tables for previous annual reports.

86   The correlation between annual violent crime arrest rates for teens age 15-19 and adults age 20-44 for the maximum time period for which consistent FBI statistics are available, 1955-1993, is 0.98; the correlation between 1993 youth violent crime and adult violent crime arrest rates by geographic region produces a similarly high 0.94. Similarly high correlations exceeding .90 in all cases exist when rates of violent death (accidents, suicides, and homicides) are compared over time, either in aggregate or individually.

87   Harris R (1993, 22 August). A nation's children in lockup. *Los Angeles Times*, pp A1, A20-A21.

88   Coleman BC (1994, 15 June). AMA wants detailed movie ratings. Washington: Associated Press.

89   American Psychological Association Commission on Violence and Youth (1993). *Violence & youth*. Washington, DC: APA, pp 25-26, 54-55.

90   Law Enforcement Information Center (1995), *op cit*.

91   FBI (1994), *op cit*.

92   Rorty R (1995, 24 September). Color-blind in the marketplace. *New York Times Book Review*, p 9.

93   Friedenberg EZ (1963). *The dignity of youth and other atavisms*. Boston: Beacon Press, p 66.

94   Hunt T (1995, 24 September). Passionate political embrace holding family values tight. Washington, DC: Associated Press.

95   Roper WL (1993). Kids, health, and the media: What can public health offer? *Journal of School Health* 63, 273-75.

96   See Males M (1993, 20 September). Public enemy number one? *In These Times*, pp 14-17.

97   See Huesmann LR, Eron LD, Berkowitz L, Chaffee S (1992). The effects of television violence: A reply to a skeptic. Freedman JL (1992). Television violence and aggression: What psychologists should tell the public. In Suedefeld P, Tetlock PE (editors) (1992). *Psychology and Social Policy.* New York: Hemisphere.

98   Huesmann et al (1992), *op cit,* p 191.

99   Blame it on Hollywood (1994, May). *U.S.,* p 60.

100   Arnett J (1991, September). Adolescents and heavy metal music. From the mouths of metalheads. *Youth & Society* 23, 76-97.

101   Singer JL, Singer DG (1986). Family experiences and television viewing as predictors of children's imagination, restlessness, and aggression. *Journal of Social Issues* 42:3, 107-124.

102   See Futrelle D (1993, 20 September). Van Damme made me do it. *In These Times,* p 18.

103   Kantrowitz B (1995), *op cit,* p 50; Blumstein (1995, August), *op cit.*

104   World Health Organization (1995). *World health statistics annual 1993.* Geneva: WHO, Table D-1, Causes of death by sex and age.

105   California Center for Health Statistics (1995). Microcomputer injury surveillance system (MISS). Sacramento, CA: Department of Health Services (diskette).

106   Associated Press (1990, 26 August). Racial outcry not heard in "other" jogger rape. Syracuse, NY.

107   Baker S, Gore T (1989, 29 May). Some reasons for 'wilding.' *Newsweek,* pp 6-7.

108   Hendrickson RC, Cook FJ (1956), *op cit,* p 194.

109   Harris R (1993, 22 August). A nation's children in lockup. Juveniles: Value of harsher punishment questioned. *The Los Angeles Times,* A1,A20-21.

110   Males M (1989, 19 November). Sex crimes and the courts: Judges getting tougher. *Bozeman Daily Chronicle,* pp 1, 8.

111   Chapman JR et al (1987). *Child sexual abuse: An analysis of case processing.* Washington, DC: American Bar Association.

112   Merida K (1994, 10 May). Pop culture takes the rap as Congress battles violence. *Washington Post,* pp A1, A4.

113   Law Enforcement Information Center (1995), *op cit.*

114   Rawls JJ, Bean W (1993). *California: An interpretive history.* Sixth edition. New York: McGraw Hill, p 505.

115   Robison C (1995, 24 September). Prison explosion only a temporary fix. Editors. Packed prisons: One way or another, crime hits Texans' wallets. *Houston Chronicle,* p 2C.

116   FBI, *op cit,* annual for years cited.

117   Fox JA (1995, 30 October). The calm before the crime wave storm. *Los Angeles Times,* p B9.

118   Wilson JQ (1994, September). What to do about crime. *Commentary,* pp 25-34.

Chapter 5: Nicoteen Fits

1   White D (1994, 30 March). Moss Landing students take concerns to Rep. Farr. *Monterey Herald,* p 1c.

2   For example, Philip Morris ad (1995, 4 September). No sale. *The New Yorker,* p 24.

3   Richter P, Cimons M (1995, 4 August). Clinton to weigh plan to curb teen smoking. *Los Angeles Times,* p A14.

4   Devoy A (1995, 8 August). Clinton calls for tough — yet practical — program to combat teenage smoking. *Washington Post,* p A8.

5   Fournier R (1995, 11 August). Analysis: Clinton hopes for political windfall. Washington: Associated Press.

6   Moon RW, Males MA, Nelson DE (1993). The 1990 Montana (United States) initiative to increase cigarette taxes: Lessons for other states and localities. *Journal of Public Health Policy* 14, 19-33; Lewit EM (1989). U.S. tobacco taxes: Behavioural effects and policy implications. *British Journal of Addictions* 84, 1217-1235; Institute for the Study of Smoking Behavior and Policy (1985, 17 April). *The cigarette excise tax.* Cambridge: Harvard University.

7   Clinton WF (1995, 10 August). Washington: News conference. See excerpts in Protecting young people from the "awful dangers" of tobacco (1994, 11 August). *Washington Post,* p A14.

8   U.S. Public Health Service (1986). *The health consequences of involuntary smoking. A report to the Surgeon General.* Washington, DC: U.S. Department of Health and Human Services, p 36.

9   *Ibid,* p 107.

10   Associated Press (1990, 7 September). Smoking parents double cancer risk for their children. Boston.

11   *Ibid,* p 169.

12   Associated Press (1991, 18 June). Study suggests children's health can be related to parents' smoking.

Washington, DC.

13   U.S. Office of Health and Environmental Assessment (1992, December). *Respiratory health effects of passive smoking: Lung cancer and other disorders.* Washington, DC: U.S. Environmental Protection Agency, p 1-1.

14   American Public Health Association (1995, November). Survey: Children's health worse than parents realize. *The Nation's Health*, p 23.

15   U.S. Public Health Service (1986), *op cit.*

16   U.S. Centers for Disease Control (1994, 4 November). Cigarette smoking among women of reproductive age — United States, 1987-1992. *Morbidity and Mortality Weekly Report*, pp 789-791.

17   Associated Press (1991, 18 June). Study: Second-hand smoke poses severe risks to children. Washington, DC.

18   National Research Council (1986). *Environmental tobacco smoke: Measuring exposures and assessing health effects.* Washington, DC: National Academy Press, p 216.

19   The petition drive collected the necessary signatures to put the issue on the ballot, but the tax lost handily in the November election after tobacco interests spent a record $1.4 million to defeat it.

20   Montana Office of Public Instruction (1989). *Montana youth risk behavior survey.* Helena, MT: Montana OPI and Montana Board of Crime Control, p 16.

21   Committee on Business and Economic Development (1991, 22 March). Testimony on House Bill 378, House Bill 849, and Senate Bill 369. Helena, MT: House of Representatives.

22   Fischer PM et al (1991, 11 December). Brand logo recognition by children aged 3 to 6 years. *Journal of the American Medical Association 266*, 3145-3148.

23   The Tobacco Institute (1990). *On youth smoking: Tobacco industry initiatives.* Washington, DC (information packet).

24   DiFranza JR, Brown LJ (1992, September). The Tobacco Institute's "It's the Law" campaign: Has it halted illegal sales of tobacco to children? *American Journal of Public Health 82*, 1271-1273.

25   U.S. Public Health Service (1986), *op cit*, p 91.

26   U.S. Office on Smoking and Health (1989, October). *Smoking, tobacco & health, a fact book.* Washington, DC: U.S. Department of Health and Human Services, pp 7, 14.

27   Office on Smoking and Health (1994). *Preventing tobacco use among young people. A report of the Surgeon General.* Washington, DC: U.S. Dept of Health and Human Services.

28   Mott F et al (1995, March). The determinants of delayed sexual activity in a high risk adolescent population. San Francisco, CA: Paper presented to the Population Association of America annual meeting, Table 4.

29   Smokers: When and why began (1991, December). *The Gallup Poll Monthly*, p 9.

30   Urburg K, Robbins RL (1981). Adolescent perception of the costs and benefits associated with cigarette smoking: Sex differences and peer influences. *Journal of Youth and Adolescence 10*(5), 353-361.

31   Landrine N et al (1994). Cultural diversity in the predictors of adolescent cigarette smoking: The relative influence of peers. *Journal of Behavioral Medicine 17*(3), 331-346.

32   Downs WR (1987). A panel study of normative structure, adolescent alcohol use and peer alcohol use. *Journal of Studies on Alcohol 48*, 167-175.

33   Fischer et al (1991), *op cit.*

34   DiFranza JR et al (1991). RJR Nabisco's cartoon camel promotes Camel cigarettes to children. *Journal of the American Medical Association 266*, 3149-3153.

35   Pierce JP et al (1991). Does tobacco advertising target young people to start smoking? *Journal of the American Medical Association 266*, 3154-3158.

36   Public Health Service (1991, March). *Health in the United States 1990.* Washington, DC: U.S. Department of Health and Human Services, Table 57.

37   Johnston LD, O'Malley PM, Bachman JG (1993). *National results on drug use from the Monitoring the Future study, 1975-1992.* Volume I. Washington, DC: National Institute on Drug Abuse, Table 13.

38   Stolberg S (1995, 21 August), *op cit*, p A16.

39   Males M (1992, 24 June). Tobacco promotion and smoking. *Journal of the American Medical Association 267*, 3282.

40   Pierce JP, Shopland D, Johnson M (1992, 24 June). Tobacco promotion and smoking. *Journal of the American Medical Association 267*, 3283.

41   Stolberg S (1995, 21 August). Joe Camel leads the pack in lighting up controversy. *The Los Angeles Times*, pp A1, A16-A17.

42   Mulvey K (1995, 17 October). Letter to *In These Times.* Boston, MA: In Fact.

43   Substance Abuse and Mental Health Services Administration (1994, July). *Preliminary estimates from the 1993 National Household Survey on Drug Abuse.* Advance report No. 7. Rockville, MD: U.S. Department of Health and Human Services, Table 14B.

44   Green G et al (1991). Like parent like child? Associations between drinking and smoking behaviors of parents and their children. *British Journal of Addiction 86*, 745-758.

45   Foshee V, Bauman KE (1992). Parental and peer characteristics as modifiers of the bond-behavior relationship:

An elaboration of control theory. *Journal of Health and Social Behavior* 33(1), 66-76.

46   Oei TP, Egan AM, Silva PA (1986). Factors associated with the initiation of "smoking" in nine-year-old children. *Advances in Alcohol and Substance Abuse* 5(3), 79-89.

47   Standing LG, Nicholson B (1989). Models for student drinking and smoking: Parents or peers? *Social Behavior and Personality* 17, 223-229.

48   Borland BL, Rudolph JP (1975). Relative effects of low SES, parental smoking, and poor scholastic performance on smoking among high school students. *Social Science and Medicine* 9(1), 27-30.

49   Gottlieb NH (1982). The effects of peer and parental smoking on the smoking careers of college women: A sex-related phenomenon. *Social Science and Medicine* 16(5), 595-600.

50   Newman IM, Ward JM (1989). The influence of parental attitude and behavior on early adolescent cigarette smoking. *Journal of School Health* 59, 150-152.

51   Marty PJ, McDermott RJ, Williams T (1986). Patterns of smokeless tobacco use in a population of high school students. *American Journal of Public Health* 76, 190-192.

52   Office on Smoking and Health (1994, July), *op cit*, p iii.

53   *Ibid*, pp 7, 129-130.

54   See U.S. Centers for Disease Control (1990). Cigarette advertising — United States, 1988. *Morbidity and Mortality Weekly Report* 39, pp 261-263.

55   For good discussions of this phenomenon, see Rosenthal R (1963). On the social psychology of the psychological experiment: The experimenter's hypothesis as unintended determinant of experimental results. *American Scientist* 51, 268-283.

56   American Public Health Association (1995, November), *op cit*.

57   Botvin EM et al (1984). Adolescents' self reports of tobacco, alcohol, and marijuana use: Examining the comparability of video tape, cartoon, and verbal bogus-pipeline procedures. *Psychological Reports* 55, 379-386.

58   Bauman KE, Dent CW (1982). Influence of an objective measure on self-reports of behavior. *Journal of Applied Psychology*, 67, 623-628.

59   Stolberg S (1995, 21 August), *op cit*.

60   Campbell DT (1969). Reforms as experiments. *American Psychologist* 24, 409-429.

61   Evans RI, Hansen WB, Mittelmark MB (1977). Increasing the validity of self-reports of smoking behavior in children. *Journal of Applied Psychology* 62, 521-523.

62   Jason LA, Ji PY, Anes MD, Birkhead SH (1991). Active enforcement of cigarette control laws in the prevention of cigarettes sales to minors. *Journal of the American Medical Association* 266, 3159-3161.

63   Public Health Service (1990), *op cit*.

64   Males M (1995, August), *op cit*, Table 3.

65   Johnston LD, O'Malley PM, Bachman JG (1993), *op cit*, Table 13.

66   Roan S (1995, 5 October). A new flap over teen smoking. *Los Angeles Times*, pp E1, E6.

67   Office of Smoking and Health (1994, July), *op cit*, pp iii, iv.

68   SAMSHA (1994, July), *op cit*, Table 14B; OSH (1994, July), *op cit*.

69   Kirn TF (1987). Laws ban minors' tobacco purchases, but enforcement is another matter. *Journal of the American Medical Association* 257, 3323-3324.

70   Newman IM, Ward JM (1989), *op cit*, p 151.

71   Anda RF et al (1990, June). Behavioral risk factor surveillance 1988. *Morbidity and Mortality Weekly Report* 39, 55-2. Atlanta, GA: Centers for Disease Control, Table 5.

72   See Rovner S (1991, 16-22 December). Up in smoke: Why do so many kids ignore all the evidence condemning cigarettes? *Washington Post National Weekly Edition*, p 11; Levy D (1994, 21 June). Lighting up young. When smoke gets in their lives. *USA Today*, pp 1-2.

73   Males M (1992). Montana's tobacco tax: Learning from defeat. Washington, DC: National Cancer Institute, paper.

74   *Mad* 107 (1966, December), back cover.

75   Bauman L (1986). *The nine most troublesome teenage problems*. Seacaucus, NJ: Lyle Stuart Inc, p 171.

76   Anda RF et al, Centers for Disease Control (1990, June). Behavioral risk factor surveillance, 1988. *Morbidity and Mortality Weekly Report* 39:SS-2, 10-11.

77   Puffing is passe, say H.S. seniors (1981, 6 March). *Senior Scholastic* 113, p 26.

78   Johnston LD et al (1993), *op cit*; Public Health Service (1991, March), *op cit*.

79   Anda RF et al (1990, June), *op cit*.

80   Jason LA et al (1991), *op cit*.

81   Johnston LD et al (1993), *op cit*; Public Health Service (1991, March), *op cit*.

82   DiFranza JR (1989). School tobacco policy: A medical perspective. *Journal of School Health* 59, 398.

83   Males M (1992). Use of a school referendum to deter teenage tobacco use. *Journal of School Health* 62, 362-365.

84   Turner C (1995, 30 September). Anti-smoking drive offers lessons for US. *Los Angeles Times*, p A2.

85   Wilson-Smith A et al (1994, 21 February). Pack of trouble. *MacLean's*, pp 10-13; Fennel T, Wood C (1994, 21 February). The worst fear. *MacLean's*, pp. 14-16.

86   Moon RW, Males MA, Nelson DE (1993), *op cit*; Lewit EM (1989), *op cit*; Institute for the Study of Smoking Behavior and Policy (1985), *op cit.*

87   Wilson-Smith et al (1994, 21 February), *op cit.*

Chapter 6: Doped on Duplicity

1   Neergaard L (1995, 20 July). Marijuana use sends teens to hospital emergency rooms. Washington, DC: Associated Press.

2   U.S. Substance Abuse and Mental Health Services Administration (1995, September). *Preliminary estimates from the 1994 National Household Survey on Drug Abuse.* Rockville, MD: U.S. Department of Health and Human Services, Table 2A.

3   Zappa F (1967). Go to San Francisco. *We're only in it for the money.* The Mothers of Invention, Verve Records.

4   Sheff D (1988, 5 May). Sex, drugs and rock & roll. *Rolling Stone*, p 57.

5   Peele S (1986, September). The "cure" for adolescent drug abuse: Worse than the problem? *Journal of Counseling and Development* 65, 23-24.

6   National Center for Health Statistics (1995). *Vital statistics of the United States, 1990.* Volumes IIA and IIB, Mortality. Washington, DC: U.S. Department of Health and Human Services, Table 1-27 (annual through 1990).

7   Federal Bureau of Investigation (1994). *Uniform crime reports for the United States, 1993.* Washington, DC: U.S. Department of Justice, Table 2.13 (annual through 1993).

8   Calculated by author from figures in references 6 and 7.

9   National Safety Council, in Famighetti R ed. (1995). *World almanac and book of facts 1996.* Mahwah, NJ: World Almanac Books, p 966.

10   U.S. Supreme Court (1995, 26 June). Vernonia School District v Acton, U.S. 94-590.

11   Whitmire R (1994, 13 December). Drug abuse rises among U.S. teens. Washington, DC. Gannett News Service.

12   Ostrow RJ (1994, 13 December). Nearly 50 percent of 12th graders linked to drug use. *Los Angeles Times*, p A38.

13   Naughton JM (1970, 15 September). Agnew assails songs and films that promote a 'drug culture.' *New York Times*, p A15.

14   Kids and marijuana: The glamour is back (1994, 26 December). *U.S. News & World Report*, p 12.

15   No one, of course, bothered to study whether "drug messages" were actually more prevalent today than in the 1980s or whether t-shirts, caps, songs, and the mere sight of the marijuana leaf has anything to do with causing teenage drug use. And of course, no one bothered to mention that on the day of Shalala's press conference, two dozen adults, many shut out of overcrowded treatment facilities, would die from cocaine, heroin, or medical drugs.

16   Johnston LD, O'Malley PM, Bachman JG (1994). *National survey results on drug use from Monitoring the Future Study, 1975-1993.* Volume I, Secondary School Students. Rockville, MD: U.S. Department of Health and Human Services.

17   Wagner HJ (1995, 15 June). Drug-sniffing dogs to be kept on duty in schools. *Los Angeles Times* (Orange County edition), p B3.

18   U.S. Supreme Court (1995), *op cit.*

19   Neergaard L (20 July 1995), *op cit.*

20   U.S. Bureau of the Census (1995). *Statistical abstract of the United States, 1994.* Washington, DC: U.S. Department of Commerce, Table 179.

21   SAMSA (1994, December). *Preliminary estimates of drug-related emergency department episodes.* Advance Report No. 8. Washington, DC: U.S. Department of Health and Human Services.

22   SAMSA (1994, March). *Annual emergency room data, 1992.* DHHS Pub #SMA 94-2080. Rockville, MD: U.S. Department of Health and Human Services, Table 2.06c.

23   National Center for Health Statistics (1995), *op cit*, Table 1-23.

24   Compiled from the Bureau of the Census, *Statistical abstract of the United States 1994.* Washington, DC: U.S. Department of Commerce, Table 179; U.S. Bureau of Justice Statistics, *Sourcebook of criminal justice statistics 1993.* Washington, DC: U.S. Department of Justice, Tables 3.94-3.99; and California Center for Health Statistics (1994). California microcomputer injury surveillance system (MISS), 1993. Sacramento, CA: Department of Health Services (diskette).

25   *U.S. News & World Report* (1994, 12 December), *op cit.*

26   Newcomb MD, Bentler PM (1988). Impact of adolescent drug use and social support on problems of young adults: A longitudinal study. *Journal of Abnormal Psychology* 97, 64-75.

27   Andersson T, Magnusson D (1988). Drinking habits and alcohol abuse among young men: A prospective longitudinal study. *Journal of Studies on Alcohol* 49, 245-252.

28   Donovan JE, Jessor R, Jessor L (1983, March). Problem drinking in adolescence and young adulthood: A follow-

up study. *Journal of Studies on Alcohol* 44, 109-137.

29   Newcomb and Bentler, *op cit.*

30   *Ibid.*

31   Shedler J, Block J (1990, May). Adolescent drug use and psychological health. *American Psychologist* 45, 612-630.

32   Newcomb & Bentler, *op cit.*

33   Hawley RA (1990, December). The bumpy road to drug-free schools. *Phi Delta Kappan* 70, 311.

34   Califano JA Jr (1995, 16 September). Adult smoking victims all started young. *New York Times*, p A14.

35   See discussion by Engs RC (1991, April). Resurgence of a new "clean living" movement in the United States. *Journal of School Health* 61, 155-158.

36   A similar effect occurred during the 1980s: When Reagan officials publicized the drug crisis, the public cited it as the worst national ill. When official proclamations lapsed, the public stopped mentioning drugs as a problem).

37   SAMHSA (1994, December), *op cit.*

38   Associated Press (1995, 13 September). Marijuana use rises among teens. Washington, DC.

39   U.S. Substance Abuse and Mental Health Services Administration (1995). *Annual Medical Examiner Data, 1993*. DHHS Report #95-3019. Rockville, MD: U.S. Department of Health and Human Services, Tables 2.01, 2.02, 2.09.

40   Maguire K, Pastore AL (1995). *Sourcebook of criminal justice statistics 1994*. Washington, DC: U.S. Bureau of Justice Statistics, Table 4.36.

41   Easton NJ (1995, 1 October). Adoption, the underclass, and America. *Los Angeles Times Magazine*, pp 14-19, 32-33.

42   Elliott DM, Briere J (1992, February). The sexually abused boy: Problems in manhood. *Medical Aspects of Human Sexuality* 26, 68-71.

43   National Victim Center (1992, 23 April). *Rape in America*. Washington, DC: p 8.

44   Blumstein A (1995, August). Violence by young people: Why the deadly nexus? *National Institute of Justice Journal*, pp 2-9.

45   Maguire K, Pastore AL (1995). *Sourcebook of criminal justice statistics 1994*. Washington, DC: Bureau of Justice Statistics, Tables 4.7, 6.67.

46   Musto DF (1991, July). Opium, cocaine and marijuana in American history. *Scientific American* 265, pp 40-47.

47   National Center for Health Statistics (1995), *op cit*, Table 1-27; FBI (1994), *op cit*, Tables 38, 43.

48   Scheer R (1995, 8 October). Justice for the rich isn't justice for all. *Los Angeles Times*, p M5; Ostrow RJ (1995, 6 October). Sentencing study finds racial divide. *Los Angeles Times*, pp A1, A19.

49   Savage DG, Richter P (1995, 27 October). Clinton to sign bill preserving stiff crack rules. *Los Angeles Times*, p A22.

50   Musto DF (1991, July), *op cit.*

51   Males M (1991, 20 February). Drugs, sex and violence: O.C.'s Fifties youth crisis. *Oklahoma Gazette*, pp 1-4.

52   Hendrickson RC, Cook FJ (1956). *Youth In Danger*. New York: Harcourt, Brace and Co, pp 172-173.

53   National Commission on Marihuana and Drug Abuse (1973, March). *Drug use in America: Problem in perspective*. Second Report. Washington, DC: U.S. Government Printing Office, pp 43-90.

54   See Stuart RB (1974). Teaching facts about drugs: Pushing or preventing? *Journal of Educational Psychology* 37, 98-201; Weaver SC, Tennant FS (1973). Effectiveness of drug education programs for secondary school students. *American Journal of Psychiatry* 130, 812-814; Goodstadt MS (1986). School-based drug education in North America: What is wrong? What can be done? *Journal of Studies on Alcohol* 56, 278-288,

55   Hawkins JD (1995, August). Controlling crime before it happens: Risk-focused prevention. *National Institute of Justice Journal*, pp 10-18.

56   Engs RC, Fors SW (1988). Drug abuse hysteria: The challenge of keeping perspective. *Journal of School Health* 58, 26-28.

57   For examples, see *New York Times* (1988, 14 January); *Los Angeles Times* (1988, 18 January); States News Service (1988, 18 January); United Press International (1988, 25 January); MacNeil/Lehrer NewsHour (1988, 18 May). Washington, DC.

58   For the statistically inclined, this negative correlation is significant: $r = -0.46$, 20 df, $p < .05$.

59   Peele S (1987). The limitations of control-of-supply models for explaining and preventing alcoholism and drug addiction. *Journal of Studies on Alcohol* 48, 65.

60   Peele S (1987), *op cit*, p 64.

61   See Morse SJ (1988, 12 April). Consider decriminalization in war against drugs. *Los Angeles Times* Syndicate.

62   Editorial (1995, 11 November). Deglamorising cannabis. *The Lancet* 346. 1241.

63   van de Wijngaart GF (1990). The Dutch approach: Normalization of drug problems. *Journal of Drug Issues* 20, 667-678.

64   Currie E (1993). *Reckoning: Drugs, the cities, and the American future*. New York: Hill & Wang, p 332.

65   van Mastrigt H (1990). The abolition of drug policy: Toward strategic alternatives. *Journal of Drug Issues* 20, 647-657.

Chapter 7: Two-Fisted Double Standards

1   Hopkins RH et al (1988, January). Comprehensive evaluation of a model alcohol education curriculum. *Journal of Studies on Alcohol* 49, p 49.

2   Milgram GG (1982). Youthful drinking: Past and present. *Journal of Drug Education* 12, p 289.

3   Zappa F, the Mothers of Invention (1967). Bow-tie daddy. *We're only in it for the money*. Verve Music.

4   Lomask M (1954, March). First report on high school drinking. *Better Homes and Gardens*, pp 72-75, 139-142.

5   Henrickson RC, Cook FJ (1956). *Youth in danger*. New York: Harcort, Brace & Co, pp 6-7.

6   Mendelson JH, Mello NK (1985). *Alcohol use and abuse in America*. Boston: Little Brown and Co, pp 3-17.

7   Critchlow B (1986, July). The powers of John Barleycorn, beliefs about the effects of alcohol on social behavior. *American Psychologist* 41, p 752.

8   Vingilis ER, De Genova K (1984). Youth and the forbidden fruit: Experiences with changes in legal drinking age in North America. *Journal of Criminal Justice* 12, pp 162-163.

9   *Ibid.*

10   Chauncey RL (1988, Winter). New careers for moral entrepreneurs: Teenage drinking. *Journal of Drug Issues* 22, pp 45-70.

11   Mosher JF (1980). The history of youthful drinking laws: Implications for current policy. In Weschler H (ed). *Minimum drinking age laws: An evaluation*. Lexington, MA: Lexington Books, pp 11-38.

12   Vingilis & De Genova (1984), *op cit.*

13   Mosher JF (1980), *op cit.*

14   Anonymous (1931, March). This moderate drinking. *Harpers Monthly*, pp 419-427.

15   Milgram (1982), *op cit*, p 297.

16   U.S. Bureau of the Census (1975). *Historical statistics of the United States, colonial era to 1970*. Series B 149-166. Washington, DC: U.S. Department of Commerce, p 58.

17   Lender ME, Martin JK (1982). *Drinking in America*. New York: Free Press, p 139.

18   Drunken driving (1936, 23 September). *The New Republic*, p 135. Primitive estimates were that 6-10 percent of all traffic crashes were due to outright drunkenness, then defined liberally as having a blood alcohol content of 0.15 percent or greater (compared to .08 percent-.10 percent today), which editors noted could mean many more were due to lesser amounts of drinking.

19   Drinking drivers dangerous as well as drunken ones (1938, 26 March). *Science News Letter* 33, p 205.

20   Drunken drivers (1938, 30 October). *Literary Digest* 124, p 8.

21   U.S. Bureau of the Census (1929-37). *Mortality statistics*. Washington, DC: U.S. Department of Commerce, Table 7.

22   Durfee CH (1937, June). A letter to my son. *Parents* 12, pp 29, 94.

23   Lomask (1954), *op cit.*

24   Hendrickson RC, Cook FJ (1956). *Youth in danger*. New York: Harcourt Brace & Co, Introduction.

25   Maddox GL (1964). Adolescence and alcohol. In McCarthy RG (ed). *Alcohol education for classroom and community, a source book for educators*. New York: McGraw-Hill Book Company, pp 35-37.

26   National Clearinghouse for Alcohol Information (1981). Fact sheet: Selected statistics on alcohol abuse and alcoholism. Washington, DC: National Institute on Alcohol Abuse and Alcoholism.

27   In McCarthy (1964), *op cit*, pp 43-44.

28   National Center for Health Statistics (1969-1975). *Vital statistics of the United States*. Part B, Mortality. Washington, DC: U.S. Department of Health and Human Services, Table 7-5.

29   Williams AF et al (1975). The legal minimum drinking age and fatal motor vehicle crashes. *Journal of Legal Studies* 4, pp 219-239.

30   Cook PJ, Tauchen G (1984). The effect of minimum drinking age legislation on youthful auto fatalities, 1970-1977. *Journal of Legal Studies* 13, pp 169-190.

31   Smart RG, Goodstadt MS (1977). Effects of reducing the legal alcohol-purchasing age on drinking and drinking problems. A review of empirical studies. *Journal of Studies on Alcohol* 38, 1313-1323.

32   *Ibid*, p 170. See also Douglass RL (1980). The legal drinking age and traffic casualties: A special case of changing alcohol availability in the public health context. In Wechsler H (ed). *Minimum-drinking age laws: An evaluation*, p 93.

33   Moskowitz JM (1989, January). The primary prevention of alcohol problems: A critical review of the research literature. *Journal of Studies on Alcohol* 50, pp 60-62.

34   Lowman C (1981/1982, Winter). Facts for planning no. 1: Prevalence of alcohol use among U.S. senior high school students. *Alcohol Health and Research World* 6, pp 41-46; Rachal JV et al (1982, Spring). Facts for planning no. 4: Alcohol misuse by adolescents. *Alcohol Health and Research World* 6, pp 61-68.

35   Blane H, Hewitt L (1977). *Alcohol and youth — an analysis of the literature, 1960-1975.* NTIS #PB-268-698. Washington, DC: National Institute on Alcohol Abuse and Alcoholism.

36   Mendelson and Mello (1985), *op cit*, p 282.

37   Chauncey RL (1981), *op cit*, pp 47-55.

38   Alcoholism: New victims, new treatments (1974, 22 April). *Time*, pp 75-81.

39   Chauncey (1981), *op cit*, pp 47-48.

40   *Ibid*, p 49.

41   *Ibid*, pp 49-50.

42   *Ibid*, p 49.

43   *Ibid*, p 51.

44   Mendelson and Mello (1985), *op cit*, p 282.

45   *Ibid*, p 100.

46   *New York Times* (1994, 15 January), p 7-A.

47   Moskowitz JM (1989), *op cit*, p 65.

48   Blose JO, Holder HD (1987, January). Liquor-by-the-drink and alcohol-related traffic accidents. *Journal of Studies on Alcohol* 48, pp 52-60.

49   See Greenfield LA (1988, February). *Drunk driving.* Special Report NCJ 109945. Washington, DC: Bureau of Justice Statistics, p 7.

50   Fell JC (1983, October). Tracking the alcohol involvement problem in U.S. highway crashes. Paper presented for the National Center for Statistics and Analysis to the American Association for Automotive Medicine. Washington, DC: NHTSA, p 10.

51   National Clearinghouse for Alcohol Information (1981), *op cit.*

52   See Peele S (1987). The limitations of control-of-supply models for explaining and preventing alcoholism and drug addiction. *Journal of Studies on Alcohol* 48, pp 61-75.

53   Males M (1986, January). The minimum purchase age for alcohol and young-driver fatal crashes: A long-term view. *Journal of Legal Studies* 40, p 192.

54   Williams AF et al (1983). The effect of raising the legal minimum drinking age on involvement in fatal crashes. *Journal of Legal Studies* 37, pp 169-175.

55   DuMouchel W et al (1987). Raising the alcohol purchase age: Its effects on fatal motor vehicle crashes in 26 states. *Journal of Legal Studies* 16, pp 249-266.

56   NHTSA (1995), *op cit*, Figure 3.

57   Males M (1986), *op cit*, p 187.

58   Hingson R et al (1983). Impact of legislation raising the legal drinking age in Massachusetts from 18 to 20. *American Journal of Public Health* 73, pp 163-170.

59   Klein TM (1981). *The effect of raising the legal drinking age on traffic accidents in Maine.* HS-806-149. Washington, DC: U.S. Department of Transportation.

60   Hingson R, Merrigan D, Heeren T (1985, February). Effects of Massachusetts raising its legal drinking age from 18 to 20 on deaths from teenage homicide, suicide, and nontraffic accidents. *Pediatric Clinics of North America* 32, 221-232.

61   Males M (1986), *op cit.*

62   Asch P, Levy DT (1987). Does the minimum drinking age affect traffic fatalities? *Journal of Policy Analysis and Management* 6, pp 180-192.

63   Barnes G et al (1986, February). Parental socialization factors and adolescent drinking behaviors. *Journal of Marriage and the Family* 48, p 75.

64   Lowman C (1981/82), *op cit.*

65   Taylor P (1991, 12 September). Minimum drinking age laced with loopholes, Novello says. *Washington Post*, pp A1, A18.

66   See Centers for Disease Control (1988, July). A public health approach to prevention of acute alcohol-related problems among adolescents and young adults. Atlanta, GA: U.S. Department of Health and Human Services, draft.

67   See radio and television Anheuser-Busch "public service" ads, 1993-95.

68   National Commission Against Drunk Driving (1988). *Youth driving without impairment.* Washington, DC, pp 23, 37.

69   Unfair drunken driving bill (1992, 17 January). *The Salt Lake Tribune.*

70   NHTSA (1994). *Traffic safety facts 1992.* Washington, DC: U.S. Department of Justice, p 36.

71   Shogren E (1995, 11 June). Clinton seeks strict drunk driving laws. *Los Angeles Times*, p A24.

72   Montana Highway Traffic Safety Division (1985). *BAC and you.* Helena, MT: Montana Department of Justice; American Automobile Association (1975). *One drink can be too many.* Falls Church, VA.

73   FBI (1975, 1993). *Uniform crime reports for the United States.* Washington, DC: U.S. Department of Justice, Table

36 (1975), Table 38 (1993).

74   NHTSA (1995), *op cit*, Figure 1.

75   *Martin's annual criminal code* (1988). Ontario, Canada: Canada Law Book, Inc, Part VI, Sections 203-242.

76   Donovan JE, Jessor R, Jessor L (1983, March). Problem drinking in adolescence and young adulthood, A follow-up study. *Journal of Studies on Alcohol* 44, pp 109-137.

77   Mauss AL (1988). The problematic prospects for prevention in the classroom: Should alcohol education programs be expected to reduce drinking by youths? *Journal of Studies on Alcohol* 49, pp 51-61; Goodstadt MS (1986). School-based drug education in North America: What is wrong? What can be done? *Journal of Studies on Alcohol* 47, 278-288.

78   Hopkins et al (1988), *op cit*.

79   Males M (1987), *op cit*.

80   National Institutes on Mental Health, quoted in Peele S (1989). *Diseasing of America*. Lexington, MA: DC Heath & Co, p 68.

81   Peele S (1989), *op cit*, p 72.

82   Males M (1987, April), *op cit*, p 16.

83   Barnes G et al (1986, February), *op cit*, p 27.

84   Chauncey R (1981), *op cit*.

85   Peele S (1987), *op cit*, p 75.

86   Preusser DF, Williams AF (1991, March). *Sales of alcohol to underage purchasers in three New York counties and Washington, D.C.* Arlington, VA: Insurance Institute for Highway Safety.

Chapter 8: Growing Up Referred

1   Hill RF, Fortenberry JD (1992). Adolescence as a culture-bound syndrome. *Social Science & Medicine* 35, 78.

2   Hill & Fortenberry (1992), *op cit*, p 73.

3   Kett JE (1977). *Rites of passage: Adolescence in America, 1790 to the present*. New York: Basic Books, pp 238, 241.

4   Holmbeck GN, Hill JP (1988). Storm and stress beliefs about adolescence: Prevalence, self-reported antecedents, and effects of an undergraduate course. *Journal of Youth and Adolescence* 17, 285-306.

5   Lavigne JV (1977). The pediatric staff's knowledge of normal adolescence development. *Journal of Pediatric Psychology* 2, 98-100.

6   Gould SJ (1981). *The Mismeasure of Man*. New York: WW Norton & Company.

7   Offer D, Ostrov E, Howard KI (1981). *The adolescent: A psychological self-portrait*. New York: Basic Books, p 5.

8   Hall GS (1904). *Adolescence: Its psychology and its relation to physiology, anthropology, sociology, sex, crime, religion, and education*. New York: D Appleton, p xiv.

9   Blos P (1961). *On adolescence*. New York: Free Press of Glencoe, p 9.

10   Freud A (1958). Adolescence. *Psychoanalytic Study of the Child* 13, 275.

11   Strong J, quoted in Gould SJ (1981), *op cit*, p 118.

12   Hollingworth LS (1928). *The psychology of the adolescent*. New York: Appleton-Century, p 17.

13   Mead M (1928). *Coming of age in Samoa: A psychological study of primitive youth for western civilization*. New York: Dell, p 12.

14   Gould SJ (1981), *op cit*, pp 74, 107.

15   Berk L (1991). *Child development*. Boston: Allyn & Bacon, p 445.

16   Offer et al (1981), op cit, pp 2-4, 63, 65.

17   Offer D (1987). In defense of adolescents. *Journal of the American Medical Association* 257, 3407-3408.

18   Montemayor R (1983). Parents and adolescents in conflict: All families some of the time and some families most of the time. *Journal of Early Adolescence* 3, 85.

19   Kett (1977), *op cit*, pp 215, 243.

20   Gould SJ (1982), *op cit*, pp 330-331.

21   Piaget J (1967). *Six psychological studies*. New York: Vintage Books.

22   Friedenberg EZ (1964). *The vanishing adolescent*. Boston: Beacon Press, pp 15, 118.

23   Friedenberg EZ (1963). *The dignity of youth and other atavisms*. Boston: Beacon Press, p 94.

24   Friedenberg EZ (1964), *op cit*, pp 114-115.

25   Warwick I, Aggleton P (1990). "Adolescents," young people and AIDS research. In Aggleton P, Davies P, Hart G (editors). *AIDS: Individual, cultural and policy dimensions*. New York: Falmer Press, pp 89-102.

26   Gardner W, Herman J (1990, Winter). Adolescents' AIDS risk taking: A rational choice perspective. *New Directions in Child Development* 50, 17-34.

27   Gardner & Herman (1990, Winter), *op cit*, pp 17-18.

28   For the mathematically inclined, the correlation between teen (age 15-19) and adult (age 20-44) violent death rates from 1955-1991 is very high: $r = .911$, 35 degrees of freedom, $p < .0001$. More than 80 percent of the

change in teenage violent deaths is explained by the same factors that cause changes in adult violent death.

29 Adler T (1993, April). Sense of invulnerability doesn't drive teen risks. *APA Monitor*, p 15.

30 *Ibid.*

31 Gardner & Herman (1990, Winter), *op cit*, pp 31-32.

32 Zwarenstein C (1994, 12 December). Teens not the problem, and tired of being told they are generation gap. *Toronto Star*, p A17.

33 Centers for Disease Control (1991, 20 September). Attempted suicide among high school students—United States, 1990. *Morbidity and Mortality Weekly Report* 40, 633-635.

34 National Center for Health Statistics (1990 and previous annual), *op cit*. Figures on suicide by age, sex, race, and time period are from the tables in *Vital statistics of the United States* (1937-1990), Vol II, Part A, Mortality, Table 1-25 (and previous annual); and its predecessor volume by the U.S. Bureau of the Census, *Mortality Statistics* (1900-1936).

35 Bayatpour M, Wells RD, Holford S (1992). Physical and sexual abuse as predictors of substance use and suicide among pregnant teenagers. *Journal of Adolescent Health* 13, 128-132.

36 Shogren E (1993, 20 October). Survey of top students reveals sex assaults, suicide attempts. *The Los Angeles Times*, p A22.

37 National Victim Center (1992, 23 April). *Rape in America.* Arlington, VA: NVC, Table 7.

38 See Dooley D et al (1989, Winter). Economic stress and suicide: Multilevel analysis. *Suicide & Life-Threatening Behavior* 19, 321; Stanley M, Stanley B (1989, Spring). Biochemical studies in suicide victims: Current findings and future implications. *Suicide & Life-Threatening Behavior* 19, 30; Green A (1978). Self-destructive behavior in battered children. *American Journal of Psychiatry* 13, 579-582.

39 Freiberg P (1991, March). Sullivan is criticized by APA over report. *APA Monitor.*

40 National Center for Health Statistics (1995). *Vital statistics of the United States* 1991. Mortality, Part B. Washington, DC: U.S. Department of Health and Human Services, Table 8-5.

41 Associated Press (1995, 21 April). Child suicide rate on rise, CDC reports. Atlanta, GA.

42 U.S. Bureau of the Census (1915). *Mortality statistics.* Washington, DC: U.S. Department of Commerce, Table 7.

43 Terman L (1913, January). The tragedies of childhood. *The Forum* 49, pp 41-47.

44 Editors (1921, 23 July). Appalling rate of child suicide. *Literary Digest* 70, p 29.

45 Editors (1920, 28 August). Child suicide increasing. *Literary Digest* 66, p 23.

46 *Ibid.*

47 Terman L (1913), *op cit.*

48 *Literary Digest* (1920, 28 August), *op cit.*

49 See Adolescent suicide. *Hygeia* (1928, March), pp 125-127. The death's head on campus. *Literary Digest* (1927, 5 March), p 30.

50 Beeley AL (1932, July). Was there a suicide 'wave' among college students in 1927? *Scientific Monthly* 35, 66-67.

51 *Science News Letter* 31 (1937, 19 June), 392.

52 Davis PA (1983). *Suicidal adolescents.* Springfield, IL: Charles C Thomas, p 11.

53 Holinger P (1978). Adolescent suicide: An epidemiological study of recent trends. *American Journal of Psychiatry* 135, 754-756.

54 Gist R, Welch QB (1989). Certification change versus actual behavior change in teenage suicide rates, 1955-1979. *Suicide & Life-Threatening Behavior* 19, 277-287.

55 Males M (1991, Fall). Teen suicide and changing cause-of-death certification, 1953-1987. *Suicide & Life-Threatening Behavior* 21, 245-259.

56 The correlation between teenage (age 15-19) and adult (age 20-44) suicide/self-inflicted-death trends over the 35 year period is .96 (34 df, p < .0001), indicating that 90 percent of the trends in suicidal deaths among adolescents are explained by the same factors governing such deaths among grownups.

57 Task Force on Youth Suicide (1989, January). *Report of the Secretary's Task Force on Youth Suicide.* Washington, DC: U.S. Department of Health and Human Services, pp 1, 5.

58 Kleck G (1988). Miscounting suicides. *Suicide & Life-Threatening Behavior* 18, 219-235.

59 Centers for Disease Control (1986). *Youth suicide surveillance.* Washington, DC: U.S. Department of Health and Human Services, p 1.

60 Pfeffer CR (1981, Spring). Parental suicide: An organizing event in the development of latency-age children. *Suicide & Life-Threatening Behavior* 13, 43.

61 See Elkind D (1989, January). The facts about teen suicide. *Parents*, p 111. See also Associated Press (1991, 2 April) dispatch on the Gallup Survey on teen suicide, quoting experts that "5,000 to 6,000 teenagers" commit suicide annually. I sent copies of vital statistics reports to AP national editors showing this figure was 2.5 to three times too high and received acknowledgement that in the figure figures would be carefully checked. They have not been.

62 CDC (1991, 20 September), *op cit*, Table 1.

63 Males M (1987, 5 April). Teen's suicide raises hard questions for Livingston youths and parents. *Bozeman Daily*

Chronicle, pp 1, 2.

64   Finch SM, Poznanski EO (1971). *Adolescent suicide.* Springfield, IL: Charles C Thomas Publishers, p ix.

65   Gould MS (1989, Spring). Suicide clusters: A critical review. *Suicide & Life-Threatening Behavior* 19, 25.

66   Lawrence MT, Ureda JR (1990, Summer). Student recognition of and response to suicidal peers. *Suicide & Life-Threatening Behavior* 20, 164-167.

67   Hendin H (1982). *Suicide in America.* New York: WW Norton & Co, pp 182-87.

68   See Shaffer D et al (1990, 26 December). Adolescent suicide attempters, response to suicide prevention programs. *Journal of the American Medical Association* 264, 3151-3155.

69   Hill & Fortenberry (1992), *op cit*.

70   Peele S (1990). *Diseasing of America.* Boston: Lexington Books.

71   Gould SJ (1977), *op cit*, p 145.

72   National Commission on the Role of the School and Community in Improving Adolescent Health (1990). *Code blue: Uniting for healthier youth.* Alexandria, VA: National Association of State Boards of Education, p 7.

73   Commission on Violence and Youth (1993). *Violence & youth.* Washington, DC: American Psychological Association, pp 54-55.

74   National Association of Private Psychiatric Hospitals (1985, 6 June). In Select Committe on Children, Youth, and Families. *Emerging trends in mental health care for adolescents.* Washington, DC: U.S. House of Representatives, 99th Congress, First Session, pp 78-79.

75   Lewis DO, Lewis M, Unger L, Goldman C (1984). Conduct disorder and its synonyms: Diagnoses of dubious validity and usefulness. *American Journal of Psychiatry* 141, 514-519.

76   Horne AM, Sayger TV (1990). *Treating conduct and oppositional defiant disorders in children.* New York: Pergamon Press Inc.

77   American Psychiatric Association (1987). *Diagnostic and statistical manual of mental disorders.* Washington, DC, pp 56-58.

78   *Ibid*, pp 53, 55.

79   Select Committee on Children, Youth, and Families (1985, June 6), *op cit*, p 9.

80   Frick PJ et al (1992). Familial risk factors to oppositional defiant disorder and conduct disorder: Parental psychopathology and maternal parenting. *Journal of Consulting and Clinical Psychology* 60, 49-55.

81   Horne & Sayger (1990), *op cit*, p 34.

82   *Ibid*, p 89.

83   *Ibid*, pp 25-26.

84   American Psychiatric Association (1987), *op cit*, p 56.

85   Horne & Sayger (1990), p 138.

86   APA (1987), *op cit*, p 55.

87   U.S. Supreme Court (1979). *Parham v J.R.* 442 U.S. 584, 99 S.Ct 2493.

88   See Matson JL, Nieminen GS (1987). Validity of measures of conduct disorder, depression, and anxiety. *Journal of Clinical Child Psychology* 16, 151-157.

89   Goleman D (1989, January 10). Pioneering studies find surprisingly high rate of mental ills in the young. *New York Times*, pp C1, C9.

90   Talan J (1988, 7 January). The hospitalization of America's troubled teen-agers. *Newsday*, p 1.

91   Goleman (1989), *op cit*.

92   Peele S (1989). *Diseasing of America.* Lexington, MA: DC Heath & Company, p 131; Talan (1988), *op cit*.

93   Select Committee (1985), *op cit*, p 31.

94   Talan J (1988, 7 January), *op cit*.

95   Select Committee (1985), *op cit*.

96   Atlas JA et al (1991). Symptom correlates among adolescents showing posttraumatic stress disorder versus conduct disorder. *Psychological Reports* 69, 920-922. See also Lewis et al (1984), *op cit*; Frick et al (1992), *op cit*.

97   See Prinz RJ, Miller GE (1991). Issues in understanding and treating childhood conduct problems in disadvantaged populations. *Journal of Clinical Child Psychology* 20, 379-385.

98   Select Committee (1985), *op cit*.

99   Metz H (1991, December). Kids in the cuckoo's nest. *The Progressive*, pp 22-25; Select Committee (1985), *op cit*.

100   Talan (1988), *op cit*, p 1.

101   Select Committee (1985), *op cit*, pp 78-79.

102   Talan (1988), *op cit*.

103   Select Committee (1985), *op cit*.

104   Metz (1989), *op cit*.

105   *Ibid.*

106   Select Committee (1985), *op cit*, p 29.

107   Select Committee (1985), *op cit*, p 10.

108   Metz (1991), *op cit*, p 22.

109   *Ibid*, p 12.

110   Horne & Sayger (1990), *op cit*.

111   Carson RC, Butcher JN (1992). *Abnormal psychology in modern life*. New York: Harper Collins Publisher, p 545.

112   Zoccolillo M, Rogers K (1991). Characteristics and outcome of hospitalized adolescent girls with conduct disorder. *Journal of the American Academy of Child and Adolescent Psychiatry* 30, 973-981.

113   Carson & Butcher (1992), *op cit*, p 544.

114   Armstrong L (1995). *Of "sluts" and "bastards:" A feminist decodes the child welfare debate*. Monroe, ME: Common Courage Press.

115   Select Committee (1985), *op cit*, p 8.

116   Lewis et al (1984), *op cit*, p 518.

117   Leon GR (1990). *Case histories of psychopathology*. Fourth edition. Boston: Allyn & Bacon, p 71.

Chapter 9: Generation Y

1   Jones CT (1994, 25 March). Iacocca cuts through weighty issues. *Daily Oklahoman*, pp 23-24.

2   Males M (1992, September). Top school problems are myths. *Phi Delta Kappan*, pp 38-40.

3   See Musto DF (1991, July). Opium, cocaine, and marijuana in American history. *Scientific American* 265, pp 40-47.

4   Youth gone loco: Villain is marijuana (1938, June 12). *Christian Century* 55, pp 812-813.

5   Davis M (1936). *The Lost Generation*. New York: McMillan & Co; see also, *The Literary Digest* (1936, 4 April). Today's lost generation, p 21.

6   Leighton GR, Hellman R (1935, August). Half slave, half free: Unemployment, the depression, and American young people. *Harper's Magazine* 171, pp 342-353.

7   Marcosson IF (1936, September). Our muddled youth. *American Magazine*, pp 24-25, 109-112.

8   National Center for Health Statistics (1939). *Vital Statistics of the United States, 1937*. Volume I, Natality, and Volume II, Mortality. Washington, DC: U.S. Department of Health, Table 14.

9   Cassidy C (1936, April). Youth faces the sex problem. *American Mercury* 37, p 436.

10   Taussig FJ (1936). *Abortions, spontaneous and induced*. Mosbey Press, in Abortions (1936, 10 March). *Time*, p 52.

11   Hart H, Hart EB (1941). *Personality and the family*. Boston: DC Heath and Company, pp 22, 190-194, 286.

12   U.S. Public Health Service (1935, May). Reprint No. 51 from Venereal Disease Information. Washington, DC: pp 12, 14.

13   Marcosson IF (1936, September), *op cit*.

14   Butler NM (1935, 7 October). The perpetual youth problem. *Vital Speeches of the Day* II, p 24.

15   *Schools and Society* (1938). The need for a permanent national youth service. p 14.

16   Crow LD, Crow A (1945). *Our teen-age boys and girls*. New York: McGraw-Hill Book Company, preface.

17   Rosenblatt RA, Feldman L (1995, 6 May). Aging conference adapts to era of limits. *Los Angeles Times*, p A17; Klein J (1995, 15 May). AARP? Arrgh. *U.S. News & World Report*, p 27.

18   Roosevelt FD (1936, 13 April). Address to young Democrats. Baltimore, MD. In *Vital Speeches of the Day* (1936, 20 April). II, pp 442-444.

19   Roving youth: CCC, FERA, NYA aid in problem of 1,500,000 wanderers (1936, 25 July). *Literary Digest* 122, pp 28-29.

20   See Eaton JS (1995, 5 January). *Investing in American higher education: An argument for restructuring*. New York: Council for Aid to Education, p 8.

21   Shogren E (1995, 29 October). GOP budget plans would put burden on the poor. *Los Angeles Times*, p A1.

22   Shogren E (1995, 27 October). Welfare report clashes with Clinton, Senate. *Los Angeles Times*, pp A1, A14.

23   Corbett J (1995, 28 June). Federal belt-tightening plans put squeeze on student aid. *Los Angeles Times*, p A5.

24   U.S. Bureau of the Census (1994). *Money income of households, families, and persons in the US, 1992*. Washington, DC: U.S. Department of Commerce, Tables 1, 3.

25   Chen E (1995, 19 October). Medicare plans fail to figure on baby boomers. *Los Angeles Times*, p A16.

26   Robinson D (1967, 5 April). Dr. King proposes a boycott of war. *New York Times*, pp 1, 3.

27   See Smith L (1991, 17 November). Oh grow up! *Los Angeles Times Magazine*, pp 14-20, 54-56; Merser C (1987), *Grown-ups*. New York: Penguin Books.

28   Osborne D (1984, November). Newt Gingrich: Shining knight of the post-Reagan right. *Mother Jones*, pp 15-20, 53.

29   Associated Press (1995, 11 August). Quit cigars? No way, Clinton says. Washington, DC.

30   Reed A Jr (1994, August). Pimping poverty, then and now. *The Progressive*, pp 24-26.

31   Rosenblatt R (1995, 8 October). The society that pretends to love children. *New York Times Magazine*, pp 60,

61.

32   National Commission on the Role of the School and the Community in Improving Adolescent Health (1990). *Code blue: Uniting for healthier youth.* Alexandria, VA: National Association of State Boards of Education, executive summary.

33   Carnegie Council on Adolescent Development (1995, October). *Great transitions: Preparing adolescents for a new century.* New York: Carnegie Corporation, p 39.

34   Gelman D (1986, 20 January). Treating teens in trouble. Can the psychiatric ward fill in for the family? *Newsweek*, pp 52-54.

35   Morain D (1994, 16 October). California's profusion of prisons. *Los Angeles Times*, pp A1, A20-22.

36   U.S. Supreme Court (1988). Hazelwood School District v Kuhlmeier. 108 S.Ct 562.

37   New York Times News Service (1994, 1 May). Censorship, budgets chill scholastic press. New York.

38   Taubin A (1995, 25 July). Skating the edge. *Village Voice*, pp 29-33.

39   Knight S (1995, 25 September). What 'Kids' leaves out of the picture. *Los Angeles Times*, p F5.

40   Offer D, Ostrov E, Howard KI (1981). The mental health professional's concept of the normal adolescent. AMA *Archives of General Psychiatry* 38, 149-153.

41   Moore DW (1994, September). Majority advocate death penalty for teenage killers. *Gallup Poll Monthly*, pp 2-4.

42   Males M (1994, May). The roles of knowledgeability, political inclination, and neuroticism in mediating graduate and undergraduate students' attitudes toward adolescents. Irvine, CA.

43   Organization for Economic Cooperation and Devopment (1995). In: Growing disparity in U.S. incomes. *Economic Notes* (14 December 1995). Loyola University, Department of Economics.

44   Liederman D (1995, 17 November). Does America really care about its teen parents? Phoenix, AZ: Address to the annual conference of the National Organization on Adolescent Pregnancy, Parenting, and Prevention. Washington, DC: Child Welfare League.

45   Wealthiest Californians (1993). *California almanac 1993.* Table 11.24.93.

46   Whitman D et al (1995, 6 November). Who speaks for the poor? *U.S. News & World Report*, p 43.

47   Peterson PG (1993). *Facing up: How to rescue the economy from crushing debt & restore the American dream.* New York: Simon & Schuster.

48   See Herman ES (1995, November). The assault on social security. *Z Magazine*, pp 30-35; Hess JL (1994). The profit of austerity. New York, NY; Cohen J, Solomon N (1993). *Adventures in medialand.* Monroe, ME: Common Courage Press, pp 28-29.

49   Du Boff RB (1995, October). Government and social insurance: A view from the left. *Monthly Review* 47, 1-13.

50   Hage D, Fischer D, Black RF (1995, 10 April). America's other welfare state. *U.S. News & World Report*, p 35.

51   Smeeding T, Torrey BB, Rein M (1988). Patterns of income and poverty: The economic status of children and the elderly in eight countries. In Palmer JL, Smeeding T, Torrey BB (1988). *The vulnerable.* Washington, DC: Urban Institute Press, pp 116-117.

52   Shogren E (1995, 10 November). White House report assails welfare plan. *Los Angeles Times*, p A4.

53   *Ibid*, p 116.

54   Skelton G (1992, 27 October). Times Poll: Voters evenly split over proposal to cut welfare. *Los Angeles Times*, pp A1, A18.

55   Florida Kids Count (1993). *Key facts about the children, a report on the status of Florida's children.* Tallahassee, FL: Florida Center for Children and Youth, p 11.

56   Ross M (1974). Suicide among physicians. *Tufts Medical Alumni Bulletin* 34(3), 16-17; This doctor will self-destruct... *Human Behavior* 3(2), 54.

57   Editors (1994, 24 October). The crashing bores. *Orange County Register*, p Metro-6.

58   See the review by Gordon P (1995, September). The truth about DARE. *The Talk of Los Angeles*, pp 72-77.

59   Geismer LL, Wood K (1986). *Family and delinquency.* New York: Human Sciences Press.

60   Novello A (1991, 12 September). *Washington Post*, pp A1, A5.

61   Hirozawa J (1995, 26 October). Speaker warns of aging baby boomers. *Daily Forty-Niner*, California State University at Long Beach, p 4.

62   Morain D (1994, 16 October), *op cit.*

63   Law Enforcement Information Center (1993, 1994, 1995). *Crime and delinquency in California, 1992, 1993 and 1994.* Sacramento, CA: Department of Justice, Table 33 (and 1994 printout).

64   Mehren E (1995, 8 November). No surrender: Jonathan Kozol lends his rare, uncompromising voice to the South Bronx. *Los Angeles Times*, pp E1, E4.

65   Kozol J (1995). *Amazing Grace.* New York: Crown Publishers.

66   O'Rourke PJ (1991). *Parliament of whores.* New York: Atlantic Books.

67   Breneman DW (1995, 5 February). Pulling the rug on students. *Los Angeles Times*, p M5.

68   Law Enforcement Information Center (1995). Willful homicide crimes, 1993, age of victim by age of offender. Printout. Sacramento: California Department of Justice.

69   Associated Press (1995, 18 December). Murder plummets in first half of 1995. Washington, DC.

70   McLellan D (1994, 4 November). Stirring up the activist passion in today's youth. *Los Angeles Times*, pp E1, E9.

71   Abcarian R (1994, 2 November). A lesson in empathy taught by the children. *Los Angeles Times*, pp E1, E5.

72   Times Poll: A look at the electorate (1994, 11 November). *Los Angeles Times*, p A5.

73   Calavita K (1995, 28 February). The new politics of immigration: Proposition 187 and beyond. Colloquium. Irvine, CA: University of California, School of Social Ecology.

74   Moreño R, Pavón JL (1995, 6 November). Curfew would target minorities. *San Francisco Chronicle*, p A21.

Index

About the Author

Mike Males is a doctoral student in social ecology at the University of California, Irvine, and a writer. He has written extensively on youth and social issues in *The Lancet*, *The New York Times*, *Phi Delta Kappan*, *In These Times*, *Extra!*, *The Progressive*, *Adolescence*, *Journal of School Health*, and in numerous anthologies.

He was born in Oklahoma City in 1950 and received a B.A. in Political Science from Occidental College in Los Angeles in 1972. He worked for environmental groups involved in recycling and wilderness preservation, and for successful initiative petitions on anti-nuclear and lobbyist disclosure topics. He has worked in numerous youth programs, including the Youth Conservation Corps, and wrote extensively about politics, government, and youth issues for the *Bozeman Daily Chronicle* (Montana) for eight years. He authored legislation and lobbied for passage of Montana's Youth Conservation Corps (now in operation), and for the student tobacco referendum in which 51,000 junior and senior high students participated in 1991. In 1989, he was appointed to the Montana Children's Trust Fund Board of Directors, which administers the state's child abuse prevention programs, and served as president of that board in 1991.

While completing his doctorate, he has spoken to conferences on youth issues, including those of the California Family Impact Seminar, the California Suicide Prevention Council, Healthy Mothers/Healthy Babies, the Population Association of America, the California Sociological Association, and the California and National Organizations on Adolescent Pregnancy and Parenting.